A TREATISE ON MIND

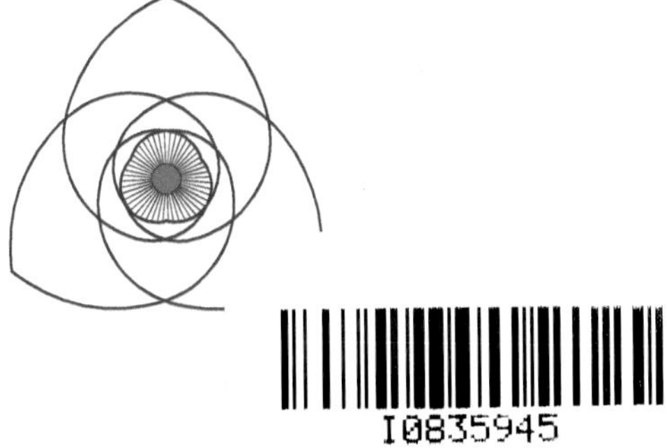

VOLUME 5

An Esoteric Exposition of the Bardo Thödol

PART A

The Deities of the Bardo Thödol

Other Titles in the Series

The I Concept

Volume 1: The 'Self' or 'Non-Self' in Buddhism

Volume 2: Considerations of Mind - A Buddhist Enquiry

Volume 3: The Buddha-Womb and the Way to Liberation

Cellular Consciousness

Volume 4: Maṇḍalas - Their Nature and Development

Volume 5: An Esoteric Exposition of the Bardo Thödol (Part B)

The Way to Shambhala

Volume 6: Meditation and the Initiation Process

Volume 7: The Constitution of Shambhala

VOLUME FIVE

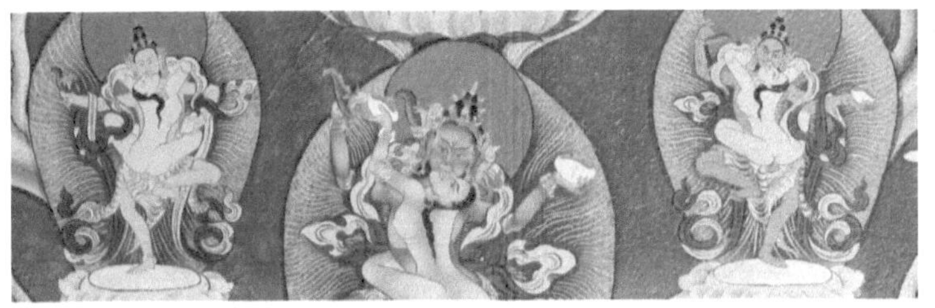

An Esoteric Exposition of the

Bardo Thödol

PART A

The Deities of the Bardo Thödol

BODO BALSYS

UNIVERSAL DHARMA
PUBLICATIONS
SYDNEY, AUSTRALIA

ISBN 978-0-9923568-4-2

2nd Edition, 2025

Āḥ!

Homage to the Lord of Shambhala.
Inconceivable, inconceivable, beyond thought
Is the bejewelled crown of this most excelled Jina.
He whose Eye has taught many Buddhas.
And who will anoint the myriad,
that in the future lives will come.
As I bow to His Feet my Heart's afire.
Oh, this bliss, this love for my Lord
can barely be borne on my part.
It takes flight as the might of the Dove.
The flight of serene *nirvāṇic* embrace.
The flight of Light so bright.
The flight of Love so active tonight.
The flight of enlightenment for all to come to
their mind's Heart's attire.

Obeisance to the Gurus!
To the Buddhas of the three times.
To the Council of Bodhisattvas, *mahāsattvas*.
To them I pledge allegiance.

Oṁ Hūṁ! Hūṁ! Hūṁ!

Dedication

Thanks to my students, past, present and future, and in particular to those that have helped in the production of this Treatise.

Oṁ

Acknowledgments

Special thanks to Angie O'Sullivan, Kylie Smith,
and Ruth Fitzpatrick
for their tireless efforts in making this
series possible.

Oṁ

Contents

Figures

Tables

Plates

Preface

This treatise investigates Buddhist ideas concerning what mind is and how it relates to a concept of a 'self'. It is principally a study of the complex interrelationship between mind and phenomena, from the gross to the subtle—the physical, psychic, supersensory and supernal. This entails an explanation of how mind incorporates all phenomena in its *modus operandi,* and how eventually that mind is liberated from it, thereby becoming awakened. Thus the treatise explores the manner in which the corporeally orientated, concretised, intellectual mind eventually becomes transformed into the Clear Light of the abstracted Mind; a super-mind, a Buddha-Mind.

A Treatise on Mind is arranged in seven volumes, divided into three subsections. These are as follows:

The I Concept
Volume 1. *The 'Self' or 'Non-self' in Buddhism.*
Volume 2. *Considerations of Mind—A Buddhist Enquiry.*
Volume 3. *The Buddha-Womb and the Way to Liberation.*

Cellular Consciousness
Volume 4. *Maṇḍalas - Their Nature and Development.*
Volume 5. *An Esoteric Exposition of the Bardo Thödol.*
(This volume is published in two parts)

The Way to Shambhala
Volume 6. *Meditation and the Initiation Process.*
Volume 7. *The Constitution of Shambhala.*

The I Concept represents a necessary extensive revision[1] of a large work formerly published in one volume. Together the three volumes investigate the question of what a 'self' is and is not. This involves an analysis of the nature of consciousness, and the consciousness-stream of a human unit developing as a continuum through time. It will illustrate exactly what directs such a stream and how its *karma* is arranged so that enlightenment is the eventual outcome.

The first volume analyses Prāsaṅgika lines of reasoning, such as the 'Refutation of Partless Particles', and 'The Sevenfold Reasoning' in order to derive a clear deduction as to whether a 'self' exists, and if so what its limitations are, and if not, then what the alternative may be. The analysis resolves the historically vexing question of how—if there is no 'self'—can there be a continuity of mind that is coherently connected in an evolutionary manner through multiple rebirths.[2] In order to arrive at this explanation, many of the basic assumptions of Mahāyāna Buddhism, such as Dependent Origination and the Two Truths, are critically analysed.

The second volume provides an in-depth analysis of what mind is, how it relates to the concept of the Void *(śūnyatā),* and the evolution of consciousness. The analysis utilises Yogācāra-Vijñānavādin philosophy in order to comprehend the major attributes of mind, the *saṃskāras* that condition it, and the laws by means of which it operates.

The enquiry into the nature of what an 'I' is requires comprehension of the properties of the dual nature of mind, which consists of an empirical and abstract, enlightened part. As a means of doing this, the *ālayavijñāna* (the store of consciousness-attributes) is explored, alongside the entire philosophy of the 'eight consciousnesses' of this School.

Volume three focuses on the I-Consciousness and the subtle body, by first utilising a minor Tantra, *The Great Gates of Diamond Liberation,* to investigate the nature of the Heart centre and its functions, then the

---

1 The book was inadequately edited hence contains many errors and grammatical mistakes that have been corrected in this treatise.

2 My earlier work *Karma and the Rebirth of Consciousness* (Munshiram Manoharlal, Delhi, 2006) lays the background for this basic question.

chakras below the diaphragm. This is necessary to lay the foundation for the topics that will be the subject of the later volumes of this treatise concerning the nature of meditation, the construction of *maṇḍalas,* and the yoga of the *Bardo Thödol.*

The focus then shifts to investigate where the idea of a self-sustaining I-concept or 'Soul-form' may be found in Buddhist philosophy, given the denial of substantial self-existence prioritised in the philosophy of Emptiness. Following this, the pertinent chapters of the *Ratnagotravibhāga Śastra* are examined in detail so that a proper conclusion to the investigation can be obtained via the *buddhadharma.* This concerns an analysis of how the *ālayavijñāna* is organised, such that the rebirth process is possible for each human consciousness-stream, taking into account the *karma* that will eventually make each human unit a Buddha. In relation to this the ontological nature of the *tathāgatagarbha* (the Buddha-Womb) must be carefully analysed, as well as the organising principle of consciousness represented by the *chakras.* I thus establish that there is a form that appears upon the domain of the abstract Mind. I call this the Sambhogakāya Flower. The final two chapters of this volume principally define its characteristics.

The second subsection, *Cellular Consciousness,* is divided into two parts. Volume four deals with the question of what exactly constitutes a 'cell', metaphysically. The cell is viewed as a unit of consciousness that interrelates with other cells to form *maṇḍalas* of expression. Each such cell can be considered a form of 'self' that has a limited, though valid, body of expression. It is born, sustains a form of activity, and consequently dies when it outlives its usefulness. This mode of analysis is extended to include the myriad forms manifest in the world of phenomena known as *saṃsāra,* including the existence and functioning of *chakras.*

Volume five deals with the formative forces and evolutionary processes governing the prime cells (that is, *maṇḍalas* of expression), and the phenomenon that governs an entire world-sphere of evolutionary attainment. This is explored via an in-depth exposition of the *Bardo Thödol* and its 42 Peaceful and 58 Wrathful Deities. The text also incorporates a detailed exposition concerning the transformation of *saṃskāras* (consciousness-attributes developed through all past forms of activity) into enlightenment. The entire path of liberation enacted by a *yogin* via the principles of meditation, forms of concentration, and related techniques *(tapas, dhāraṇīs)* is explained. In doing so, the soteriological purpose of the various wrathful and theriomorphic deities is revealed. This volume is published in two parts. Part A explores chapter 5 of the *Bardo Thödol* concerning the transformation of *saṃskāras* via meditating upon the Peaceful and Wrathful Deities. This necessitates sound knowledge of the force centres (*chakras*) and the way their powers (*siddhis*) awaken. Part B deals with the gain of such transformations and the consequence of conversion of the attributes of the empirical mind into the liberated abstract Mind.

The third subsection, *The Way to Shambhala*, is also in two parts. They present an eclectic revelation of esoteric information integrating the main Eastern and Western religions. Volume six is a treatise on meditation and the Initiation process.[3] The meditation practice is directed towards the needs of individuals living within the context of our modern societies.

Volume six also includes a discussion of the path of Initiation as the means of gaining liberation from *saṃsāra*. The teaching in Volume five concerning the conversion of *saṃskāras* is supplementary to this path. The path of Initiation *is* the way to Shambhala. As many will choose to consciously undergo the precepts needed to undertake Initiation in the future, this invokes the necessity of providing much more revelatory information concerning this kingdom than has been provided hitherto.

How Shambhala is organised is the subject of Volume seven, which details the constitution of the Hierarchy of enlightened being[4] (the Council of Bodhisattvas). It illustrates how the presiding Lords who govern planetary evolution manifest. This detailed philosophy rests on the foundation of the information provided in all of the previous volumes, and necessitates a proper comprehension of the nature of the five Dhyāni Buddhas. To do so the awakening of the meditation-Mind, which is the objective of *A Treatise on Mind*, is essential.

---

3 The word Initiation is capitalised throughout the series of books to add emphasis to the fact that it is the process that makes one divine, liberated. It is the expression of divinity manifesting upon the planetary and cosmic landscape.

4 The word 'being' here is not pluralised because though this Hierarchy is constituted of a multiplicity of beings, together they represent one 'Being', one integral awakened Entity.

How to engage with this text

In this investigation many new ways of viewing conventional Buddhist arguments and rhetoric shall be pursued to develop the pure logic of the reader's mind, and to awaken revelations from their abstract Mind. New insights into the far-reaching light of the *dharma* will be revealed, which will form a basis for the illustration of an esoteric view that supersedes the bounds of conventionally accepted views. Readers should therefore analyse all arguments for themselves to discern the validity of what is presented. Such enquiry allows one to ascertain for oneself, what is logical and truthful, thus overcoming the blind acceptance of a certain dogma or line of reasoning that is otherwise universally accepted as correct. Only that which is discovered within each inquiring mind should be accepted. The remainder should, however, not be automatically discarded, but rather kept aside for later analysis when more data is available—unless the logic is obviously flawed, in which case it should be abandoned. There is no claim to infallibility in the information and arguments presented in this treatise, however, they are designed to offer scope for further meditation and enquiry by the earnest reader. If errors are found through impeccable logic, then the dialectical process may proceed. We can then accept or reject the new thesis and move forward, such that the evolution of human thought progresses, until we all stand enlightened.

This treatise hopes to assist that dialectical evolution by analysing major aspects of the *buddhadharma* as it exists and is taught today, to try to examine where errors may lie, or where the present modes of interpretation fall short of the true intended meaning. The aim is also to elaborate aspects of the *dharma* that could only be hinted at or cursorily explained by the wise ones of the past, because the basis for proper elaboration had not then been established. This analysis of *buddhadharma* will try to rectify some of the past inadequacies in order to explore and extend the *dharma* into arenas rarely investigated.

There will always be obstinate and dogmatic ones that staunchly cling to established views. This produces a reactive malaise in current Buddhist ontological and metaphysical thought. However, amongst the many practitioners of the *dharma* there are also those who have clarified their minds sufficiently to verify truth in whatever form it is presented, and will follow it at all costs to enlightenment. The Council of Bodhisattvas heartily seek such worthy ones. The signposts or guides upon the way to enlightenment have changed through the centuries, and contemporary practitioners of the *dharma* have yet to learn to clearly interpret the new directions. The guide books are now being written and many must come forth to understand and practice correctly.

If full comprehension of such guide books is achieved, those *dharma* practitioners yearning to become Bodhisattvas would rapidly become spiritually enlightened. Here is a rhyme and reason *for* Buddhism. The actual present dearth of enlightened beings informs us that little that is read is properly understood. The esoteric view presented in this treatise hopes to rectify this problem, so as to create better thinkers along the Bodhisattva way.

The numbers of Buddhists are growing in the world, thus Buddhism needs a true restorative flowering to rival that of the renaissance of debate and innovative thinkers of the early post-Nāgārjunian era. In order to achieve this it must synthesise the present wealth of scientific knowledge, alongside the best of the Western world's philosophical output.

Currently the *buddhadharma* is presented as an external body of knowledge held by the Buddha, Rinpoches, monks and lay teachers. This encourages practitioners to hero worship these figures and to heed many unenlightened utterances from such teachers, based on a belief system that encourages people to *uncritically* listen to them and adopt their views. When enlightened teachers *do appear* and find consolidated reasons for firing spiritual bullets for the cause of the enlightenment of humanity, then all truth can and will be known. The present lack of inwardly perceived knowledge from the fount of the *dharmakāya* on the part of many teachers blocks the production of an arsenal of weapons for solving the problems of suffering in the world. Few see little beyond the scope of vision in what they have been indoctrinated to believe, allowing for only rudimentary truths to be understood. While for the great majority this suffices, it is woefully inadequate for those genuinely seeking Bodhisattvahood and enlightenment. The cost to humanity in not being given an enlightened answer as to the nature of awakening, is profound.

We must go to the awakening of the Head lotus to find the most established reasoning powers. Without the 1,000 petals of the *sahasrāra padma* ablaze then there is little substance for proper understanding, little ability to hold the mind steady in the dynamic field of revelation that the *dharmakāya* represents. How can the unenlightened properly understand Buddhist scriptures, when there is little (revelation) coming from the Head centres of such beings? Much still needs to be taught concerning the way of awakening this lotus, and to help fill the lack is a major purpose of *A Treatise on Mind.*

Those who intend to reach enlightenment must go beyond the narrow sectarian allegiances promoted by many strands of contemporary Buddhism. Buddhism itself unfolded in a dialectical context with other heterodox Indian (and Chinese, etc.) traditions, and prospered on account of those engagements. When one sees the unfolding of enlightened wisdom in such a fashion, the particular information from specific schools of thought may be synthesised into a greater whole. Each school has various qualities and types of argument to resolve weaknesses in the opposing stream of thought. This highlights that there are particular aspects in each that may be right or wrong, or neither wholly right or wrong. Through this process we can find better answers, or if need be, create a new lineage or religion which is expressive of a synthesis of the various schools of thought.

The Buddha did not categorically reject the orthodox Indian religio-philosophical ideas of his time, nor did he simply accept them—he reformed them. He preserved the elements that he found to be true, and rejected those 'wrong views' which lead to moral and spiritual impairment. If the existing system needs reformation it becomes part of a Bodhisattva's meditation. The way a reforming Buddha incarnates is dependent on how he must fit into such a system. Thus he is essentially an outsider incarnating into it to demonstrate the new type of ideas he chooses to elaborate. If there is a lot of dogmatic resistance to the presented doctrine of truth, then a new religion is founded. If there is some acceptance then we see reformation. There is always room for improvement, to march forward closer to enlightenment's goal, be it for an individual or for a wisdom-religion as a whole. There is a need for reform throughout the religious world today.

By way of a hermeneutical strategy fit for this task, we ought look no further than the Buddha himself. The Buddha proposed that all students of the *dharma* should make their investigations through the *Four Points of Refuge.* These are:

1. The doctrine is one's point of refuge, not a person.
2. The meaning is one's point of refuge, not the letter.
3. The sacred texts whose meaning is defined are one's point of refuge, to those whose meaning needs definition.
4. Direct awareness is one's point of refuge, not discursive awareness.[5]

These four points can be summarised or rephrased as: the doctrine (*dharma*), true or esoteric meaning, right definition, and direct awareness are one's point of refuge, not adherence to sectarian bias, semantics, the dialectics of non-fully enlightened commentaries, or to illogical assertions. What may be long held to be truthful, but is not, upon proper analytical dissection, needs rectifying. Also, in other cases, a doctrine or teaching may indeed be correct, but the current interpretation leaves much to be desired, and hence should be reinterpreted from the position of a more embracive or esoteric view.

Hopefully this presentation finds welcoming minds that will carefully analyse it in line with their own understandings of the issues, and as a consequence build up a better understanding of the nature of what constitutes the path to enlightenment. Their way of walking as Bodhisattvas should be enriched as a consequence.

For a guide to understanding the pronunciation of Sanskrit words, please visit our website.

http://universaldharma.com/resources/pronounce-sanskrit/

Our online esoteric glossary also provides definitions for most of the terms used in this treatise.

http://universaldharma.com/resources/esoteric-glossary/

5 Griffith, P.J., *On Being Buddha, The Classical Doctrine of Buddhahood,* (Sri Satguru Publications, New Delhi, 1995), 52.

My eyes do weep as I stare into this troubled world,
For I dare not place my Heart in my brother's keep.
He would grapple that Heart with hands so rough
So as to destroy the fabric of its delicate stuff.
Oh to give, to give, my Heart does yearn,
But humanity must its embracive,
Humbling, pervasive scene yet to learn.
To destroy and tear with avarice they know,
But little care to sensitive rapture they show.
How to give its blood is my constant fare,
For that Love to bestow upon their Hearts I bemoan.
But they hide their Hearts behind mental-emotional walls.
No matter how one prods these walls won't fall,
So much belittling emotional self-concern prop their bastions.
Oh, how my eyes do weep as I stare.
I stare at their fearsome malls and halls.
That lock Love out from all their abodes
And do keep them trapped in realms of woe.

Oṁ Maṇi Padme Hūṁ

Guru Rinpoche as the King of Sahor

1

Padmasambhava and the Bardo Thödol

Introductory statements

The teachings of the *Tibetan Book of the Dead (Bardo Thödol)* contain multiple levels of meaning and symbolism. It is traditionally used as a liturgy to be read out continuously for forty-nine days for the recently deceased as means to guide them through the travails of the after death (Bardo) state. However, the *Bardo Thödol* is also an important meditation treatise, because the processes associated with what happens when one dies is similar to dying to the physical body in meditation. This book will concentrate upon the section of the *Bardo Thödol* relating to the transformation of base *saṃskāras*[1] into their enlightenment attributes. In doing so it will present much technical information concerning the nature of and the relationship between the deities and the processes involved in this transformation. The book thereby aims to guide the reader through the realms of illusion to eventual enlightenment.

The Tibetan term *Bardo Thödol* is translated as *'The Great Liberation by Hearing in the Intermediate States'* by Gyurme Dorje,[2]

---

1 *Saṃskāras* are mental-emotional propensities of present and past actions carried through from life to life. The *saṃskāras* are expressed in the form of the five different types of *prāṇas* conveyed throughout the *nāḍī* system. They are thus collectivised in various groups of five consciousness-attributes. Literally, *saṃskāras* are one's karmic accumulations which must be worked with, and inevitably transformed in any one life and transmuted into the seeds of enlightenment.

2 Gyurme Dorje, Trans., *The Tibetan Book of the Dead: The Great Liberation by Hearing in the Intermediate States*, (Penguin Books, London, 2005), xxxvi.

and '*The Book of Spontaneous Liberation from the Intermediate State*' by Lama Anagarika Govinda. Govinda states:

> Those who have not yet attained the strength and maturity to see the unveiled reality are led by way of symbol and initiation ritual with the appropriate exercises to gradual understanding and personal experience. That is why the *Bardo Thödol,* the Tibetan book of spontaneous liberation *(thos-grol,* pronounced *thö dol*) from the intermediate state *(bar-do)*—that intermediate state between life and rebirth that we call death—is written in symbolic language.[3]

Govinda explains his use of the phrase 'spontaneous liberation' in the translation of the title:

> Who are those that have ears to hear? Here we come to the decisive point in our judgement of the *Bardo Thödol:* the "hearing" that is meant is not mere reception through the outer ear, but spontaneous grasping through inner hearing, described in the *Surangama Sutra* as an intuitive hearing that transcends the ordinary senses. In this text, Mañjuśrī says to the Buddha:
>
>> We receive this doctrine of yours first through our hearing; but as soon as we are capable of fully grasping it, it becomes our own through a suprasensorial, intuitive hearing. This fact makes the awakening and perfection of such a supersensorial hearing of the greatest importance for every novice. The deeper the wish to gain *samādhi* is established in the mind of a pupil, the more surely can he gain it by means of this supersensorial organ of hearing.[4]
>
> This is the spiritual background which makes intelligible the expression *Thödol (thos-grol),* which I have rendered as "spontaneous liberation," and which literally means "hearing liberation." It is a liberation through inner, intuitive hearing, through a spontaneous grasp of reality.
>
> The understanding of the *Bardo Thödol* depends on one's inner maturity and readiness. While it is, for those who are unprepared, a book sealed with the seven seals of silence, it begins to reveal itself

3 Lama Anagarika Govinda, *Buddhist Reflections,* (Motilal Banarsidass, Delhi, 2007), 130-131.

4 The footnote given: *The Surangama Sutra,* Charles Luk (Lu K'uan Yü), tr., (London: Rider & Co., 1966).

> to those who have learned silence in the schools of meditation, in the practice of self-absorption. For the ordinary person there is no hearing when there is no sound. But for the spiritually awakened, the inner hearing is most lively in stillness, in the silence of all the other senses, and above all, of one's own thoughts.[5]

My explanation of the significance of selected chapters of the *Bardo Thödol* should be read in the spirit of the development of this 'inner, intuitive hearing', as some of the secrets of this 'book sealed with the seven seals of silence' are unravelled. There are various levels of interpretation of these 'seven seals' veiled by each cycle of seven days of the *Bardo Thödol:* the seven *chakras,*[6] seven Rays, seven sheaths of expression to the human persona, the seven planes of perception and seven Initiation levels into the mysteries of being/non-being.

Govinda further states in the introductory foreword of Evans-Wentz's rendition of the *Bardo Thödol:*

> It is a book which is sealed with the seven seals of silence,—not because its knowledge should be withheld from the uninitiated, but because its knowledge would be misunderstood, and, therefore, would tend to mislead and harm those who are unfitted to receive it. But the time has come to break the seals of silence; for the human race has come to the juncture where it must decide whether to be content with the subjugation of the material world, or to strive after the conquest of the spiritual world, by subjugating selfish desires and transcending self-imposed limitations.[7]

---

5 Lama Anagarika Govinda, *Buddhist Reflections,* 131-132.

6 The proper transliteration is *cakra,* but I use the term *chakra,* to denote how this important term is actually pronounced. The term *chakra* means a 'wheel, or disc', of any one of the major or minor energy vortices. The major ones stem from points in the spine. They are divided by means of spokes of energy into regions that have been likened to the petals of lotus blossoms in the etheric body of a person. These psychic centres allow the entry of light of differing qualities and potencies from one dimension of perception into another. Depending upon the energies *(prāṇas)* conveyed, so is seen the manifest quality or characteristic of that being. The major endocrine glands are their physical plane externalisations. The seven major centres are: the Base of Spine centre, the Sacral centre, the Solar Plexus centre, the Heart centre, the Throat centre, the Ājñā centre (the 'third eye') and the Head centre.

7 W.Y. Evans-Wentz, *The Tibetan Book of the Dead,* (Oxford University Press, 1960), liv.

In the process of unlocking these 'seals of silence' much formerly esoteric information can be provided concerning the theriomorphic deities, the functions of the Peaceful and Wrathful Deities, plus that dealing with liberation through knowing the Mind.[8] To explain the context of the entire text would take a major treatise, thus only the key chapters shall be interpreted, allowing the information to be extrapolated into much of the *Bardo Thödol* by interested readers.[9] The readers will thereby be led to a detailed comprehension of the nature of the practices concerning this higher yoga Tantra *(uttarayogatantra).* Consequently they should be able to utilise the information in their own meditation practices. Such comprehension will provide an important background for the teachings in Volume 6 of this treatise, *Meditation and the Initiation Process.*

The *Bardo Thödol* was said to have originally been penned by the great Tantric *yogin* Guru Rinpoche (Padmasambhava).[10] He was invited by king Thrisong Detsun to come to Tibet because the great *dharma* teacher Śāntarakṣita could make little headway in converting the Tibetans to Buddhism in that early time. The main reason was the amassed adversity of the evil spirits and sorcerers in Tibet. Śāntarakṣita thus told the king 'In order to subdue the savage spirits and demons of Tibet, there is a mantra adept called Padmasambhava, who is, at present, the most powerful in the world. I will send him an invitation, and Your Majesty should do the same'.[11] It is within the context of the subjugation of the 'savage spirits and demons' of Tibet (the embodied, externalised aberrant *saṃskāras* of the nation, plus the forces generated by the dark brotherhood) that the *Bardo Thödol* came to be written. The text was the expression of the specialised knowledge of Guru Rinpoche, of his own 'spontaneous liberation' through inner hearing.

---

8 The word mind is capitalised when it refers to the enlightened (abstract) Mind, and in lower case when referring to the unenlightened mundane mind.

9 They are chapter 4 of Gyurme Dorje's translation, entitled 'The Introduction to Awareness: Natural Liberation through Naked Perception', and chapter 5, 'The Spiritual Practice entitled Natural Liberation of Habitual Tendencies'. (Pages 35 and 59 of his book.)

10 It was given in the form of a Terma, a spiritual treasure, said to be hidden by his most important disciple, Yeshe Tsogyal, to be found by an inspired one (the fourteenth century treasure revealer, Karma Lingpa) at the time when people were ready for the teachings.

11 Dudjom Rinpoche, Jikdrel Yeshe Dorje, *The Nyingma School of Tibetan Buddhism,* (Wisdom, Boston, 1991), 513.

The respective images of the Wrathful Deities; the Iśvarī, Mātaraḥ, and Piśācī, therefore fall within the context of what a *yogin* must accomplish internally if enlightenment is to proceed. Guru Rinpoche mastered this subject, as well as demonstrated external exorcisms of the demons in Tibet, so that Buddhism (the pure white *dharma)* could take hold there, and to supplant (convert) the Bön-pa religion of that time (circa 800 A.D.).

With respect to how much of the iconography of the indigenous religion of Tibet was incorporated into the *Bardo Thödol* teachings, Govinda states:

> Even though Padma-Sambhava did adopt into the Buddhist system some of the local Tibetan deities, to serve as guardians of the Faith, in doing so he did not give up one inch of Buddhist ground to the Bön-pos, but acted in perfect conformity with the principles of orthodox Buddhism, wherein, in all Buddhist countries, the deities of the Earth and of space have always been honoured and propitiated, as being protectors of the *Dharma.*[12]

Govinda further states in this respect:

> The Buddhist universe is alive through and through; it has no room for inert matter and mere mechanism. And what is more, the Buddhist is alert to all possibilities of existence and to all aspects of reality. If we have read of the fearful apparitions which surrounded the Buddha during the night preceding His Enlightenment, we need not search for Bön influences in relation to the animal-headed monsters that appear from the abyss of the subconscious mind at the hour of death, or in the visions of meditation. Wrathful deities, demons in animal form, and gods in demonical guise are as much at home in Indian as in Tibetan tradition.[13]

How the *Bardo Thödol* is 'a key to the innermost recesses of the human mind, and a guide for initiates, and for those who are seeking the spiritual path of liberation',[14] can now be detailed. What shall be revealed

12 Evans-Wentz, *The Tibetan Book of the Dead*, lv.

13 Ibid., lvii.

14 Ibid., lix.

in this book will indeed prove to be a treasure trove of enlightening material for serious practitioners. They will discover the joys of what the visualisations in their meditations provide, as they successfully master their own *saṃskāras*. The associated deities of the *Bardo Thödol* will produce their vital revelatory experiences, if the meditations are carried through by means of the activity of the Heart's Mind, and not by means of the force of the personal will or imaginative desire. One must learn to *listen* to the Heart, and thereby *hear* the instructions from the guru within. Thus do all *śrāvakas* (pious disciples of the Buddha, 'hearers') begin to discern the real from the unreal, between what is the product of their imaginations and what appears in consciousness, freed from the image-making faculty of the mind. The various deities are not to be imagined to be real, they will simply appear at the appropriate time, and so act in their transformative and transmutative dance to signal that an appropriate stage has been achieved in the meditation. Then the development of the next stage is possible.

Sincerity in motive is the key. Earnest aspiration to transform base *saṃskāras* into enlightenment-attributes is the need. Steadfastness in applying the liberating aspects of the *buddhadharma* is the method. For others, the detail concerning the qualities associated with the various deities is a labour of mind, as the eye-doctrine develops its own belief system, its own accepted forms of images associated with the world of its accustomed ken.

There is an application of these Bardo teachings that would pave the way to the science of the future, if logically pursued with an awakened Mind. For the development of this future science the words of this treatise have also been written. Much can be understood concerning the natural world and its formation and evolution once the attributes and workings of the mind are properly comprehended. Many lines of enlightened investigation are therefore possible for future students of the *dharma* as these Bardo teachings come to be properly analysed and applied. Concerning the various Bardo states, Govinda says:

> At every moment something within us dies and something is reborn. The different *bardos,* therefore, represent different states of consciousness of our life: the state of waking consciousness, the normal consciousness of being born into our human world, known in Tibetan as the *skyes-nas bardo;* the state of dream-consciousness *(rmi-lam*

> *bar-do);* the state of *dhyāna,* or trance-consciousness, in profound meditation *(bsam-gtan bar-do);* the state of the experiencing of death *(hchhi-kha bar-do);* the state of experiencing of Reality *(chhos-nyid bar-do);* the state of rebirth-consciousness *(srid-pa bar-do).*[15]

Of these states, the waking consciousness is well known to all that function via their sense-perceptors. It produces the sense-consciousnesses, as integrated by the sixth sense, the intellect. Many also experience the dream-consciousness, with its usual mix of distorted memories of what has been experienced when out of the body at night. Subliminal desire-thoughts and all drug-induced hallucinations can enter into consciousness in this Bardo, plus those that enter in from the enlightened planes of perception. The *Book of the Dead* is recited to firstly assist the deceased to recognise the bright lights of the deceased's sojourn that lead to the liberated domains. The experiencing of Reality is to be revealed via the primary or secondary[16] Clear Lights in the Bardo of experiencing death (Chikhai Bardo, *hchhi-kha bar-do)* within the first week of being deceased.[17] Either light, if recognised, brings the deceased to high attainment, akin to a *yogin's* liberation.

There are five types of Clear Light implied in the *Bardo Thödol,* as Lauf states:

> In a Tibetan work about the clarification of all meanings of the bardo the dawning of the clear light from the centre of awareness is outlined in five stages:
>
> In the first, one catches sight of it in its fivefold radiance like a visionary reflection; in the second it is like a moon; in the third like the sun; in the fourth it is like a dawning. These are the signs of the clear light, and then in the fifth stage it itself appears like the cloudless vault of heaven.[18]

---

15 Ibid., lx-lxi.

16 Evans-Wentz, *The Tibetan Book of the Dead,* 89-101.

17 Gyurme states that for the timing of the experience of the primary Clear Light, 'as most sūtras and tantras state that the period of unconsciousness [following the moment of death] may last for three and a half days, generally one should persevere for that length of time, in making this introduction to inner radiance'. Gyurme Dorje, *The Tibetan Book of the Dead,* 229.

18 Detlef Ingo Lauf, *Secret Doctrines of the Tibetan Books of the Dead,* (Shambhala,

In terms of the philosophy presented in this *Treatise on Mind* the first three of these five levels of the Clear Light relate symbolically to the three abstract mental sub-planes. Here the sun and moon refer to relative levels of clarity of vision upon this domain of Mind. The fourth stage that is 'like a dawning' refers to the juncture between the abstract Mind and *śūnyatā*. The fifth stage, 'like the cloudless vault of heaven', can be equated with the *dharmakāya*. From this perspective the primary Clear Light refers to the integration of the fourth and fifth of these levels. The secondary Clear Light then refers to the three sub-planes of the abstract Mind. The *śūnyatā-saṃsāra* nexus[19] is where the primary and secondary Clear Lights meet.

The trance-like Bardo *(dhyāna, bsam-gtan bar-do)* relates to the experience obtained through the mental domain, where perceptions from the abstract Mind come to supersede those from the concrete mind. The term *dhyāna* means 'concentration, a one pointed abiding in an unwavering state of mind'. It is a state of absorbed contemplation, of deep meditation and abstraction into the causal realms of the abstract Mind or higher, according to the abilities of the meditator.[20] The objective inevitably is to experience the lucid Clear-Mind state of enlightenment, of residence at the *śūnyatā-saṃsāra* nexus. In the mastery of *dhyāna* lies the key to the experiencing of Reality, the *Chönyid Bardo (chhos-nyid bar-do)* and therefore controlling the entire rebirthing process. In this Bardo the forty-two Peaceful Deities are said to be experienced

---

Boston, 1989), 95. The source given is: *Bar-do'i spyi'i don thams-cad rnam-pa gsal-bar bsyed-pa dran-pa'i me-long,* Fol. 18a.

19 The place of interrelation between *saṃsāra and śūnyatā* wherein the *dharmakāya* finds its place of application in the meditation-Mind. This nexus can also be viewed as the *Śūnyatā Eye* at the heart of the Sambhogakāya Flower (*tathāgatagarbha),* but it is also more than that, as it may be experienced directly when the Flower is no more. In fact the building of the bridge (*antaḥkaraṇa*) from mind to *dharmakāya* produces the death of the Sambhogakāya Flower, as once this bridge is built, that most subtle of forms (the flower) no longer serves a function. The interrelation between the *ālayavijñāna* and the *dharmakāya* via the *śūnyatā-saṃsāra* nexus is the great Seal (*mahā-mudrā*).

20 *Dhyāna* is one of the six *parāmitas* (great virtues) of perfection. There are said to be four types or levels of *dhyāna.* 1) Joy and pleasure obtained because of the relinquishing of desire and wrong thoughts. 2) Joy due to one-pointed concentration to produce clarity of thought. 3) Bliss due to relinquishing all forms of subtle emotions. 4) Obtainment of equanimity and pure lucid awareness, the Clear Mind.

for the next seven days, and the fifty-eight Wrathful Deities for the next seven days. Thus in these fourteen days the entire panoply of the *maṇḍala* of deities normally come and go. For a meditating *yogin,* however, the process is not that easy. These Deities are expressions of the trance Bardo, whereby the process of experiencing the death of any unruly *saṃskāra* becomes manifest. This activity is fostered by the meditator with the assistance of the energies of the Wrathful Deities. These *saṃskāras* are expressions of the theriomorphic entities, which need to be transformed into enlightenment-qualities. This takes considerable time, and often more than one lifetime is needed.

The cleansed *saṃskāras* are consequently birthed into a higher reality zone, where a new cycle of expression manifests the attributes of the Peaceful Deities as seen in the *Chönyid Bardo.* (The forces of one's own Heart centre—the guru within.) The rebirth Bardo then manifests, to bring one back into the waking consciousness. Upon awakening from this cycle the memory of what happened is enacted in a lucid dream-like state. The process happens again and again whilst transforming subtle *saṃskāras*, until eventually the livingness of the reality of the Clear Light of the Mind is obtained. The normal waking state is then illumined bright prescience, where the cycles of converting *saṃsāra* into *nirvāṇa* are completed.

If the deceased cannot accept the intensity of the bright lights of the liberated domains then the dull lights of *saṃsāra* appear. This process interrelates one with various states of perception, from the various hell states, to the effects of the mental emotions of people's thought life, as one dies to one experiential zone and enters another. This is symbolically undertaken in the twenty-first to the forty-ninth day in the rebirth Bardo *(srid-pa bar-do).* We see that effectively the sum of astral plane phenomena[21] is incorporated here according to the directives of *karma.* The hope is then for the deceased to make the right choice in

21 The astral plane is explained on pages 137-146 in Volume 4 of this treatise, and is the plane of perception where the deceased is normally found after the experience of the *chhos-nyid bar-do.* One can then speculate that the Yid-kyi lus mentioned by Lauf is but a Tibetan name for the astral body: 'The Yid-kyi lus is absolutely capable of experiencing the events of the bardo, as if it were equipped with all the corresponding senses for earthly life'. Lauf, *Secret Doctrines of the Tibetan Books of the Dead,* 96.

the rebirth Bardo which concerns the process of transition to any of the Six Realms. The forces of the *saṃskāras* generated in past lives lay the foundation for the direction of the individual's consciousness. This Bardo refers to the start of every new cycle of experience, rather than just being born out of a mother's womb. One can be born into any of the Six Realms or into the liberated domains. In its simplest connotation it concerns seeking out new experiences in an experiential zone to which one is newly born into.

This outline is a yogic interpretation of the process implied through the symbolic 49 days or stages that are effectively enacted when the *Bardo Thödol* is continually recited for the deceased. The deceased represents an embodied consciousness-stream that will wander to a better cyclic existence if the meaning of the words recited are appropriately understood and acted upon. The number 49 represents the 7 x 7 subdivisions of the sheaths of substance that one can experience and via which one incarnates,[22] as synthesised by the seven *chakras*. The number also refers to the Rays and sub-rays delineating one's consciousness-states, thus the various permutations of the *saṃskāras* that must be transformed and inevitably converted into the Jina[23] wisdoms. (The five wisdoms must also eventually merge into a higher two that represents the function of the Ādi Buddha and his Consort.)

As one delves into the technicalities of the *Bardo Thödol,* so then the significance of various numbers (2, 3, 4, 5, 6, 7, 8, 10, 12) and some of their permutations become quite meaningful. Much background information has been provided concerning these numbers in the former volumes of this *Treatise on Mind* and the earnest practitioner should refer to this foundational wealth to assist in understanding what the *Bardo Thödol* reveals.

---

22 Those sheaths are explained in Volume 6 of this treatise, *Meditation and the Initiation Process*. They can be delineated as three *dharmakāya* levels; *ādi, anupādaka,* and *ātma,* then the mirror *(buddhi, śūnyatā)* which reflects *dharmakāya* into *saṃsāra*. *Saṃsāra* is represented by the mental plane, the astral zone of desire-emotions, and the dense physical plane.

23 *Jina* (Tib. rgal ba): 'Conquerer', an epithet of the Buddha, however, it specifically refers to the five Dhyāni Buddhas.

Padmasambhava and the four cardinal directions

Investigating the significance of the Tantric life of Padmasambhava[24] would be a worthy study. However, this would be a lengthy disquisition in itself that would diverge us too far from the main theme of the *Bardo Thödol*. Revealing a small portion of the biographical detail surrounding him may, however, be of value to earnest students, who can then begin to research the deeper meaning of the import of his life for themselves. Consequently, I shall focus upon the eight names of Guru Rinpoche, and the four cardinal directions veiled in the symbolism of his apparel as the King of Sahor.

I shall use my system of assigning positions of the Buddhas and Bodhisattvas, etc., to the directions of space, which sometimes may supplant the generally accepted assignments. In my system, the direction *north* refers to that pertaining to the liberated realms, the *dharmakāya*. The direction *east* refers to the way inwards to the heart of liberated Life *(śūnyatā)*. The direction *south* refers to the dissemination of compassionate purpose to the little lives ensconced in *saṃsāra*. The direction *west* relates to the outward field of expression representing humanity, who must be brought to an enlightened stance by Bodhisattvic activity. These four directions represent the attitudes of an enlightened one tied to a fixed cross of resolute compassionate purpose.

When the intermediate positions of mutable enlightening activity are added it produces the eight armed cross of direction in space. These intermediate positions manifest as a mutable cross or swastika of energies that interrelate the various arms of the fixed cross in such a way that underlying compassionate purpose can be engendered as one moves from one form of activity to the next. The *northeast* arm of this mutable cross is characterised by the quality of *unity*. By 'unity' is meant that which unifies the forces of the enlightened one, and of the *maṇḍala* to which such a one belongs, so that they can be appropriately utilised to produce the most skilful and effective means to produce the objective.

---

24 Guru Rinpoche, meaning the precious teacher, is the name given by the Tibetans to the founder of the Lamaistic system in their country, Padmasambhava, the lotus born one.

The *southeast* direction directs that unified purpose into the field of *expression.* It is sown in the domains of *saṃsāra,* where hopefully the imparted ideas and energies produce fruit in enlightening response. The *southwest* direction produces the resultant gain in the form of *understanding* from those that worked with what was sown in the field of expression in the southeast. Right comprehension via the *northwest* then allows them to aspire upwards to liberation. Northwest signifies the response or gain of that comprehension as joy and *goodwill* demonstrated to all around as they become harbingers of the teachings of liberation. Such is the pattern of liberating activity found in all lists of four or eight, which abound in the *Bardo Thödol,* depending upon the level of interpretation one pursues.

The symbolic representations of all enlightened beings signify the status of their accomplishments and of the types of realisations they were Initiated into. Padmasambhava is no exception, and a wealth of information can be gleaned from the mythos surrounding him. After first describing some of Padmasambhava's more important attributes Lama Anagarika Govinda states:

> The eight forms in which Padmasambhava is depicted are therefore not different incarnations, as popularly believed, but the representations of his eight main initiations, in each of which he assumed a new personality, symbolized by a new name (as gained in higher forms of initiation), and a form of appearance corresponding to that name. Because initiation is equivalent to entering a new life, it is a form of rebirth.
>
> In his most important and characteristic form Guru Padmasambhava appears in the royal robes of the king of Zahor, but holding the insignia of spiritual realization.[25]

The meaning of these insignias are important and deserve deeper analysis. They relate to the qualities of expression of the four cardinal directions, in which they indirectly symbolise attributes of the Dhyāni Buddhas. Govinda also states that:

> Over the head of Padmasambhava often appears the red Dhyani-Buddha Amitabha, the Buddha of Infinite Light. He is the spiritual

---

25 Govinda, Lama Anagarika, *Insights of a Himalayan Pilgrim,* (Dharma Publishing, California, 1991), 71-73.

> source of Padmasambhava, who thus may be called an embodied ray of Amitabha on the earthly plane.[26]

This infers that Guru Rinpoche, in the form of the king of Sahor, symbolises the attributes of the *nirmāṇakāya* of Amitābha. Of the three bodies (*trikāya*) of a Buddha the highest is the *dharmakāya,* the ultimate nature, body of Truth, the primordial, eternally self-existing essentiality of *bodhi* (enlightenment). Next is the *sambhogakāya,* the 'bliss body' of sublime vision of a Buddha or great Bodhisattva found upon the abstract domain of the Mind. It is the ecstatic transformation body of the form of the great ones depicted in Buddhist art. Finally we have the *nirmāṇakāya,* the transformation body, the emanation (form) body of a Buddha. It is the outer or phenomenal appearance, the tangible something that can be contacted on the realms of illusion, the incarnation body. With respect to Padmasambhava, the three bodies of a Buddha are provided in the dedicatory prayer of part one of the main section of the *Bardo Thödol:*

> I bow down to the spiritual teachers, [embodiment of] the Three Buddha-bodies:
>
> To the Buddha-body of Reality, Infinite Light, Amitābha;
>
> To the Buddha-body of Perfect Resource, the Peaceful and Wrathful Lotus Deities;
>
> And to the Buddha-body of Emanation, Padmākara, protector of beings.[27]

The 'Lotus Deities' relate to the emblem of Amitābha, which is the lotus. It signifies the powers of the *chakras,* embodied by the various deities that denote the attributes of these psychic centres. They can thus be peaceful or wrathful, depending upon the nature of the *saṃskāra* that they convey. The term Padmasambhava means 'the lotus born one', thus he can be considered one of these 'Deities'. The other emblems

---

26 Ibid., 76.

27 Gyurme Dorje, *The Tibetan Book of the Dead,* 225. Note that the term Padmākara is another name for Padmasambhava. Thurman's rendering is: O Amitabha, boundless light of the Truth Body, O mild and fierce Beatific Body Lotus Deities, O Padma Sambhava, incarnate savior of beings—I bow to the Three Bodies in the Spiritual Mentors! (Robert A.F. Thurman, The *Tibetan Book of the Dead: Liberation through understanding in the Between,* Bantam Books, New York, 1994, 117.)

for the *maṇḍala* of the Dhyāni Buddhas (Jinas) are the eight-spoked wheel of the *dharma* for Vairocana and his Dharmadhātu Wisdom, who occupies the central position of the *maṇḍala*. Akṣobhya (the Mirror-like Wisdom) occupies the eastern position, holds the *vajra,* with its five Rays embodying the immutable power of the *maṇḍala* of the Dhyāni Buddhas. Amitābha possesses the Discriminating Inner Vision and his direction in the *maṇḍala* is west. Ratnasambhava, of the southern direction, manifests the Equalising Wisdom and holds the adamantine jewel, the diamond-mind or wish fulfilling gem, the intrinsic energy field of enlightenment, and which is the *nāḍī* system from which the *chakras* stem. Finally we have Amoghasiddhi and his All-Accomplishing Wisdom, whose emblem is the *viśvavajra,* which extends the power of the *vajra* in all directions and localities of space.[28]

The western direction that Amitābha embodies in the *maṇḍala* of the Dhyāni Buddhas rules the realm of the mind/Mind, specifically everything associated with the *ālayavijñāna* (wherein resides the Sambhogakāya Flower[29]). He therefore embodies the essence of whatever consciousness signifies, and the way of its transmutation into the *dharmakāya.* Residing in the Clear Light of Mind and by utilising its Fires, Padmasambhava's miraculous supramundane *siddhis* (psychic powers[30]) were evoked through the complete subjugation of the Watery disposition that qualify most humans. The *siddhis* are gained when all attributes and aspects of desire-mind *(kāma-manas),* its illusions, demons, attachments and phantasms can be subdued, conquered, and transmuted into enlightened principles.

Being an attribute of the *padma* family, the entire *Bardo Thödol* is set

---

28 These Wisdoms and emblems are taken from the *maṇḍala* on the Dhyāni Buddhas on page 121 of Govinda's *Foundation of Tibetan Mysticism.*

29 The Sambhogakāya Flower was explained in detail in Volume 3 of this treatise, *The Buddha-Womb and the Way to Liberation.* It is an alternate name for the *tathāgatagarbha,* the reincarnating principle, in the form of a *chakra* (a flower) existing upon the domain of the abstract Mind.

30 *Siddhi:* psychic powers (spiritual accomplishments) developed through yogic practices. They may be supramundane (attained by a Buddha) or 'common' (attained by an ordinary *yogin).* They can be of the left or right hand variety, and are of many types. We distinguish between the lower *siddhi,* derived from the *chakras* below the diaphragm, and the higher *siddhi,* the powers associated with the evocation of the qualities of the Heart centre, coupled with the *chakras* above the diaphragm.

to detail the powers attributed to the *chakras*. This subject is intimately linked to the *prāṇas*[31] circulating through them. When viewed in terms of the *skandhas*[32] incorporated by means of consciousness via sense-contact with the phenomenal universe, we then have the appearance of *saṃskāras*. This is the basis to comprehending the theriomorphic, Wrathful and Peaceful Deities of the *Bardo Thödol*. They are the (mind-born) personifications of the *saṃskāras* incorporated by the *nāḍīs* as *prāṇas* course through them. They are modified or converted by means of conscious volitions via any of the *chakras*. The process of conversion from gross *saṃskāras* (constituting base desire-mind attributes) to the refinement pertaining to enlightened attributes then constitute the nature of the path signified by the various coloured lights depicted in the text of the *Bardo Thödol*. The quality of the *saṃskāra* involved determines the nature of the colour of the *prāṇa* observed.

Grosser *saṃskāras* are converted in the *chakras* below the diaphragm, where we have the activity of the theriomorphic deities. The conversion zones of transference (Initiation) from a lesser consciousness state to a more exalted level is enacted by the custodians of transference, the Wrathful Deities, who embody the forces pertaining to the major *chakras*. The Peaceful Deities represent the enlightened outcomes in the *chakras* above the diaphragm. This outline of the yogic process depicted in the *Bardo Thödol* shall be detailed later in this book.

31 *Prāṇa:* derived from the Sanskrit roots *pra*, meaning 'forth', and *na*, meaning 'to breathe, move, live'. It is a 'wind', a current of psychosomatic energy, of which there are five types activating the subtle body. It is the 'breath of life', the energy drawn to the physical world from the etheric aspect of all phenomenal life, and is the sum total of the vital energy composing a body, be it human, planetary, or solar. The process of liberation from bondage to the dense form is directly concerned with the transmutation and right projection of the grossest forms of *prāṇa* in the body.

32 *Skandha:* the bundles or groups of attributes that together constitute the human personality and are responsible for the evolution of consciousness. Exoterically, there are five such groupings (attributes of consciousness): 1. Form, or body, the sense organs, sense objects and interrelationships (*rūpa*), 2. Perception or sensation, feelings and emotions (*vedanā*), 3. Aggregates of action, or the motives to thus act (*saṃskāra*), 4. The faculty of discrimination (*samjñā*), 5. Revelatory knowledge (*vijñāna*).
For an explanation of the view of the *skandhas* utilised in this series see Volume 1, chapter 2, where the esoteric account is provided. There they are relegated more purely to considerations of form (*rūpa*) and of the mental substance that incorporates the body of expression of the material world

With respect to Padmasambhava, we must conceive a *maṇḍala* of the Dhyāni Buddhas that has Amitābha as the central figure. This *maṇḍala* is focussed upon the dissemination of the Fiery energy of Mind into manifestation. Vairocana and his Dharmadhātu Wisdom occupies the northern position. One then meditates with vertical alignment upwards to the 1,000 petalled lotus, to awaken the full potency of its petals. Only when the sum total of these petals are awakened can the reception and stabilisation of *dharmakāya* manifest. Akṣobhya and the Mirror-like Wisdom in the eastern direction signify the qualities related to the awakening of the Heart centre — where pacified and transformed *saṃskāras* from below the diaphragm are received into the Void Elements of the liberated Mind. It is therefore the place where generation of the Peaceful Deities occur.

Amoghasiddhi manifests the All-Accomplishing Wisdom in the southern direction. His 'gesture of fearlessness' helps to dispel the phantasms and to transform the most ferocious, noxious and malevolent forces lurking in the depths of *saṃsāric* life.

Ratnasambhava works in the western direction to harmonise human emotional attributes in accord with the modifications of the enlightened Mind (the Equalising Wisdom) so that the patterns of liberation manifest. These patterns are the pathways that inspire people to walk the way of the Heart.

The *maṇḍala* with Amitābha at the centre, or with Padmasambhava substituting for Amitābha (being his *nirmāṇakāya),* represents the locality of the *saṃsāra-śūnyatā* nexus, the place of 'explosion' (if one may so term the process) of *dharmakāya* into *saṃsāra,* and 'implosion' of the attributes of *saṃsāra* into the Void. All happens as a consequence of being able to express the rarefied Fires of cosmos. Literally from this perspective Mind is all there is, wherein *saṃsāra* becomes the vehicle of expression for the manifestation of *dharmakāya.* To obtain this view the obscurations of mind must be converted to Mind by means of the transformation and transmutation process indicated in the *Bardo Thödol.* Here lies the potency of the realisation of rDzogs-chen, the Great Perfection,[33] and of the Yogācāra-Mādhyamika view of the Nyingma.

---

33 Or more specifically the Dharmakāya Way, explained in this *Treatise on Mind.*

The western direction

Having analysed the central figure of the *maṇḍala* associated with Padmasambhava as king of Sahor we can now look to the detail of its other major aspects. The *first* of the insignia of spiritual realisation to be considered is the *khaṭvāṅga.* The use of the *khaṭvāṅga* represents the expression of the *western* direction of outwards to serve humanity. It therefore summarises the attributes of the Bodhisattva path, of the means of transforming 'greed, hatred and ignorance' into enlightened attributes.

> The *khatvanga*, a staff, surmounted by a double-vajra *(vishvavajra),* the symbol of universality and the "Wisdom that Accomplishes All Works"; a vessel containing the elixir of immortality (Skt. *amrita-kalasha*); and two human heads and a skull, symbolizing greed, hatred, and ignorance, which have been overcome by the knowledge of the Three Worlds and the Three Times, symbolized by a flaming trident (*trishula*). The staff itself represents the *sushumna* or the central current of psychic energy, which combines the solar and lunar forces (*pingala* and *ida*, respectively) in one mighty uprush of conscious realization. Thus, all these symbols constitute various aspects of insight into the nature of reality.[34]

The staff is surmounted by seven symbolic representations. We first come across the trinity of:

a. The *viśvavajra*, the symbol of universality and of immutable power over all elements and forces in the material domain. It governs the potency of the united wisdoms of the Dhyāni Buddhas, and of all the attributes of their full *maṇḍala* of expression. It represents the demonstration of the first Ray energy of the Will through yogic prowess projected to the four directions in space to awaken its potency.

b. A *vessel* containing the elixir of immortality. This elixir is the ambrosia of *bodhicitta*, the energy of Love-Wisdom that confers immortality to all who can partake of this intoxicating, enlightening and liberating liquor.

---

34 Govinda, *Insights of a Himalayan Pilgrim*, 73.

c. A *flowing scarf* (not mentioned by Govinda) symbolising the free-flowing spaciousness of Mind, and which technically envelopes the vessel of immortality. In the nature of the energy flow from the *viśvavajra,* the third Ray of Mathematically Exact Activity is represented, producing the activity of the awakened Mind.

Above this trinity are three heads surmounted by a flaming trident.[35] The heads consist of a normal face, a distressed one, and a skull. The normal face symbolises happy ignorance, the state into which one is born. Thus it refers to the foundational quality or Earthy Element that one must learn to overcome. The distressed face refers to the consequence of attachment to phenomena, the expression of the quality denoted as 'speech', thus to the sum of the Watery Element that drives our passions, avarice and all emotional attributes. The skull refers to the death-like nature of the wheel of *saṃsāra,* thus to the fact of being in corruptible physical forms that eventually sicken and die. Hatred is implicated (and the Fiery mental Element) because this passion most produces aggressive attitudes and the wars that cause so many deaths.[36]

Ignorance, hatred, and greed are 'the three poisons' that stand at the centre in depictions of the *saṃsāric* Wheel of Life (and its Six Realms). They manifest in the form of a *red cock* (greed, passionate desire and attachment to things desired), a *green snake* (for all forms of aversion, irritation, separativeness and hatred), and a *black hog* (symbolising the darkness of ignorance and of all forms of blindness). They are the consciousness-attributes to be mastered and transmuted by means of the power of the *khaṭvāṅga* upon which they rest. We thus have:

a. The extreme of hatred that develops when the Fires of mind manifest separative qualities. This quality is symbolised by

35 A trident is represented in the case of a male holding the *khaṭvāṅga*, as it represents his female consort. If a *yoginī* holds it then it is surmounted by a *vajra.* The interrelation then symbolises the non-dual fusion of male and female—of compassion (method) and wisdom, emptiness and bliss.

36 I shall not here deal with other aspects of the symbolism of these heads, such as their colours (usually red, green and white) or of the symbolism of the *khaṭvāṅga* to Tantras such as the Chakrasamvara. Such symbolism is masterly explained in Robert Beer's book *The Encyclopedia of Tibetan Symbols and Motifs,* (Shambhala, Boston, 1999). His work complements well my account.

the skull, as the mind is the ruler of the death-like *saṃskāras* developed by the individual. Eventually a 'hatred' or aversion for the conditions of *saṃsāra* develop, propelling the individual upon the yogic path to mastery over all the attributes of form. The *yogin* and *yoginī* therefore frequent the charnel grounds of their meditative lives to dance upon the corpses of the deceased *saṃskāras* that become the victims on the road to liberation.

b. Greed, exemplifying the clinginess of the Watery desire principle, is the main energy that ties one to the sum of *saṃsāric* allurements, empowering the potency and longevity of the cycles of pain and suffering and is depicted as the distraught face. This face also symbolises the eventual realisation of the practitioner that all of the base *saṃskāras* that were developed in this and in previous lives must be transformed and transmuted into enlightenment principles. The distraught face also manifests as a realisation of the consequences of the *karma* that must be worked off upon the path.

c. Lack of knowledge of the true nature of the form, of phenomena (the Earthy principle), epitomises the extent of one's ignorance, and represents the normal head. It is the conditioning that most people find themselves in. Ignorance has a special place in the dialectic dissertations of Buddhists. It is the foundational basis to the twelve links of Dependent Origination (*pratītyasamutpāda*), thus of the entire wheel of birth and death.

The practitioner must therefore strive to overcome all forms of ignorance by learning the main attributes of the *dharma,* and then ardently practice the yogic precepts and meditation instructions so that enlightenment ensues.

Ignorance is relative to where one stands upon the ladder of attainment, and is never really mastered in its entirety. Even enlightened ones have forms of ignorance to master relative to the staggering immensity of the multidimensional cosmos they are newly born into, though they have mastered all forms of knowledge states concerning our earthly life.

The Fiery Element must be developed upon the path to liberation to fully master the vicissitudes of all the attachments to life so that the wheel of *saṃsāra* can eventually be surmounted. It is the consequence of developing the mind to comprehend the nature of it all. Body, speech and mind are thereby viewed in terms of the transformations that eventually lead to enlightenment.

The *flaming trident* symbolises the function of the abstract Mind, the Clear Light, after the attributes of the three heads on the *khaṭvāṅga* have been transformed into the *saṃskāras* of enlightenment. The prongs of the trident then represent the Fiery expressions of the combined *iḍā, piṇgalā* and *suṣumṇā nāḍīs,* and every associated ramification. Eventually they produce the three bodies of a Buddha, the *dharmakāya, sambhogakāya,* and *nirmāṇakāya.*

The symbolism of the *khaṭvāṅga* can also relate to the three major tiers of the Sambhogakāya Flower existing upon the abstract levels of the mental plane. The *viśvavajra,* the flowing ribbon and cup of *amṛta* represent attributes of the three Knowledge petals of the Flower, where the attributes of mind that were developed are contained. They must eventually be transformed into the qualities of the Mind (the Wisdoms of the five Jinas) that inevitably transcend the ability of containment by this form. Much spiritual power must be used to transform the five sense-consciousnesses via knowledgeable pursuits, thus the need for the use of the *viśvavajra* at this level of development.

The three heads represent the development of the compassionate aspects *(bodhicitta)* of human livingness, thus the qualities of the attributes of consciousness that are stored in the Love-Wisdom triad of petals. Ultimately, these petals are responsible for transmuting the basic qualities of the three heads into their enlightened aspects. This process manifests through selective rebirths of the sequence of personal-I's and the rightful overshadowing of each 'I' so that *saṃskāras* are eventually transmuted.

The *three prongs* of the trident represent the Sacrifice triad of petals because they indicate the high point of attainment of the *khaṭvāṅga.* The abstracted attributes of the *iḍā, piṇgalā* and *suṣumṇā nāḍīs* are stored in these petals. When the *prāṇas* of this triad are added to the two other triads, then we have the nine qualities symbolising the functions of the nine major petals of the Sambhogakāya Flower. All aspects of the Flower must be abstracted into their most rarefied expression and projected towards the *dharmakāya* realisation.

The major tiers of the Head lotus (*sahasrāra padma*) similarly incorporate the *prāṇas* of the conscious volition of a personality via the activity of the Ājñā, Throat and Heart centres. (The *prāṇas* are processed in the Head lotus before being directed to the Sambhogakāya Flower.) The rectified and transformed *prāṇas* of the three poisons are directed to the Head lotus by these major *chakras*. *Ignorance* is transformed into revelatory knowledge with the assistance of the combined Head and Ājñā centres. (These two centres overlap and are esoterically viewed as a unity.) *Hatred* is transformed into acceptance and comprehension of underlying causes, or else to meditative realisation of how to affect beneficent change, with the assistance of the Throat centre. (This centre deals with all *manasic*[37] *prāṇas* in the body.) *Greed* is transformed with the assistance of the Heart centre focussed upon the centres below the diaphragm. The Heart centre works to convert all self-centred based emotions into egoless attributes of compassion. All selfish tendencies to amass things for oneself must be converted into selfless service to others. The process of the conversion of all mental-emotional *prāṇas* is the work of the dual Splenic centres via their interrelation with the Solar Plexus and some of the minor *chakras* below the diaphragm.

If we look to the overall symbolism of the *khaṭvāṅga* then we find seven major components, which relate to the seven Ray aspects governing all life. These seven aspects relate to a *western* orientation of outwards to the field of service, the major life orientation for the Bodhisattva.

1. The *viśvavajra* represents the first Ray of Will or Power, which expresses the combined power of the wisdoms of the five Dhyāni Buddhas. All *saṃsāric* allurements must be mastered and converted to wisdom-attributes by means of the Will-of-Love if these wisdoms are to be obtained.
2. The *vessel of amṛta* containing the nectar of immortality, which represents the function of the second Ray of Love-Wisdom, conveying enlightenment upon all who can sup this ambrosial energy.
3. The two *strands of the scarf* represent the qualities of the third Ray of Mathematically Exact Activity. They move this way and that (via the *iḍā* or *piṅgalā* streams) according to the way the winds of

37 *Manas:* (from the Sanskrit root *man*, 'to think') is literally the domain of the mind.

enlightenment (*buddhi*) flow, and to the perceived need in the material domain. Therefore this scarf is seen to manifest a dual function, which also symbolises the mode of the manifestation of mind/Mind.

There is also an implicit septenate in these three, with the four outer prongs of the *viśvavajra* representing the powers needed to process and overcome the afflictions of the personality quaternary and to transform them into enlightenment principles. This quaternary constitutes the dense form, the etheric substratum containing the *nāḍīs,* the emotional body, and the empirical mind. The vessel of *amṛta* symbolises the abstract Mind wherein enlightened consciousness resides, and which induces immortality when all of its attributes are fully expressed. (Here it is an extension of the central prong of the *vajra.*) From this perspective the two strands of the scarf signify the *iḍā* and *piṇgalā nāḍīs* gathering *prāṇas* in the vicissitudes of *saṃsāra.*

4. The *trident* symbolises the qualities of the fourth Ray of Beautifying Harmony overcoming Conflict, which is a mirror reflecting the qualities of the triune abstracted universe into the three concreted realms, and *vice versa.* The long prong and handle of the trident integrates all of the component parts of the *khaṭvāṅga* into a unity, similar to the fourth Ray, which interrelates the three higher to the three lower Rays. The mechanism of the prongs either reflect divinity into the form, or project power from the form to conquer attributes of manifest space. The fourth Ray, or middle principle, works similarly with respect to receiving the gain from *saṃsāric* involvement, or to project into *saṃsāra* the attributes of divinity. The role of Ratnasambhava's Equalising Wisdom for this western direction is exemplified here.
5. The *manasic* overtones of the head relating to *hatred* is an expression of the fifth Ray of Scientific Reasoning. Hatred is an extreme version of the separative, dissecting nature of the analytical use of the mind, when coupled with strong emotion.
6. The head relating to *greed/desire* refers to the sixth Ray of Devotion, which is a refined form of desire, where the focus is for things divine or inspirational in nature.

7. The skull relates to the seventh Ray of Ceremonial Cyclic Activity which governs all of the cycles associated with the material world. This symbolises repeated incarnations of birth and death.

All of these attributes are conveyed to the personal-I (here interpreted at the level of the *nirmāṇakāya* of Padmasambhava) by means of the shaft of the staff, representing the *antaḥkaraṇa,* the consciousness-link between the 'I' and the Sambhogakāya Flower. They therefore represent the sum of the manifesting divinity that is mastered by the accomplished *yogin.* They are his prowess, the mechanism and qualities possessed to help humanity in the manner that this western position implicates.

The eastern direction

The *eastern* direction of inwards toward the Heart of Life is represented in the skull-bowl (*kapāla*):

> The skull-bowl (*kapala*), in which the vessel with the elixir of immortality is placed, rests in the left hand of the Guru, because the knowledge or conscious experience of death (as gained in the higher forms of initiation) leads to the realization of immortality, to the experience of the Greater Life. The elixir of immortality is the attribute of Amitayus, the Buddha of Infinite Life, the Sambhogakaya reflex of the Dhyani-Buddha Amitabha.[38]

The skull bowl is held in the left hand, its position is below the Heart centre and symbolises the transmuted Watery qualities (of desire, lust, etc.) of the Solar Plexus centre (*maṇipūra chakra*) contained as an offering to the Heart of Life. The *amṛta* ('elixir of immortality') is the fusion of all transmuted *prāṇas* of the Inner Round grouping of *chakras* synthesised by the Solar Plexus centre and integrated by *bodhicitta* from the Heart. It necessitates deep inner introspection to accomplish the translation of the *prāṇas* from the Solar Plexus centre so that they can be accommodated by the Heart centre. This is the basis for the expression of the *siddhis* developed by accomplished ones. The inward

38 Govinda, *Insights of a Himalayan Pilgrim*, 73.

meditation concerns dedicatory offerings of all awakened *siddhas*[39] to serve all sentient beings. Every form of transience (symbolised by the skull bowl) must be converted into the accomplishment of this elixir of immortality as an offering for all to drink its essence. This is the way of the Heart, the boundless expanse of the Waters of Love.

The southern direction

The symbolism of the *southern* direction (downward towards the little lives that constitute the body of manifestation), concerns controlling the entire field of *saṃsāra* wherein the lives reside. The mechanism of control is the *vajra* in the guru's right hand that is raised in 'the gesture of fearlessness and blessing'. Govinda describes the *vajra* as:

> the sceptre of spiritual power, the means through which wisdom is put into action. It may also be displayed in a threatening attitude, the hand above the right knee, in the act of subduing evil forces. In a devotional Tibetan text Padmasambhava is described in the following words:
>
> > Being the end of confusion and the beginning of realization,
> > He wears the royal robes of the Three Vehicles (of liberation),
> > He holds the Vajra of Skillful Means in his right hand
> > And in his left the Skull-bowl of Wisdom with the Elixir of Life.
> > He cuts off the heads of hatred, greed, and ignorance
> > And carries them like ornaments on his trident.[40]

This gesture represents the projection of the spiritual power that will subjugate the demons and the forces of the dark brotherhood that control much of the material domain. It also represents the potency needed to subdue all of one's materialistic incentives, to overcome the allurements of attachment to the world of material plane living. The potency is a veiled form of the wisdoms of the Dhyāni Buddhas. Therefore, it represents the Guru's ability to wield control over the externalised form of *karma*, whilst the bowl of *amṛta* represents the ability to control the *karma* of the internalised *saṃskāras*. Together they make him the

---

39 Accomplished *yogins* that have awakened *siddhis*, such as that of psychic heat.

40 Govinda, *Insights of a Himalayan Pilgrim*, 73-75. Govinda does not provide his source.

all-conquering Lord of Nature and the denizens inhabiting the *lokas*[41] of all manifest life. He is a Buddha for the entire material domain, as all of its forces and potencies come under his control.

The northern direction

Finally, we have the symbolism of the *northern* direction of upward towards Life supernal as symbolised by the insignia on his hat.

> His hat (known as the "lotus cap") is adorned with the symbols of the crescent moon, the sun-disk, and a small flame-like protuberance, which signifies the union of lunar and solar forces (Tib. *thig-le*), the realization of the Dharmadhatu wisdom. The hat is surmounted by a vajra and an eagle's feather. The latter indicates the Guru's soaring mind, penetrating the highest realms of reality.[42]

As this cap adorns the head, signifying the Head lotus *(sahasrāra padma),* it expresses the direction north to the highest realisations. The crescent moon refers to the energies of the *iḍā nāḍī,* which are lunar (astral) in nature when compared to those of the *piṇgalā nāḍī,* which are radiantly luminescent (solar) in constitution. By 'lunar' is meant that which shines by reflected light, and is a satellite to the greater luminary. Here the 'satellite' is the personality and the greater luminary is the Sambhogakāya Flower. The Fires of mind are kindled in the personal-I residing in *saṃsāra* via the development of the sense-consciousness. This awakens the *iḍā* flow, however, the supernal liberating light of the Sambhogakāya Flower directs the overall *karma* and generates the flashes of illumination that produce enlightenment. The light from this Flower consequently shines upon the personality to direct its purpose. The solar forces are those whereby consciousness develops compassionate attributes to awaken the potency of the Heart centre and eventually the experience of *śūnyatā*.

The 'small flame-like protuberance' refers to the qualities of the *suṣumṇā nāḍī,* which grows into a fierce incandescence when fully awakened. The Head lotus absorbs and processes all *prāṇas* associated

41 Planes of perception.

42 Govinda, *Insights of a Himalayan Pilgrim,* 75.

with these *nāḍīs,* and will eventually transform them into the highest enlightenment-attributes, synonymous with the Dharmadhātu Wisdom of Vairocana, once an aspirant is rightly focussed and can utilise the higher Wills. We know the *vajra* to symbolise the immutable power of the Dhyāni Buddhas. The eagle is able to soar high in the sky and with an extremely keen vision spot the minutest activity in the valley below, which symbolises the qualities of the All-seeing Eye, the Ājñā centre.

All told, this cap is a composite of seven symbols that express the potencies of the seven *chakras* in the body, the *prāṇas* of which are absorbed into the 1,000 petalled lotus. For this reason they sit on Guru Rinpoche's head, where the Head centre is also situated.

1. The lotus cap—the Base of Spine centre, which supports all of the other *chakras,* the insignia of which are incorporated in this cap.
2. The cap is adorned with three, four or five small circles, and sometimes a *viśvavajra.* The three circles symbolise the three wish-fulfilling gems and their liberated qualities. They flow up the three major *nāḍīs* from the Sacral centre once the three poisons are converted. If four circles, then they symbolise the four main Elements that constitute the *saṃskāras* that fulfil people's earthly wishes. Five circles, or the *viśvavajra,* represent the wisdoms of the Jinas, the transmuted correspondences of the sense-consciousness. The entire process of the retrieval of the associated *saṃskāras* and their eventual conversion find their repository in the various petals of the Head lotus.
3. The crescent moon symbolises the lunar forces in the body. They are the *prāṇas* generated below the diaphragm and synthesised by the Solar Plexus centre. These *prāṇas* are incorporated as the general *iḍā* stream.
4. The solar disc symbolises the solar forces in the body, which pertain to the Heart centre. These *prāṇas* represent the *piṇgalā* stream.
5. The flame-like protuberance, which Govinda says represents 'the union of solar and lunar forces', relates to the Throat centre, which regulates the Fiery Element, the forces of the mind, thus of the way that these *prāṇas* come to be incorporated into the Head lotus. Eventually the process associated with the liberation of *kuṇḍalinī* is also generated by the use of this centre.

6. The eagle's feather represents the All-seeing Eye, the Ājñā centre, which allows one to soar high in spiritual vision, to purvey the sum of the spiritual and *saṃsāric* landscape at need.
7. The *vajra,* with its prongs focussed northward, represents the immutable spiritual power of the fully awakened Head centre.

The complete body of Guru Rinpoche, with all of its adornments, also needs mention as it symbolises the central position of the *maṇḍala,* the *dharmakāya* from which all stems. The significance of the quote Govinda extracted from a devotional text: 'Being the end of confusion and the beginning of realization, He wears the royal robes of the Three Vehicles (of liberation)' may be illustrated. These three vehicles of liberation are the *nirmāṇakāya, sambhogakāya* and *dharmakāya* of a Buddha.

The eight appearances of Guru Rinpoche

The eight directions of space will be utilised to explain these appearances to derive a far greater meaning from them. It is useful to study these qualities because it provides a better understanding as to the nature of Tantric philosophy and the way that all aspects of a great One can be utilised to convey important esoteric truths. The eight appearances that are depicted around the central figure of Padmasambhava as the king of Sahor are:

> 1. Padma Jungnay *(Tib. Padma-'byung-gnas,* "the Lotus-born," Skt. Padmasambhava) in his Vajrasattvic form, dark-blue, embraced by his *Prajna*, the embodiment of his Wisdom (generally light-blue, sometimes white), because—according to his symbolical biography—Padmasambhava took on the aspect of *Vajradhara* when he was initiated into the doctrine of the Great Perfection (Tib. *rDzogs-chen*), in which the indestructible and transparent diamond-nature of our innermost being is realized.[43]

The direction indicated here is *north* (upward to the domains of liberation), because here we have the doctrine of The Great Perfection

43 Ibid., 77.

exemplified, bringing us to the highest realisations. Vajrasattva (white in colour) is the *sambhogakāya* of the Ādi (primordial) Buddha (known as Samantabhadra in the *Bardo Thödol*). He holds the *vajra* (signifying the wisdom of the five Jinas) in his right hand at his Heart centre (the seat of *śūnyatā)* and a bell *(ghaṇṭā*, signifying the natural emptiness of the Mind) with his left hand supported at his hip (signifying mastery of the lower centres by means of the clarifying sound). As such, the *maṇḍala* of Peaceful and Wrathful Deities of the *Bardo Thödol* are said to be emanations of his Heart (the Peaceful Deities), and of his Mind (the Wrathful Deities). The name Vajrasattva can be translated as the vehicle of the unexcelled pristine Diamond-Mind (when the *vajra* is viewed as a diamond-sceptre).

> 2. Guru Shakya Senge (Tib. *Shakya-seng-ge*, "The Lion of the Shakya Clan"). In this form Padmasambhava is identified with Shakyamuni, the historical Buddha, thus indicating Padmasambhava's initiation into the teachings of the earliest schools of Buddhism, as represented by the Small Vehicle (Hinayana).[44]

Shakya-Seng-ge refers to the direction *south* (downward to the material domains), because here the most basic expression of the *buddhadharma* is established, the Hīnayāna vehicle. This vehicle laid the foundation of the qualities to be developed and the later development of the Bodhisattva path espoused by the Mahāyānists. Also, Gautama gave out the foundational teachings (the *mūlādhāra chakra* level) upon which all later Buddhistic development was based. From this southern direction one learns to travel upwards to liberation by mastering *saṃsāra.*

> 3. Guru Padmasambhava as a *bhikshu* or pandit of the Great Vehicle, indicating his initiation into the teachings of the Mahayana School and his entering upon the Bodhisattva Path.[45]

A *bhikśu* of the Mahāyāna refers to the direction *west* (outward to the field of service that represents humanity), because here the Bodhisattva path is exemplified. The ideal being to serve all sentient

44 Govinda, *Insights of a Himalayan Pilgrim, 77.*

45 Ibid., 77-78.

beings and humanity in general, by bringing them to liberation, before the Bodhisattva takes the final step of *parinirvāṇa.*

> 4. Guru Lodan Chogsed (Tib. *Blo-ldan mchog-sred*), the "Guru Possessing Wisdom and the Highest Aspirations." He appears here in kingly robes, his right hand raised with a *damaru*, from which the eternal sound (*shabda*) of the Dharma rhythmically emerges and pervades the universe. The left hand holds a skull-bowl brimming with the elixir of immortality.[46]

Guru Lodan Chogsed embodies the direction *east* (inward to the Heart of Life), because the way to the liberating Heart of all that is concerns the development of wisdom, realised through 'the highest aspirations'. The eternal sound of the *dharma* perpetually emanates from the Heart centre. This sound can be considered to be the word of the liberation of consciousness—Oṁ. Technically, the drum *(ḍamaru)* beats out the rhythm 72 times per minute, similar to the pulsing of the blood in the veins.

> 5. Guru Padma Gyalpo (Tib. *Padma-rgyal-po,* "the Lotus King"), is very similar to the previous figure; he distinguishes himself mainly by holding the Mirror of Truth in his left hand. Sometimes he is also depicted with the mirror held up in his right hand, in which case the left hand holds the skull-bowl. In some thankas the emblems of these two kings are reversed, so that it seems these two figures are more or less interchangeable.[47]

Padma Gyalpo refers to the direction *northeast* of unity of all forces directed towards one common field of expression. This lotus king holds 'the mirror of truth', which effectively reflects the combined wisdom of his fellow Bodhisattvas into the sacred and temporal space of the *maṇḍala* of which he is a part. It also refers to the mirror-like wisdom, staring into the face of the intrinsic emptiness[48] of one's own being. This quality is projected from this direction into the activity of the entire wheel of this cross of direction in space.

---

46 Ibid., 78.

47 Ibid.

48 For a detailed explanation see Volume 4, chapter 3.

6. Guru Dorje Drolog (Tib. *rDo-rje-gro-lod),* "the Diamond Comforter," manifests in a wrathful appearance (*krodha-bhairava*), red in colour, surrounded by flames (symbolizing knowledge in its "terrible" illusion-devouring aspect), riding on a tiger, holding a vajra in his outstretched right hand, and in his left hand a *phur-bu,* a magical dagger which destroys evil influences, exorcises demons, and drives away the powers of darkness. The prostrate human form underneath the tiger represents a conquered demon.[49]

Dorje Drolog represents the direction *southeast,* of the expression into manifestation of the qualities possessed by the divinity contacted in the northeast direction. The 'wrathful appearance (*krodha-bhairava*)' that repels all phantasms and demons of the material world is necessary if the projection of the pure white *dharma* is not to be immediately consumed by the denizens of the encompassing *māyāvirūpa* and converted into the vilest *saṃskāras*. Psychic protection is a necessity in all true meditation work, as there are many *saṃskāras* of past life activities related to the dark arts that come to the surface when *yogins* awaken minor *siddhis*. The externalisations of the *siddhis* manifest in the form of demons and the like. They must all be transformed into enlightenment-attributes by the fierceness of this wrathful one. The work is accomplished by means of right ritual practices, invoking the power symbolised by the *phur-bu (phur ba,* the ritual dagger), that potently grounds the power of the wisdoms of the five Dhyāni Buddhas. The three blades and three faces of the *phur ba* represent the three planes and three times of human livingness; of body, speech, and mind, all of which must be transformed by means of yogic ritual and *dhāraṇīs.*[50] The blade is capable of liberating the serpent power *(kuṇḍalinī),* thus it has entwined serpents running down it. The point projects the power of this liberating potency, as directed by the Knowingness of Secret Mantra, to whatever the object of the ritual is. Dorje Drolog rides upon the tiger, symbolising his fearlessness in dealing with any aspect of *saṃsāra*.

7. Guru Nyima Odzer (Tib. *Nyi-ma-od-zer*), "the Sun-ray Guru," appears as an ascetic of the Heruka (unclad) type. His left (sometimes

---

49 Govinda, *Insights of a Himalayan Pilgrim, 78.*

50 *Dhāraṇī:* a mechanism for fixing the mind to an idea, vision or experience gained in meditation.

> his right) hand holds the sun by a ray, his right (sometime his left) hand holds a three-pointed staff (*khatvanga*). He wears a crown of skulls and a tiger-skin around his loins. His colour is yellow.[51]

Guru Nyima Odzer represents the direction *southwest* of understanding the expression formerly seeded in the southeast position. Thus he holds the sun disc, signifying the evocation of the wisdom associated with the *piṇgalā nāḍī* stream *(bodhicitta).* The 'crown of skulls' signifies the wisdom that has been gained through perpetual rebirths into transient material forms, and through the mastery of *saṃskāras* that produce death-like *saṃsāric* attributes. The tiger skin indicates that he is the victorious conqueror over the entire desire principle that gained power over the course of many lives. The entire turning about in the seat of consciousness has occurred and the triumphant *yogin* has mastered *saṃsāra.* He can thus experience the Void (the empty hand), or else sound out the note of Emptiness to clarify all temporal space. (The use of the bell.)

> 8. Guru Senge Dradog (Tib. *Senge-ge-sgra-sgrogs*), "the Guru with the Roaring Voice of a Lion", is a dark blue demoniacal figure, clad in a lion skin dangling from his shoulders and a tiger-skin as a loin-cloth. He is surrounded by flames; in his right hand he wields a vajra in a menacing way, and the left hand is either empty or holds a bell before his chest. He stands on the bodies of two conquered demons.[52]

Guru Senge Dradog represents the *northwest* position of emanatory goodwill to all beings. 'The Roaring Voice of a Lion' symbolises victory over all *saṃsāric* vicissitudes as one treads the path of enlightenment, and is the unique sound of accomplishment emanated out into all space to hearken the residing brethren of his coming prowess. His menacing *vajra* is a warning to all dark foes that their days of manipulating base human desires are now numbered, as he has gained the power to make their spells and conjurations of demons ineffective. The sound of warning therefore emanates out into the space he is yet to travel, preceding his arrival. He is master of the entire material domain and hence is seen trampling demons of desire and divisiveness.

51 Govinda, *Insights of a Himalayan Pilgrim, 79.*

52 Ibid.

The Guru and the Heart centre

The eight names of Guru Rinpoche are not just appellations signifying his Initiations, but they also imply the qualities to be developed by all who would wish to emulate his prowess to gain a similar enlightenment. As aspirants come to master each of the qualities of these directions, so then they can be Initiated into the related mysteries. Upon mastery the Initiates can take similar appellations for themselves, and so it will be for all true seekers on the path.

The two main female disciples (consorts) generally depicted at the bottom right and left hand sides of the king of Sahor are the Tibetan Ḍākinī Yeshe Tsogyal and the Indian princess Mandarava. They obviously manifest an important trinity with the Guru, and as always with such representations the central figure signifies the potency of the qualities of the *suṣumṇā nāḍī.* The left hand figure (in this case Mandarava) embodies the *iḍā nāḍī* qualities, and the right hand side (Yeshe Tsogyal) the *piṇgalā* aspect. The symbolism of each can be properly analysed with respect to the functioning or qualities of the central figure. Something less obvious to the devotees of the Guru shall be analysed here, namely that the symbolism of the four cardinal directions plus the eight names define the characteristics of the twelve petals of the Heart centre, or more specifically, the Heart in the Head centre of Guru Rinpoche. They therefore symbolise the qualities each of us must develop if we are to emulate his magnificent achievements.

The characteristics of each petal of the Heart centre were given in Volume 3 of this treatise, in the chapter entitled 'Zodiacal Consideration of the Heart Centre', to which the reader must refer for detail. The associated figure shall be presented for reference. The main components of the Guru Rinpoche *maṇḍala* can then be related to these petals. Taking the attributes of a Heart lotus, Padmasambhava stands in the guise of Avalokiteśvara, lord of compassion, who is one of the Bodhisattvas ascribed to Amitābha.

We will proceed with the wheel turning in a clockwise direction starting with the western direction, which governs the process related to the resolution of the *karma* of the entire path to enlightenment. The four main attributes of the king of Sahor represent the four cardinal petals of the Heart *chakra* (N,S,E and W.) The eight names of Guru Rinpoche then represent the qualities of the intermediate petals of this centre.

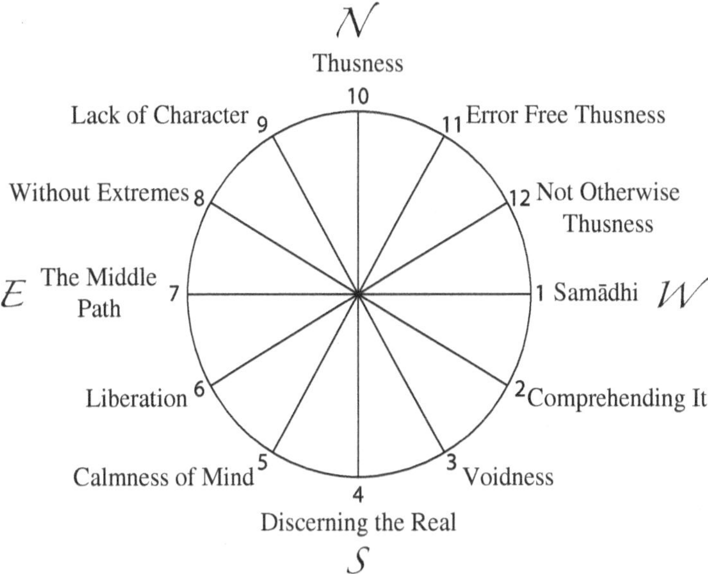

Figure 1. Qualities of the petals of the Heart centre

1. For the direction *west*[53] the enlightened quality is the development of 'Samādhi'. The entire symbolism associated with the *khaṭvāṅga* comes into active manifestation when one learns to attain the meditative quietude that will allow analysis of all aspects of life. One then learns that it is not this, not that, not other than what one can find within the Clear Light of the precincts of a Mind stilled in *samādhi.* The power of the *khaṭvāṅga* can then be used to drive the entire wheel forwards to liberation. The *khaṭvāṅga* symbolically depicts the major achievements of the meditative one, used both for vertical alignment with higher principles and for projection of spiritual power.
2. For the direction *west-south* the enlightened quality is 'Comprehending It'. This direction of the Heart lotus is assigned to Dorje Drolog, who as *krodha-bhairava,* 'devours all phantasms and demons of the material world'. They are aspects of the phenomena produced by others that must be repelled or psychically transformed

53 For an explanation regarding the placement of the east and west directions on the figure, refer to Volume 4 of this treatise, page 197.

by one upon this petal of the Heart. Then all aspects of phenomena upon the road to liberation can be comprehended. Also upon this path the various demons of one's own corporeal *saṃskāras* must be overcome. Once these *saṃskāras* have been transformed then enlightened principles replace them.

3. For the direction *southwest* the enlightened quality is 'Voidness'. Travelling upon the Bodhisattva path will produce true Voidness, this relates to a follower of the Mahāyāna, not the *arhat* form of *śūnyatā* aspired to in the Hīnayāna path. (The *arhat* attainment is illusional in that the condition lasts for that life only, rebirth is necessary to discover the way of the Bodhisattva.) The path to liberation necessitates cleansing all types of *karma* obscuring affiliations. One must earnestly follow the Bodhisattva path if liberation from tyranny of the 'self' concept is to ensue.
4. In the direction *south* the enlightened quality is 'Discerning the Real'. To distinguish the real from the unreal, one must fearlessly confront all extraneous attributes of Nature including those manifesting in the psychic domains and the phantasms of mind. As one battles the allurements of *saṃsāra* so the qualities of the *vajra* (the wisdoms of the Jinas) are developed, assisting one to reach the domain of the *śūnyatā-saṃsāra* nexus. The discernment of the real from the unreal at every level of perception thus awakens the powers of the *vajra* held in the Guru's right hand and raised in 'the gesture of fearlessness and blessing'.
5. The direction *southeast* posseses the enlightened quality 'Calmness of Mind'. It is embodied by the attributes of Guru Shakya-Seng-ge. The Hīnayāna vehicle introduced the practice concerning the development of Calmness of Mind *(śamatha)* by meditating upon the Buddha's teachings. The endeavour here is to observe all causes of *māyā* so that *saṃsāric* attributes are cut at their roots. The *bhikśu* establishes the foundational practices by this means that will eventually lead deeply to the heart of the inner sanctuary of revelation.
6. The direction *east-south* is given the enlightened quality 'Liberation'. This direction is embodied by Guru Lodan Chogsed, whose *ḍamaru* beats out the 'eternal sound of the *dharma*'. This sound then

produces liberation when earnestly listened to. It awakens wisdom and the compassionate insight that allows the Guru to assist all needy ones in *saṃsāra*.

7. The direction *east* posseses the enlightened quality 'The Middle Path'. It refers to the symbolism of the skull-bowl *(kapala)* that holds the *amṛta*, the nectar of immortality. The ability to sup the *amṛta* from the skull cup is the leitmotiv of the existence of the Heart centre. It is the energy that is the mainstay of this centre and feeds the *nāḍīs* with the draught of the Void. This path is exemplified by the middle way of the Buddha. It instigates a cycle of progression around the twelve petals of the Heart centre, which generates the *amṛta* that fills the *kapala* of blissful revelation. The *prāṇas* leading to all petals of the Heart centre must be mastered, and consequently the attributes of the twelve signs of the zodiac, before liberation is possible. Many lives go into such an undertaking.
8. In the *east-north* direction the enlightened quality developed is 'Without Extremes'. Here the functions of Padma Gyalpo holding 'the mirror of truth' come to the fore. The mirror of the Clear Light truthfully reflects whatever is perceived in terms of the Real. Things are perceived as they actually are, without any of the extremes that would come from a mental-emotional analysis of manifesting phenomena. The perceptions are conjunctly produced, integrating the realm of enlightenment and the mundane domains. The link formed, the *śūnyatā-saṃsāra* nexus, allows *dharmakāya* (cosmos) to contain *saṃsāra* and vice versa.
9. In the *northeast* direction the enlightened quality developed is 'Lack of Character'. Here the qualities of Padma Jungnay (the lotus-born) is exemplified, signifying the development of *rDzogs-chen*. The Great Perfection is without mentalistic characterisations, as it stands in the Void. All forms of volition that come from a concept of 'self' must be overcome if the Great Perfection is to be achieved, where *śūnyatā* and *saṃsāra* stand in mutual embrace, both being empty of intrinsic characteristics. They are expressions of a potent energy that integrates both, which allows *saṃsāra* to be used as a vehicle to reveal *śūnyatā,* which is the basis of *rDzogs-chen*.

10. The *northern* direction is embodied by the *cap* that adorns the head *(sahasrāra padma)* of the Guru. The enlightened quality is the 'Thusness' that is achieved when the Heart in the Head centre is fully awakened. The Heart knows not a 'self', only of the needs of 'the other'. The awakened 1,000 petals of this lotus allows the gnosis of the full potency of the *dharmakāya* to become integrated with *saṃsāra.*
11. For the direction *northwest* the enlightened quality developed is 'Error-free Thusness'. Here we have Guru Senge Dradog's 'Roaring Voice of a Lion' demonstrating the victory over all *saṃsāric* vicissitudes. For the *yogin,* this necessitates mastery of aberrant self-produced *saṃskāras.* Arrows of righteousness, and of one-pointed focus, must be directed to manifest the potency of the adamantine *vajra,* repelling spells and conjurations of demons, or wrong thought constructs. Overcoming all fanciful emanations of mind, the enlightened one then resides in the Thusness that is exact, precise, pristine, with respect to what must be repelled or achieved.
12. The direction *west-north* expresses the quality 'Not Otherwise Thusness'. This direction is held by Guru Nyima Odzer, who wields the sun disc, the developed wisdom associated with the *piṇgalā nāḍī* stream, the 'crown of skulls', and the tiger skin of victorious control over the entire desire principle. Many are the tests and trials on the path that must be passed, myriad the *saṃsāric* allurements that must be overcome if the material domain is to be mastered and the Thusness that signifies liberation be gained. All types of *karma* must be cleansed upon the way. The mechanism concerns pouring into the murkiness of one's own *saṃskāras* the supernal spiritual light of the internal radiant sun that comes from applied wisdom. One must then stalk tiger-like the aberrant *saṃskāras* in the jungles of materialism to convert them into enlightened qualities. So the battle rages with the demons of lust, desire and hatreds until the 'not otherwise Thusness' is achieved.

Yogic austerities and right discernments manifest, specifically in relation to control of the *prāṇas* of the Watery Element, allowing the major *siddhis* associated with the awakened Heart centre to be developed. We therefore have the image of the *yogin* or *yoginī,* victoriously dancing in the charnel ground of overcome *saṃskāras.*

Having analysed part of the symbolism concerning the author of the *Bardo Thödol* we are now better equipped to deduce the more esoteric meanings of this Tantra. There are always many levels of interpretation to consider, which should inevitably provide assistance in the quest for revelation and ultimate enlightenment. As we do so, some of that which was formerly 'ear whispered' can be revealed for earnest practitioners of the Tantric *dharma*. Revelations abound when the knots veiling the esoteric lore are untangled.[54] So let us untangle what is possible, leave some for heuristic investigation, and pave the way for the gnosis of the unmitigated vastness of cosmos that is *dharmakāya* to reveal itself in the Thusness of the awakened Heart that is the Mind.

---

54 The term for the intentional veiling or incorporated code in Tantric texts is *sandhyābhāṣā* (secret, esoteric, intentional) hence 'twilight language'. There is some controversy amongst scholars as to whether this word or *sandhābhāṣa* is the correct term for the esoteric code in the Tantras.

Samantabhadra and Consort

2

The Deities of the Bardo Thödol Part One: Thought Constructs in Nature

The Dhyāni Buddhas as the source of thought constructs

This analysis begins with the Dhyāni Buddhas and their Consorts. They are archetypes whose qualities can be found to have correspondences on all planes and states of awareness. Together they embody and regulate the substance of mind/Mind in all its attributes, when viewed upon a universal scale. This substance consists of aggregate streams of *saṃskāras* that come into expression by merging 'moments' of conscious activity. The aggregates exist as part of a bundle of *saṃskāras* that move in relation to similar 'bundles' within the greater life of the *maṇḍala* (a cellular unit) of which they are a part.

Aggregate streams appear in the mind as patterns which then create images according to the realities the mind recognises as true. With respect to that mind, illusionality generally manifests in relation to the bigger picture outside the *maṇḍala* proportionate to the distance one travels from the place of generation of the *saṃskāras*. Images concerning the larger expansive vista can be expanded to the size of the universe. A human mind can conceive of such vistas, but what is directly experienced upon earth by a humanity as a whole is microscopic in size. What exists beyond the scope of the eye of a beholder, however, is generally considered illusional because the mind perceives as real only that which it can cognise in terms of the experience of its sense-consciousnesses.

The minutiae are arranged as patterns of memory, generally manifesting like a flower with variegated petals representing the different degrees and lengths of moments of consciousness. Consciousness has many aspects to it and pathways to former ideas that retrieve what it needs from what is stored from the past.

The process concerning the generation of memory is of interest because it produces consequences, namely a sequence of actions incorporating experiential results that are garnered by a mind as a present schema of consciousness-moments. Each schema flows into the next one, manifesting finite consciousness-bubbles of interrelated ideas or images. These then constitute the basis to the manifestation of a cellular unit. A consciousness-bubble can become especially vitalised with an increasing number of *saṃskāras* drawn from memory and interwoven with the present experiential moment. It can gather denser substance from the lower strata of one's empirical space, i.e., become Watery and then Earthy, until a precipitation (a manifestation or birthing) occurs in the phenomenal realms. Other consciousness-units can then contact and even mistake this to be 'real'.

The smaller the consciousness-unit involved, the more illusional the cellular structure produced. This is because actions manifest more fleetingly relative to the larger (picture or cellular) unit the smaller unit may be a part of. The vaster unit's process of recalling *saṃskāras* will appear to happen at a slower speed with respect to the smaller units. The vaster stream of consciousness-moments are much more expansive, involving a larger amount of substance and vital entities (*prāṇic* lives, *devas*) to be moved. The *saṃskāras* called forth must move over a comparatively vaster arena of space than those of the smaller consciousness-unit. Different consciousness-units therefore come to inhabit *different time zones* in the scheme of things. This makes the happenings (thought structures) of the thinker of the vaster schema relatively real, non-transient, with respect to that of the minute unit. (Which is normally below the awareness-horizon of the larger unit.)

The expanse of Mind of the Dhyāni Buddhas and Consorts will thus be seen to manifest on a far vaster time-scale than does the limited awareness of the self aggrandising minds of the units of our human kingdom. This is one reason why the *dharmakāya* space of the Jinas is attributed as 'the Real'. From *dharmakāyic* space emanate the prototypic wills engendering the *five types of instincts* that influence all forms of

Life upon our planet. The sequence is:

1. *Vairocana*, the instinct of self-assertion. Here the Dharmadhātu Wisdom projects the originating thought into space, creating a 'bubble' of a time-space continuum where previously there was none. This 'bubble' incorporates entities whose actions are self-sustaining, exerting their own spheres of influence as part of the original projection (of the will to exist) of the Jina.
2. *Akṣobhya*, the group or herd instinct. The thought form expands to be inclusive of *saṃskāric* streams of ideas and idealisms mirrored into it from the primordial store by means of the Mirror-like Wisdom of this Jina. Integrated unities (the seminal *bījas* in space) coalescing into harmonious forms of interrelatedness is the paradigm for the group or herd instinct in Nature. The thought-form has now become a cellular construct.
3. *Amitābha's* Discriminating Inner Wisdom produces the instinct towards knowledge. Once major structures have been created, with increasingly detailed *saṃskāras* being introduced into the originating bubble, then the tendency will be the distinguishing of one image or set of images from another. This also produces *manasic* propensity within the components of the construct. The differences are utilised and interrelated according to their inherent properties with respect to need or purpose. The propensity for further and greater detail is the paradigm on which the instinct towards knowledge is propagated, this impetuses naming to signify differentiation.
4. *Ratnasambhava*, the sexual instinct, derived from his Equalising Wisdom. This concerns the polarities of existence that come into play through the evocation of the various *saṃskāras* from the past, as all of the opposing forces in the *maṇḍala* need to be balanced and fused into a harmonising unity through a properly structured governing law. The polarities become integrated in terms of sexual union, to produce the child or progeny (symbolising union or 'equalising') that is the outcome of co-emergent evolution. Despite the competitiveness between entities that Darwinian Theory is based upon, we find that different polarities of manifestation (species) produce a fruition of commingled harmonious activity. There is an

integrated biodiversity found throughout Nature, where every niche in our biosphere is filled by both competitive and non-competing entities, producing a symbiosis of interrelatedness. Everywhere we see the activities of one species serving to assist the growth, viability, and evolutionary abilities of its neighbours whether by competitive or non-competitive action. This is the basis for the modern Gaia Theory.[1] Chaotic activity is the illusion which hides the Intelligent order that governs evolution in Nature; there is no blind chance.

5. *Amoghasiddhi*, whose All-Accomplishing Wisdom generates the instinct of self-preservation. All *maṇḍalas* that manifest need to be sustained for the duration of their purpose. Some gain must be built into that purpose to justify the entire play of manifestation and its preservation. Once achieved, the play can be extinguished as that particular thought-bubble is no longer needed. A repeat upon a higher cycle of expression must then come into play, as the divine Thinker continues to evolve the paradigms of the *manasic* thought until the entire ideogram is perfected. The mind continually recycles thoughts until the idea has become complete in every detail and can bear no further improvement. Thus the entire rebirthing process is sustained via this instinct of self-preservation of an image needing processing until perfected.

The inevitable death of a cell is the process whereby the *saṃskāras* that constituted it will be either annulled, transformed, transmuted or transferred to another time zone in space. The integral Life (the consciousness) has effectively withdrawn the presence of its energising breath of thoughts, and focussed its energies elsewhere in a different thought-stream. As conscious units evolve in Nature so then they develop the propensity to mimic the form of activity of the Dhyāni Buddhas. This is driven at first by instinctual urges and later the exemplifications of those urges in the five types of sense-consciousnesses, which are transmuted into their ultimate correspondences, the five wisdoms of the Dhyāni Buddhas.

We see from the above that the Dhyāni Buddhas are not just archetypes. They are also liberated entities from far distant aeons,

---

1 A term coined by James Lovelock, when viewing the biosphere of the earth manifesting as a vast self-regulating interrelated organism.

existing in Shambhala, that play an important role in embodying the substance of all that is, and to effect the liberation of all lives.

The information concerning the five Jinas provided in the earlier volumes of this treatise shall be expanded below to provide a comprehensive listing of their qualities:

1. *Vairocana* (meaning 'the intensely luminescent one'). His Dharmadhātu Wisdom embodies the central point of the *maṇḍala*, as well as the central jewel of the Sambhogakāya Flower. The comprehension of His reality ('Truth', *satya)* is said to be the antidote to delusion and ignorance. His *mudrā* is the 'gesture of the wheel (of the *dharma*)'. This is the eight-spoked wheel of direction in space via which the purpose and luminosity of Vairocana can flow. He has no Mahābodhisattva directly associated with him, as all directions in space emanate from him. Thus he embodies the Element Aether, from which the other four Elements differentiate. It is their carrier. He governs that which is veiled by the *śūnyatā* experienced by a Buddha as the base for the complete liberation of a Bodhisattva, away from earth experience and humanity altogether.

- Colour—intense white, with blue emanation.
- Consort— Ākāśadhātviśvarī, the vehicle or body of space (*ākāśa*).
- Prāṇa—*vyāna,* the sum total of all *prāṇic* energies, directed by the combined Head and Ājñā centres. They govern all possible consciousness extensions into all directions of space, and to all orders of being/non-being. The Ājñā centre governs immaculate vision and direction of the energies and processes of meditative Life.
- Sense—Smell, quality: sense of unity, producing perfection and abstraction through the awakened universal consciousness.
- Ray energy—the first of Will or Power[2].
- Emblem or family—the *dharma* wheel, wherewith he is able to direct truth to all directions in space wherever it is needed.

---

2 The Ray energies assigned to the Jinas here relate to their bodily hues. In the case of Vairocana the white is taken to veil the red of the first Ray of Will or Power, as it embodies all of the other colours. If one takes the Jinas to be emanations of the attributes of Mind, then their subsidiary emanations would be the third, fourth, fifth, sixth and seventh Rays respectively, from Vairocana to Amoghasiddhi.

Plate 1. Vairocana and Consort Ākāśadhātviśvarī

- Vehicle supporting his throne: a lion, who is the ferocious ruler of the jungle that is *saṃsāra*.

2. *Akṣobhya* (meaning 'the unshakable, or immovable one'). His Mirror-like Wisdom embodies the *eastern* direction. This is the way inwards, to the Heart of Life, *śūnyatā*, and the expression of *bodhicitta*, which is carried lightning-like through the Airy Element.[3] His *mudrā* is the 'earth touching gesture', to ground the highest revelations and spiritual power throughout the corporeal form. This was the gesture (calling forth the earth Mother for witness) that Gautama used as a symbol of his final accomplishment

3 The orthodox assignment is Water for Akṣobhya, Earth for Ratnasambhava, Fire for Amitābha, Air for Amoghasiddhi and Aether for Vairocana. For the reasons for my assignment of the Elements see Volume 1, chapter 6.

Plate 2. Akṣobhya with Consort Locanā and surrounding Bodhisattvas

under the *bodhi* tree. This way of serene inward contemplation produces the spaciousness associated with Air, and is said to be the antidote to anger or hatred (but necessitates mastering all emotions). Akṣobhya governs the human kingdom *śūnyatā* as the base to attain the *dharmakāya* experience, as well as for experiencing the three central bud petals of the Sambhogakāya Flower.

- The Bodhisattvas associated with him are Kṣitigarbha (east) and Mañjuśri (northeast). Their consorts are Lāsyā and Ālokā respectively.
- Colour—deep blue. The 'deep blue space of undifferentiated consciousness'.[4] His emanation is white.

4 Govinda, *Foundations of Tibetan Mysticism,* (Century Paperbacks, London, 1987), 118.

- Consort–Locanā, the 'Buddha-eye'.
- Prāṇa–*prāṇa,* the *nāḍī* from the nose to the Heart. The energy of the Heart centre that reveals the way of the Lord of Life. The path thereto necessitates mastery of the entire *piṅgalā nāḍī* system.
- Sense–Taste, quality: tendency to discriminate, producing enlightenment through intuition, flashes of illumination.
- Ray energy–the second of Love-Wisdom.
- Emblem or family–the *vajra.* The two pronged *vajra* here symbolises the awakening of the All-seeing Eye (Ājñā Centre), allowing the wielder contemplative insight into all possible levels of being/non-being. The five rays to each prong project the wisdoms of the Jinas outwards into manifestation, with the help of Akṣobhya's unsullying, non-differentiating meditation.
- Vehicle supporting his throne: the elephant, symbol of great strength, stability, and steadfastness.

3. *Amitābha* (meaning 'boundless light'). His Discriminating Inner Wisdom embodies the *western* direction, which is said to manifest as the antidote to selfishness, lust and greed. His *mudrā* is the 'gesture of meditation'. With respect to this direction the way of such meditation is outwards toward the field of human interrelations. It necessitates the wise use of the mind in all fields of application. Consequently the Element is that of Fire, the mode of expression of consciousness. Amitābha governs the animal kingdom *śūnyatā* as the base for the evolution of consciousness, as well as the Knowledge petals of the Sambhogakāya Flower.
   - The Bodhisattvas associated are Avalokiteśvara (west) and Viṣkambhin (southwest). Their Consorts are Gitā and Ghandhā respectively.
   - Colour–red.
   - Consort–Pāṇḍaravāsinī, 'White robed' mother.
   - Prāṇa–*udāna,* the *nāḍī* from the nose to the top of the head, generated via the Throat centre by all who learn to speak the creative Word. It necessitates the mastery of the use of the Fires of the mind, of the entire *iḍā nāḍī* system to do so.
   - Sense–Sight, quality: darkness (ignorance), producing revelation, the reasoning facilities of the mind.

- Ray energy–the fifth of Scientific Reasoning, the Light of Reason and Intelligent Design.
- Emblem or family–the lotus blossom. Amitābha therefore governs the way that the *chakras* unfold in humanity and in Nature. He rules the *manasic* expression of the kingdom of the Sambhogakāya Flower, which exists upon the abstracted realms of Mind.
- Vehicle supporting his throne, the peacock. This bird's feathers are adorned with eyes, which exemplifies the function of seeing attributed to Amitābha. The great floral display of the male bird also symbolises the nature of the mental aura of an enlightened being, the 'eyes' representing different *maṇḍalic* universes, thought constructs through which one can peer for revelatory insight.

Plate 3. Amitābha with Consort Pāṇḍaravāsinī and surrounding Bodhisattvas

4. *Ratnasambhava* (meaning 'jewel born'), who with his Equalising Wisdom embodies the *southern* direction and the Element Water. His *mudrā* is the 'gesture of giving', the development and awakening of the force of *bodhicitta* needed for all that aspire to tread the Bodhisattva path. The Watery Element acts as an equalising agent in a similar way that water dissolves so many substances, making them part of the same solution. They then come to flow in a common stream. With this Element (the emotions/desire) the major defilements are churned and precipitated in consciousness. These emotions manifest the glaze via which consciousness generally works and looks through to produce concrete actions. Most human actions are sustained by desire, centred around concepts of a 'self'. Eventually the enlightenment-path is trod, generally because of first experiencing the Equalising Wisdom, which is said to be an antidote to pride. Ratnasambhava governs the plant kingdom *śūnyatā* as a base for all planetary vitalisation, as well as the Love petals of the Sambhogakāya Flower.

- The Bodhisattvas associated are Ākāśagarbha (south), and Maitreya (southeast), and their Consorts are Dhūpā and Puṣpā respectively.
- Colour–yellow.
- Consort–Māmakī, 'mine-ness', signifying that all children are viewed as hers, of identical nature.
- Prāṇa–*samāna*, the *nāḍī* from the Heart to the Solar Plexus. It is generated by the Solar Plexus centre, which directs these Watery *prāṇas* in the body so that eventually aspiration to a high ideal is brought about, allowing *bodhicitta* to be conveyed throughout the body. All evolving Life is inevitably sustained and integrated through the flow of the purified aspect of this Watery stream.
- Sense–Touch, quality: desire, eventually transformed into equanimous Love for all.
- Ray energy–the fourth of Beautifying Harmony overcoming Conflict.
- Emblem or family–the wish-fulfilling gem *(cintamaṇi)*, the philosopher's stone that grants all of the attributes of enlightenment to its possessor.

- Vehicle supporting his throne, the horse. Govinda states that 'the horse is a solar symbol, associated with the south, and the sun in its zenith'.[5] However, the true meaning of the horse here is that it is the vehicle or carrier of the mind.[6]

Plate 4. Ratnasambhava with Consort Māmakī and surrounding Bodhisattvas

5. *Amoghasiddhi* (meaning 'unfailing success or accomplishment'). His All-Accomplishing Wisdom takes the *northern* position of the *maṇḍala* of the Dhyāni Buddhas in the texts. The north represents the direction upwards toward the higher spheres of enlightenment.

---

5 Govinda, *Foundations of Tibetan Mysticism,* footnote 1, 120.

6 Thus it represents the animal nature, i.e., the emotions with respect to humanity, but which can be considered the truly human attribute.

His *mudrā* is the 'gesture of fearlessness' that is employed to convert all demons preventing one's path to liberation, and to overcome dark brotherhood predations. He governs the Element Earth, the expression of the instincts, and oversees the physical activities of those incarnate. Only upon the dense plane, where all Elements are mingled and interrelated, can a person truly turn about in consciousness to aspire upward to enlightenment; to *dharmakāya*. Amoghasiddhi embodies perfect action, which is said to be the antidote to envy and jealousy. The mineral kingdom *śūnyatā* is represented, as a base for all evolutionary progression. He governs the Will/Sacrifice petals of the Sambhogakāya Flower.

- The Bodhisattvas associated are Vajrapāṇi (north) and Samantabhadra (northwest), and their Consorts are Nṛtyā and Mālā respectively.
- Colour—green.
- Consort—Tārā (Tib. Dölma), the divine compassionate mother.
- Prāṇa—*apāna,* the *nāḍī* from the Solar Plexus to the feet, generated by the combined Sacral and Base of Spine centres that are the support of all manifest life. As there are four major petals of the Base of Spine centre, so each petal is responsible for the overall functioning of one or other of the four kingdoms in Nature. Amoghasiddhi's energy is thus said to be 'All-Accomplishing'. It is responsible for the overall pattern of the way Nature manifests materially.
- Sense—Hearing, quality: limitation, producing eventual freedom.
- Ray energy—the third of Enlightening, Mathematically Exact Activity.
- Emblem or family—*viśvavajra*, exemplifying the spiritual power of all the Jinas. The *siddhi* producing the power of this omnidirectional *vajra* is needed to overcome attachment to all materiality, to produce absolute command of the atoms of substance. It resists all evil machinations, converting these grey and black projections of force to the most brilliant forms of light.
- Vehicle supporting his throne: Garuḍa, a mythic sun bird-man, usually shown with a raptor's beak. He is an enemy of serpents, and as such represents the mechanism of the transmutation of evil forces, the tainted *saṃskāras,* depicted in the form of serpents

(nāgas). As the sun he controls the *nāgas*, who have power over Water. Garuḍa is also the vehicle of Viṣṇu, the second person of the Hindu *trimūrti*.

Plate 5. Amoghasiddhi with Consort Tārā and surrounding Bodhisattvas

Stages of the development of Nature's *maṇḍala*

There are ten stages to be discussed in all. They can also be considered the ten stages of the evolutionary process. Five of these stages shall be dealt with in this chapter and the remainder in the following ones. If we are to analyse the birthing process in Nature, the activity associated with the appearance of any *maṇḍala*, then we must first look to *involution*. The term is here viewed as a progressively downward motion of the incepted *maṇḍala* from higher, subtler *lokas* (zones of activity) to the grosser, more concrete planes of *saṃsāra*. There are also two supplementary stages to produce the perfection and final abstraction to the ten stages of a *maṇḍalic* construct. The stages happen according to a certain sequence. (Viewing the process from the point of view of the meditator that is objectivising the mental construct.)

The list below outlines the ten stages of evolution of consciousness in the form of an unfolding *maṇḍala*:

1. *Conception of all forms and processes in the material universe.*
2. *Duality, the emergence of interrelated opposite forces, the activation of the karma that sets all into motion.*
3. *The balancing of forces, producing a coherent form, seen as the appearance of the manasic level of the manifested realms.*
4. *Physical incarnation, the downward projection of the ideation that fully establishes the maṇḍala.*
5. *The point of greatest divergence prior to the actual appearance of the phenomena of human consciousness.*
6. *The individuation of a human kingdom from out of the animal kingdom.*
7. *The development of the mind in all of its attributes.*
8. *The development of unselfish idealism and compassionate action.*
9. *The psycho-spiritual striving to wisdom by the aspirants, world innovators, and helpers of mankind.*
10. *Evolutionary perfection, the appearance of liberated beings.*

These stages of the unfolding *maṇḍala* and evolution of consciousness can now be explained in more detail.

Stage 1. Conception of all forms and processes in the material universe.

This involves a complete understanding of all the processes that are to occur, necessitating a visualisation of the sum of the webs of *karma* to be projected to their inevitable conclusion. It concerns dynamically holding in meditative rapture the sum of all forthcoming activities until the process has reached its consummation. Such a process, therefore, is a *manasic* function with respect to humanity and the idea of what is to transpire.

Primordially, this process is an expression of the Mind of the Ādi Buddha, Samantabhadra,[7] the first of the forty-two Peaceful Deities presented in the *Bardo Thödol.* The complete translation of this text by Gyurme Dorje shall be utilised as the reference for the nature of the various deities in the *Bardo Thödol.* They will therefore be analysed in relation to these ten stages of generation. Concerning Samantabhadra and his Consort Gyurme states:

> Within the expanse of a seminal point located at the centre of one's heart,
> The primordial lord, the unchanging buddha-body of light,
> Samantabhadra, the Buddha-body of Reality, blue in colour,
> And Samantabhadrī, the expanse of reality, white in colour,
> Are indivisibly united, both in the posture of meditative equipoise,
> Seated upon lotus, sun and moon cushions,
> [Symbolising the union of] radiance and emptiness.[8]

The Ādi Buddha Samantabhadra, the radiant Awareness principle of all Buddhas, impregnates his Consort, Samantabhadrī, with the idea of the completed *maṇḍala* and its purpose. Consequentially, the Dhyāni Buddha Vairocana and his *prajñā* Ākāśadhātviśvarī emanate forth. The effective boundaries of the full *maṇḍala* can now be delineated. This necessitates a dynamically focused Will to integrate all of the necessary potencies and to project the purpose of the *maṇḍala.*

In Nature, the fertilisation of the seed *(gotra*[9]*)* of all that is to come happens upon the *ātmic* plane (the lowest *dharmakāya* level), and the growth of the impregnated form manifests in the Womb of the Divine Mother Ākāśadhātviśvarī. By the name 'Ākāśa' we see that the form of emptiness that specifically concerns us here is that attributed to abstract space, *ākāśa,*[10] from which all proceeds. The associated *chakra* is the combined Ājñā—Head lotus. The 'centre of one's heart' from the quote above refers to the Heart that is in the Head centre rather than the Heart centre *per se.* (Both of which are in the form of a twelve petalled

---

7 Alternatively we could use the names Dorje Chang or Vajrasattva.

8 Gyurme Dorje, *The Tibetan Book of the Dead,* 67.

9 *Gotra*: Lineage, germ, seed.

10 *Ākāśa* (Tib. nam mkha): space, subtle and ethereal energy pervading the totality of the universe, and a vehicle of Life.

lotus.) The Head lotus establishes the thought-construct of the entire paradigm of future purpose of the *maṇḍala.*

Stage 2. Duality, the emergence of interrelated opposite forces, the activation of the karma that sets all into motion.

This is the mirror that reflects the conceived *gotra* into the actuality of divine manifestation. Now the appearance of the five Jinas are brought into active expression via the extension of Vairocana's deliberation. The Love-Wisdom quality of the thought-construct is vivified through the reflective meditation of the Divine Mother Locanā (the *prajñā* of Akṣobhya). The four major Void-Elements that sustain the four quadrants of manifest space can now be properly integrated into the *maṇḍala.* It brings into expression, therefore, the various *chakras,* and the entire *nāḍī* system that sustains the projection of the Elements in manifestation, and thereby all of *saṃsāra.* Everything is incubated in the embracive energies of the Jinas via their Consorts. Their qualities are therefore integrated into the entire panorama of *saṃsāra.* All is built upon the foundation of their Wisdom.

In Nature this activity happens via the *śūnyatā-saṃsāra* nexus. The *chakra* activated is the Heart centre. The principle of Life is thereby expressed to sustain the activities of the entire corporeal form. This Life principle implicates the involvement of the 42 Peaceful Deities. Inevitably, *saṃskāras* are generated as part of the activities of all that manifest.

The focus of this and following chapters is upon the fifth section of the *Bardo Thödol,* entitled 'The Spiritual Practice entitled Natural Liberation of Habitual Tendencies' in Gyurme's translation.[11] Habitual tendencies cause the generation of *saṃskāras,* therefore this section concerns the methods of mastering, transforming and transmuting these *saṃskāras.* Enlightenment is the result. The main practice consists of firstly visualising oneself as Vajrasattva residing in one's Heart centre. As a consequence:

> One clearly discerns a seminal point [formed of] the five lights,
> Whose nature is the five pure essences [of the five elements],
> [And from this], the thirty-six peaceful buddhas radiantly manifest,
> Amidst a radiant and vibrant maṇḍala suffused by the five pristine cognitions,

11 Gyurme Dorje, *The Tibetan Book of the Dead,* 59.

> Their bodies composed of five lights, the unimpeded [union of] emptiness and radiance,
> [Seated] upon a tier of lotus, sun and moon [cushions],
> Supported by lion, elephant, horse, peacock and cīvaṃcīvaka [thrones].[12]

In this way the entire *maṇḍala* of the generation of the Peaceful Deities is introduced. Samantabhadra and his Consort are said to eminate from the seminal point in the following section of Gyurme's translation. After that the five Dhyāni Buddhas manifest, then the Guardians (Gyurme uses the term 'gatekeepers'), followed by the rest of the entourage of Peaceful and Wrathful Deities. The 'thirty-six peaceful buddhas radiantly manifest' are counted as: Samantabhadra and Consort, the five Dhyāni Buddhas and their Consorts, the four male Guardians and their Consorts, plus the eight male Bodhisattvas and their Consorts. The Buddhas of the Six Realms are not counted here as they technically are emanations of Avalokiteśvara in his desire to liberate all beings from *saṃsāra*.

The number 36=3 x 12 is important because it introduces the necessary powers of twelve. Firstly there are the twelve main petals of the Head centre that govern the generation of enlightenment-producing wisdom. Next we have the twelve petals of the Heart centre in the chest cavity, governing the ability to achieve liberation through the generation of *bodhicitta*. Finally we have the twelve petals of Splenic centre I (it is a dual centre) below the diaphragm, wherein *saṃskāras* are refined and transformed before being sent to the centres above the diaphragm. There is a trinity represented here, each of which reflects the attributes of the highest centre, so if we multiply the number 36 x 3 we also get the sacred number 108.

In the 'lion, elephant, horse, peacock and cīvaṃcīvaka' (a Garuḍa or 'bird-man') we have the vehicles of the Dhyāni Buddhas, which introduces the third stage of the evolving *maṇḍala* of the awakening of consciousness.

Stage 3. The balancing of forces, producing a coherent form, seen as the appearance of the manasic level of the manifested realms.

Saṃsāra proper now appears, allowing the consequent projection of all related lives into concretised objectivity. All of the active elements

12 Ibid., 67.

of cognition then come into manifestation, which are seeded into the thought-construct by the Divine Mother Pāṇḍaravāsinī (the *prajñā* of Amitābha). The complete *maṇḍala* of Jinas and Consorts is established and impregnated with the purpose of the originating Buddha-Mind. Samantabhadra's seminal thought has expanded to produce its progeny in the Womb of Samantabhadrī. The entire construct is constituted to obey the laws of Mind unfolding, which allows the processes of karmic law to govern. The fifth Ray of Scientific Reasoning thus governs this stage of activity. The *devas*, the agents of karmic law, embody the mental substance and manifest under the law to impetus this evolutionary development.[13]

In Nature, the process of externalising phenomena happens in the concrete realms of the mind. Here the ability to segregate, classify and name comes to the fore, as all the functions of the intellect are established. The *chakra* activated is the Throat centre.

Stage 4. Physical incarnation, the downward projection of the ideation that fully establishes the maṇḍala.

The conception becomes materialised, and the related sentient streams now manifest their forms of experiences. At first we look to the etheric substratum of the physical wherein the entire reticulation of energies that sustain all forms of activities flow. This energy body is the *true* corporeal form of everything that is considered sentient, 'alive', as it is the medium of interchange between the higher strata of revelatory expression and the moving appearance of things. All impulses that manifest through the etheric body automatically effect the gross physical forms via the force plexuses (*chakras*) in the etheric. The physical body thereby becomes an automaton whereby phenomena is experienced by means of fleeting impressions contacted via the five senses. Consequently, we have the appearance of the great illusion. All life forms possess etheric bodies and *nāḍī* systems, and all such systems are interrelated in a truly harmonised, 'equalised' fashion via Ratnasambhava's meditation. His Equalising Wisdom integrates diversity into one grand coherent system.

---

13 The *devas* (meaning 'shining ones') come under the general auspices of the third Ray of Mathematically Exact Activity, which is directly allied to the fifth Ray. They are the feminine procreative Intelligences that embody the substance of all that is, rather than the gods of the Hindu Pantheon.

The energy field governing all of Nature is thus the expression of the Womb of the Divine Mother Māmakī, the *prajñā* of Ratnasambhava. The *chakra* established at this stage is the greater Solar Plexus centre that governs all formative forces. The energising potency of the sixth Ray of Devotion comes into play to drive the *prāṇa* through the earth's *nāḍīs*.

Ratnasambhava and Māmakī govern the overall process of forms appearing into and constituting *saṃsāra*. Ratnasambhava's Equalising Wisdom infuses all with the principle of *bodhicitta*, in its hidden universal expression. This then is the driving force of the *karma* that integrates all forms of action and projects everything that incarnates towards liberation. The driving force therefore lays the foundation for the motion that allows every entity to develop consciousness. What is known as *māyā* is consequently the continuous, rapturous meditation of Māmakī, as she sways the forces therein towards the goal set for all to achieve by her Lord. *Śūnyatā* is both the sustaining power and the end of the process of the driving force of *karma*.

Energies are distributed by Māmakī in the eight directions of space by means of the Guardians of the four Gates of the *maṇḍala* and their Consorts. The Guardians occupy the cardinal positions and their Consorts the intermediate positions, thereby manifesting as a moving swastika of energies.

To understand the greater Solar Plexus centre in Nature (which posses ten petals) we note that two times five main Rays of consciousness projection cause the phenomena of manifestation as a product of the meditative activities of the Dhyāni Buddhas and their Consorts. The *vajra* that manifests projects the basis for the evolution of the sense consciousnesses and the generation of the related wisdoms. There is also a continuous stream of returning energies and *saṃskāras* from the active participants in the world-play. The associated perfumes are received by the Dhyāni Buddhas as part of their ongoing commitment to the evolutionary process. This allows them to make the necessary adjustments to ensure that everything proceeds according to their united meditative Plan.

We must look to two types of *viśvavajras*. The first has its main spokes oriented in the cardinal directions, and obeys the symbolism of a fixed cross. Its 4 x 5 Rays allow for twenty energy streams altogether. Of these twenty streams we find that ten flow along the north to south axis and another ten flow in the east to west axis. Generally, at any one time there are predominantly *iḍā* or *piṅgalā prāṇas* in either of these major directions. This *viśvavajra* represents the general power of the masculine deities that direct the functioning and energy flow of the higher attributes of a ten-petalled Solar Plexus centre, according to the quality of energy it is receptive to at any time. The power of the *viśvavajra* is also awakened by humans in their later evolutionary progress on the path to liberation, via developing the refined qualities of the Mind through treading of the Bodhisattva path.

Next we have the *viśvavajra* with its main spokes oriented in the intermediate directions of the eight-armed cross of direction in space. It forms a mutable cross that revolves according to the law of *karma* that conditions the evolutionary progression that is *saṃsāra*. It is similarly composed of 4 x 5 Rays, allowing for twenty energy streams of either *iḍā* or *piṅgalā prāṇas*.[14] This *viśvavajra* represents the powerhouse of the *maṇḍala* of the feminine deities associated with the general evolutionary process of the *prāṇas* that produce evolutionary changes throughout Nature's kingdoms. From this perspective the northeast direction governs the conditioning group law or type of instinct to be evolved. The southeast direction relates to the expression of the associated activity of the lives conditioned by this cross. The southwest direction relates to the evolutionary gain, and the northwest position to progression to the next higher level or kingdom of evolution.

Figure 2. Orientations of the *viśvavajra*

14 Generally one type of *prāna* is the focus, followed by the next. In this way the necessary qualities are best developed.

If we combine the Rays from the two *viśvavajras* and add the central points we get the number 42, the number of Peaceful Deities in the *maṇḍala* of the *Bardo Thödol.* Their Rays therefore manifest through the spokes of the *viśvavajras* according to need. (The power of the central point manifests through any group of five Rays.) The Buddhas of the Six Realms are thus added to the list of Peaceful Deities and take male or female dispositions according to need.

The *viśvavajra* held by Amoghasiddhi can be of either orientation, depending upon the focus of the particular meditation. It is the symbol of the ultimate power he wields over all affairs in *saṃsāra*. Therefore he presides over the conversion process, the 'turning about in the seat of consciousness' for humanity, as they defocus from materialistic incentive and begin to work instead for liberation from *saṃsāra*. The *viśvavajra* changes from the feminine form to its masculine counterpart as this conversion takes place.

The twenty spokes or Rays represented in the *viśvavajra* express the power of a *maṇipūra chakra*. Within our planetary system there are two major *maṇipūra chakras* for human evolution, one superimposed upon the other. The *first* exists upon the *ātmic* plane[15] and is created by the direct meditative concentration of the Dhyāni Buddhas and their Consorts. It is formed to project into manifestation the ideal qualities needed for planetary evolution. The *second* exists upon the abstract level of the mental plane. It processes the evolved *manasic* attributes gained from the activities of the incarnate lives that are developing higher perceptions as part of their evolutionary progression. Here *manasic* proclivity is also viewed in terms of the evolution of the instincts and the sense-consciousnesses. This second *maṇipūra chakra* projects the upwards aspiration (or essence) of the evolved *prāṇas* towards the Jinas who direct the overall processes. This focus of planetary evolution takes all of the kingdoms of Nature into account. Such Solar Plexus activity was dominant prior to the appearance of a human kingdom. Human evolution is based upon the paradigm of the twelve petals of a Heart centre. Together they constitute certain petals of the Dharmakāya Flower. (The cosmic version of the Sambhogakāya Flower, possessed

---

15 The lowest *dharmakāyic* level. This plane of perception is the store of primeval *karma* which is utilised by the Jina Consorts to effect their planetary purpose. Volume 6 of this series puts these planes of perception into perspective.

by the Logos informing a planetary system such as the earth.[16])

Evolutionary progression in Nature therefore consists of a similar dynamic to what is found in the human *nāḍī* system concerning the generation of theriomorphic attributes below the diaphragm, and their eventual transformation into purely human attributes so that they can be absorbed by the centres above the diaphragm. Instead of theriomorphic entities in Nature we have the various members of the animal kingdom slowly evolving the aspects perfected by human units. Below the diaphragm the Solar Plexus centre rules. All entities evolving through Nature's kingdoms can be considered part of a (planetary) Womb. Outside of it are the controlling agencies emanating from the cosmic Heart centre, which are delineated in terms of the twelve signs of the zodiac.

In the dynamics between the interrelation of the Heart centre to the Solar Plexus centre is much of the mystery hid. From this perspective the Throat centre is a construct that interrelates the two, existing as it does to contain the evolved attributes of mind, and then their transformation into those of Mind, with the assistance of the energies from the Heart centre. We can see here that the symbolism of the *Bardo Thödol* can be interpreted from this vast scale of events. It is a view I wish to explore somewhat in this book. Buddhists need to expand the horizons of their minds so as to encompass far more than the human conditioning, if they are to gain a better view of what constitutes enlightenment. Significant territory will therefore be introduced that can be expanded on by later researchers. Consequently, the symbolic context of such esoteric texts as the *Bardo Thödol* will be significantly clarified.

Only the perfumes, the most abstracted qualities of the lower *maṇipūra chakra*, enter into the domain of the higher superimposing one. The *prāṇas* of the lower *maṇipūra chakra* are generated by the four kingdoms in Nature,[17] though the focus is generally upon the kingdoms

---

16 The nature of the Dharmakāya Flower was briefly explained in Volume 3 of this treatise with reference to the existence of *karma* external to a human unit, and the functions of an Ādi Buddha (a Logos). A Logos can be conceived of as a great One that embodies the Mantric Word governing the manifestation of the evolution of a world-sphere, such as our earth.

17 The reader should be reminded here that these 'four kingdoms' are viewed esoterically rather than in modern scientific terms. Thus we have the mineral, vegetable, animal, and human kingdoms.

below that of humanity. The animal-like *prāṇas* generated by humans, signifying their desires and emotions, can also be included in this list. The Consorts of the Guardians of the four Gates process these *prāṇas*.

A third level of *viśvavajra* comes into being for humanity in their Head centres. It regulates the functioning of normal human consciousness. In fact, three *viśvavajras* can generally be found in the human body, organising the activity of the Solar Plexus centre, the Throat centre, and the Head lotus. The one in the Solar Plexus represents control of the feminine forces in the human persona: the mental-emotions and desire. The methodology of controlling these forces by rightly empowering this *viśvavajra* concerns the making of a *siddha* via awakening the minor *siddhis*. Upon such attainment one emulates the attributes of a *ḍākinī*. The *viśvavajra* in the Throat centre also manifests in a feminine form whilst thinking is tainted by the emotions, or concreted. When the energies from the Heart centre rule (producing wisdom) then it manifests in the masculine orientation. This centre is constructed to empower the activity of the *viśvavajra* because it embodies the power of the mind/Mind to direct energies. It therefore has a quadrant of four main petals surrounding an inner twelve. This allows the Throat centre to be the organ of mantric command and to direct the creative Words of *manasic* import to any direction in space.

The higher correspondence of the Solar Plexus is established in the Head lotus, which integrates the attributes of normal waking consciousness into the petals of that centre. The Head lotus also expresses the fixed cross version of the *viśvavajra,* which dominates the unfoldment of its petals once the Heart in the Head is activated. This allows the expression of *bodhicitta* in its wisdom attribute, and thus the complete gain of the attributes of enlightenment. There are five stages to the unfoldment and full awakening of each *viśvavajra,* which are responsible for the expression of the higher *siddhis* in the accomplished *yogin* when fully unfolded. We then have the appearance of a *mahāsiddha*.

These types of *viśvavajras* develop from the central *bindu* of the *maṇḍala* of the 1,000 petalled lotus. Together they allow the *maṇḍala* of the five Jinas to form and establish the *nirmaṇakāya* of an incarnate great One. They are thereby subservient to the *dharmakāya* aspect ensconced in the *ātmic* realm.

The Ājñā centre, Heart centre and the Base of Spine/Sacral centre combination mainly embody the attributes of the simple *vajra*. The two main lobes of the Ājñā centre absorb the *prāṇas* of the *iḍā* and *piṅgalā nāḍīs,* process them and direct the results of the refined *prāṇas* to the Head lotus. It is also the organ of vision for the awakened thinker, in a manner that will be explained later.

The Heart centre, being central to the entire *prāṇic* circulation can manifest as a masculine *viśvavajra,* but its major mode of expression is in the form of the simple *vajra*. It then manifests in the form of triads of petals and their polar opposites, which direct *prāṇas* from one arena of the *nāḍī* system to another. The Heart centre is the Son in incarnation, generating the compassionate aspect of *bodhicitta*. The demonstration of the full potency of such a 'Son' represents the unfathomed purpose of all human activity.

Splenic centre I functions similarly to the Heart centre, but its main purpose is in purifying base *saṃskāras* so that they can be projected to the Heart and Throat centres.

The Base of Spine/Sacral centre supports the activities of both types of *vajras* in their most elementary form.

The Guardians of the four Gates of the *maṇḍala*

The evolution of human consciousness involves a special stream of meditation for the Dhyāni Buddhas, the focus being upon the Sambhogakāya Flowers, which manifested upon the abstracted levels of the mental plane when an entire human kingdom came into existence from out of an animal kingdom.[18] The way *prāṇa* manifests in the *nāḍīs* of human evolution, within the overall scheme of the *maṇḍala* of Life, is the concern of the Dhyāni Buddhas. They direct these *prāṇas* so that they eventually produce fruitful consequences. This is governed by the fixed cross position of the cardinal directions (N-S-E-W). The *maṇḍala* of these Flowers is established, 'grounded' upon the abstract realm of the Mind and organised by these Guardians.[19] They regulate the overall karmic flow through this kingdom via the distribution of the

18 The technical term for this event is Individualisation.

19 They are the Mahārājas of Hinduism, and their agents are the Lipika (scribes), Lords of *karma*.

Yamāntaka and Vajrapāśī

Hayagrīva and Vajraśṛṅkhalā

Vijaya and Vajrāṅkuśī

Amṛtakuṇḍalin and Vajraghantā

Plate 6. The Guardians of the four Gates of the *maṇḍala*

substance of the four main Elements. The four directions are protected by the Guardians of the four Gates of the *maṇḍala.*

These Guardians are explained by Lauf:

> They are of human form with wrathful faces, and they have the third eye of higher knowledge. With their wild hair and their crowns of five skulls, they guard the four cosmic directions of the maṇḍala and at the same time become the guides of the awareness-principle in the transcendent world.[20]

The crowns of skulls refer to the five types of *saṃskāras* (the effect of unwholesome moribund activities) to be transmuted in the phenomenal realms. The *saṃskāras* are the Void Elements (associated with the Dhyāni Buddhas) that have been modified by means of the activities and attributes of desire-mind by humans or creatively modified by *devas.* They are then conveyed in the *nāḍī* system in the form of the five types of *prāṇas.* The *prāṇas* then become the factors governing the awareness principle conditioning all of Nature when regulated by the *devas.* Human units have defiled the pristine qualities of the originating emanations of the *saṃskāras* with emotional attributes and often foul attitudes of mind, plus the aggrandisement of desires, materialistic attachments and ego-clinging. Such defilements are moribund, because they produce the necessity for repetitive cycles of birth and death, which is symbolised by the characteristics of these skulls. The Guardians stand at the junction between the realms of enlightenment and those of Dependent Origination. They therefore help guide the worthy from one realm to the other and block entry for the unworthy. (Those still too afflicted with base *saṃskāras.* The process associated with their transmutation is what manifests as the wrathful forms of the Guardians.)

We can count four kingdoms in Nature, and for each of these

---

20 Lauf, *Secret Doctrines of the Tibetan Books of the Dead*, 137. I shall generally use Lauf's descriptions of the Peaceful and Wrathful Deities throughout my work because he presents good succinct descriptions of their appearance and qualities. There are, however, differences in the names of some of the deities between his depictions and Gyurme's, which shall be noted. Note also that all representations of Buddhist deities are Mind-born emanations, created by Mind to cleanse aberrations of mind and to test the attributes of mind in the process of transformation into their liberated, enlightened correspondences. (The liberated aspects of mind are here denoted 'Mind' because they are *dharmakāyic* potencies or form the abstracted mental domain.)

there can be attributed a gate[21] from one kingdom to the next wherein the species at the end of their respective evolutionary attainment are prepared to enter the next kingdom. This is accomplished by means of evolving the characteristics of that new domain. Therefore the *prajñās* (Consorts) of each of these Guardians wield the conditions, or limiting factors wherein this transferring process occurs for each species that appropriately meet their challenges. 'Limiting factors' represent that which must be overcome before transiting through one or other of the gates is possible. If we take the mineral kingdom as the base level, then we can look to the Consort of the southern Guardian to be responsible for the transference of mineral sentience states into the next highest level of the most primitive plant forms. The plant kingdom can thus be understood to be the domain of enlightenment for the elementary mineral 'blinded' lives. This process for the mineral, plant and animal kingdoms is controlled and delineated by the *dharmakāya* type of *karma*. If the process is relegated purely to humanity then the *sambhogakāya* type of *karma* becomes the controlling factor.[22]

When we limit our view only to the factor of the human kingdom, then each of these gates represent zones of transference of human consciousness, wherein Initiation is undertaken. Initiation is the gain of the *bhūmis* that designate each stage of accomplishment of the Bodhisattva. Each Initiation necessitates the process of passing certain tests that signify that the candidate has mastered significant qualities before he/she can move along the Bodhisattva path towards full enlightenment. Initiation defines what has been mastered and the experiential revelations possible at any major step to liberation, and beyond. The subject of Initiation is detailed in Volume 6 of this treatise, *Meditation and the Initiation Process,* thus the information presented in this section shall be brief. The serious student will have to integrate the information here with the later exposition.

---

21 Each gate is also a septenary to admit the streams of Life passing through them, according to the qualifying conditioning of the seven Rays governing the divisions of Life. These Rays can be considered as five exoteric, with which we are concerned with above, and two esoteric. The subject of the Rays needs to be mentioned here for the sake of the completeness of the teachings. Our focus here is upon the five Rays of Mind, as exemplified by the attributes of the five Dhyāni Buddhas.

22 These types of *karma* are explained in Volume 2 of this treatise.

The concept of Initiation here has correlations to, but differs significantly from that given in traditional accounts, as for instance described by Thurman:

> Initiation rituals are immensely complicated. The Unexcelled Yoga Tantras use four main categories of initiation: the "vase initiation," which focuses on the body and empowers you for creation stage visualisation practice; the "secret initiation," which focuses on speech and empowers you for the initial stages of the perfection stage transformation practice; the "wisdom-intuition initiation," which focuses on the mind and empowers you for the higher stages of the perfection stage; and the "precious word initiation," which focuses on body, speech, and mind indivisibly, and empowers you for the highest integration level of the perfection stage, which corresponds to the Great Perfection teachings.[23]

The Initiations I speak of relate to demonstrating mastery of the major Elements: Earth for the first Initiation, Water for the second, Fire for the third Initiation, etc. The ceremonies related to their attainment also happen as part of one's meditation experiences. The higher Initiations happen in Shambhala and are coordinated by the inner and outer spiritual preceptors working as a team in conjunction with the attendance of the Council of Bodhisattvas. Furthermore, the instructions in this book mostly relate to 'the perfection stage', where the focus is upon the awakening of the Heart centre and its correspondence in the Head lotus. The process is, however, more arduous than what is implied in the texts because *saṃskāras* must be appropriately converted and consciousness consequently transformed. Thurman states:

> The opening of the heart centre is a delicate untangling process, highly dangerous if forced, and therefore the vajra recitation can take many years even for the most capable yogi or yogini. Its goal is reached when all impediments in the heart centre are gone, and the dissolutions can lead to the orgasmic ecstasy that engages the indestructible consciousness-energy drop in the centre of the heart. This is then called the "mind isolation," as the mind is isolated from any nonexperience of great bliss. The subtlest mind becomes the

---

23 Robert Thurman, *The Tibetan Book of the Dead,* (Bantam Books, New York, 1994), 65.

> mind of great bliss, which becomes the ultimate subjectivity for the cognition of the still metaphoric clear light of universal voidness or of selflessness.[24]

The full awakening of the Heart and Throat centres producing Clear Light and great Bliss are very difficult because the *saṃskāras* pertaining to *saṃsāric* affiliation are deeply ingrained. Generally, decades are needed to achieve the goal. Indeed, only a few of the many that aspire so are capable of attaining the third or fourth Initiations, to which most descriptions of high attainment in the texts, such as 'mind isolation' refer.

The Guardians stand at the portals between where the candidate was and must be if the tests for Initiation are to be mastered. They represent the forces assisting the transformation and transmogrification of *saṃskāras,* to produce increasing refinement of attributes. These forces therefore guard the doors to the higher spheres of attainment. By the colours attributed to the Guardians we see that they represent the transformative reflex of the Dhyāni Buddhas. They oversee the transformations that must be accomplished before an aspirant can finally stand enlightened in the domain that the associated Dhyāni Buddha embodies.

The Guardians ensure that no unworthy candidate can cross the threshold into the sacred portals of the domain of the Initiated ones. Those that fail their prospective testings cannot progress psychically, because their own unsubdued *saṃskāras* effectively manifest the attributes of the wrathful qualities of the Guardian, blocking their access to the mysteries of Initiation. They can only gain entry when later they are more capably endowed by having transmuted defiling *saṃskāras.*

Yamāntaka, ruling the southern gate, regulates the path of probation and the first two Initiations that stand on the threshold of the *ālayavijñāna* enlightenment, when the complete mastery of the mind is attained. At this gate Earthy and Watery *saṃskāras* have to be mastered in the process of being transformed into enlightened attributes. This allows the development of the *siddhis* associated with the control of the Waters. As these *siddhis* can also be developed by the members of the dark brotherhood, it is important for the wrathful force represented

---

24 Ibid., 77.

by Yamāntaka to exclude the unworthy. Lauf states:

> At the south gate of the maṇḍala the wrathful yellow Yamāntaka appears (T. gShim-rje gshed-po) with his Ḍākinī, Vajrapāśī, in red flames and standing on a lotus throne. Yamāntaka carries a sling and a bell. The Guardian of the south gate appears in order to dissolve the five corporeal senses, and he further ensures that the "five poisons" (cardinal failings) are overcome by the five wisdoms. In addition he represents the divine state of great compassion (S. mahākaruṇā; T. sNying-rje chen-po) and leads the dead person's awareness beyond the doctrine of the boundedness of things. For neither thinking exclusively along the dimensions of bounded appearances nor thinking in terms of eternal conditions alone can ensure access to indescribable nirvāna, which lies beyond Being and non-Being. Thinking in mental conceptual constructions must be subjective and dualistic, and it thereby misses the experience of absolute reality (T. Don-dam-pa).[25]

The name Yamāntaka means the one who overcomes the god and judge of death (Yama), and is an epithet of Vajrabhairava. By virtue of his southern position in this *maṇḍala,* Yamāntaka is responsible for laying the conditionings that will allow undertaking the first and second Initiations by aspirants. The first Initiation concerns overcoming Earthy allurements ('the boundedness of things'), necessitating a proper understanding of everything concerning sexuality, material comforts, avaricious propensities (for money), and of mundane considerations of social allurements and man-made laws. All these attitudes produce moribund attachments to the domains of form. They necessitate an in-depth analysis of the true effects of the five sense-consciousnesses and the attachments caused by addiction to the pleasurable experiences they provide. Yamāntaka's sling allows him to fire the mineral-like projectiles associated with the Earthy level of expression to help overcome the defilements preventing the attainment of the first Initiation.

Comprehension begins the process of mastery of material plane illusions and of striving upwards towards higher identifications. Inevitably such striving causes the material *prāṇas* to be 'dissolved' into the next higher level of expression, of the plant-like qualities associated with the Inner Round set of minor *chakras* that are synthesised by

25 Lauf, *Secret Doctrines of the Tibetan Books of the Dead,* 137-138.

the Solar Plexus centre. The tests to be undertaken to pass the second Initiation produce an enrichment of the candidate's ability to love and consequently serve others. As each Initiation testing can be successfully passed, so the wisdoms of the Jinas are accordingly generated.

Yamāntaka dances upon the conversion of all the *saṃskāras* generated in the centres below the diaphragm: those of the Inner Round, the Solar Plexus and Sacral centres. (The Base of Spine centre is awakened at the higher Initiations.) Desire-emotions are therefore transformed into *bodhicitta* under Yamāntaka's guardianship.

The lord of death (Yama) is overcome by means of the entire Initiation process introduced under the watch of, and firmly established by, Yamāntaka's vigilant dance within those working to eliminate defiling *saṃskāras*. As each progressive Initiation is undertaken, more of the mysteries of being/non-being become clear to the consciousness concerned. By mastering the life processes, comprehension manifests that there is no such thing as death, only transference of consciousness from one state to another, and the eventual transmutation of consciousness into *dharmakāya*.

Yamāntaka's yellow colour indicates his relation to Ratnasambhava. Ratnasambhava governs the expression of the Watery Element, the sixth Ray of Devotion, and the *prāṇas* processed by the Solar Plexus centre. Candidates seeking the second Initiation must develop mastery of the emotions and desire (the Watery Element). The equalising energies of Ratnasambhava are utilised to produce this mastery, signifying generation of compassionate, loving *saṃskāras*. As the various trials on the path unfold, so wisdom and love are wrought from the struggle to overcome base emotions. Eventually sensitive attunement to the source of pain and suffering other people possess is developed, and the candidate vouches to help them overcome the causes. Love-Wisdom *(bodhicitta)* is thereby evoked upon the upward way as the basis to establishing Ratnasambhava's Equalising Wisdom. Such mastery seeds the compassion developed by all Bodhisattvas. Compassion is the end result of the devotion and high aspiration (other Watery attributes) the candidate utilises to strive towards high ideals. *Bodhicitta* is then generated by the candidate (as well as being directed by him/her) to assist the effort to serve all sentient beings because the focus of the individual has shifted from the *chakras* below the diaphragm towards the Heart centre, wherein this energy is stored, making such energisation possible.

The development of a more refined awareness is the basis where the cardinal failings of the five poisons are overcome through receptivity to the *prāṇas* of the five wisdoms that will take their place. They drive perception away from the mundane world of the empirical senses. Once having started on the path of transformation of the poisons, the process will naturally continue through all of the higher Initiation levels until full liberation is attained. The mysteries of the true nature of the various Bardo states (associated with the Watery astral realm) are also accorded to the Initiate as testings in the field of Life are passed. Meditation then reveals all subsequent consequences, including the way of warding off fearful emanations and attacks from members of the dark brotherhood.

Each of the Guardians carries a bell. The bell allows mantric sounds to resonate throughout the *nāḍīs* concerned, transforming the obstructions to clear thought on the issues that are to be confronted at their respective level. Eventually the note of all-pervading emptiness (signified by the bell) is achieved.

Yamāntaka's Consort Vajrapāśī[26] transfers the *prāṇas* and associated sentient lives in Nature from the mineral to the plant kingdoms. With respect to humanity she controls the *karma* of the Earthy *prāṇas* that are generated. The name Vajrapāśī can be translated as the adamantine power to use the sacred noose *(pāśa)* to bind the fetters that strangle the *yogin's* ability to obtain liberation. It is especially used in connection with overcoming the effect of Yamā, the god of death, who carries a noose. Vajrapāśī therefore regulates the *karma* of those that are attached to the objects of the senses in such a way that they learn the related lessons and ardently strive to not be attached. She therefore assists those upon the path to liberation to overcome the fetters that bind them.

We should note that the functions attributed to the Guardians are of importance with respect to the changes undergone within the consciousness of the struggling disciple/*yogin*. The Consorts on the other hand embody the substance of all phenomenological processes. They represent the matrix within which all changes occur, and therefore direct the *karma* of the changes so that they manifest according to the purpose of the established *maṇḍala*. Thus they establish the conditions wherein

26 Gyurme uses the name Pāśā. In Lauf's depiction the word *vajra* is added to these Consorts, whereas Gyurme omits this, otherwise the meanings of the deities are the same.

humanity can flourish. Technically, however, only those attributes of the Consorts that should be considered here are from the fourth to the tenth stages of Nature's *maṇḍala.*

The work of the first Guardian (Yamāntaka) should also be placed at the eighth evolutionary stage, which sets the preconditions for the taking of the first two Initiations by disciples. This being a consequence of overcoming the *saṃskāras* associated with the animal-headed deities. (These *saṃskāras* are controlled at the attainment of the third Initiation.) The remaining Guardians would then play a similar role in the ninth and tenth stages. One then enters into the domain of the Peaceful Deities to undertake the higher Initiations.

The western Guardian is represented thus:

> At the west gate of the maṇḍala is the red Guardian Hayagrīva (T. rTa-mgrin rgyal-po) with his female counterpart, the Ḍākinī, Vajraśṛṅkhalā (T. rDor-je lcags-sgrog-ma). Hayagrīva with the horse's head in his hair carries an iron chain (or else a club entwined with snakes) and a bell, and his Ḍākinī also has an iron chain. The wrathful Hayagrīva appears in order to dissolve all feelings and to ensure that the path of compassion is not abandoned. The deity is associated with the doctrine of self-contemplation and of reflective inner vision (T. bDag-tu lta-ba) and represents the divine virtue of sympathetic joy (S. muditā; T. dGa'-ba).[27]

All desires, feelings, and animal-like passions must eventually be dissolved into the *amṛta* of pure compassion. The horses' head (the bearer of the guiding human principle of mind) in the hair reminds us that all of the animal-like *prāṇas* associated with the Solar Plexus centre need to be controlled. All such *prāṇas* developed in the centres below the diaphragm must be dominated by the compassionately focused mind. The battles of the various tests that convert mind to Mind are thereby undertaken under Hayagrīva's guidance. The focus is upon the Inner Round of *chakras,* of which all *prāṇas* are animal-like, or even beastly (gross emotions, desires and passions). They are to be firmly chained to the Heart and Mind by the steely will, so that they no longer produce an afflicted mind.

One of the problems concerning the mind is its distinct self-focus and separativeness. There are many subtleties to be mastered concerning

27 Lauf, *Secret Doctrines of the Tibetan Books of the Dead,* 138.

these qualities. Most Initiation candidates for instance are the product of a particular school of belief, where often the supposition is that it embodies the most enlightened or assuredly correct form of teaching. Insight into the nature and validity of all paths to enlightenment is however of value to any seeker. There must be no condescension or derision, no arrogance of mind for anyone upon the Initiation path. Hayagrīva's club is used to bash all such unruly thoughts into submission. The Fiery Mind fuelled by the wind of *bodhicitta* must be developed to overcome the concretions of mind, if the third Initiation is to be attained upon the mountaintop of experience. Here complete identification with the *ālayavijñāna* happens, and consequently fusion with the Sambhogakāya Flower that eliminates all concept of ego. For this a hefty club is used to pummel all elements of 'self-ness', until all that is left is the consciousness of the Sambhogakāya Flower, which knows not this 'self'. It is utterly group conscious. The Throat centre, which regulates the Fires of Mind, is properly awakened at this gate or door of Initiation.

Iron hooks hook unruly *saṃskāras* (that are serpentine in motion) so they can be disciplined and chained to the mind's forthright will to convert all types of mental-emotions. The discipline utilises forms of *dhāraṇīs* that allow the *yogin* to control the modifications of mind. This path is well described in the meditation manuals, thus needs no elaboration. Sympathetic joy is the expression of the mind's own illumination once it has mastered the task at hand.

Only once the Waters have been fully stilled can the calm reflective mirror develop, where undistorted images are gained via the inner vision. Consequently, clairvoyance, the ability to envision the future or past lives, etc., can manifest. Transmuting the Waters of desire, lust and greed, produces devotion to the *dharma*, aspiration to liberation, and joy in the knowledge that the pain others experience can be eliminated. They but need to be educated to travel the path to liberation. Psychically these *saṃskāras* are represented as poisonous serpents of different sizes, which are effectively controlled by the club that Hayagrīva is sometimes depicted as wielding. The fact that the club is 'entwined with snakes' indicates that those vying for the third Initiation need to master all types of psychic perceptions and hallucinatory illusions. The club must be used upon the myriad serpents of desire-mind and psychicism. Joy is also produced whenever any of the qualities associated with one or other of the serpents is forever vanquished.

Hayagrīva's Consort Vajraśṛṅkhalā[28] controls that door in Nature wherein the members of the plant kingdom can gain entry into the type of sentience attained by the animal kingdom. We can note the spiral-cyclic motion of the interlinked eights associated with the chain she wields that illustrate the constitution of the *nāḍīs*. They are literally chains of small *vajras*, constituted by weaving in and out from common loci of five types of *prāṇas* that the *vajras* wield. The plant kingdom, which conveys the *prāṇas* of Life to the animal and human kingdoms, synthesises the sun's energy into food. To do so it must build the links of each chain of *prāṇic* vitality to be consumed by animal forms. This vitality is combined with the vibrancy and sentience developed by animals who posses a nervous system and experience pain. This synthesising process and reaction to pain is necessary for the development of consciousness. Animals are also conditioned by the essentially interminable unyielding instincts that govern their activities.

The iron chains that Vajraśṛṅkhalā wields also chains the *karma* of human mental-emotions to the perpetuators, so the consequences of the hell states they created for others will be experienced by themselves. The strongest Will is needed, indeed the powers of the *vajra* (implied in her name) must be invoked, to tame these beasts of mental-emotions when the cycle of retributive or corrective aspects of *karma* return.

The red colour assigned to Hayagrīva invokes the quality of Amitābha, who embodies the Fires of Mind via his wisdom of Discriminating Inner Vision.[29] After the battles over mental illusions have been won the *yogin* will completely control the mind. The Mind then becomes king of this domain through the development of Amitābha's wisdom.

Next, we have the eastern Guardian:

> At the east gate the white Guardian Vijaya (T. rNam-par rgyal-ba)

---

28 The term *śṛṅkhalā* refers to the chain used to subdue, bind, or destroy enemies of the *dharma*. The name Spoṭha given for this Consort by Gyurme has a similar meaning.

29 Hayagrīva is considered the wrathful aspect of Avalokiteśvara, who takes Amitābha as his Lord.

> appears together with his Ḍākinī, Vajrāṅkuśī. The symbols carried by the wrathful Vijaya are a kapāla and a bell, and his female counterpart carries an iron hook. The Guardian of the east gate appears in order to enlighten body-consciousness (T. Lus-kyi rnam-shes), and he effects the final physical dissolution of all beings. At the same time he represents one of the four divine boundless states (S. catur-pramāṇa; T. Tshad-med bzhi) and stands for the virtue of immeasurable kindness (S. mahāmaitrī; T. Byams-pa chen-po). With the appearance of the dynamic figure of Vijaya, flaming red upon a lotus, the doctrine of the immortality of things and of psycho-personal structure (T. rTag-par lta-ba) is overcome.[30]

In this gate, representing the way of the Heart, true liberation from all concepts of form occurs. All *saṃskāras* from below the diaphragm must be transformed and transmuted into the refined attributes of the Jinas if they are to be incorporated into the Heart centre. The process eventually leads one to being Initiated into the Void of consciousness-attributes that *śūnyatā* represents. The *kapāla* (skull cap) carried by Vijaya (meaning the victorious subduer)[31] represents the complete cutting away of the mind by the Initiate who holds it, so all that is left of what was once the full panoply of mental activity is the Void and the bliss it conveys. We thus have the *śūnyatā* experience represented and of the 'immeasurable kindness' that is the natural expression of the Heart centre. 'Kindness' here refers to the removal of all fetters preventing liberation. Dujom Rinpoche presents 'the four divine boundless states' as 'the four immeasurables', and states they are 'Loving kindness *(byams-pa,* Skt. *maitrī),* compassion *(snying-pa,* Skt. *karuṇā),* sympathetic joy *(dga'ba,* Skt. *muditā),* and equanimity *(btang-snyoms,* Skt. *upekṣā)'*.[32] They are boundless because these attributes of the Heart centre awakening are expressions of *bodhicitta* and are universal, immeasurable in their scope. There are no bounds in the universe that can limit their expression.

In continuing the line of reasoning re the functions of the Consorts

---

30 Lauf, *Secret Doctrines of the Tibetan Books of the Dead,* 137.

31 Gyurme has Trailokyavijaya, meaning the victorious subduer of the three worlds of human livingness.

32 Dujom Rinpoche, *The Nyingma School of Tibetan Buddhism,* section two, 132.

we can conclude that Vijaya's Ḍākinī, Vajrāṅkuśī (Gyurme gives Āṅkuśā), is concerned with assisting the transference from the human kingdom into that of enlightened being/non-being. This is because in this direction *śūnyatā* can be fully accessed, causing the termination of all concepts of ego, even that relating to one's human disposition. Her focus is thus with the type of *karma* causing the death of all types of mentalistic attributes related to the concept of 'self'. This concerns the *karma* that produces the liberation of consciousness from its fetters of mind. The hook she carries can be considered to pull all enlightenment-attributes out from the *manasic* pool that once contained them.

An *ānkuśā* is an elephant goad used for controlling elephants. It is a staff containing a hook and in Buddhist Tantricism contains *vajras* on top and on the opposite side of the hook. The elephant symbolises great strength and the wisdom utilised in overcoming *saṃsāric* allurements.

The white colour of Vijaya is that attributed to the Dharmadhātu Wisdom of Vairocana. Its purpose is to eventually bring about the *dharmakāya* enlightenment in the aspiring Initiate. This confers the immortality of the real and the dissolution of things[33] once considered real, when the nexus between *saṃsāra* and *śūnyatā* has been bridged. Standing at this nexus allows attainment of Initiations higher than the fourth. The dissolution we look to is that of the consciousness responsible for the segregation of 'things' by considering them to be real. It is converted to the flaming drop (red victorious *bindu*) that symbolises the fount of the body of *dharma* working to enlighten all aspects of the body-consciousness, especially when the higher interpretation of this 'body' is considered to be that of the *ālayavijñāna*.

The quality of the Dhyāni Buddha not represented in the consideration of the Guardians is the blue colour of the Mirror-like Wisdom of Akṣobhya. This means that Akṣobhya stands at the centre of this *maṇḍala,* as his Wisdom is that which the others are expressions of. His quality exemplifies the way of the Heart. Esoterically this Heart

33 The term 'things' is preferable here rather than 'physical dissolution of all beings' because the actual 'physical dissolution' of 'all beings' is wracked with many philosophical conundrums relating to eschatological considerations of the ending of days, and of ontological considerations of what 'beings' actually are, and how their 'dissolution' may actually occur. Simple physical plane death on the other hand needs no great enlightenment to achieve.

mirrors (or projects) the qualities of cosmic Love into the earth sphere. Vijaya's white colour therefore can also be considered the principle mechanism of transmission of Akṣobhya's radiance here.[34] (White referring not so much to that which is empty of colour, but rather the full scintillating potency of the seven Rays.)

Finally we have the Guardian of the northern gate:

> The Guardian of the north gate is the green Amṛtakuṇḍalin (T. bDud-rtsi 'kyil-ba) with his green Ḍākinī, Vajraghaṇṭā. He carries a crossed vajra and a bell and appears in order to enlighten the awareness of all bodily sensations. In addition he effects transcendence through infinite compassion. Amṛtakuṇḍalin represents the divine state of equanimity (S. upekṣā; T. bTang-snyoms) and overcomes all thinking in signs and forms. He stands to the north as the cosmic place of Buddha Amoghasiddhi, and thereby symbolizes the perfection of all earthly and karmically conditioned works. The four Ḍākinīs of the Guardians are also associated with the doctrine of the signs of the four boundaries (T. rTags-chad mu-bzhi), those boundaries within which alone all empirical experience of life can take place. These four boundaries of our physical and mental capabilities are birth and death (T. sKyed-'gag), immortality and dissolution (T. rTag-chad), existence and non-Being (T. Yod-med), and appearance and emptiness (T. sNang-stong).[35]

This northern direction governs the Initiation process from the first to the fifth Initiations. It thus assists one to overcome the impediments preventing entrance into the next higher dimension of perception, which is symbolised by this northern position of ascension or liberation from the former *maṇḍala* of expression. The green colour of Amoghasiddhi signifies that the All-Accomplishing Wisdom must be invoked with mathematical certainty at each stage of the path, relative to the quality to be mastered, if the next step is to be realised. It inevitably produces perfected activity in the material domain through complete comprehension of the nature of everything that is 'karmically conditioned'.

Effectively, the Initiate cycles through each of the gates in turn, overcoming *saṃskāras* and mastering qualities, whilst striving for

34 Akṣobhya has a blue body and a white emanation.

35 Lauf, *Secret Doctrines of the Tibetan Books of the Dead*, 138.

any Initiation. There are thus four sub-Initiation levels for every Initiation. (With a fifth sublevel producing the Initiation.) At each sub-level the defiling qualities of a particular Element are worked upon, to eventually produce the appearance of the Void Elements at the fourth Initiation. At the southern gate the qualities of Earthy and Watery *saṃskāras* as a subset of the fundamental Element one is focused upon (e.g., Fire) are mastered and transformed. In the western gate we have the corresponding Fiery *saṃskāra* focused upon. In the eastern gate the refinement of the remaining Watery attributes into those of the Airy Element occurs. In the northern gate the final vestiges of Earthy considerations (relating to the sum of *saṃsāra* and one's ego-posturing with it) are converted into the Aetheric propensities of the *dharmakāya*. In this way the potency of Amoghasiddhi's All-Accomplishing Wisdom is wrought in the crucible of transformatory experience.

The 'four boundaries' have a relation to the cycles of experiences (obscuring *karma)* associated with these five Initiation levels. 'Birth and death' and its consequence of pain and suffering because of attachment to transience, desire, and emotional volatility, is therefore mainly the focus of candidates for the two Initiations on the threshold. It thereby becomes an expression of the southern boundary. 'Immortality and dissolution' (the northern boundary) is the focus of the candidate for the fifth Initiation, who is firmly fixed upon the *dharmakāya,* the absolute mastery of all phenomena and the laws conditioning *saṃsāra*. 'Existence and non-being' (the western gate) relate to the focus of the forces of the mind of those that are vying to attain the third Initiation. All queries as to what phenomena ('existence') really is, what its purpose may be, leading to (non-being) must be answered by the enquiring mind of the Initiate vying for this degree. 'Appearance and emptiness' (the eastern gate) are the focus of the candidate for the fourth Initiation, who has *śūnyatā* firmly in his/her sights.

For the northern gate to be opened the Fiery *saṃskāras* of the Mind must be mastered, as the Head lotus is to be awakened in full. It therefore rests upon the laurels that the third Initiation accords. Consciousness is understood for what it is and its faculties are rightly utilised for the good of all. All forms of defiled mind and *saṃsāric* attachments, 'thinking in signs and forms', are overcome to produce 'the perfection of all earthly and karmically conditioned works'. Mastery of the mind automatically produces complete control of the Earthy Element, as the phenomena of the form (*saṃsāric* illusionality) are an extension of what constitutes the mind. The wisdoms of all the Dhyāni Buddhas can now be fully invoked, therefore this Guardian has a *vajra*, signifying that attributes of their potency is his to command. The equanimity attributed to this Guardian is developed at each of the Initiation levels after the crises of the tests have been passed. Equaniminous poise then manifests at increasingly subtler levels, until serenity beckons the composure at all times.

The name Amṛtakuṇḍalin is important, as *amṛta* is the elixir of immortality, a transmutation of the *saṃskāras* of ego clinging, whilst *kuṇḍalin* refers to the *kuṇḍalinī* Fire, the 'procreative' energy binding all forms into cohesive unities. This Fire is awakened through yogic practices. We are reminded here that the fearsome Fiery flames surrounding each of these Guardians is constituted of this Fire. Consequently, the wrath of the Guardians are evoked whenever one tries to awaken *kuṇḍalinī* before one is ready, no matter which Initiation level one is at. Supping the *amṛta* is only possible once the associated Wrathful one has been assuaged and thoroughly pacified through proper transformation of the *saṃskāras* concerned. After the fourth Initiation the Guardians are no longer needed because *kuṇḍalinī* comes to be supplanted in the *nāḍīs* by the rarefied *ātmic* Fire, and the Initiate is so imbued with Bodhisattvic qualities that psychic transgression is no longer possible. The Guardians can be considered to be aspects of *kuṇḍalinī,* and are responsible for its dissemination in Nature.

The Guardians govern the points of integration between this Fire and *śūnyatā.* The Herukas embody the transforming potency of this Fire, whilst the Wrathful Deities in general prepare the candidate for its arousal.

In Nature's kingdoms the green Ḍākinī, Vajraghaṇṭā,[36] can be considered to be responsible for the process wherein members of the animal kingdom prepare for Individualisation into the human through the nascent development of the ability to think. In this way they will eventually come to develop and comprehend the nature of 'the awareness of all bodily sensations'. This represents the *iḍā* line

36 Gyurme uses the name Ghaṇṭā.

of such development. The *piṅgalā* line comes via strong devotion. The name Vajraghaṇṭā means the *vajra* (common to all the Consorts) and the bell. Here it implies the feminine creative sounds delineating their ineffable power through the all-pervasive consciousness-space.

With respect to humanity Vajraghaṇṭā guards the types of *karma* produced through their *manasic* (Fiery) activity, of *cittavṛtti* manifesting all of the vicissitudes of mind. This allows the overcoming of 'all thinking in signs and forms' once the abstract Mind is properly developed and expressed.

In summary, the Guardians of the four directions are:

- *East,* we have Vijaya, white in colour, his Consort is Vajrāṅkuśī, and the developed *parāmita* is kindness.
- *South,* we have Yamāntaka, yellow in colour, with Consort Vajrapāśī, the *parāmita* being compassion.
- *West,* we have Hayagrīva, red in colour, and Consort Vajraśṛṅkhalā, with joy as the corresponding *parāmita.*
- *North,* we have Amṛtakuṇḍalin, green in colour, with Consort Vajraghaṇṭā. The *parāmita* is equanimity.

When we take the Guardians of the four directions into account, and add them to the 20 energy streams associated with the *viśvavajra,* then we have an energy field based upon the number 4 + 20. All similar *vajras* can interrelate with this one to produce a *maṇḍalic* pattern to the fabric of systemic space. This expression empowers the central 24 petals of the *chakras* that condition the formation of things. The *chakras* grow according to a prearranged pattern, with a consequent manifestation of *prāṇic* flow between the flowers as they grow. The Guardians stand at the junction between the *maṇḍala* proper and that which exists external to it. The Guardians therefore represent the doors of admission of extraneous energies to the *maṇḍala.* (They effectively have one foot inside and another outside of it.) This energy assists the successful candidate at each level of Initiation to move upwards into the next dimension of perception, the next enlightenment level.

There are thus four cardinal and 20 subsidiary positions, and if we include a central point, then there are 25 altogether that ties the entire *maṇḍala* into a unity. For the sake of completeness we should broaden our vision of the *maṇḍala* to represent the Dharmakāya Flower. It consists of a unity of 5 x 25=125 subsidiary interrelated Flowers, as each Dhyāni Buddha has his own *maṇḍala* of 25 to fully manifest his qualities. This paradigm is then reflected into the construction of each Sambhogakāya Flower.

If we multiply the 4 + 20 by 4, to adequately represent the nature of the manifestation of all qualities into the four directions into space, then we get the number 96, which is the base number of all subsidiary petals of any major *chakra*. This important number was explained in Volume 4 of this *Treatise on Mind.*

The relationship of the Dhyāni Buddhas to humanity manifests in a triune fashion:

a. The Father-Will aspect, governing the overall schema of the originating *maṇḍala* of five as emanations of the primordial Ādi Buddha. The focus here is upon the *ātmic*[37] portion of the Dharmakāya Flower. Here the *karma* that conditions all that is, and which is yet to be for human evolution exists in *bindu* form. The discovery of this Flower represents the way of escape out of the *maṇḍala* of space-time of Bodhisattvas when they become Buddhas. Preparation for such eventual expulsion from our planet happens as a consequence of instructions from the kingdom of Shambhala.

b. The Son or pure Consciousness aspect, the appearance of the Sambhogakāya Flowers of humanity. (We also have the *sambhogakāya* representation of the various deities.) This aspect represents the mechanism whereby the Wisdom-attributes of the Dhyāni Buddhas can flood human consciousness at the appropriate time to effect liberation from *saṃsāra.* It necessitates the development of the inward contemplative practices of a *yogin,* as exemplified in the higher yoga Tantras, where *śūnyatā* becomes a mechanism of escape. The focus, however, is upon the nature of

---

37 The substance of the fifth plane of perception (counting from below up), from where primordial *karma* originates. From this we have the appearance of 'unities' via which *karma* acts in *saṃsāra* (for *karma* must work through focal points of action). (Around such an idea is derived the concept of *ātman* by Hindus). The *ātmic plane* represents the lowest level of expression of cosmic Mind (*dharmakāya*) attainable by a Master of Wisdom. See also Volume 6, pages 276-284.

consciousness, as that represents the appropriation of the space from which the *maṇḍala* of time-space is constructed, and expresses the dynamics of the full Wisdom-principles of the Jinas. Therefore, the *śūnyatā-saṃsāra* nexus comes to the fore.

c. The Mother-Activity aspect, the *manasic* portion of the Dharmakāya Flower, as embodied by the work of the Consorts of the Dhyāni Buddhas. This concerns the way that forms appear and evolve in Nature. It allows an outwards meditation of the nature of *saṃsāra,* and a consequent liberation from it by desirelessly, spontaneously, and effortlessly following the laws and processes stemming from beyond the domain of mind. The method of liberation is found in Tantric works where the focus is upon the *dharmakāya.* The true nature of the *maṇḍala* as a unit first comes to be experienced at this level. The Father-Will aspect can then unite with the Mother. This requires the evolution of a substantial wisdom to directly obey the dictates of the laws of Life that originated from the primordial Buddha.

The fifth stage of the genesis of a *maṇḍala,* and the Vidyādharas

The explanation of the nature of the evolutionary process concerning the genesis of a *maṇḍala* will now continue.

Stage 5. The point of greatest divergence prior to the actual appearance of the phenomena of human consciousness.

This stage of evolution is the point at which the appearance of continuums of human mind-streams, with their separative attitudes of mind, are born from Nature. Form has now developed its own peculiar traits, with myriads of karmic agents (*devas*) working under the auspices of their great Lords (*ḍākinīs,* the Consorts of the Jinas and Mahābodhisattvas). They ensure that all of the processes in Nature flow in accord with the ideation of the great Mother Samayatārā,[38] the *prajñā* of Amoghasiddhi. Samayatārā is the loving, faithfully devotional one, who has completely surrendered and pledged herself to Amoghasiddhi's

38 The shortened version of the name Samayatārā (yum dam-tshig sgrol-ma) is Tārā (sgrol-ma). The term '*samaya*' means 'bound by an oath, agreement, or a convention'.

Plate 7. The five Vidyādharas and Consorts

purpose, and to maternally assist all sentient beings regardless of their merits. The focus is the dense physical plane, and the *chakra* concerned is the combined Sacral and Base of Spine centers, which now come into active manifestation.

By now all Consorts are actively manifest, producing the *maṇḍala* of their united interplay. The Consort of the primordial Ādi Buddha embodies the central *bindu* from which the overall structure develops. At the level of the phenomenal appearance of things there are nine Consorts altogether, making the nine-spoked *vajra*, with Amoghasiddhi's Consort as the central spoke. The four remaining Consorts of the Jinas represent the cardinal positions and the four Consorts of the Guardians as the intermediate positions. They thereby manifest as a swastika as they move to produce the transitional phases of any sentient grouping from a lower to a higher sentient state, and the interlude to final Initiation into the next kingdom for them. The Consorts of the Jinas stand relatively fixed as they project the *prāṇas* of the five Elements down and outwards. They can then establish the forms of sense-consciousness in Nature that are the bases to the formation and activity of a human mind.

We can now analyse the activity of the five secret Vidyādharas and their Consorts that appear on the seventh day, prior to the appearance of the Wrathful Deities on the eighth day.

> On the seventh day of the bardo visions the last of the peaceful deities appear, namely, the five "knowledge-holding deities," or Vidyādharas (T. Rig-'dzin lnga), who occupy a special position within the bardo maṇḍala. Certain texts fail to consider them at all. The Vidyādharas are heroic tantric deities (S. vīra; T. dPa'-bo), and they form a maṇḍala in the sambhogakāyacakra of the throat centre (T. Longs-spyod 'khor-lo). They stand at the place of the mystical mantric lute and are symbolic figures of the spiritually enlightened verbal plane of human activity. By way of their assignment to the cakra of the throat centre, they belong neither to the sphere of the wrathful deities of the mental plane (the forehead center) nor to that of the peaceful spiritual plane of the heart lotus[39]...
>
> The mantric path of the Mahāyāna (T. sNgags-kyi theg-pa) belongs to the secret paths of liberation through knowledge of the condensed meaning of the mantras and their recitation. Thus, the Vidyādharas, as deities on the mantric plane of pure speech (T. gSung-gi dkyil-'khor), even become guides on the path of liberation before the great cycle of wrathful deities dawns on the eighth day.
>
> The first deity to appear from the heavenly spheres (T. mKha-spyod zhing-khams) in the fivefold radiant light of "simultaneously born wisdom" in the centre of the lotus is the red Knowledge-holder, "Lotus Lord of the Dance" (T. Padma gar-gyi dbang-phyug), in tantric union with his red Ḍākinī. Like the other four knowledge-holding deities, he carries as symbols the tantric kapāla and the ritual sickle (T. Gri-gug). Then on the eastern lotus petal follows the white "Knowledge-holder of the Earth" (T. Sa-la gnas-pa'i rig-'dzin), on the southern lotus petal the yellow "Life-Ruling Knowledge-Holder" (T. Tshe-la dbang-ba'i rig-'dzin), in the west the red "Knowledge-Holder of the Great Symbol" (T. Phyag-rgya-chen-po'i rig-'dzin), and in the north the green "Spontaneously Arisen Knowledge-Holder" (T. Lhun-gyi grub-pa'i rig-'dzin). All have the same symbols and are accompanied by their mystical Ḍākinīs.[40]

39 Lauf, *Secret Doctrines of the Tibetan Books of the Dead*, 139.

40 Ibid., 140.

The five Vidyādharas[41] ensure the methodology of evolution throughout Nature, that the five instincts and sense-consciousnesses develop into the five-fold *manasic* propensity whereby human units can evolve wisdom. The developed sense-consciousnesses must be utilised as a base for the full maturation of mind. Once established, it produces the necessary requirements that will allow humanity to gain the characteristics of the five Jinas, 'the fivefold radiant light'. Gyurme's version states:

> *In the centre of [this maṇḍala], suffused by rainbows and light, the unsurpassed [Vidyādhara] known as the 'awareness holder of maturation', Padmanarteśvara, will simultaneously arise, his body resplendent with the radiance of the five lights.*[42]

The Vidyādharas are reapers of the *karma* of the five streams of Life in *saṃsāra*,[43] thus they all carry sickles (curved knives), symbolising their function as karmic agents.[44] They flay the skin and cut the flesh off the bones of ordinary life, so that the related *prāṇas* can eventually be converted to wisdom-principles. Implicit is the entire course of Life over many cycles of time, where sentient streams gradually develop mental *saṃskāras*. The consequences are perpetually recycled to produce a congruous evolution via the effort of the Consorts. Their main work, however, is with the field of human consciousness, which is effected by mantras emanating from the Throat centres of the Jinas to which the respective colours assigned to the Vidyādharas refer. Thus they figuratively 'stand at the place of the mystical mantric lute and are symbolic figures of the spiritually enlightened verbal plane of human activity'. They carry the streams of the mental organisation of those upon the path of Light to its conclusion in the *dharmakāya*. Their main work is therefore upon the higher mental plane via the constitution of the Sambhogakāya Flower.

41 *Vidyādhara*: 'knowledge holders', from the term *vidyā*, (Tib. rig pa) to know, be aware; the knowledge and sacred lore found in the magical power of mantra or spells. The term also refers to all consciousness perceptions, mental aptitude, empirical science, and direct illumined perception.

42 Gyurme Dorje, *The Tibetan Book of the Dead*, 251. *Padmanarteśvara* means 'the lotus lord *(padma*-Īśvara) of the dance'.

43 The four kingdoms of Nature, plus the *deva* hierarchy. (The Vidyādharas, the fifth Creative Hierarchy, whereas humanity are the fourth.)

44 Gyurme's version has the *ḍākinīs* holding the implements.

The sickle cuts the chaff from the golden grains of the harvest of Life that will eventually produce the Love-Wisdom conveyed by each Flower.

The awareness attributes they reap can also be correlated to the lives coursing through five planes of perception[45] as far as they can be expressed upon the abstract domains of the Mind. They bear the imprint of the *karma* that these lives weave into planetary manifestation. All is interrelated by means of sound. Each of the Knowledge-holders hold a *kapāla,* the skull cup containing the 'blood', the *prāṇa* of transmuted *saṃskāras* (the intoxicating bliss of Mind) obtained by those that drink its contents. This 'bliss' is constituted of the essence of the five streams of awareness developed by the five kingdoms of Nature[46] that come into manifestation and undergo evolutionary progression under the auspices of the Jinas. The skull cup thus contains the total experiences, the essence of the gain from any cycle of incarnation in the material world.

The *karma* is stored from cycles of activity of previous *maṇḍalas* carried through to the present purpose. The Vidyādharas have knowledge of all lines of lives and their former karmic interrelationships, hence they are 'Knowledge-Holders'. They know when any form of sentient life is to appear in the *saṃsāric* play and when it is to recede again. *Bījas* then manifest for future karmic propensity. Their Consorts, however, are the actual builders of the forms and shapes containing the categories of sentient lives. We thus have the appearance of all the species of lives that have evolved throughout the aeons of time, guided through each successive (genetic) transformation to an ultimate evolutionary purpose.

These deities are arranged in the general manner of the five Dhyāni Buddhas, of which they are emanations, via the paradigm of the *maṇḍala* emanated by Amitābha, who is responsible for the dissemination of the Fiery Element throughout space. The centre of the *maṇḍala* of the Vidyādharas is the red 'Lotus Lord of the Dance', 'the Supreme Knowledge-Holder Who Ripens *Karmic* Fruits, radiant with all the five colours'.[47] He can therefore be considered the 'Son' born from the Womb of Amitabha's Consort, a product of their ecstatic union. This

45 These 'five planes' are expressions of the five Elements, Aether, the *ātmic* plane; Air, the *buddhic* realm; Fire, the *manasic* realm; Water, the astral realm; and Earth, the physical domain.

46 The mineral, plant, animal, human and the liberated kingdoms.

47 Evans-Wentz, *The Tibetan Book of the Dead,* 127.

dance concerns the movement of Fiery *manasic* energies according to the way that they must be directed to all the streams of Life occupying the rest of the *maṇḍala*.

The specific concern with respect to humanity is the dissemination of mind in the context of developing wisdom.[48] For most of human development the evolution of the empirical mind is of paramount importance. It holds central stage until enlightenment is sought. Therefore, the sickles the Vidyādharas hold reap the *karma* generated by each individual in humanity's *manasic* environment (the *ālayavijñāna*). The Consorts then sow the *karma* back into the human field of Life in such a way that human units become wiser over time. They thus help empower the Throat centre of humanity, so that eventually selfish thoughts are converted into those of goodwill that are the basis to wisdom. The development of wisdom necessitates the right activity of speech. At first profanities and common articulations of speech manifest, and later wisdom awakens, to propagate the *dharma*. Eventually we have the mantric observances of *yogins* in their *sadhana* to educate others.

The Vidyādharas and the Sambhogakāya Flowers

The Vidyādharas and Consorts comprise the substance of the form aspect of the Sambhogakāya Flowers when human Soul-forms come into existence. In this process of Individualisation the Vidyādharas provide a vortex of five energy streams. The aspiring animal sentience incorporated in the form of elementary lives *(lunar pitṛs)* that are attributes of the four female Gatekeepers of Pristine Cognition, provide the other four to make the necessary nine whorls of petals. These four energy streams are in the form of elementary mind, the principle of desire, the *prāṇas* associated with the etheric double and the dense form, via which all lives gain evolutionary experiences. We therefore have the foundation for all subsequent *manasic* development by humans.

Incorporating this prepared nine-fold whorl of substance upon the *sambhogakāya* domain via its central point constituting the Śūnyatā Eye is a *dharmakāyaic* Monadic form instigating the principle of human Life. This Monadic form is a unit of cosmic Mind needing

48 They appear in stage six of the evolutionary process, when the *tathāgatagarbha* for each human unit has been established.

further evolutionary impetus, but can descend no further than the abstract domain of Mind. It incarnates into the form of the newly constituted Sambhogakāya Flower and through it manifests cycles of human incarnations within the fields of *māyā* until it gains the required experiences and the generated wisdom of a Buddha, allowing it to completely free itself from phenomena. This is the secret of the formation and existence of a *tathāgatagarbha*. Compassion is inherent because the purpose for this aeonic sacrifice is the redemption of substance, the elevation of the sentient lives constituting that substance into the domain of the human mind, so that eventually they evolve into human units. A symbiosis consequently exists between the *deva* hierarchy denoted as the Vidyādharas and the Monadic Presence which has always been veiled by the coital integration between a Buddha and his Consort. This subject of the grand evolutionary scheme of all forms and entities in the universe has always been relegated as part of the mysteries of Initiation. It is introduced here for a Buddhist audience because it is now time for the revelation of the true content of the symbolism of their Tantras, and what is also veiled in many treatises.

Most of my later writings will be concerned with the ramifications of this topic, as the associated philosophy is vast. Buddhist ontology lays the foundation for its revelation, re detail concerning the nature of the attributes of mind/Mind and its relation to *śūnyatā*, as well as in all the other topics so far discussed in this series. This represents the *piṇgalā* approach in the overall scheme of things esoteric. The general Hindu belief system represents the *iḍā* approach, wherein the deities associated with cosmological considerations and that concerning the cycles of time (*kalpas*) lay an epistemic basis concerning the nature of the appearance of phenomena. The exoteric ontology concerning the nature of an *ātman* may be flawed, but nevertheless contains the seed of truth, as also does the Buddhist concept of the *tathāgatagarbha*. The veils of both systems need removing so that the *iḍā* and *piṇgalā nāḍīs* of these sibling religions can be merged into the liberating *suṣumṇā* stream of revelation herein called the Dharmakāya Way. The two religions should not be thought of in terms of their competitiveness, or even of their main differences, but rather how one manifests relative to the other, of their complimentary qualities.

Welcome to the new expanded view of the *buddhadharma*. There is no ending to the limitless vistas of cosmos once Monadic perception has been attained. Shambhala (the planetary Head centre) exists to process this Monadic Way. As Buddhas appear they must choose their paths away from this little speck in cosmos called earth. These 'thus gone' Ones have much still to learn in the vast vistas of never-ending space populated with innumerable stellar zones of attainment.

The Sambhogakāya Flowers are Buddha-Wombs (*tathāgatagarbha*) because not only is a Monadic (elementary Buddha) presence incarnate, but because of the Vidyādharas' embodiment of manasic substance that facilitates the path to enlightenment. Manifesting as the substance of the causal forms of humanity, the Consorts can thereby regulate the overall karmic stream of humanity's progress to liberation. The overseeing Jinas working via the agency of the Vidyādharas can consequently also make broad scale karmic adjustments for humanity's benefit. In this way each human unit is destined to eventually evolve into a Buddha. Following such a path is only a matter of evolutionary time, right guidance and karmic adjudication, plus the development of the Will-to-Love and the Will-of-Love by humans. The Vidyādharas and Consorts are a combined *deva*[49] hierarchy, a subject that can only be introduced here, but shall be elaborated on in Volume 7, *The Constitution of Shambhala*.

Note that each Sambhogakāya Flower bears three groups of petals that can be categorised according to a five-fold dispensation, as explained in Volume 3 of this *Treatise on Mind*. The Vidyādharas process the gain of the accumulated qualities of mind for the entire human kingdom as first the Knowledge tier of petals awaken, then the Love-Wisdom tier and finally the Sacrifice tier. (This is a generalisation, as the awakening of the petals is generally quite staggered, according to the focus of the qualities to be developed by the Flower concerned.) The role of their Consorts is to integrate the *prāṇas* from the Head lotus into the Sambhogakāya Flower. The Vidyādharas then assist in the coordination of group *karma* between the Sambhogakāya Flowers and help bathe their domain with aspects of cosmic Mind. Their Consorts inevitably manifest a marriage with the human unit, with the human and this *deva* kingdom merging into one as the higher Initiations are

49 The third and fifth Creative Hierarchies.

accomplished. The Monadic presence consequently takes the role of a Vidyādhara, freeing the Vidyādharas to take higher roles in cosmos.

With respect to a human unit the awakening of the Throat centre effectively unfolds the five Knowledge petals of the individual. The awakening of the Heart centre develops the Love-Wisdom petals. Finally the Sacrifice petals absorb the *prāṇas* of the awakening Head lotus when the path to enlightenment is consciously trod. The entire development is controlled by the *manasic* propensity of the Fires of Mind via the Throat centre, because the Sambhogakāya Flower is a vehicle of the Fiery domain that is the *ālayavijñāna*.

Once the Sacrifice petals are in the throes of bringing into manifestation the liberating qualities from the *dharmakāya* then *kuṇḍalinī* can be roused and the entire 1,000 petalled lotus of the Head centre can be awakened. We can see, therefore, that the process is but an expression of various states of Fire:

1. The liberating Father Fire, the *dharmakāya*.
2. The Fiery Son in incarnation (the Sambhogakāya Flower-*tathāgatagarbha)* wherein the exchanges take place, within the fluxial sea of Fire that is *ālayavijñāna*.
3. The awakening Mother Fire *(kuṇḍalinī)*, prepared and adorned at the Base of Spine centre.
4. The vibrant *manasic* Fires of the Head lotus that become intensified and made ablaze, awakening the *yogin*.
5. The Fires of substance that become liberated, allowing the various *siddhis* to manifest via the development of the yoga of the psychic heat. Energy is thereby invigorated and every atom of the form is brought totally under the *yogin's* direct control.

Gaining knowledge on the earth happens slowly for humanity. Guided by the Lords of Life, first the physical apparatus had to be mastered, then the psychic attributes of humans developed. This was the onus of the Atlantean civilisation, which was cataclysmically destroyed at the time of the ending of the last ice age.[50] In the new

50 Thus we have the story of the 'great flood' recorded in virtually every ancient religion, and nowadays taken as myths. For those with internal vision the existence of this former continent is a fact. A significant portion of humanity's *karma* can be traced to Atlantis.

cycle, focused upon the development of mind, agrarian civilisations came into existence; the stone age, copper age, bronze age, and then the technologically superior iron age where humanity learnt to refine metal and utilise metal instruments. When farming and village life became the mainstay of human interaction it facilitated the type of contemplative lifestyles such as were found in the Buddha's era, where mendicants could wander from place to place seeking alms and spreading the *dharma.* An understanding of the nature and place of *karma* in people's lives could therefore be taught so that they could positively respond and ameliorate its effects.

Over time a technologically advanced civilisation has evolved manifesting an advanced use of the Element Fire.[51] This development necessitated the full use of the discriminative, separative, analytical, deductive, creative aptitude of the mind. It also produces philosophical speculation. The inevitable consequence is the ability to gain all knowledge through direct *yogic* perception (necessitating the taming of *kuṇḍalinī).* The Vidyādharas are entities that helped direct this course of evolution so that consciousness could integrate the Fiery attributes of the animal sentience developed in Nature. These animal-like potencies *(kāma-manas)* are integrated into the mind, and inevitably find themselves as the *saṃskāras* stored within the petals of the Sambhogakāya Flower. The petals of this Flower are constituted of the Fiery Element, but the main characteristic is the factor of Love-Wisdom, to help direct the conversion of *saṃskāras.*

When these potencies are to be converted into the peaceful qualities that are the true heritage of the human persona so that *kuṇḍalinī* can be awakened, then the doors to the focus of the Wrathful Deities are accessed. It takes great Wisdom and Love to properly handle and channel the serpent-Fire. The overall guiding role of the Vidyādharas, therefore, is to help safely liberate this Fire.

The centre of the *maṇḍala*

The role that the Vidyādharas play with respect to the Sambhogakāya Flower can now be analysed. The symbolism of their role here indicates

---

51 Often the driving impetus for the growth of such technology was the desire to wage war against known enemies and for territorial expansion.

how their forces manifest with respect to the paradigm established by the Dhyāni Buddhas. That which possesses the most refined and intensified energies, which are then modified in the other directions, embodies the centre of the *maṇḍala*. Here we have Kāya-Vidyādhara,[52] the red 'Lotus Lord of the Dance'. He governs the overall organisation and function of the petals of the Sambhogakāya Flower and the assimilation of their *prāṇas* into the Śūnyatā-Eye, when the sacrificial path is trodden by those seeking liberation from *saṃsāra* by means of the developed Will based upon Love. 'Sacrifice' refers to the most intense form of energy possible to engender, often conceived of in terms of 'the destroyer-regenerator' that sacrifices all for the benefit of the All. The term 'Lotus Lord' has an esoteric reference to the lotus form that this Flower takes. Kāya-Vidyādhara represents the vehicle (*kāya*) for holding the sum of the Fiery energies of the *maṇḍala* of the Sambhogakāya Flower. The dance therefore refers to the way that the multihued and resplendent sacrificial Fiery energies are seen to interplay within this floral form. Unregenerate *saṃskāras* of mind are sacrificed for this purpose. The *prāṇas* flowing in all subsidiary *chakras* can also be accounted for here.

This dance first awakens the Throat centre of an incarnate individual because it distributes the *manasic* energies generated to the mind. Eventually the entire 1,000 petalled lotus of the Head centre will be awakened when *kuṇḍalinī* has arisen and the pathways to the higher Mind are developed. In Nature, *kuṇḍalinī* integrates all forms into coherent unities and gives them the internal heat to sustain life.

As Lord of the Dance, Kāya-Vidyādhara's symbolism is similar to that of Lord Śiva's (of the Hindu pantheon) in his guise as Naṭarāja. Naṭarāja is depicted as a cosmic dancing *yogin* (who destroys the universe so that it can be recreated by Brahmā) within a halo of flames and with cobras (*kuṇḍalinī*) wrapped around him. He is dancing on a dwarf that represents ignorance.

In Nature we see the purveyance of all attributes of the Fiery Element by the activity of Kāya-Vidyādhara's Consort in such a way that forms are sustained, allowing rudimentary aspects of mind to be evolved and eventually developed in a humanity. With respect to the

52 The terms Kāya, Citta, Guṇa, Vāc and Karma Vidyādhara are provided by Lauf, *Secret Doctrines of the Tibetan Books of the Dead*, 140.

tathāgatagarbha, her energies integrate the most vibrant attributes of the Head lotus into the Sacrifice petals of the Sambhogakāya Flower.

All the deities wield the same implements. Gyurme has the knife the Vidyādhara wields pointing to the sky, whereas Evans-Wentz calls it 'the *mudrā* of fascination'.[53] 'The sky' relates to enlightenment, and the 'fascination' is with what it veils (e.g., the Sambhogakāya Flower).

The north

Karma-Vidyādhara, the 'Spontaneously Arisen Knowledge-Holder', holds the direction north that signifies focussing upwards to *dharmakāya.* Evans-Wentz terms this Vidyādhara 'the Self-Evolved Knowledge-Holder, green in colour, with a half-angry, half-smiling radiant countenance'.[54] Gyurme uses the phrase 'spontaneous presence'.[55] The half wrathful, half smiling countenance indicates the combination of Will or Sacrifice with Love-Wisdom. The wrathful, sacrificial stance is necessary to ensure that all *saṃskāras* have been appropriately converted and transformed so that the *dharmakāya* can flower at the *saṃsāra-śūnyatā* nexus after the qualities of the Sacrifice petals have been gained. The northward looking focus is therefore towards that nexus. The name Karma-Vidyādhara means that this knowledge holder reaps the consequence of the actions (*karma*) of gaining knowledge in the material world in such a way that all *karma* associated with *saṃsāric* activity can be finally resolved. The ability to annul the *karma* is 'self-evolved' and 'spontaneously arisen' as a natural consequence of receiving impressions from the sacrifice petals of the Sambhogakāya Flower.

The path necessitates dispassionately following the way of the manifesting *karma,* no matter where it leads, so that the consequences of past actions are lived out, and no new *karma* is created. The corresponding impetus of Love-Wisdom *(bodhicitta)* will then also ensue the treading of the Bodhisattva path to liberation. Long is the evolutionary struggle that human units undergo in the material domain before they are capable of spontaneously working off their *karma.*

---

53 Evans-Wentz, *The Tibetan Book of the Dead,* 127.

54 Ibid., 128.

55 Gyurme Dorje, *The Tibetan Book of the Dead,* 252.

Karma-Vidyādhara's Consort is focused on the general absorption of the *prāṇas* from the tier of petals that represents the Throat in the Head centre. The five Sacrifice petals of the Sambhogakāya Flower absorb these *prāṇas*.[56] She also works via the *manasa devas* that regulate the activities of all thought processes in the mental domain. The energy field governed by them is that of the northwest direction of emanatory 'good will'. They work to assist all beings, to help them to cleanse their *karma* with the material domains, so that they can inevitably rise to worlds supernal. This is an integrated service with respect to the dissemination of the *karma* governing the entire *maṇḍala*. The colour governing the general expression of the law of *karma* is green.

The east

This petal concerns the way of inwardly focussing the aspects of mind *(citta)* to produce contemplative realisations. Here we have the derivation of compassion, the significance of the colour white assigned to Citta-Vidyādhara, the 'Knowledge-holder of the Earth' who governs this direction. Gyurme has the 'awareness holder who abides on the levels', whilst Evans-Wentz has 'the Earth-Abiding Knowledge-Holder'. We see that 'the Earth' here does not refer to the Element, but rather to the entire earth-sphere. Knowledge (*citta*) concerning evolution upon it is gained, and the earth is then valued for its true worth, devoid of emotional constraints and distortions. Eventually right knowledge is used to generate the Will-to-Love where the person learns to sacrifice selfish concerns because of knowledge of the inevitable consequences of self-focus. This makes one a true master of *saṃsāra*. The Bodhisattva path is consequently trod. First, however, all of the major battles of mastering emotional *saṃskāras* must be fought.

The concept of *'citta'* here is used in its pure sense of the mind substance wielded by all the Vidyādharas, as an expression of Amitābha's Discriminating Inner Vision, which this eastern direction specifically embodies. 'The Earth' from this perspective can refer to the ground that is the substance of Mind that all liberated Ones tread upon.

56 They are the Sacrifice–Sacrifice, the Sacrifice–Love-Wisdom, the Sacrifice–Knowledge, the Love-Wisdom–Sacrifice, and the Knowledge–Sacrifice petals.

Citta-Vidyādhara's Consort sows *citta* into manifestation from a primarily northeast direction (of 'unity'), the focus being upon the development of mind by animal groups, so that the goal of establishing the kingdom of the *tathāgatagarbha* can be accomplished upon the domain of the higher Mind. Later, the problematic battle of converting animal-headed *saṃskāras* will manifest by the resultant humanity. This Consort governs the general *citta* that embodies the substance of the petals of the Sambhogakāya Flower, and specifically the five Love-Wisdom petals.[57] This sets the general resonant note for the activities of all the Flowers. She works to help incorporate the *prāṇas* from the Heart in the Head centre into the Sambhogakāya Flower.

The west

The direction here is that of outwards into the field of service representing humanity. Both Lauf and Evans-Wentz give us the red 'Knowledge-Holder of the Great Symbol' (Vāc-Vidyādhara), whereas Gyurme provides the phrase *'awareness holder of the great seal'*.[58] Knowledge necessitates speech (*vāc*), and its extension as writing, to convey all of the levels of understanding of any human civilisation, culminating in great wisdom. The 'speech' that is implied here reflects this transformation. Wisdom is the spontaneous loving knowledge conveyed by the Throat centre when integrated with the *prāṇas* of the Heart. The mantric words spoken therefore by this Knowledge-Holder are those emanating from the Heart and directed by the Throat centre.

The Great Symbol (or 'Seal', the *mahāmudrā),*[59] at its lowest

57 They are the Sacrifice–Love-Wisdom, Love-Wisdom–Sacrifice, Love-Wisdom–Love-Wisdom, Love-Wisdom–Knowledge, and Knowledge–Love-Wisdom petals.

58 Gyurme Dorje, *The Tibetan Book of the Dead,* 252.

59 *Mahāmudrā:* literally 'great Seal', or 'great Symbol', referring to the state of the attainment of the emptiness that is the ultimate attainment of reality, Buddhahood. It is a *mudra* (gesture) because realisation of the three bodies of a Buddha in one is sealed in supreme unchanging bliss. It involves realisation of enlightenment in one lifetime through the 'seal' that integrates the masculine compassion with the feminine wisdom aspect. In the Kagyupta tradition it denotes the experiential attainment of the Buddha-Mind through the practice involving the stages of the preparatory ground, the path (using the calm abiding and insight meditations) and the result being liberation. It is the absoluteness of being/non-being, which unites all duality, male and female into a unity,

connotation, refers to the mind's ability to conceptualise in terms of symbols and images of all types, and to integrate the different ideas in terms of a harmony. Next we have refinement of those images into the abstractions associated with the enlightened Mind. Finally, the method of integrating the masculine (human) and feminine (*deva*) principles in Nature into a unity must be discovered and the powers of the associated *chakras* 'sealed' in accomplishment. Inevitably this enables the experience of *śūnyatā* via the development of Love-Wisdom *(bodhicitta),* where the Love part *(bodhi)* refers to the human and the Wisdom part *(citta)* to the *deva* method of expression. *Śūnyatā* becomes the place of mergence or marriage (consummation) between these two Life streams. The Void, as the mirror of the *dharmakāya,* then becomes the Symbol itself. The finalising of such experience (by utilising the Will and Love that are the leitmotiv of the human hierarchy) integrates *ālayavijñāna,* the ground of all consciousness (ruled by the Vidyadhāras), with the impress from *dharmakāya* once the *śūnyatā-saṃsāra* nexus is found.

We see, therefore, that the control of speech (*vāc*) refers here to the method of integration (in a coital, yab-yum synthesis) of wisdom with compassion in such a way that sacred, secret mantras can be uttered to control all of Nature's forces, because everything is intrinsically 'empty'. The outward field of expression of this western direction then necessitates control and conversion of all unruly *saṃskāras* generated as a course of human interactions with substance. The methodology then incorporates the expression of the Wrathful and theriomorphic deities, as explained in the subsequent chapters of this book.

With respect to the colours attributed to the Consorts of the Vidyādharas we see that two of them are red (for Kāya and Vāc Vidyādhara), and we even have this colour indirectly implied in the word *citta,* because Amitābha's realm is the environment of the Sambhogakāya Flowers, and orange is their general colour. (Orange being the overall hue, which in the colour schema of the *Bardo Thödol* is taken as red.) This colour is also exemplified in the petal of the western direction because *manasic* substance is embodied by the Vidyādharas, and is the main quality to be developed by humanity, being necessary

---

completeness. This Symbol can be depicted as the cypher zero, and involves the sum of the entire cause-effect world play, as it impresses itself upon consciousness.

for the development of wisdom. The remaining colours are yellow, green and white, which are oriented according to the qualities to be mastered from the perspective of the Sambhogakāya Flower.

Vāc-Vidyādhara's Consort reaps *manas* throughout the sum of the petals of the entire *chakra* system of Nature via the southwest position (of 'understanding'). *Citta* is inherent throughout *saṃsāra,* as the *devas* embody this substance and convey it as karmic lore. The purpose is to assist the development of intelligence amongst the animal population. They can then develop the ability to use speech, which is one of the defining distinctions between them and humans. Vāc-Vidyādhara's Consort incorporates *saṃskāras* of *kāma-manas* from the outermost tier of petals of the Head lotus (the Solar Plexus in the Head) into the five Knowledge petals of the Sambhogakāya Flower.[60] This then becomes the basis to the expression of the *ālayavijñāna* environment for that (human) consciousness-stream.

The south

This direction is denoted 'downwards to the little ones' and is governed by Guṇa-Vidyādhara, the yellow 'Life-ruling Knowledge holder'. Gyurme states that this awareness holder has 'power over the lifespan',[61] whilst Evans-Wentz states that he has 'Power Over Duration of Life'.[62] *Guṇa* translates as 'merit', but also in the Hindu philosophy we have the three *guṇas: sattva* (mobility), *rajas* (kingly rhythm) and *tamas* (inertia).[63] They refer to the natural order or flow of energies, causing the

---

60 They are the Sacrifice–Knowledge, Love-Wisdom–Knowledge, Knowledge–Sacrifice, Knowledge–Love-Wisdom, and Knowledge–Knowledge petals.

61 Gyurme Dorje, *The Tibetan Book of the Dead,* 252.

62 Evans-Wentz, *The Tibetan Book of the Dead,* 127.

63 *Guṇa* (Tib. Yon tan): 'fundamental quality'. All manifest objects are structurally composed of the three *guṇas: sattva, rajas* and *tamas. Sattva* (truth) embodies what is pure and subtle, *rajas* (kingly) embodies activity, and *tamas* (darkness, inertia) embodies heaviness and immobility. *Sattva,* signifying rhythm or balance, is the nature of that which must be realised; *tamas* is the obstacle that opposes this realisation; and *rajas* is the force that overcomes *tamas.* In terms of consciousness, *sattva* is expressed as peace and serenity, the base for the realisation of the truth of whatever is. *Rajas* is the activity of the mind that establishes knowledge, and *tamas* represents laziness, lack of interest, and stupidity arising from ignorance.

way things appear in Nature and human society. It represents the trinity of Father-Son-Mother. All life is conditioned thus, and the relationships in human society produce attributes according to the way of action of the *guṇas*. The *saṃskāras* of active life manifest upwards in this triune fashion (seen also in terms of the *iḍā, piṅgalā* and *suṣumṇā nāḍīs)* and are absorbed into and regulated by the similarly conditioned trinity of petals of the Sambhogakāya Flower. The mind is thereby fed through all forms of knowledgeable pursuits. Attachments to temporal understandings prove insufficient, producing a yearning for further higher, enlightened learning. This process is termed 'merit' above. Eventually refined *(sattvic)* forms of knowledge are born.

From the southernmost direction one must turn one's direction upwards (north), to seek liberation from *karma's* effects. Knowledgeable pursuits are needed to sustain one's material life. One then moves to religious aspiration, and finally yoga, in order to master the entire world of phenomenon into which one is born.

In Nature, Guṇa-Vidyādhara's Consort, occupying the southeast position (of 'expression'), organises the panoply of interrelationships of animal lives unfolding as a foundational basis for developing the later five sense-consciousnesses of humanity. Such development necessitates incarnating into dense forms. The mineral kingdom is an automatic reflex of the impulses originating from the *manasic* domain, the concretisation of the originating impulses. Therefore this exposé will help to develop a proper scientific application of the statement that all is considered to be an expression of mind.

This Consort deals with the overall organisation of the *prāṇas* in the Sambhogakāya Flower to produce a harmonious note, and so that appropriate characteristics are gained by the incarnating personalities. The aims for the development for any sequence of lives by the Sambhogakāya Flower must be rightly monitored and expressed so that the *guṇas,* the appropriate Knowledge, Love-Wisdom and Will attributes are developed as needed.

The way of mind/Mind

The Yogācāra affirmation that all phenomena are an expression of the variegations and structural arrangements of mind can be extended to the way of the organisation of elemental atomic life. The purpose of phenomena is so that the will can be developed through mastery of its phenomenon. The related experience is carried forth as developed wisdom to enlightenment's shore (one's true place of residence). This is effected by means of inherent *karma* and the way of the Heart via the impetus of will. Such is the effect of the march of events becoming the flow of time. In the same way that thoughts are structured and arranged by human minds, atomic forms and sentient life streams are the components of the *manasic* input of the greater *deva* lives. Such lives have various names in the many religious dispensations: fairies, angels, Seraphim, *ghandarvas, devas, ḍākinīs,* of which there are many classifications. We can now add such terms as Vidyādhara's, Īśvarī, Mātaraḥ, etc., to the list.

The Vidyādharas and their Consorts' governance evolve sentient streams of lives and convert them into intelligent life. They are transmuted into higher dimensional attributes with the assistance of the Guardians and their Consorts. These lives are all held in a coherent pristine form by the Ādi Buddha and Consort. All is the expression of their union. The focus of the work of the Guardians and their Consorts is upon the lives in the *arūpa* (formless) levels. The Jinas and Consorts work with both *arūpa* and the most abstract *rūpa* levels, whilst the focus of the Vidyādharas and their Consorts is to transform *rūpa* attributes into the *arūpa.* (They work under the auspices of Amitābha and the red Kāya-Vidyādhara.) The masculine deities control the direction of the consciousness streams, whilst their Consorts control the *karma* of the ever-changing manifesting forms that are the vehicles of the integral sentient lives. Thus all of the laws of Nature come into existence. They manifest *from above down* to influence the little lives in *saṃsāra,* and to effect the diversification of all forms from the atomic world, plant life, and so on upwards.

One day the scientific community will discover the principle of organised Thought-life throughout Nature and apply their discovery logically, utilising the Buddhist philosophy herein presented, and consequently move forward into a new hylozoistic universe of discovery.[64]

64 This process of discovery has begun with, for instance, the clairvoyant investigations of Besant and Leadbeater on the nature of the atom, and Dr. Hauschka, whose *The Nature*

They will then reveal to humanity the effects of the arcane wisdom known to the *mahāsiddhas*. Such awareness will consequently benefit human progress, divorced from avaricious pursuits that disadvantage the majority for the connivance of a power elite. (As a consequence, true scientific development is stifled or skewed.) Only then will humanity be truly able to master the ability to travel in space by transcending physical plane limitations via complete comprehension of the laws of Mind. Their journey throughout cosmos will be with the speed of thought in vehicles of Mind. The statement 'verily all is mind/Mind' will then be the basis of the fount of their evolved wisdom.

One can also compare the five stages of the evolutionary process so far presented purely in terms of the appearance of a human form from out of the womb of its mother:

- Stage one, *conception,* concerning the implanting of the seed of the child in the womb.
- Stage two, *duality*, the emergence of interrelated forces, activating the *karma* that sets all into motion. The development of the foetus now begins in earnest, with the dividing of cells producing increasingly complex organelles. We also have the evocation of *saṃskāras* from past life cycles to be built into the constituency of the child to be.
- Stage three, the *balancing of forces,* producing a coherent form, the final preparation of the child prior to its emergence into the light of day.
- Stage four, *physical incarnation*, the downward projection of the *maṇḍala.* The child is born and utters its first cry (or mantra from a Logoic perspective), and thus begins the new cycle that activates the *karma* of all that is to follow.

---

of Substance pioneers the field of esoteric chemistry. We can look to the work of other Anthroposophists, and also the advocates of the new biology, such as Rupert Sheldrake (*A New Biology of Life*), and James Lovelock's Gaia theory. Then there are the physicists who have compared the discoveries of modern physics specifically to Buddhist philosophy, and the concept of the Anthropic Principle. We should also add the anti-Darwinian scientists to the list, such as Michael Behe (*Darwin's Black Box*) and William Dembski (*Signs of Intelligence*) etc., and some modern cosmological theorists, such as Hannes Alfvén. Alchemical investigation and biological transmutations are other fields of study.

- Stage five, the *point of greatest divergence* in Nature, thus producing the stages of development of the child to adulthood.

The next chapters shall continue the theme of the *ten stages* of the development of the *maṇḍala* of evolution, beginning with stage six and the overcoming of human *saṃsāric* afflictions. Much detail concerning the nature and functioning of the *chakras* will then be forthcoming, plus the mechanics that underlie gaining enlightenment. Little will be said concerning the eight Mahābodhisattvas and their Consorts, for which Volume 4 should be consulted.

3

The Deities of the Bardo Thödol
Part Two:
Controlling Factors of the Human Condition

Stage six of the genesis and evolution of a *maṇḍala*

I shall now analyse the deities responsible for human evolution, the subjective factors assisting the overcoming of *saṃsāric* afflictions created by people. The concern, therefore, is with that which constitutes the making of enlightened beings, their drive to liberation and inevitable Buddhahood. This involves an analysis of the sixth to tenth stages of the evolutionary process, with an added two needed to produce a Buddha. In continuing on to stage six of the genesis and evolution of a *maṇḍala,* where the *maṇḍala* designated is the *Bardo Thödol*, our focus shall be the process of evolution in Nature and the development of humanity. The generation of human *saṃskāras* and their eventual resolution and transformation into enlightenment-attributes follows. This process is incorporated into the *maṇḍala* itself and inevitably produces the appearance of wrathful and animal-headed human entities.

Stage 6. The individuation of a human kingdom from out of the animal kingdom.

This stage necessitates the formation of a Sambhogakāya Flower, a *tathāgatagarbha,* for each human unit. We then have the manifestation of individual *karma* instead of the shared group *karma* that affects the animal kingdom, and the development of noetic sensory awareness.

The background information for this chapter can be found in the teachings on the Sambhogakāya Flower provided in Volume 3 of this

Treatise on Mind. Further information is provided here as a supplement to show how the *tathāgatagarbha* actually comes into existence, and consequently of the way that it is organised, to extract and to store *saṃskāras* of the evolving consciousness-stream that represents each human life. The reader should be reminded here that the work of building forms and the direction of the resultant *karma* rests in the domain of the feminine principle in Nature. They (the *ḍākinīs, devas)* embody the substance from which it is all wrought. Their masculine compliment (humanity) directs the consciousness-principle that evolves out of and via this substance, undergoing the tests and trials that eventually produce enlightenment and liberation from *māyā.*

With respect to the Sambhogakāya Flower, the Consort of the Ādi Buddha (Samantabhadrī) expresses the substance of the central pupil, literally that which the Śūnyatā Eye of the *tathāgatagarbha* looks through to view the domain of the *dharmakāya.* She is, as the text states, the 'source of the origination of all maṇḍalas'.[1] The Consorts of the Vidyādharas, assisted by the Consorts of the Guardians and the Jinas, are responsible for building the actual petals of the Sambhogakāya Flowers of humanity. The Consorts of the four Guardians help build the central structure of the *tathāgatagarbha,* the iris part, plus the three shielding buds. The role of all these Consorts, which was only generally introduced in the previous chapter, will be further elucidated.

The influences of the Jina Consorts are more general; they integrate the five tiers of the Flower (the three main whorls of petals, the three bud petals as a unit, plus the iris portion) into one coherent structure. They also help build the links that allow the general five-ness of the Flower to manifest. We thus have the five Sacrifice petals,[2] when the three direct ones (Sacrifice—Sacrifice, Sacrifice—Love-Wisdom, and Sacrifice—Knowledge[3]) are integrated with the Knowledge—Sacrifice

---

1 Lauf, *Secret Doctrines of the Tibetan Books of the Dead*, 102.

2 These Sacrifice petals express a combination of Sacrifice and Will, as described with respect to Figure 27 in Volume 4. The attributes of Will and Sacrifice must be utilised to awaken the Sacrifice petals, producing demonstrable spiritual power upon the physical domain.

3 The nature of these petals are explained in Volume 3 of this *Treatise on Mind,* in the chapter entitled 'The Uttaratantra of Maitreya and the Sambhogakāya Flower'.

and Love-Wisdom—Sacrifice petals. Ditto for the Love-Wisdom and Knowledge petals. (The Love-Wisdom—Sacrifice, Love-Wisdom—Love-Wisdom, and Love-Wisdom—Knowledge petals integrated with the Sacrifice—Love-Wisdom petal and Knowledge—Love-Wisdom petal, etc.) Because knowledge is organised by the expression of the five sense-consciousnesses, seeded by the Jinas into Nature's panoply, the five Consorts of the Jinas also focus on the Knowledge petals of the flower. These Consorts direct the resultant *karma* and establish the paradigm for all subsequent groups of five. The number five incorporated into the general structure of the Flower is important because it allows proper integration of the *saṃskāras* derived from the sense-consciousnesses to be processed by the Flower.

The Vidyādharas and their *prajñās* come into active expression almost purely in the form of a symbiosis with human evolution via all the attributes of mind/Mind. They also help direct the lesser kingdoms in Nature so that bearers of *manas* can evolve from them. The Consorts of the Guardians and Jinas possess other significant roles with respect to the entire *maṇḍala* of Life, as already explained.

The Consorts of the five Vidyādharas focus upon building the nine main whorls of petals, specifically via that of the Love-Wisdom grouping. (Love-Wisdom being the major quality of this Flower, the basis of the *bodhicitta* that it embodies.) We saw also that the Consort of Guṇa-Vidyādhara embodies the general form of the Flower and its integration with a person's Head lotus. The Consort of Kāya-Vidyādhara integrates the qualities of the three main whorls of petals with the three central bud petals. The process of transmutation and refinement of *saṃskāras* is then possible, allowing the awakening of the bud that reveals the jewel in the heart of the lotus as a consequence of the Initiation process. The remaining three Vidyādhara Consorts govern the evolution of the three main whorls of petals. Their specific purpose is to oversee the general evolution of the Sambhogakāya Flowers, the way they karmically unfold upon their own domain. Each Consort can therefore be considered to represent a triad of *devas*. Each triad reflects the overall attributes of the three types of Consorts (of the Guardians, Vidyādharas and Jinas) governing the attributes of the Sambhogakāya Flowers. Each triad also accommodates attributes gleaned from the three worlds of human evolution; the mental, astral, and physical, described as 'body, speech, and mind' in Buddhism.

There is also a commingling of energies from the Consorts of each of the groups with respect to the three major tiers of petals of the Sambhogakāya Flower. The energies of the Guardians' Consorts impress the three Sacrifice petals, those of the Vidyādharas' Consorts impress the Love-Wisdom petals, and those of the Jinas stimulate the qualities of the Knowledge petals. These 3 x 3 groupings also come under the general auspices of Amoghasiddhi, Ratnasambhava, and Amitābha. They thereby govern the resolution into their enlightenment-attributes the consciousness generated in the three worlds of human evolution.

Ratnasambhava's Consort Māmakī assists the overall process of building the Sambhogakāya Flowers, as far as the general floral shape of their exterior forms are concerned, and taking the entire *maṇḍala* of the Sambhogakāya Flowers into account. This involves integrating the Flowers of all individual units into one overall floral arrangement. 'Equalising Wisdom' is the qualifying principle or basic *saṃskāra* of the Flowers, in a similar sense that *manas* (mind) is the overriding force governing the evolution of each personal-I. Ratnasambhava principally utilises the form and consciousness-building attributes of the five Wisdom *ḍākinīs*, as this process happens in the realms of the *ālayavijñāna* (the abstract levels of the mental plane).

Through the factor of *manas,* Amitābha's Consort, Pāṇḍara, oversees the general evolution of all the groups of petals. Amitābha governs the abstract levels of the domain of mind, where all Sambhogakāya Flowers exist. This is the esoteric reason why Amitābha's paradise realm (the blissful western domain, *sukhāvatī)* is offered as a place to aspire to for the masses of people in certain Buddhist texts. It is simply a way of stating that the devotees of those texts will gain the resplendent experience of the domain of the *tathāgatagarbha* via the methodology proffered. It necessitates passing into an egoless state to enter this Bardo. This experience prepares people for rebirth.

Amoghasiddhi's Consort, Samayatārā, works specifically with the way that the Flowers are organised into groups and the general process of assimilating *karma* from those incarnate in the three worlds. The mechanism of expressing such *karma* via these Flowers produces a nine-fold integration of *deva* forces that are specifically responsible for directing the attributes of the nine whorls of petals of the Sambhogakāya Flower towards their ultimate sacrificial resolution of absorption into *dharmakāya*. This process will ultimately spell the death of the flower.

Akṣobhya's Consort, Locanā, oversees the generation of the *saṃskāras* of *bodhicitta* for this Flower so that they produce a general expansion of the petals. Similarly for the overall *maṇḍala* of this Flower.

Vairocana's Consort, Ākāśadhātviśvarī, oversees the process that expands the bud lotus and reveals the Śūnyatā Eye. The three bud petals build the mechanism that allows the Śūnyatā Eye to be focussed in three directions:

1. Towards the domain of the personal-I.
2. Towards the Sambhogakāya Flowers within the *ālayavijñāna*.
3. Towards the *dharmakāya*.

The Ādi Buddha's Consort, Samantabadrī, oversees the general development of the entire *maṇḍala* of the Sambhogakāya Flower.

The above then supplements, from a Buddhist perspective, what was earlier presented to the world via Alice A. Bailey on the evolution of the petals of this Flower, called 'the egoic lotus' in the extract below:

> It should here be remembered that, subtle though the material may be, the egoic lotus is as truly substance of a particular vibration as is the physical body, only (owing to the rarity) physical plane man regards it practically as non-substantial. It is in fact, as earlier pointed out, the result of the dual vibration of the fivefold Dhyanis or Gods in conjunction with the fourfold Quaternary, or the Pitris of the lower vehicles. Through a conscious effort of the planetary Logoi, these Dhyanis and lower Pitris are brought into a close relationship. This produces (upon the third sub-plane of the mental plane) a ninefold vibration or whorl in the gaseous matter of the plane—for this is the cosmic gaseous sub-plane—which, after a certain period of persistence, assumes the form of a nine-petalled lotus. This lotus is folded over in bud shape upon the central point, or heart of the lotus—that spark of electric fire which by its action or innate vitality working upon the substance of the lotus, attracts to itself sufficient of that substance to form three inner petals, which closely shield the central spark; these are nevertheless of the same substance or essence as the nine other petals. The student must be careful not to materialise his concept too

> much and it might therefore be wise for him to view this manifestation from other angles and employ other terms to express the same idea. For instance, the body of the Ego may be viewed in the following four ways:
>
> *As nine vibrations,* emanating from a central point, which, in its pulsation or radiations produces three major vibrations of great force pursuing a circular activity around the centre; the nine vibrations pursue a diagonal path, until they reach the periphery of the egoic sphere of influence. At this point they swing around, thus forming the well-known spheroidal form of the causal body.
>
> *As nine petals* of a lotus, radiating from a common centre, and hiding within themselves three central petals, which conceal a central point of fire. The radiations from the tip of each petal are those which cause the illusion of a spheroid shape.
>
> *As nine spokes* of a wheel, converging towards a central hub, which is in itself threefold, and which hides the central energy or dynamo of force—the generator of all the activity.
>
> *As nine types* of energy which produce definite emanations from a threefold unit, again itself an outgoing from a central unit of force.[4]

'The fivefold Dhyanis' referred to are the Vidyādhara Consorts as presented in my account. Their purpose is to reap the *karma* and related *saṃskāras* of the evolving consciousness-stream of humanity, and to direct the related life towards the evocation of Love-Wisdom, which is the true gain or purpose of human evolution. Lords of Love and Will we come to be, but *manasaputras* (containers of mental input) we are for the great bulk of our journeying through the Wheel of Birth and Death.

The 'fourfold Quaternary, or the Pitris[5] of the lower vehicles', are directed by the *deva* agents of the Consorts of the four Guardians. These agents control the lives that constitute the substance of the corporeal form through which we incarnate. Their purpose is to integrate the

---

4 Bailey, Alice A. *A Treatise on Cosmic Fire,* (Lucis Publishing Company, New York, 1982), 816-818.

5 *Pitṛs,* meaning the Fathers of the form, governing therefore the qualities of the four-fold lower vehicle that a human Life stream incarnates into: the Fiery *manasic* principle, the Watery emotional or astral constitution, the Earthy etheric/dense physical duo. The term *lunar pitṛs* refers to the elementals (elementary lives) constituting the embodied form. In my account the governing entities directing all such elementary lives shall be denoted *pitṛs.*

qualities of the four Elements and the abstracted substance (sentience) of the four kingdoms of Nature into the constitution of this Egoic form.

The *deva* agents of the five-fold *dhyānis,* the Consorts of the Vidyādharas, then integrate the two groups of *deva* potencies. They are brought together by the mantric call of the Vidyādhara Consorts. Once the basic structure has been built through the union of the five with the four (allowing the incorporation of the sense-consciousnesses into the Sambhogakāya Flower) then the Vidyādhara Consorts build into the construct the essential qualities of this Flower, which is the receptivity to and expression of *bodhicitta.* This energy then becomes the guiding principle of the *karma* of each Flower.

As soon as these two groups of lives first interrelate (at the time of Individualisation) we get an ovoid patchwork of interweaving energies comprised of the nine-primal whorls of energy. Over time this primal form develops into the nine radiant petals of the Sambhogakāya Flower. This form is established upon the domain of the abstract Mind, utilising the substance of the Vidyādharas, under the auspices of the primary energy qualifications of the Consorts of the Dhyāni Buddhas, who govern the expression of the five planes of perception wherein *karma* rules. Each central bud is linked into a unified purpose by the meditation of the Consort of the Ādi Buddha. Thus the *tathāgatagarbha* (the Buddha-embryo for each human unit) is established.

Conditioning influences to the Sambhogakāya Flowers

We can now analyse the petals of the Sambhogakāya Flowers in relation to the way that the conditioning forces of the *ḍākinīs* influence the mode of activity of these Flowers. The Vidyādhara's and Consorts must also be taken into account here. They embody the *manasic* substance and are guiding Minds helping to direct the evolutionary course of each human unit. The development of Love-Wisdom is the objective, but for the unit to truly become liberated, attributes of sacrifice have to be developed. The work of the Consorts of the four Guardians then come into account, with the overall liberating pull coming from the domain of the Dhyāni Buddhas. The appropriate karmic cycles for when *saṃskāras* are to be activated in the mind of a personality can then be rightly directed. The process does not, however, just involve consideration of an individual unit's development, but must be extended to include the context of the sum total of the united meditations of the Sambhogakāya Flowers upon human civilisation. This is because no *saṃskāra* is developed in a vacuum, many types of human interrelationships go into the production of each one. The instigating impetus from the *dharmakāya* should also be taken into account to fully comprehend this subject.

The allocation relates to the effect of the energies of the Consorts of the five Dhyāni Buddhas and the *lunar pitṛs,* the *deva* agents of the Consorts of the four Guardians. They can be so considered because that is their en-Souling influence, but they are in fact a sub-order of the Vidyādharas. The reason for this is that the mental plane is dual, consisting of an abstract and a concrete portion. From this perspective we see that the Vidyādharas embody the sum of the substance of mind/Mind. They consist of the substance of everyone's thoughts. In reasoning this out properly one will receive many revelations. Here we have the basis to the substantiality of the theriomorphic deities, as they are the disguises, or forms that these elemental *manasic* lives take when moulded by human mental-emotions. They are experienced upon the path of return when the human creator must consciously deal with the associated *saṃskāras* to transform and annul the *karma.*

The transformation process is directed from the domain of the Sambhogakāya Flowers. This concerns the way the *karma* of returning *saṃskāras* is regulated so that Initiation is eventually attained. Initially the Initiation process is primarily guided from the precincts of this Flower. For the first three Initiations this process involves three factors:

a. The directive impulses from the kingdom of Shambhala (the domain of the Dhyāni Buddhas and Guardians, and their Consorts), and from members of the Council of Bodhisattvas.

b. The preparatory efforts by the Sambhogakāya Flowers.

c. The positive response from the rightly focussed personal-I, or *yogin.* The *karma* is wisely regulated to produce the right circumstances and events. The internal promptings causes the aspiring one to manifest the necessary disciplines and efforts to so achieve, once the ability to listen to these intuitions has been gained. The concern is then with one's mode of interaction with the higher mental plane and the *ālayavijñāna* environment.

The vision is from above down (the way of directing the evolution of sentient substance by the Consorts of the Guardians) and from within-without that the inspiration comes to seek liberation. The below-up response concerns the resolution of the *saṃskāras* developed. They had their genesis in the evolutionary progress of the lives lived by members in the various kingdoms in Nature, directed by the Consorts of the Dhyāni Buddhas. The evolution of the human desire factor, coupled with that of *manas,* greatly hastened their development. They are the causes of perpetual rebirth and must be rectified upon the Initiation path, so that attachment to *saṃsāra* is eliminated.

The three Sacrifice petals

Of the three major whorls of petals of the Sambhogakāya Flower we shall first consider the three *Sacrifice petals* whose purposeful direction is governed by Amoghasiddhi's Consort, Tārā. These petals come under the general influence of Amoghasiddhi because of his role as the overseer of the physical plane, where *saṃsāra* must be rightly confronted so that it can be mastered. This involves commitment of the greatest sacrifice and Will. The general purpose of all flowers on the Sambhogakāya realm comes under the rulership of Tārā. This is an esoteric reason why she is so popular in Tibetan Buddhism, as collectively the *tathāgatagarbha* is the group-soul of humanity. It is what humans really *are*, as the manifest personal-I is part of the great illusion. Devotees have an innate recognition that Tārā's compassion truly represents the most exalted liberating energy possible to aspire to. It is the embodiment of the green compassionate Will governing the *karma* of the evolution of Nature.

Under the auspices of Tārā the work of the Guardian Consorts can then be taken into account. They are specifically responsible for the mode of conversion of the *saṃskāras* of the four main Elements into the Void Elements via the agency of the Sambhogakāya Flower. This process of transformation of the characteristics of substance necessitates the development of the greatest amount of Will and sacrificial attributes for the personalities that must do the conversion. Effectively here, the transformation of the elemental Lives *(pitṛs)* into their *manasic* (solar) correspondences must occur through the agency of the human mind.

(Nature's alchemical retort.) The Guardian Consorts therefore oversee the overall process for the human kingdom via their Sambhogakāya Flowers. This lays the foundation for the Initiation process, not seen so much in terms of the crises of the needed transformations of human consciousness, but rather in terms of the alchemicalisation of the basic substance of the periodical sheaths (the triune personality vehicle). Such transformations involve the lives constituting that substance, so that all become *arūpa,* void of the forms of activity associated with *saṃsāra.* This represents the true gain of the entire evolutionary process for the kingdoms of Nature below the human.

The Guardian Consorts therefore empower the energy of the Wrathful Deities and the Will energy that must be used to effect the transformations. The human unit must develop the compassionate Will so as to appropriately ignite and transform the *pitṛs* of the fourfold form (*manasic,* astral, etheric, and dense) with intensified Fire so that they are converted into the radiance of the Clear Mind that is the outcome.

There are three main Elements that are the focus of this alchemicalisation process, which is the substance of the three sheaths incarnated into by a human; denoted body, speech, and mind.

1. *The body,* the Earthy Element: *Sacrifice–Sacrifice petal.*

This petal is built through the agency of the Ḍākinī Vajraghaṇṭā, who is the Consort of the green Guardian Amṛtakuṇḍalin of the north gate.[6] At first the process of the transformation of the mineral kingdom and its conversion into a plant kingdom is instigated. (Involving thus what might be termed the alchemicalisation of substance.) Human units later perform a similar conversion within their *nāḍī* systems, where the flowers therein (the *chakras)* convert the mineral-like substance of consciousness into more vibrant attributes.

Alchemical transformation requires more than just what people regard as 'mineral', i.e., physical matter, but also the conversion of the

6 This and similar statements from the other petals of the Sambhogakāya Flower (taking the Sambhogakāya Flower as a kingdom rather than an individual Flower) informs the reader that each *ḍākinī* is the head of an office in the kingdom of Shambhala. There is a hierarchy of *deva* agents administering to their purpose. Their concern is the karmic adjudication of various streams of Lives, but in this case our vision is upon the Sambhogakāya Flower and the directing forces governing its overall evolution.

entire structure of *saṃsāra*. One must use the will upon all levels of substance for complete success in the purpose of converting elemental *citta*. One must ride the horse of conversion via the Initiation path upon all levels of expression of the five Elements, to eventually transform the originating cycle of *karma*. Vajraghaṇṭā thus lays the seeds for the eventual undertaking of the fifth Initiation.

The entire *manasic* substance of the Sambhogakāya Flower must become more lucid, radiant and expansive as a consequence of this transforming process. The energy contained by the form becomes so intense that it can no longer contain its potency because of the sacrifice here implied. This process is a prelude to the 'death' of the Sambhogakāya Flower as it becomes incorporated into the Void. *Saṃskāras* are thereby converted into the Void Elements.

The process, however, starts by overcoming the Earthy allurements by aspirants and thereby attaining the first Initiation. It then continues until the substance of all levels of perception is likewise mastered. Because such attainment must happen in a physical body the Earthy Element is the first to be mastered. To be achieved, all Initiations require the sacrifice of long cherished beliefs and the development of more refined perceptions. The candidate must develop abstract reasoning and thus awaken the Clear Light of Mind. This inevitably involves the complete transformation of the *ālayavijñāna* so that it becomes the natural vehicle of expression of *dharmakāya,* the empirical substance of a Buddha-Mind.

We can see, therefore, that all the allurements and attachments to *saṃsāric* life must be sacrificed and transmuted for such an event to manifest. Much material plane *karma* is consequently rectified, producing the ability to undertake the path of Initiation, from the first to the fifth Initiations. This is the foundation upon which is based the *ālayavijñāna* enlightenment that the third Initiation accords. The Flower will then stand in full glory upon its own domain and be fully integrated with the consciousness of a human unit's Head lotus.

2. *Speech,* the Watery Element: *Sacrifice–Love-Wisdom petal.*

This petal is built through the agency of the Consort of the yellow Guardian Yamāntaka of the south gate, the Ḍākinī Vajrapāśī. (For which reason Yamāntaka was earlier said to help in producing the first two Initiation experiences.) This gate represents mastery of the Watery *saṃskāras* necessary for gaining the second Initiation.

The purpose here is to develop the capacity to contain the most intense form of *bodhicitta* that the Flower is capable of expressing, and to first project it upwards through the Śūnyatā Eye. This facilitates a guiding response from the Council of Bodhisattvas that will fan the spirit of compassion, and who introduce the Plan to rectify the problems of human society, or of the group an individual belongs to for any particular cycle. The Waters of Love-Wisdom flood the Flower and the part of the Plan that the Sambhogakāya Flower is to play is acceded. This energy is then used to assist in projecting images and ideas into the mind of the incarnate personal-I so that right aspiration is fostered and charitable deeds are contemplated and acted upon. The personal-I thereby receives the inner directives in accordance to what was meditated upon by the entire Council of Bodhisattvas as the need for the now, according to the Ray disposition of the individual concerned.

The Watery allurements are the most difficult for the average aspirant to overcome, as they involve the field of strong desire, emotional attachments and all of the sex urges. The theriomorphic deities consequently are brought into play upon this battle field at this stage, when all desires, feelings, and animal-like passions are to be converted to attributes of compassion so that the Plan can be fulfilled. This manifests in the form of the *amṛta* of pure compassion and held in the vessel *(kalaśa)* of the Heart centre. We thus have the foundation for treading the Bodhisattva path in general through converting all *kāma-manasic* impulses with the fount of wisdom. The forces and potencies of the entire Flower come to bear upon the individual so that *bodhicitta* will be discovered and evoked. This necessitates the control of the *prāṇas* of the general *nāḍī* system. The process first generates the energy of goodwill, and later the Will-to-Love from the realms of the Sambhogakāya Flower, thus rerouting the *arhat* meditation to produce revelation of the nature of the Bodhisattva path.

This way of the Heart eventually produces liberation from all concepts of form as one is Initiated into the Void of consciousness-attributes *(śūnyatā)*. By incorporating the specific activity of developing the Will-of-Love all base attributes of human nature can be overcome. It paves the way for the attainment of the fourth Initiation and the annihilation of the Sambhogakāya Flower's form. The Guardian of this direction ensures that the process happens in appropriate, gradual stages for humanity, so that all transformations produce beneficent results. The misuse of the will, producing destructive or reifying effects is all too common amongst people. The generation of spiritual will is however needed if one is to overcome all of the hurdles to Initiation. The will must be rightly directed to produce the principle of sacrifice upon the path of compassion.

The last vestiges of the 'self' concept must be eliminated, even subtleties associated with the splendid Sambhogakāya Flower, so that the *śūnyatā* experience is possible. The Wisdoms that are expressions of the Heart of the Jinas are then fully accessed.

Upon this path the second Initiation is difficult for most to achieve because it involves much personal sacrifice to master the theriomorphic forces in the *nāḍīs*. The transformative battles, the conversion of the *prāṇas* of animal-headed entities into compassionate attributes occurs via the awakening of this and the following Sacrifice petal.

3. *Mind*, the Fiery Element: *Sacrifice–Knowledge petal.*

This petal is built via the agency of the Ḍākinī Vajraśṛṅkhalā, who is the Consort of the red Guardian Hayagrīva of the west gate. Much of the work of Vajraśṛṅkhalā is to assist the Consort of Vairocana in laying the foundational conditions that will assist taking the third Initiation by aspirants, by way of mastery of all the elements of the mind. Vajraśṛṅkhalā helps the *yogin* to develop the Aetheric Element from out of the attributes of mind, so that the *dharmakāya* can be experienced as an expression of Mind.[7] This process is the mainstay of all higher yoga teachings, and will be explained in the remainder

7 Aether is the substance of the third of the seven planes of perception, and conveys the *dharmakāya*. It is developed when *manas* is thoroughly refined and converted to Mind in such a way that Mind is integrated with Logoic Thought. Once awakened, the abstract Mind then becomes the vehicle of expression of the five Jina Wisdoms. There is a direct line of expression between the Divine Will (cosmic Mind), Aether, the domain of the mind/Mind, and the dense physical plane. The physical domain is the most concreted expression of the energies of mind/Mind.

of the *Bardo Thödol*. The *suṣumṇā* line of development can then be followed through until the highest Initiation is attained, making one a Master of Wisdom. We see, therefore, that the entire sacrificial tier of petals is concerned with undertaking the path of Initiation by a candidate, thus the process of the mastery of all the attributes of the three periodical vehicles residing in *saṃsāra*. The third Initiation is the apogee of attainment for the Sambhogakāya Flower. It represents the *ālayavijñāna* enlightenment, when knowledge of the Mysteries pertaining to this entire kingdom is attained.

This Initiation is the accomplishment of the Sambhogakāya Flower as it works to impress the incarnate personality with the full weight of the Knowledge, Love-Wisdom and Sacrificial intent that it possesses. The separative will and persona of the personal-I dies as it transforms itself through meditative practices to merge with the overshadowing consciousness of the Flower. As a consequence of this Initiation only the Sambhogakāya Flower remains,[8] manifesting through a thoroughly prepared and consecrated personality vehicle, and the awakened Mind, in order to manifest the impress from the Council of Bodhisattvas. The personal 'self' has died to be replaced by the selflessness of the Sambhogakāya Flower.

After this the Initiate aspires to attain the fourth Initiation, which spells the death of the Sambhogakāya Flower's form upon attainment of this *śūnyatā* enlightenment.

The *śūnyatā-saṃsāra* nexus is first built within the domain of the Flower as the Initiate begins to peer through the central Śūnyatā Eye towards the *dharmakāya*. In doing so bridges are built from the domain of Mind bypassing the Flower straight to the *dharmakāya*. Increasingly more Fiery energy descends, intensifying the energies contained by the Flower. The stable base has, however, been established in *dharmakāya* through this bridge building process, for the Initiate to remain in the Clear Light of Mind that integrates *śūnyatā* with *saṃsāra*, preparatory to the death of the causal form of the Flower. The way of cosmic ascent has begun.

---

8 For those that had attained the fourth Initiation in a former life and are recapitulating the third in the present life there is a direct Monadic presence overshadowing them.

The Airy Element is expressed via the Love-Wisdom petals in general. This Element conveys the principle of Love, and is the general carrier of all the five *prāṇas* conveyed in the *nāḍī* system. The Love-Wisdom conveyed via *manas* is the main attribute of the Vidyādharas. The Consort of the white Guardian Vijaya of the east gate, the Ḍākinī Vajrāṅkuśī also conveys this principle *(bodhicitta).* Vajrāṅkuśī therefore integrates the activity of the Guardians with the general activity of the Consorts of the Vidyādharas. Her focus is via the *Love-Wisdom–Sacrifice* petal in order to help engender the sacrificial attributes that will produce the Initiation process amongst humans. This particular petal therefore absorbs the effect of the development of loving *saṃskāras* and directs the personal-I towards the Bodhisattva path. Entering this path is that of aspiration to undertake Initiation. In this way then the entire domain of the Guardians becomes infiltrated with the effects of human aspiration, and later sincere yogic *tapas,* to overcome obstreperous *saṃskāras* on the way to enlightenment.

The fifth Element (Aether) does not need a specific Guardian Consort to convey it, because it is intrinsic to the *dharmakāya,* via which the Guardians emanate to control the functions of the *arūpa* domains. *Dharmakāya* is visualised via the Śunyatā Eye, but this experience necessitates bridge-building via the way of the abstract Mind. Aether is the foundational support for all the other Elements that need to be transformed in Nature. The conversion of all the Elements into their Void Elements needs to be wrought by human consciousness from below up. The Consorts of the Dhyāni Buddhas assist in this process, therefore there are five Consorts to take into account. Part of their purpose is to facilitate the integration of the Fiery gain obtained through meditation and the life experience into the petals of the Sambhogakāya Flowers so that inevitably the Jina Wisdoms are the outcome. Their focus is therefore specifically upon the Knowledge petals of the Sambhogakāya Flowers and the transformation of knowledge into wisdom via the awakening of the 1,000 petals of the Head lotus of an individual. Egoistical pursuits thereby need to be transformed into enlightened ideals. For this purpose they help organise the *karma* of humanity to help them discover the Bodhisattva path wherein such transformations happen.

As far as the Initiation process is concerned there are five petals specifically involved with establishing its eventuation, and there is considerable overlapping of functions. (As also with the development of the petals generally. They normally awaken unevenly because of the way that *saṃskāras* are evolved.) The highest Initiation possible for the Sambhogakāya Flower to attain is the third, however it also lays the foundation for taking the fourth and fifth Initiations. The development of the spirit of sacrifice and the generation of Love-Wisdom, based upon a foundation of much empirical knowledge, is necessary for this. The general sequence for the process is as follows:

a. The *Love-Wisdom—Sacrifice* petal lays the foundation for the first Initiation, and is concerned with the path of aspiration.

b. The *Love-Wisdom—Love-Wisdom* petal lays the foundation for taking the second Initiation; the way of discipleship proper. This Initiation happens as a consequence of the disciple coming under the dominance of *bodhicitta*, the major energy characteristic of this Flower.

c. The *Sacrifice—Knowledge* petal lays the foundation for the third Initiation, and the first Initiation is taken under its sway.

d. The *Sacrifice—Love-Wisdom* petal lays the foundation of the fourth Initiation, and the second Initiation is undertaken because of its full awakening.

e. The *Sacrifice—Sacrifice* petal lays the foundation for undertaking the fifth Initiation and the third Initiation is taken as this petal awakens.

The *Sacrifice—Knowledge* petal is built under the auspices of Vairocana's *prajñā,* Ākāśadhātvīśvarī. She helps control the *prāṇas* flowing to this petal by humanity and embodies the highest of the Elements, Aether *(ākāśa),* assisting its development by those transforming the *saṃskāras* of mind into enlightenment-attributes. (This is symbolised by the effects of the inbreathing of the highest of the sense-consciousnesses; smell.) Ākāśadhātvīśvarī synthesises the work of all the Consorts of the Jinas by gathering in the qualities of the sense-consciousness and abstracting them in such a way that the attainment of Initiation is possible. The aim then is to assist the candidate to eventually take the third Initiation. At first the personal-I works to change the basic focus of consciousness away from the material domain and selfish pursuits. Increasingly abstract thoughts are developed and all grosser attitudes of mind are sacrificed on the path to enlightenment. The quest for knowledge therefore is no longer materialistic or selfish, but the higher Will-to-Good is sought, allowing the first Initiation to be taken. The objective from then on is to cleanse all thought-structures so that they will inevitably reflect the Ideations found in *dharmakāya* via the *saṃsāra-śūnyatā* nexus.

This petal integrates the function of the Ḍākinī Vajraśṛṅkhalā, the Consort of the red Guardian Hayagrīva of the west gate. The reason for this is that the evoked Aetheric Element derived from knowledgeable pursuits via the awakened Head centre of a personality can be integrated into the *dharmakāya* via the open door that Hayagrīva's Consort represents. Here Vairocana's *prajñā* is really an agent for Amitābha's Discriminating Inner Wisdom, for as we saw in the second chapter, the kingdom of the Sambhogakāya Flower exists in/as Amitābha's Paradise realm.

The Love-Wisdom petals

The *Love-Wisdom* triad of petals come under the general auspices of Ratnasambhava's Consort, Māmakī. The colour assigned is yellow. This quality represents a major characteristic of the *tathāgatagarbha*. Ratnasambhava's Equalising Wisdom flavours all of the Flowers because it is an emanation of the second Ray line adapted to convert the substance of consciousness into *bodhicitta*, as a prelude for the journey to *śūnyatā*. Here also the work of the Vidyādharas is focused specifically via the Consort of the Citta-Vidyādhara, the 'Knowledge-holder of the Earth', as far as the general substance of the Sambhogakāya Flowers is concerned. The focus is upon the Heart centre in a human, to help transform unregenerate *saṃskāras* from the Solar Plexus centre.

Ratnasambhava's quality represents the overriding function of the love and wisdom derived from the Watery domain whilst a person is incarnate. This function then qualifies the activities of the Vidyādharas within the context of the general characteristics of the Fiery attributes of the *manasic* domain within which the Sambhogakāya Flower is found. This incorporates Amitābha's Wisdom into the equation, under the auspices of Vāc-Vidyādhara, the red 'Knowledge-Holder of the Great Symbol'. Together they produce a fusion of Heart with Mind, as exemplified by the term *bodhicitta*. Ratnasambhava's Equalising Wisdom is then focused upon Guṇa-Vidyādhara, the yellow 'Life-ruling Knowledge holder' governing the overall organisation of the petals of the Sambhogakāya Flower and its integration with the Head lotus of the incarnate human unit. Within this context this Floral form created by the Vidyādharas is geared to reap the attributes of the consciousness developed by incarnate humans. The symbiotic relation between the human and *deva* kingdoms is thereby brought to the fore.

The true 'human unit' is the Monad (the 'Spirit') that incorporates the Sambhogakāya Flower (thus the Vidyādharas) as its vehicle of expression at the time of the Individualisation of the Sambhogakāya Flowers. These Flowers *(tathāgatagarbha,* the 'Buddha-Womb') are therefore the corporeal forms of the human *Monads* in a similar sense that the human personality is the corporeal or illusional body of manifestation for the Sambhogakāya Flower. The human form is therefore the 'great illusion'. It exists to develop Buddha-qualities (wisdom), and by expressing its innate compassion, it plays a prime role in converting the former primordial substance *(mūlaprakṛti),* incorporated as the *māyāvirūpa* of a planetary or solar sphere, into consciousness-bearing units. Here then we have the significance of the mystery of human evolution outlined. Under the rubric of the activity associated with the Wrathful and theriomorphic deities, this exposé of the *Bardo Thödol* explains the process of this conversion of the substance (*prakṛti*) that has been incorporated as our *saṃskāras.*

The Greek term Monad means 'the One', 'the Indivisible'. Esoterically it refers to the Spirit or Father aspect, our highest principle. It is the 'God', or Buddha within us, the highest part of the triplicity: Monad (Spirit), Soul (consciousness), personality (the illusional appearance). Here is represented the triune Deity: Father-Son-Mother in one indivisible Unity. This triplicity is also veiled by the three bodies of a Buddha: the *dharmakāya, sambhogakāya* and *nirmāṇakāya.* The Monad resides upon the second systemic plane, *anupādaka*, the second *dharmakāyic* level,[9] and is said to be a Lord of Sacrifice and Love, in that the Sambhogakāya

9 The nature of the various planes of perception shall be explained in Volume 6 of this *Treatise on Mind. Anupādaka* is a dimension of perception above the third plane, the *ātmic,* the plane of the emanation of primordial *karma,* and of its eventual resolution.

Flower (the *tathāgatagarbha)* is the vehicle that it incorporates to achieve its goal. It's true home is cosmos. At the time when the human unit can gain enlightenment and liberation from *saṃsāra* as a liberated Buddha (the true Monadic form), it then sets upon that magnificent journey to 'the other shore' of being/non-being that is cosmos. All this concerns the mysteries of Monadic evolution, which can only properly begun to be known by an Initiate of the fourth degree. Accordingly, we see that a Buddha from this perspective represents a human unit that is completely awakened and Identified with the Monad.

One should note the fact that Entities have evolved in cosmos to beyond the human stage long before our earth existed. Buddhas have long ago evolved to become Logoi incorporating stars, constellations, galaxies and beyond. Everything in the universe is embodied Life and that Life is relevant to where one stands upon the evolutionary ladder. The yogic conversion of *saṃskāras* is the true beginning of becoming such a Logos.

The petal of the Sambhogakāya Flower omitted in the lists of the petals ruled by the Consorts of the Guardians and the Jinas is that of *Love-Wisdom–Love-Wisdom.* This represents the pure home of the Vidyādharas, who as previously stated, embody the qualities of the function of the Sambhogakāya Flowers as a unit. From this perspective we can deduce that the Vidyādharas exist in three groups (as per the overall organisation of the petals of the Flower). They thus incorporate the substance of the three higher sub-planes of the mental. One group embodies the substance of the Will or Sacrifice pentad, interrelating with the function of the Guardian Consorts. This group involves the work of the male Vidyādharas, who organise the kingdom of the Sambhogakāya Flowers into twelve main groups assisted by the Ādi Buddha, in the form of Vajrasattva and his Consort. The Consorts to the Vidyādharas, interrelating with the Jina Consorts, form a group that are concerned with the Knowledge pentad. The third group embodies the pure substance of the Sambhogakāya Flowers, and can be considered 'the Hearts of Fiery Love'.[10] This group, being the substance of the *tathāgatagarbhas,* can be considered the 'child' of the other two, the containment of Love-Wisdom, in terms of the nine-fold genesis (Individualisation) of the Sambhogakāya Flowers earlier explained.

10 A.A. Bailey, *Esoteric Astrology,* (Lucis Press, London, 1968), 46.

The general work of the Vidyādharas is firstly to interrelate with the karmic direction of knowledgeable pursuits controlled by the Jina Consorts, so that knowledge is converted into wisdom attributes. The Vidyādharas do this by directing *karma* in such a way that the kind, loving, compassionate attributes of the human persona are engendered. Material and *manasic* Fire must therefore be envigorated with Love by means of the agency of the Vidyādharas. Next they fan the sparks of Fiery Love with the impetus of the *Will* to overcome all obstacles upon the path to liberation. This also necessitates the integration of the Airy Element in such a way that it assists the transformation and transmutation of base *saṃskāras* into spiritual gold. The aim is therefore towards the production of the Void Elements via consciousness. This is how the Vidyādharas thereby work with the Consorts of the Guardians to assist humanity to tread the Initiation path to liberation.

The consideration so far involves two groups of nine potencies (5 + 4 each), balanced by the central five of the Love-Wisdom grouping. The number 5 + 4 is found in the five Vidyādharas and the four Guardians focussed in the northern direction, as well as the Vidyādhara Consorts integrated with the four-fold attribute of the personality (or the four sub-planes of the concrete mental domain), the projection in the southern direction. This makes 23, and when the unitary energy of the complete Flower is added we have 24 altogether. This is a base number governing the Head lotus, which consists of 1056 petals (44 x 24), or of the Ājñā centre, which has 96 petals (4 x 24). When the Ājñā and Head centres are taken as a unity, then we have 44 + 4 = 48 x 24 petals altogether, which signifies the number of petals to either lobe of the Ājñā centre multiplied by 24. In terms of units of twelve, the number 48 x 24 = 96 x 12, which signifies the number of petals to the Ājñā centre multiplied by twelve. This indicates the way that each individual petal of the Ājñā centre can organise the activities of the Head lotus and direct *prāṇas* into any grouping of twelve therein.

The number 24 represents the inwards and outwards focus of the twelve main petals of the Heart centre. It also indicates the arrangement of *saṃskāras* that can be processed by the Ājñā centre to be projected at any time into the Head centre, as was explained in Volume 4,[11] then

11 The process will also be detailed in the later chapters of this book.

from the Head lotus to the Sambhogakāya Flower. The number 24 allows the important groups of *saṃskāras* to be incorporated into the Sambhogakāya Flower from the Head lotus. First we have the number 3 x 8 = 24, allowing the eight *vijñānas* to be incorporated via the three divisions or tiers of petals of the Flower. The *vijñānas* can also be expressed in terms of the three *guṇas* explained above. Next we have the number 4 x 6, referring to the six consciousnesses being able to be incorporated according to the four main Elements that these *saṃskāras* are arranged by. Also, the Sambhogakāya Flower is well organised to absorb the five main *prāṇas/saṃskāras* by means of the above-mentioned five-fold arrangement of petals. Finally, any triad of qualities, or even individual *saṃskāras* can be similarly absorbed.

The Knowledge petals

The Knowledge triad of petals are under the general auspices of Amitābha's Consort, Pāṇḍara. These petals have a general orange colour. When the red of Amitābha's energy is added to that of Ratnasambhava then we obtain the orange-yellow flame conditioning the *tathāgatagarbha*. This is a major esoteric reason why the saffron hue was adopted as the hue for the robes of the early monks. Orange is the natural colour of the Fiery domain of the mind/Mind. Pāṇḍara therefore oversees the general evolution of *manas* in this *maṇḍala*. The Consort of Vāc-Vidyādhara, the red 'Knowledge-Holder of the Great Symbol', works to reap all knowledgeable input from the sense-consciousness, according to the mode naturally expressed in terms of the three *guṇas*. The focus of the energies of these two Jinas is upon the Throat and Solar Plexus centres (thus also the minor centres). The objective is to transform the general knowledge *(kāma-manas)* obtained from *saṃsāra* into Love-Wisdom, by evoking the energies from the Heart centre.

The five Knowledge petals can now be considered in terms of the governing influences of the Consorts of the Dhyāni Buddhas.

1. The *Sacrifice–Knowledge petal* governed by Vairocana's *prajñā*, Ākāśadhātvīśvarī, was explained previously. The *prāṇas* of the smell sense-consciousness are generally processed here.
2. *Love-Wisdom–Knowledge petal.* Akṣobhya's *prajñā*, Locana, helps build this petal and regulates the *saṃskāras* flowing to it by

humanity. She works with the transmutation of all base Airy *prāṇas* that manifest an emotional flavour into the *bodhicitta* that is the major attribute of the *tathāgatagarbha*. The energy of goodwill is expressed by this petal as it awakens, laying the foundation for the later taking of Initiation. The *prāṇas* of the taste sense-consciousness are generally processed here. It is now possible to derive the evocation of the 'merit' of true wisdom from all knowledgeable pursuits in *saṃsāra*. Thus the orientation is to comprehend the nature of the Bodhisattva path and the direction thereto of all generated *saṃskāras*. The turning about in the seat of consciousness in an individual's mind therefore mainly happens as a consequence of the activities of this petal.

3. *Knowledge–Sacrifice petal.* Amoghasiddhi's *prajñā,* Samayatārā, helps build this petal and regulates the effects of all physical plane actions, so that too much *karma* is not unduly created, necessitating untold lives of karmic adjudication. The *prāṇas* from the hearing sense-consciousness are generally processed here so that complete knowledge of the physical domain can eventuate, leading to the eventual mastery of its qualities. The limitations of forms and actions relating to desire and attachment to ephemeral things and comforts will be eliminated when comprehended for what they are. The concretised manasic *saṃskāras* flowing to this petal thus come to be transmuted into more refined or embracive thought propensities. The orientation is to accumulate all the useful mental *saṃskāras,* producing abstract reasoning via the sacrifice of non useful thoughts, or those which would prove harmful. Often the *saṃskāras* of much personal ambition and self-focus have to be processed here, producing the effect of what is regarded as retributional *karma*.
4. *Knowledge–Love-Wisdom petal.* Ratnasambhava's *prajñā,* Māmakī, helps build this petal and controls the *saṃskāras* flowing to it, as she works with the regulation of all Watery *prāṇas*. We thus have the slow conversion of the various permutations of the defiled-mind into wise and loving attributes. The *saṃskāras* of the touch sense-consciousness generally come to be processed in this petal, helping to produce more loving interrelationships in individuals, and the generation of general goodwill. Ordinary social interrelationships of

a generous nature, affectionate family, social, or tribal ties are thus explored to produce a sense of companionship, of belonging. The orientation here is to ensure that the emotional *saṃskāras* developed are eventually converted into those of love and aspiration to high ideals. Therefore the focus is on the transformation of base selfish concerns, the lifting of human consciousness away from realms of the gross form, to be more compassionate, and to provide a better, harmonious quality of life in social and family situations.

5. *Knowledge—Knowledge petal.* Amitābha's *prajñā,* Pāṇḍara, helps build this petal and controls the *saṃskāras* flowing to it, as she works with the assimilation of all basic Fiery *prāṇas.* The general qualities of the sight sense-consciousness concerning the basic gathering of all knowable impressions from *saṃsāra* are processed here. The orientation is to fan all knowledgeable impression with the Fiery wind from the higher mental plane, so that enlightened perceptions eventually come to shine. All *manasic saṃskāras* are therefore stored and arranged so that they can later be converted into their corresponding wisdom-attributes.

With respect to the *colouration* of the petals of the Sambhogakāya Flower it should be noted that *A Treatise on Cosmic Fire*[12] assigns the colour orange for the Knowledge triad, with the subsidiary hues being green and violet for the Knowledge—Knowledge petal, rose and blue for the Knowledge—Love-Wisdom petal and yellow and indigo for the Knowledge—Sacrifice petal. For the Love-Wisdom petals the general colour assigned is rose, with the subsidiary colour being orange, then green and violet for the Love-Wisdom—Knowledge petal, rose and blue for the Love-Wisdom—Love-Wisdom petal, and yellow and indigo for the Love-Wisdom—Sacrifice petal. For the Sacrifice triad the major hue is yellow, with orange and rose as subsidiary colours. The Sacrifice—Knowledge petal is also coloured green, violet and rose; the Sacrifice—Love-Wisdom petal has an additional rose and blue hue, and the Sacrifice—Sacrifice petal possessing an additional blue and indigo hue.

12 Bailey, *A Treatise on Cosmic Fire*, 822-824.

The colours indicate the nature of the hues of the *devas* that have sacrificed their substance to incorporate the petals of this Flower. The purpose is to contain and facilitate the transformation of the types of *saṃskāras* that each petal processes. The red associated with the development of the Will is a higher octave of the green colour of Amoghasiddhi, who governs the abstracting process from the Sacrifice petals towards the planes of liberation for the Sambhogakāya Flower. Sacrifice at first principally concerns rightly transforming all *saṃskāras* of attachment to physical plane activities. Harder to overcome are the mental-emotional *saṃskāras*. Amoghasiddhi's All-accomplishing Wisdom stems from the proper control of all aspects of human activity. This concerns rectification of the engendered *karma*. The green colour is the hue of the third Ray, the governing Ray of *karma* in general. This colour then effectively veils all of the five Rays of Mind, of which orange-yellow dominates upon the mental plane, where transformations of consciousness occur. Rose-violet refers to highly refined emotional attributes. However, the objective of human activity is to generate the indigo blue of Love-Wisdom, which allows abstraction into *śūnyatā*.

The colours imbued into the Sambhogakāya Flower represent the abstracted *saṃskāras* developed as a consequence of normal human evolution. They are then integrated with the colourings of the Consorts of the Vidyādharas, which as presented in the text are exoteric, generalised with respect to the hue of the associated Dhyāni Buddha. (More colourations in fact exist in the spectrum than just the five presented.) The focus is upon the Vidyādhara Consorts because they are the general builders of the Sambhogakāya Flowers. The general rose colouration of the Love-Wisdom petals is taken to be the red of the Consort of the central Kāya-Vidyādhara in the *maṇḍala* of the Vidyādharas.

The three Sacrifice petals have a general yellow colouring, as the most refined quality generated by human physical plane activity dominates. This colour represents the fourth Ray attribute that governs humanity, the fourth kingdom in Nature. It thereby signifies their overall sacrificial nature, first to bring harmony out of the general miasma and conflict people find themselves in, then to tread the path to liberation. This is the colour assigned to Guṇa-Vidyādhara's Consort, who is assigned the southern direction of the *maṇḍala*. The attributes of the Knowledge–Love-Wisdom petal she embodies transforms via use of the sacrificial Will into their most refined form in order to be incorporated into the Sacrifice petals. Here we must note the colour of the associated Jina, Ratnasambhava, is yellow. It was earlier stated that Ratnasambhava's quality represents the overriding quality of the Vidyādharas within the context of the red-orange Fiery manasic attributes expressing Amitābha's Wisdom. Together they produce the overall orange hue of the Sambhogakāya Flowers.

Ratnasambhava's yellow colour generally vitalises the astral realms, in which the deceased find themselves. This yellow colour signifies the *prāṇic* energy of the spiritual sun that shines upon these inhabitants. (Though not noticed by the denizens in the hell realms.) The general pink colour of the Love-Wisdom petals is the colouration of human emotions in their higher attributes; affection, aspiration and devotion to noble ideals. They are the highest Watery characteristics developed by humanity. From this we can gather that Citta-Vidyādhara's Consort, who governs the evolution of the Love-Wisdom petals, though being ascribed a white colour (symbolising immaculate purity), also takes the hue of the rose colouring attributed to these petals. The pristine white being toned rose by the *saṃskāras* developed by human loving affections.

Other colourations are developed by the human aura, such as the sky-blue of human aspiration, often with a touch of violet for the creative imagination. Violet is the general colouration of the etheric double underlying the dense form, wherein exists the *chakra* and *nāḍī* system. It therefore relates to the development of psychic abilities. It also represents the seventh Ray attribute of power over the material domain, facilitating the progress of yogic austerities (or similar wilful activity enacted upon the material domain). Indigo is generated as an expression of the highest form of Love, the manifestation of *bodhicitta* (which awakens the central bud shielding the Śūnyatā Eye at the heart of the Flower as this force is increasingly developed.) All of the above colourings are synthesised by the indigo hue engendered by humanity on the pathway to developing attributes of *bodhicitta*.

To Amitābha is attributed the red of wilful *manasic* activity, which humans also prostitute into selfish will. We can however determine that Vāc-Vidyādhara's Consort under Amitābha's influence embodies and disseminates the associated orange hue of normal *manasic* development of the human mind, which colours the Knowledge petals of the kingdom of the Sambhogakāya Flower.

Duller orange, grey-greens, grey-violets, reddish and brownish hues manifest in the auras for those who are predisposed to much selfish, self-centred *saṃsāric karma*-engendering activity, but such characteristics are not incorporated into the Sambhogakāya Flower.

The wrathful Herukas and the integration of the Head lotus with the *tathāgatagarbha*

In Volume 3 a generalised account of the work of the wrathful Herukas with respect to the Sambhogakāya Flowers, and transforming the *saṃskāras* of the five sense-consciousnesses was introduced. The emphasis of their work is upon the *gotra* (the Tathāgata Womb), and the *bīja* seeds obtained from *saṃsāric* involvement with all phenomena and consciousness volitions. The gross consciousness-volitions of desire, envy, lust, etc., must be transformed into their corresponding virtues before they are acceptable to the Sambhogakāya Flower. Being the protectors or guardians of the *dharma* the five Herukas are the fierce emanations of the Jinas, hence such transformations come under their auspices.

In this present account much more detail shall be presented to show how they work from the domain of the petals of the Head centre to help accomplish this end. The wrathful Herukas can therefore be considered to be Mind-born emanations, as perceived by consciousness, that assist the conversion of unruly *saṃskāras*.

The Consort of the yellow 'Life-ruling Knowledge Holder' Guṇa-Vidyādhara focuses upon the links of consciousness-transference from the Head centre of the incarnate personality to the Sambhogakāya Flower. The main input is in terms of the qualities of the 'five-ness' associated with the sense-consciousnesses. Guiding impressions directed by the Jina and the Vidyādhara Consorts from the *tathāgatagarbha* are also incorporated in the Head lotus with the assistance of the Herukas. They embody the transformative forces enthroned within that lotus. These masculine forces are the counterparts to the Consorts governing the Sambhogakāya Flower. The Consorts of the five wrathful Herukas direct and store the *saṃskāras* incorporated in the mind. The

Herukas assist in their refinement and transformation so that they can be incorporated into the luminous form of the *tathāgatagarbha*. Upon the Initiation path the Herukas are the emanations of the Fires of Mind and the Consorts prepare for the awakening *kuṇḍalinī* by challenging the formation of unworthy thoughts. They are thus attributes of one's own mind and for this reason the text says that *'he who is called Great Glorious Buddha Heruka will [now] arise, vividly manifesting before you from within your own brain'.*[13] All Herukas appear in this fashion to play their appointed roles.

It is only possible to present an elementary account here of the interrelation between these entities and the Head lotus. The subject would involve considerable detail necessitating the extended geometry of the petals of the Head centre and the way they function.[14] Each major petal of this centre and its polar opposite are viewed as a male-female pair. The Detail of the way the Heruka Consorts work in transforming *saṃskāras* in the centres below the diaphragm (particularly Splenic centre I) will be presented in the next chapter.

It has already been discussed how the nine petals of the Sambhogakāya Flower can also be categorised in terms of three groups of five, providing a fifteen-fold flavour of petals derived from the major nine.

The description above of the nine-fold whorl of petals of the Sambhogakāya Flower was primarily concerned with the *deva* builders of the form, and its mode of organisation, that allows for the retrieval of *saṃskāras* generated in *saṃsāra* by the incarnation of each personal-I. (Rayed into manifestation for that purpose.) The focus was upon the assimilation of *manasic saṃskāras*, and the expression of *karma* in such a way that Love-Wisdom is developed. The Consorts of the Guardians also provide the gateways (conditions) for the taking of Initiation via the development of sacrificial Love. All Consorts are thus by necessity sowers and directors of *karma*.

The present analysis concerns the arrangement of five tiers of petals in the Head centre that access the *prāṇas* of the five Elements and direct them to the Sambhogakāya Flower after refinement. This then

---

13 Gyurme Dorje, *The Tibetan Book of the Dead*, 259.

14 See Volume 4, chapter 7, for a basic explanation of the Head lotus.

concerns the activity of the Herukas. They do not work directly with the *karma* of the *saṃskāras,* but rather with the effect of the interplay between the various factors of mind (knowledge) as directed from the Sambhogakāya Flower so that eventually wisdom is produced. Their function is to assist in the transformation of all forms of defilements of mind, so that opportunities for Initiation in the quiet zones of *manasic* space are possible. Consciousness-transformations of attributes of mind into the higher wisdoms, and eventual liberation from *saṃsāra* is the objective.

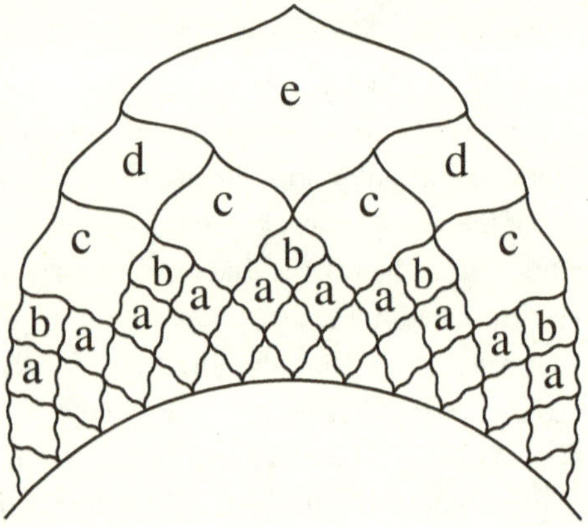

Figure 3. Five tiers of petals in the Head centre

Figure 3 is an example of one of the twelve major petals of the Head lotus. We see that there are five different levels of petals arranged in size from the smallest to the large synthesising petal. Each group was said to contain places to process *saṃskāras* of a specific Element. The concern here is with the Head lotus at a relatively advanced stage of development, namely when major *saṃskāras* are being refined, when goodwill is being generated by the incarnate personal-I's, leading eventually to the Initiation and Bodhisattva paths. Prior to this the activity of the Consorts of the Herukas are dominant. The Herukas control the activity of the petals of the Head lotus in the following manner.

a. First we have the smallest petals, of which there are three rows of petals containing twelve, eleven and ten petals each, to make 33 petals all together.[15] We can also view them in terms of ten groups of six petals each. Each group of six petals can be considered to process the attributes of the six consciousnesses when the synthesising attributes of the intellect are added to the five sense-consciousnesses. At this level of expression of the Head lotus the number ten (2 x 5) signifies the control by the Herukas and their Consorts of the intake of *prāṇas*. They specifically process the *prāṇas* generated through the entire field of desire and experiences in the material domain associated with the Earth Element. Here the activity of Karma Heruka, the emanation of Amoghasiddhi, organises associated mineral-like *saṃskāras* so that they can be absorbed into the Knowledge—Knowledge petal of the *tathāgatagarbha*.

b. The next largest petal contains ten smaller petals in its field of expression. There are also two groups of six petals incorporated into one of these petals, to take into account the work of the Herukas and Consorts, the *piṇgalā* and *iḍā* expression of *prāṇas*. This petal processes the Watery *prāṇas* generated by the individual, and the related *saṃskāras* inherited from previous lives of activity. There are five such groups in one major petal of the Head lotus. Ratna Heruka, the emanation of Ratnasambhava, organises these *saṃskāras* in such a way that they can be integrated into the Knowledge—Love-Wisdom petal of the *tathāgatagarbha*.

c. The next major petal synthesises the *prāṇas* of a group of two of the Watery petals, admixing them with *manasic* (Fiery) attributes. There are eighteen petals altogether in this petal. We can also view them as incorporating four groups of six minor petals in one overall Fiery *(kāma-manasic)* petal. There are four such petals in one major petal of the Head lotus. Each of these four can be seen to consist of two of the Watery petals, which then take the attributes of the *piṇgalā* and *iḍā* expression of *prāṇas*. Amitābha's emanation, Padma Heruka, processes this group of petals of all forms of mental-emotional energies in their four categories of earth-like, desirous, emotional, or the more purely mental impulses. These can then be absorbed by the Knowledge—Sacrifice petal of the *tathāgatagarbha*.

15 This number is found in the 330,000,000 creative Intelligences of the Hindu Pantheon.

d. The fourth largest petal of the Head lotus processes the Airy *prāṇas* that are generated. These are the general *saṃskāras* flowing throughout the *nāḍī* system that transform mental defilements (*kliṣṭamanas*[16]) into *bodhicitta*. Akṣobhya's emanation, Vajra Heruka, processes these *saṃskāras* and integrates them into the main body of the *tathāgatagarbha*. There are 27 petals if we count them simply as they appear. If, however, we count them in terms of two units of Fiery petals of eighteen smaller petals each then there are 36 petals synthesised by the major Airy petal. However, the actual way that these petals function is more complex than these simple numbers indicate. Each of these Fiery petals also contain four units of six smaller petals, which makes eight such units altogether. The Airy petal also contains three Watery petals, each containing two units of six smaller petals, making six units of six smaller petals. In the numbers 4, 8 and 6 we have all of the classifications of the Wrathful Deities implicated that are found in the *Bardo Thödol*; the Mātarah, Piśācī, Īśvarī and Gatekeepers. The number three integrates their *prāṇas* into the triads of petals of the Sambhogakāya Flower. As shall be detailed later, the domain of the theriomorphic deities are concerned with the interrelation of *prāṇas* associated with this Head lotus and the places of generation below the diaphragm.

e. Finally, the major synthesising petal represents the processing of the abstracting Aetheric *prāṇas* that allow the development of the type of perceptions pertaining to the *dharmakāya*. It contains two of the Airy petals, allowing for the classification of all the above mentioned Wrathful Deities in terms of their *piṇgalā* and *iḍā* expression. Vairocana's emanation, the central Buddha Heruka, directs these *saṃskāras* to the Sacrifice petals of the *tathāgatagarbha*.

---

16 *Kliṣṭamanas*, afflicted mind, the many types of afflictive emotions (*kleśas*), stored as *bījas* (seeds) in the *ālayavijñāna*. They are projected in the form of related *saṃskāras* when the personal-I is focussed upon an object of desire. When these emotional *saṃskāras* surface they immediately fuse with the mental consciousness (*manovijñāna*), to produce such things as desire-mind, self-will, or forms of ego-clinging. The emotions always manifest in relation to a concept of 'self', executing the will to appropriate things desired. They thus produce attachments for all things deemed pleasurable, glamorous, or needed by the personality, and react to that which they dislike.

As well as governing the overview of these five levels of petals, for the most part the five blood-drinking Herukas stand at the junction between the Watery and the Fiery petals. They thereby assist the conversion of base Watery emotions, attachments and desire into the refined qualities of *manas* and abstract thought. Their wrathful nature therefore converts the *saṃsāra*-addictive attributes of the Waters into those attributes that will inevitably bring liberation. Stern force and forms of wrathful application are needed to effect this conversion.

This process is generally thought of in terms of conversion of the 'five poisons': delusion, hatred, pride, passion (the emotions that form attachment to sensory objects), and envy. When Mahottara Heruka is taken into account then the central base of all *saṃsāric* attachment, ignorance, is also tackled. The Herukas provide the antidotes to these poisons. Thus ignorance is converted to pristine awareness, delusion to cognition of reality via Buddha Heruka's activity, hatred to loving attributes (Vajra Heruka), pride to a cognition of selflessness (Ratna Heruka), passionate attachments to right discernment (Padma Heruka), and envy to compassionate acceptance (Karma Heruka).

There are also three major tiers of petals of the Head centre, and five altogether. When we analyse the influences between the Herukas and the Jina Consorts specifically (via the mediatorship of Guṇa-Vidyādhara's Consort) then we must manifest a dimensional approach, as well as view the structure of each tier to properly comprehend the way that the Head centre functions. (The symbolism of the five tiered *stūpa* can also be applied to this arrangement of the Head centre.) We must also take into account the stages of development of the Head centre itself, of the rearrangement of the petals from that associated with normal *manasic* development to that associated with the path of Initiation.

In observing the twelve major petals of the Head lotus we can view them in terms of four quadrants of three petals each. Each of these quadrants can then be considered to convey *prāṇas* to the Sambhogakāya Flower, according to the symbolism of the orientation of the four cardinal directions of the fixed cross. Depending upon whether the orientation of the person is downwards to the material world, outwards to the field of human interrelations, upwards to high aspiration or lofty contemplation, or inwards to the Heart of Life, so the *saṃskāras* can flow to either the Sacrifice, Love-Wisdom or Knowledge petals of the Sambhogakāya Flower.

The number of petals to each quadrant can also be expanded to five (with consequent overlap in the intermediate positions, effectively making an eight-spoked wheel). From this perspective they can be considered to project *prāṇas* to any grouping of five petals of the Sambhogakāya Flower.

As the Sambhogakāya Flowers are Tatāgata-embryos the constitution of the petals are so arranged to bring about the appearance of Buddhas in time. Because the Flower exists upon the abstracted mental plane we can deduce that it stores *saṃskāras* pertainable to the development of wisdom. The factor of *manas* reigns supreme in *saṃsāra,* and therefore a great deal of evolutionary time is involved with the process that converts its attributes into wisdom qualities. We can therefore see why the activities of the wrathful Herukas are so important. They are an offshoot of the work of the Jina Consorts, thus specifically of the Knowledge petals of the Sambhogakāya Flower. These Knowledge petals absorb the refined extracts, the 'perfumes' of the five types of perceptions obtained by the sense-consciousnesses. The logic is simple enough. We can think of these perfumes being developed in the 'wombs' of the Jina Consorts every time a new personal-I is rayed into *saṃsāra* to gather further experiences and to reap the consequences of appropriately directed *karma* in the fields of mind. They are the most refined characteristics developed by the consciousness-stream during any incarnation. What should also be considered is that the Herukas are the 'Sons' born from the Wombs of the Jina Consorts, with respect to being agents of transforming *manas.*

The relation of the Herukas to the Knowledge petals is straightforward. We have:

The Sacrifice—Knowledge petal: Buddha Heruka,
The Love-Wisdom—Knowledge petal: Vajra Heruka,
The Knowledge—Sacrifice petal: Padma Heruka,
The Knowledge—Love-Wisdom petal: Ratna Heruka,
The Knowledge—Knowledge petal: Karma Heruka.

There are three major influences conditioning the interplay and evolution of the Knowledge petals of the Sambhogakāya Flowers, viewing them as a triad of petals.

1. The Knowledge—Sacrifice petal. The five Jina Consorts are responsible for this petal and for building the forms wherein the Jina's seeds can find expression for evolutionary growth.
2. The Knowledge—Love-Wisdom petal. The Vidyādhara Consorts are responsible for this petal and integrate aspects of consciousness.
3. The Knowledge—Knowledge petal absorbs the main result of the work of the five wrathful Herukas who work in the Head lotus to transmute *saṃskāras* stored by the consciousness-principle. The *saṃskāras* are the qualities from the consciousness-stream projected into the mind of a personal-I to produce necessary experiences. Within this mind all transformations of consciousness are effected. The *saṃskāras* are also generated by each new consciousness-volition of that individual.

Next we can consider the three Love-Wisdom petals. The list below is focussed upon the agents that actually build the petals and which work (with the Mahābodhisattvas) to effect the transmutation of *saṃskāras* so that *bodhicitta* can be awakened and Initiation accomplished. Consequently, the development of this set of petals is most important for humanity, because the true purpose of human evolution lies in the expression of *bodhicitta*. It produces the development of the Bodhisattva *bhūmis*, thus the way of travelling the path to liberation. This produces a three-fold influence conditioning the Sambhogakāya Flowers:

1. The Love-Wisdom—Sacrifice petal. The Consorts of the Guardians are concerned with the final transformations of the Flowers, to bring about Initiation, through first awakening *bodhicitta* and then developing its sacrificial aspects to fully overcome *saṃsāra*.
2. The Love-Wisdom—Love-Wisdom petal. The entire structure of the Sambhogakāya Flowers constitutes the 'wombs' of the Vidyādhara Consorts. Therefore all conveyance of the *saṃskāras* happen within their forms, making them karmic adjudicators when the development of the *saṃskāras* are to be regulated so that *karma* is eventually equilibrated.
3. The Love-Wisdom—Knowledge petal. Bodhisattvas work from the outside to stimulate the general development of the petals

of the Flowers. Being embodiments of Love and Wisdom the Mahābodhisattvas are the active forces in Nature that produce the evolution of these qualities among humans. The main mechanism is through right education, to produce eventual enlightenment. They therefore significantly help the evolution of the Love-Wisdom petals of the Sambhogakāya Flowers. The Mahābodhisattvas capitalise upon qualities originally seeded in *saṃsāra* by the Consorts of the Jinas.

In analysing the Sacrifice petals we find that there are three main influences bearing upon them.

1. The Sacrifice-Sacrifice petal. The Ādi Buddha's Consort, bearing the transmutative energies of the Jinas into manifestation, helps in the process of drawing the vital Life of the Flower into *śūnyatā*. The floral form is then extinguished in a supernal burst of multihued brilliance. Life, Love and Wisdom however persist.
2. The Sacrifice—Love-Wisdom petal. The Consorts of the four Guardians establish the gateways to Initiation with the Vidyādhara Consorts, who embody the formed structure of the Sambhogakāya Flower. Here the Love-Wisdom principle that is the basis to undertaking Initiation is expressed.
3. The Sacrifice—Knowledge petal. The preparatory background for Initiation concerns the transformative effects of the wrathful Herukas upon the play of consciousness, and is then incorporated in the Flower via the work of agents of the Jina Consorts.

There are consequently three main directions of the influence impacting upon the Sambhogakāya Flowers.

1. From below, the generation of *saṃskāras* and the *prāṇas* by each personal-I, to be absorbed by the petals of the Flowers.
2. Within the kingdom itself through interconnections between the Vidyādharas, Consorts, and the effect of the Bodhisattvas. They stimulate the general unfoldment of the Flowers as part of a *maṇḍala* of expression, within which each individual Flower forms a part.
3. From above, the steady pull from the Jinas and Guardians, so that liberation from incarnation can be gained by developing the

attributes of the Jinas. This necessitates transmuting the base attributes of the *saṃskāras* (viewed as substance) into the five Void Elements, and extracting the wisdom qualities into the Clear Light of the *dharmakāyic* Mind. The Void Elements are the five qualities originally seeded into manifestation that became the basis of the five sense-consciousnesses of humanity.

There are seven general influences that produce or effect the development of each *tathāgatagarbha* in conjunction with the characteristics generated by each incarnation of a personal-I.

1. The Consort of the Ādi Buddha, demonstrating the attributes of the first Ray of Will or Power, to produce the abstraction of everything into the *dharmakāya.*
2. The five Jinas, to draw out of the Flowers the propensities and characteristics of Buddha-like qualities. Their general effect demonstrates as *bodhicitta,* the attributes of the second Ray of Love-Wisdom.
3. The Consorts of the Jinas that sow the wisdom elements of their partners into the evolving form in terms of the five sense-consciousnesses that constitute the basis of the activity of the five Knowledge petals. This conditions the *manasic* propensity of the Flowers as a whole. These Consorts manifest the attributes of the third Ray of enlightening, Mathematically Exact Activity.
4. The Consorts of the Guardians, to open the gates to Initiation, the way of escape from *saṃsāric* turmoil. They present the pathways wherein humans can transform *saṃskāras* into liberation-attributes in the Sacrifice petals. This expresses the fourth Ray characteristics of Beautifying Harmony overcoming Conflict.
5. The Consorts of the Vidyādharas, who establish the basis of the Love-Wisdom petals, which transform the knowledgeable attributes derived via the five sense-consciousnesses into the expression of wisdom. Being *manasic* they manifest the attributes of the fifth Ray of Scientific Reasoning.
6. The Mahābodhisattvas and Bodhisattvas, who work both with the Flowers and the incarnate lives to produce loving attributes,

devotion to noble ideals, idealism, high aspiration, and eventual enlightenment. They prepare disciples for the testings of Initiation. With respect to the above qualities we have the manifestation of the attributes of the sixth Ray of Devotion.

7. The wrathful Herukas, who assist in the processes associated with the transformation of the sense-consciousnesses in the Head centre. They help upon the path of transmuting knowledgeable attributes into great wisdom. Their wrathful emanations manifest as a consequence of this process of transformation. The resultant *saṃskāras* can then be projected to the respective petals of the Sambhogakāya Flower. As these testings can occur upon any of the Ray lines, so therefore the Herukas embody the characteristics of the seventh Ray of Ceremonial Cyclic Activity—Demonstrable Power, which grounds the manifestation of all the seven Rays.

Humanity generates defilements by clinging to *saṃsāra* through sensual passions, lust, anger, violence, etc. This causes them to fully experience and then come to terms with suffering and its consequences via treading the wheel of birth and death. Upon the way they develop and then overcome the emotions. Emotion, coupled with the principle of desire that is developed in the higher species of animals, is the foundational attribute for the later theriomorphic qualities in humans. The advent of human units prescribes the free will that is the basis to determine individual karmic propensities. This produces the formation of the Six Realms, wherein the rulership of the six Sages is possible, according to the *Bardo Thödol* symbolism.

With respect to the above orientations and affiliations there is thus a steady progressive push upon, within, and through the kingdom of the *tathāgatagarbha* to ensure that the necessary qualities to be transmuted will be developed by this Buddha-germ. Inevitably, the consequences of all this activity is abstracted into *dharmakāya* (via *śūnyatā),* for which purpose all the above exalted lives have sacrificed themselves. Thus all sentient beings will inevitably evolve to become Buddhas. It is so written and so it shall be.

The general iconography of the Herukas

The concern here is with the overall symbolism of the Herukas as a unit, specifically as it relates to the way of integration of *prāṇas* into the Sambhogakāya Flower. Images and the detail of many aspects of the symbolism shall be provided in chapter 4, when the Herukas and their Consorts are dealt with individually.

First we have the central *Mahottara Heruka*[17] *(Che-mchog Heruka),* who is the wrathful aspect of the Ādi Buddha Samantabhadra, of which all the other Wrathful Deities are emanations. He does not appear in the main account of the appearance of the Wrathful Deities from the eighth to the fourteenth day, nevertheless because all the Herukas derive from him his presence is implicated, and thus appears in the various thangkas depicting the *Bardo Thödol*. Lauf describes the appearance of Mahottara Heruka as:

> The maṇḍala of the great wrathful blood-drinking deities is a fivefold lotus in the brain cakra, with a centre and four petals. "There first appears there from the centre of the lotus and amidst the radiance of fiery light the great, wrathful blood-drinking Che-mchog Heruka," with three heads, nine eyes, six arms, and four legs, upon a lotus, and in a flaming aureole. His right face is the colour of smoke, the middle white, and the left red. In his three right hands he carries the vajra, the trident (S. khaṭvāṅga), and a drum with a handle (T. rNga-chung), and in his left hands he carries the bell, the kapāla, and a sling made from innards. The powerful Heruka appears in inseparable union with his Ḍākini Krodheśvarī, whose colour is pure white.[18]

As the other Herukas embody the qualities of the *saṃskāras* of the sense-consciousnesses, so Mahottara Heruka embodies the functioning of the sixth sense, the intellect. The intellect integrates all of their qualities in its central store, and acts as a collating and deductive organ embodied by the empirical mind. The symbolism associated

---

17 Mahottara Heruka means 'great unexcelled' Heruka. Lauf presents the term Mahāśrī Heruka. The great honorific, radiant or glorious Heruka.

18 Lauf, 144-145.

with his appearance and implements shall be treated generically in the account of the other Herukas. The main distinguishing factor is however his smoke coloured body and right face. This colour represents the normal obscuration of mind that must be overcome upon the path to enlightenment. One must learn to clarify the haze of the smoke in order to see the intensity of the blaze that it veils. The colouration therefore represents a veil signifying the unknown, which can only be cognised as a consequence of gaining enlightenment.

By embodying the 'intellect' with respect to the Head lotus we see that Mahottara Heruka embodies the sum of the organisation of all the petals of this centre. He integrates the mode of transference of the *saṃskāras* from one arena of activity to another, and the general flow of *prāṇas* to and from the Sambhogakāya Flower. The main organising agent for these *prāṇas,* however, is the central Buddha Heruka, who appears on the eighth day of the Bardo recital. He takes the role of Mahottara for the deceased. The appearance of the central Buddha Heruka is described thus by Gyurme:

> *O, Child of Buddha Nature, he who is called Great Glorious Buddha Heruka will [now] arise, vividly manifesting before you from within your own brain. His body, blazing in a mass of light, is dark brown in colour, having three heads, six arms and four legs, which are [firmly] set apart. His right face is white, the left red and the central face dark brown. His nine eyes are fixed in a fearsome wrathful gaze, his eyebrows are quivering like lightning, his fangs are bared and gleaming, and he is laughing loudly, uttering the sounds of Alala and Haha, and Shoo oo – like whistles, in loud piercing cries. The golden-auburn hair of his head blazes and rears upward, sun and moon-discs, black serpents and dry skulls adorn each of his heads, and black snakes and fresh skulls form a garland around his body. In his six hands he holds, on the right in the first hand, a wheel, in the middle one, an axe and in the last hand a sword and to the left, in his first hand, he holds a bell, in the middle one, a plough-share and on the last a skull. The female Consort Buddhakrodheśvarī is embracing his body, her right hand clasped around his neck and her left offering a skull-cup filled with blood to his mouth. Amidst loud pounding palatal sounds of 'Thuk-chom', and an [echoing] roar like the reverberation of thunder, the fire of pristine cognition*

> *blazes from the fiery indestructible pores of their bodies, and thus they stand together, [with one leg] extended and [the other] drawn in, on a throne supported by garuḍas.*[19]

Being central, Buddha Heruka energises and integrates the remaining four Herukas, similar to the action of the central prong of a *vajra*. All of the Herukas are depicted in thangkas with the same ornaments, skulls and serpents in their hair, and wrathful gazes. Similarly the fact that they each have three heads, nine eyes, four legs solidly planted on the ground, and six arms. The related symbolism can therefore be treated together. Each Krodheśvarī (meaning 'fearsome one') are similarly attired, standing on one leg, embracing their Consort and offering him a *kapāla* to drink. The colours for each Heruka and Consort differ according to that of their respective Jina. The implements they hold also differ, as well as the colouring of the central head.

The laughter symbolises the glee of trampling upon the corpses of the elements of mastered attributes of *saṃsāra* and of all the Bardo experiences. The three sets of mantric syllables control the attributes of all the triune permutations of the Herukas—the three heads, with three eyes in each, and two sets of three arms, each holding an implement. It signifies mastery of the three worlds of human livingness, of body, speech and mind. All attributes that cause so much pain, trouble and hardship for normal humans are a subject of mirth by this conqueror.

The skulls in the crown symbolise the mastery of the five poisons and all of the other attributes of life in *saṃsāra* with its death-dealing aspects. The serpents in the hair symbolise the same quality of hatred and enmity found in the serpent at the centre of the Wheel of Life. In this case, however, the 'hatred' is towards all the attributes of *saṃsāra's* allurements. They also represent the *nagas* (serpents) that are the expressions of lower psychic powers, of psychicism of all types, which must also be controlled, subjugated and transformed into higher spiritual accomplishments by those aspiring to gain liberation. The fierceness of the Heruka's gaze and wrathful countenance indicates there will be no mercy given in any quarter relating to the transformation of unruly and

---

19 Gyurme, 259.

unregenerative *saṃskāras.* All must be vanquished and transformed into the Jina wisdoms. Nothing can prevent their transformation into liberating bliss. Thus the Krodheśvarī is similarly wrathful, offering to her Lord the elixir that is the gain of their united dance upon the corpses of the vanquished. He sups the blood of blissful 'pristine cognition' from the flow of the five types of wisdoms that come from transmuting the five poisons. Every major *saṃskāra* that is converted represents another sip to be drunk from this cup that signifies the brain of the *yogin,* wherein the actual conversion is being undertaken.

The Fiery blaze around each Heruka is the burning ground, the transformative furnace for all of the attributes that are to be stripped bare of their ephemeral attributes. The Heruka's glory consumes the flammable substance of *saṃsāric manasic* propensities in the blaze. All permutations of mind must be increasingly refined in this fire until only the most refined essence remains, which will be found as the sublime radiance of the Peaceful Deities.

The sun and moon relate to the expression of the *iḍā* and *piṇgalā nāḍīs,* reminding us of the tantric nature of this work, and the ultimate goal of uniting male and female forces in the body. Wisdom and compassion are generated, then their fusion into consummate bliss is developed. The process, however, necessitates first transforming the dull coloured serpents of aberrant *saṃskāras* into enlightening attributes, awakening the full glory of the 'garland of flowers', the intricate *nāḍī* and *chakra* system.

The four legs 'firmly set apart' of each Heruka signify the four corners of the material domain from which all experiences are derived, and which are the basis to the entire liberating and transmutative dance. Each of these 'corners' represent one of the four main Elements governing the material domain, and conveyed by means of one or other of the four petals of the Base of Spine centre. Yogically this centre is the foundation of all that is to come, of the entire wheel of *saṃsāra,* governed by the six petals of the Sacral centre. Here is the seat of the principle of desire which is the driving energy turning the entire wheel.

These legs can also symbolise the qualities of the four sub-planes of the concrete mind wherein all this activity occurs so that the attributes of the abstract Mind can be developed. We can also look to the four-fold personality structure of mind, emotions, etheric and dense forms, as well as to the qualities of the four kingdoms of Nature that the personal-I resides in and from which all *saṃsāric* attributes are derived.

The passionate embrace of the Heruka by the Consort at first represents the ordinary sexual embrace between normal human units, wherein the rebirthing principle is effected with each new child born into the world. Without perpetual rebirth no *saṃskāric* generation and consequent conversion would be possible. All are needed upon the drive to liberation (Āḥ La La), all are needed for the generation of wisdom and invoking the internal Fires (Haṁ Haṁ). All are needed to evoke compassion for all sentient beings (Sa Huṁ Oṁ). The 'loud pounding palatal sounds of 'Thuk-chom', and an [echoing] roar like the reverberation of thunder' from the Consort symbolises the general sounds of the *prāṇas* circulating within the mind and *nāḍīs.*

Five toes symbolise the need to extract the *prāṇas* of the five sense-consciousnesses from the earth terrain that is the ground of all experiences via each of the main elements: Earth, Water, Fire and Air. Four times five are the energies needed to awaken the pentads of the matrix of Life. Twenty are the *prāṇas* needed to effect the awakening of the ten main petals of the Solar Plexus centre in both the *iḍā* and *piṇgalā* attributes.

When the Consort's single foot is added to this dance (upon the corpses of *saṃsāric* defilements), as the other is held around the waist of her companion, then we have the necessary twenty-five *prāṇas* needed for the awakening of the mind/Mind. The leg held around the waist symbolises the circulating of *prāṇas* from the Inner Round set of minor *chakras* to the Solar Plexus centre.

The Consort's other foot (though not in the centre) symbolises the central prong to an effective *vajra* with the four feet of the Heruka applied to the earth in order to extract from it all of its 'nutrients', every form of experience possible, and to tie it into one unified demonstration of mastery of all forces pertaining to *saṃsāra. Saṃsāra* and *nirvāṇa* are integrated in the form of one embrace by both masculine and feminine principles.

Here we see that the feminine adds the fifth, central integrating Element (Aether), as all the forces of Mother Nature represent the great Womb wherein this entire play is carried out. It is the sum of *saṃsāra* that makes all this possible. Therefore the agents of conversion in the *Bardo Thödol* of all the mental-emotional forces generated by a human unit are feminine, or theriomorphic female deities. The consequences are reaped by the masculine deities, and who also guard the entry into the next higher state of awareness or Initiation level of the *maṇḍala* of Life. All of the *prāṇas* of transformations (as well as generation of unruly *saṃskāras)* happen below the diaphragm, therefore the other leg is wrapped around the waist of the companion Heruka in the form of a sideways Tau cross ⊣.[20] It represents the vertical alignment of Spirit to matter *(dharmakāya* to *saṃsāra*) passing through the feminine horizontal line that allows the entire phenomenological attributes of the world to appear. The eastern arm of the cross (the principle of the Heart of Life) is established, but the western arm (of mastery of *saṃsāra)* still needs to be completed to make the four arms of a fixed cross. One can also reverse the symbolism[21] to indicate that the western form of activity of interrelating between humans is established, and the inward way to the heart is still to be accomplished. This way necessitates the conversion of *saṃskāras* by means of the activity of the dual Splenic centre. Only after the transmutative battles with all the elements associated with the five poisons can the true way to the heart be found and the cross completed. It then becomes the ankh, with the circle of life representing the *chakras* in the chest cavity, rising out of the diaphragm from the *chakras* below it (which are simply represented by a vertical line). The gain of all this activity then rises to the Head lotus and is lovingly offered to the Heruka to drink, to produce the blissful experiences of awakened perceptions.

Next we can consider the symbolism of the set of right and left hands, each holding implements, and the three heads of each Heruka, each containing three eyes. Each triplicity can be viewed in terms of the attributes of the *iḍā, piṇgalā* and *suṣumṇā nāḍīs,* or the three *guṇas.* Here also is provided the symbolism of the type of rectified *prāṇa* directed to the three tiers of petals of the Sambhogakāya Flower in accord with the particular type of sense-consciousness and corresponding 'poison'. Each particular face and hand group of the Heruka embodies a different process of transmutation. The three left hands symbolically direct *prāṇas* to the Knowledge petals, the right

20 The normal way that this cross is portrayed is in the form of a T.

21 Depending upon the orientation of one's view of east and west in the symbolism.

hands direct *prāṇas* to the Love-Wisdom petals, and the three heads act similarly with respect to the Sacrifice petals. The three eyes in each of the Heruka's heads act as the means of transmission of the refined *prāṇas* from these triplicities to the Sambhogakāya Flower. Each set of eyes also completes the symbolism of the number twelve (for the twelve petals of the Heart in the Head centre) with any set of nine.

Altogether there are fifteen different implements carried by the hands. The symbolism associated with these implements relate to the qualities of the five Elements, to which there are three implements applicable to each of the Elements. The actual meaning of the implements shall be provided in the next chapter, what shall be given here are the triads of expression they embody with respect to the Elements. Each triad manifests in the form of a Will, Love-Wisdom and Activity aspect.

- Aether, the subtlest and most refined Element, which synthesises the properties of the other four, expresses the attributes of the *dharmakāya*. Here we have the *khaṭvāṅga* manifesting the Will aspect, which as we saw earlier, symbolises the entire domain of liberation and its relation to *saṃsāra,* as well as the mode of treading the path. All of the *khaṭvāṅga's* attributes are integrated and aligned on a vertical line of ascent to the highest domain. The *vajra* then embodies the Love-Wisdom aspect by means of its five prongs of energy that express the potencies of the five Jinas. Finally, the *noose of entrails* carried by Mahottara Heruka represents the Activity mode because it symbolises all of the attributes developed in the centres below the diaphragm. It captures wayward desire-mind *saṃskāras* of the digestive process and firmly holds them so that they can be transformed and transmuted into their Void aspects. This Aetheric Element is governed by the supreme endowment of the Wheel of *dharma* and its Jina family.

- Air, being intrinsically empty of attributes is the general carrier of all the *prāṇas*. The Will aspect is symbolised by the Consort offering the *kapāla* containing the elixir gained from her transformative dance in *saṃsāra*. The Love-Wisdom attribute is the *bell (ghaṇṭā)* that intones the immaculate Void of space. The *vajra* and bell are often used together in rituals, as the first represents the immutable power of the Jina, and the bell the intrinsic emptiness of his Consort.

The Activity aspect is embodied by the *drum* which rhythmically beats out the modifications of space in the form of a mantric sound. It integrates *saṃsāra's* domain with the emptiness of the all. This Element is governed by the Vajra family.

- Fire, the substance of the mind in all of its attributes. The Will aspect is symbolised by the *sword,* which is used for discriminative compassionate activity. It can quickly cut asunder truth from untruth, to smite the serpents of deceit and lies. It is double-edged, fusing wisdom and compassion in one Fiery embrace, according to the purpose of its wielder. The Love-Wisdom aspect is the *lotus,* which is the store of the various attributes of consciousness, each *chakra* also being the place for the transmutation of *saṃskāras* by means of the application of the Fires of mind/Mind. The Activity aspect is the *wheel* (of the *dharma),* which organises the Fiery elements within the *chakras* and consciousness, according to their orientation of the directions in space. This Element is governed by the Padma family.

- Water, the fluid carrier of the emotional attributes of consciousness, and of the 'blood' representing the Waters of Life. The Will aspect is the *trident* that controls the flow of the Watery substance according to the symbolism of its three prongs, which represents the potency of the three main *nāḍīs* or *guṇas.* The Love-Wisdom aspect is the *kapāla,* the skull-cup, which contains the *bodhicitta-amṛta* that is the essence of the transmuted *saṃskāras.* The Activity aspect is the *jewel,* here viewed in terms of its wish-fulfilling attributes. At first it grants whatever the object of desire may be. Later it clarifies and becomes the diamond-Mind of enlightenment. This Element is governed by the Ratna family.

- Earth, the substance of the material domain and of one's dense body of manifestation, wherein all accomplishments must be wrought. The Will aspect is the *axe,* with which the heads of the most stubborn attributes of mind must be cut off. There is no room for the sows and serpents of materialistic incentive in a *yogin's* life. The Love-Wisdom attribute is the *ploughshare,* to plough the earth with righteousness so that the seeds of the transformed *saṃskāras* can be recycled. The Activity aspect is the *club or mace* with which to pound the most obstinate *saṃskāras* of desire-mind into submission. This

Element is governed by the Karma family wielding the *viśvavajra* of omni-directional immutable power to transform all aspects of material plane living.

All Herukas have white faces facing the right, signifying immaculate purity, the spotless application of the *dharma*. The central face is the colour of the body of the Heruka and signifies his fundamental attribute in relation to the Jina of which he is the wrathful expression. In the case of the brown colour of Padma Heruka, we see that this colour is really a composite of the red, green and blue of the three primary Rays (Will, Love-Wisdom and Divine Activity) which govern the dispensation of all of the triplicities of expression in the *maṇḍala* of the Herukas. It conveys the bear-like ferocious power of the wrathful aspect of all the Herukas. The left face of each Heruka is red, signifying the nature of the will that is needed to subdue all of the defilements and attributes of mind confronted by the Herukas. In the case of Padma Heruka the colouring is the blue of compassion because the colour of the central face is dark red. The red and white faces of the Herukas also refer to the exoteric account of the red and white *prāṇas* flowing through the *nāḍīs*. Here the white energy is considered to represent the masculine energy of compassion, and the red energy the female attribute of wisdom.[22]

We see that the offering of blood from the Consorts is common to all of the Herukas because of the Airy conduit of *prāṇa* that this activity implies. It signifies the general *nāḍī* system through which all *prāṇas* flow.

The five Herukas are mainly concerned with channelling *prāṇas* into the Knowledge petals of the Sambhogakāya Flowers. The role of Mahottara Heruka is the generation and absorption of the *prāṇas* pertaining to the Love-Wisdom (the right hands) and Sacrifice petals (the left hands). For this reason the implements he wields relate to the Aetheric or Airy Elements, or the Will aspect of the Watery domain *(kapāla)*. The noose of entrails he also wields (not possessed by any of the other Herukas), if viewed as a sling, governs the forceful firing of the transformed *prāṇas* from below the diaphragm towards the Flower. It therefore relates to the Will (most abstracted) aspect of this Element.

22 See Volume 4, chapter 10, of this treatise for a detailed account of the meaning of these colours as *prāṇas*.

The throne is *'supported by garuḍas'*, which is indicated in the thangkas by the wings of this bird emanating from behind each of the Herukas. The Garuḍa (Tib. khyung), meaning 'devourer', is a vehicle of Amoghasiddhi. It is a mythic sun bird-man, usually shown with a raptor's beak, and is an enemy of serpents. (He is often depicted with a serpent in his mouth.) As such it represents the mechanism of the transmutation of evil forces, the tainted *saṃskāras* depicted in the form of serpents. The Garuḍa represents the Mind that can soar high and consume all forms of serpent-like aberrant *saṃskāras.* Garuḍa is also the steed of Viṣṇu (the second person of the Hindu *trimūrti* signifying the Love-Wisdom principle) in the form of a great bird in the ancient Hindu religious epic, the Ramayana. We see, therefore, that the Herukas take the guise of these serpent eaters in their rapacious consummative capacity to overcome all obstacles to final liberation within the minds of the aspiring ones.

The Six Realms

The *seventh stage* of the genesis of a *maṇḍala* concerning the evolutionary process can now be analysed.

Stage 7. The development of the mind in all of its attributes

The mind has clearly evolved to be distinguished as a separative entity that names and identifies the variegated, segregated principles and entities existing in the environment it experiences. This produces the full interplay of all human relationships. It involves the evolutionary progress of humanity from primitive animal-man to the harbingers of modern technologically advanced societies. First, we have the generation of all the major types of *saṃskāras* that necessitate continuous rebirth into the wheel of the Six Realms, taking the factor of Dependent Origination into consideration. Inevitably the reaction to a continuous, cyclic, painful activity produces the evolution of Bodhisattvas and the path that leads to Buddhahood. The Bodhisattva path has its genesis after the formative period of human evolution has run its course. It necessitates the existence of organised societies, wherein methods of articulation of higher ideals and handing down superior forms of knowledge to successive generations can manifest.

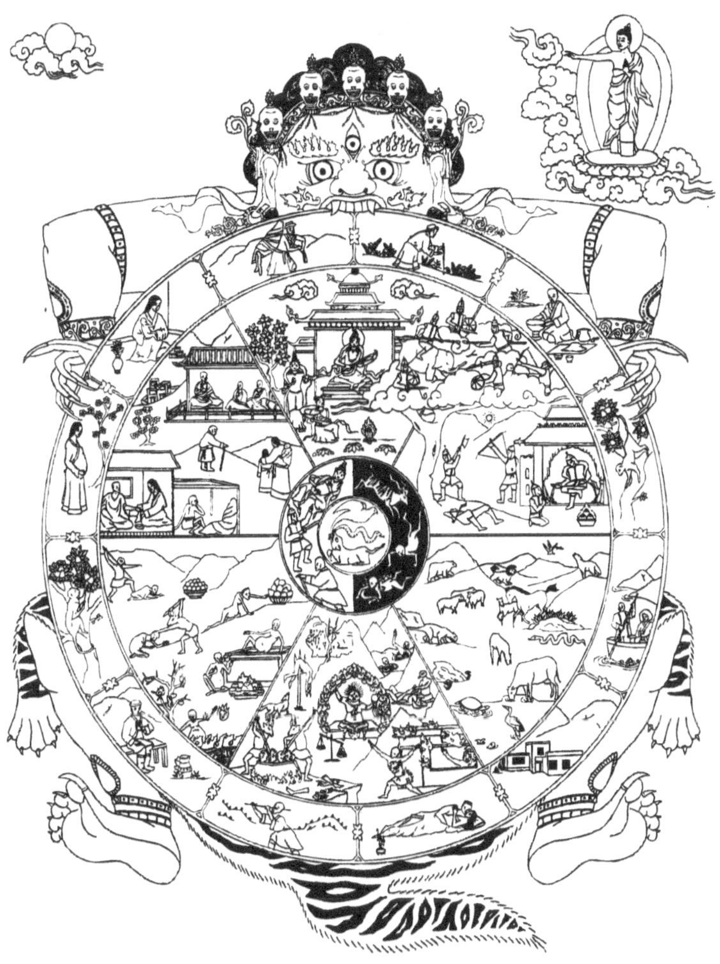

Figure 4. Illustration of the Six Realms

All are familiar with the attributes of this seventh evolutionary stage because that is what governs us today, wherein the desire-mind, glamour, selfishness, self will, all forms of *karma*-producing activities, are generated. As the great bulk of the teachings in this and all other books on the *dharma* deal with the consequences of such actions so there is no need to repeat them here. Some further information, however, can be provided concerning the nature of the Six Realms to help clarify the subject. A major exposé on the Six Reams shall not be delved into, however some of what was posited in Volumes 3 and 4 of this *Treatise on Mind* can be included here.[23] We saw also in *Karma and the Rebirth of Consciousness* the impossibility of direct human rebirth into the animal kingdom, but a symbolic and psychic truism is posited.

Lauf states:

> With the six Buddhas of the so-called wheel of life (S. bhavacakra; T. Srid-pa'i 'khor-lo), who appear on the sixth day of the bardo visions together with the five Tathāgatas and the eight Bodhisattvas, we come to the central ritual and symbolic portion of the Tibetan Book of the Dead. The six Buddhas are, among all the visionary figures of the bardo, the only ones to appear under the aspect of the nirmāṇakāya, that of the incarnated body. They are the six incarnated Buddhas (T. sPrul-sku thub-pa drug) as reincarnations of the great compassionate Bodhisattva Avalokiteśvara, and appear in the Srid-pa'i bardo as figures of salvation in the six realms of existence of karmically conditioned rebirth.[24]

Here a few extra comments can be made to what was earlier said concerning these realms in Volume 3, chapter 3 of this *Treatise on Mind*. From a *prāṇic* perspective the Six Realms can be viewed as:

a. The *human realm* is the place of generation of *prāṇas* conditioning all human relationships. Self-centred concepts and pride rule, but inevitably loving attitudes appear and once attachment to the

23 Anagarika Govinda presents an excellent account of the role of Avalokiteśvara, as well as that of the Dhyāni Buddhas in the Six Realms (as depicted in the *Bardo Thödol*), in his masterly *Foundations of Tibetan Mysticism*. The reader should supplement his account with my explanation, to gain an excellent appreciation of the teachings in the *Bardo Thödol* about this subject.

24 Lauf, 118.

attributes of *saṃsāra* are eliminated through the development of wisdom, then the evocation of *bodhicitta* is possible.

b. The *animal realm* concerns *prāṇas* generated via the Inner Round circulation carrying general emotions that are animal-like, hence delusional.
c. The *hell realms* are constituted of *prāṇas* generated by the most avaricious or violent human emotions of hateful or malicious intent, especially those engendered by sorcery.
d. The *preta realm* is generated by Watery *prāṇas* of pure desire or selfish emotional intensities.
e. The *asura realm* is generated by the *prāṇas* of intensified mental-desire, of thoughts that perpetuate love for aspects of *saṃsāra*. This produces a jealousy or envy of those that possess superior ethics, virtuous 'god-like skills', positions of authority or wealth, or who have developed enlightened attributes.
f. The *god realm*[25] in its lowest expression is generated by the *prāṇas* of lofty and even altruistic thoughts and idealisms (associated with the centres above the diaphragm), but which are still tainted by sentimentality, the 'self' concept, or loving-mind, hence demonstrate subtle illusions and forms of ignorance about the nature of phenomena. The more esoteric connotation is that it represents the liberated domains, wherein all such considerations have been eliminated.

The *prāṇas* that are completely rejected, being no longer useful to the incarnate individual, enter a zone of containment, called *the Eighth Sphere*. It is styled the 'eighth' because it contains that which cannot be sustained by the qualifications of the seven major *chakras*. It is a hell zone *(naraka)* when experienced because it contains the *prāṇas* that consciousness has eliminated and which would sicken it or stifle its growth if perpetuated in. Someday it must be re-experienced for conversion to more wholesome attributes, because it was created by

25 Note that the term 'god' here is a translation of the Sanskrit word *deva* (Tib. lha), which means 'shining one'. Though this word is generally interpreted as gods or deities it should not be confused with my rendering of the term in this *Treatise on Mind*, which refers to the feminine parallel kingdom in Nature to humanity. As elsewhere stated *devas* are agents of *karma*.

consciousness in a period of degenerate activity. It is unregenerate, and consequently has not been transformed into an expression useful for inclusion into the Sambhogakāya Flower. (There are permanent atoms that act as a store of such substance in the afterlife, prior to reincarnation.[26]) The Eighth Sphere therefore consists of the most concreted aspects of the substance of the Six Realms, however, ultimately all substance is resurrected through later cycles of outpouring and transmuted through wise, inspired activity.

There are said to be eight hot hells and eight cold hells. We can see by the number eight that they are assigned according to the wheel of direction of consciousness orientation in space. One octet embodies the *iḍā nāḍī* attribute, of those that manifest strong vile *saṃskāras* of the type associated with hatred and vituperation against others. Those who are extremely selfish and avaricious, where every action pertains to the accumulation of resources for oneself at the expense of all others, are found in the octet of the cold (murky and muddied) hells. (The *piṅgalā nāḍī* attribute.) The attributes of those in the hells are organised according to the orientation in space of the respective spokes of the wheel that best depicts the associated characteristic. They are relegated thus also by means of the eight spokes of Splenic centre II.

This said, it should be noted that the depictions of the types of torments and the reason why the occupants are in these hell states, as well as of the *asura, preta* and god realms, is an exoteric account, biased in terms of religious symbolism, and exaggerated. They should thus be modernised to tally with the truth of the way *saṃskāras* clothe the deceased and are actually experienced when the physical 'robe' is no longer possessed.

Because all phenomena is transitory, so even the worst of the hell states, *avīci* ('endless torture'), indicating never-ending flames or torment, said to be experienced by those (i.e., the dark brotherhood) that have reviled the *buddhadharma,* or killed monks or saints, ends sometime. (These dark, evil ones have destroyed the promulgators of

---

26 The permanent atoms are consequently important. They exist within the precincts of the Sambhogakāya Flower, and are the mechanism of incarnation, via which the substance of the periodical sheaths are built. The explication of their nature, however, lies outside the main theme of this treatise.

goodness and wisdom in any society.) There is said to be a transition hell *(pratekya hell,* a type of purgatory) through which those escaping a hell state travel after they begin to overcome some of the aspects that put them into the original hell state. *Avīci* should not be considered a locality, but rather a karmic set of conditions that follows one, even whilst physically incarnate. Indeed, it is easy to perceive many in the world that experience such conditions.

We should also note that the twelve petalled Splenic centre I is a lower expression (the activity aspect) of the Heart centre and therefore they can be analysed together. Similarly with the eight petalled Diaphragm centre and the eight petalled Splenic centre II. Each pair is actually part of a triplicity, making an esoteric grouping of six *chakras*, from which are derived the Buddhist concept of the Six Realms. As a mental-emotional construct[27] the Six Realms are the results of the reject *prāṇas* from these six *chakras*, and are processed by Splenic centre II. The number of petals involved is 36 + 24, making 60 in all, or twelve streams of the five different types of *prāṇas*.[28] We thus have:

The triplicity of the twelve petalled lotuses.

1. The twelve petals of the Heart in the Head lotus. The rejected *prāṇas* from this centre go to constitute the realm of the gods.
2. The twelve petals of the Heart centre, the rejected *prāṇas* producing the qualified conditionings of the human realm.
3. The twelve petalled Splenic centre, the rejected *prāṇas* of which produce the realm of the *asuras*. Effectively the *asuras* are jealous of the conditions experienced by those that reside above the diaphragm.

The triplicity of the eight petalled lotuses.

1. The eight petalled Diaphragm centre produces the realm of the *pretas*, as its refined Airy nature rejects the type of moisture (Watery

27 They are a construct of the human kingdom within the precincts of Nature's domain. After all, they are an expression of the *karma* of human folly. This is another reason why direct incarnation into the animal kingdom is not possible, as the animals play no part in the construction of the Six Realms, thus they have no *karma* with it.

28 From the viewpoint of the doctrine of the six consciousnesses we could also consider that they are processed by the ten petals of the Solar Plexus centre.

prāṇas) that feeds basic desire for *saṃsāric* allurements. The desires and emotions that remain after the activity of the Splenic centre must be removed from the *prāṇas* directed to the Heart centre. They are thus recycled to the centres below the diaphragm. The *karma* for strong attachment to things desired can thereby be cleansed.

2. The eight petalled Splenic centre II processes the various animal-like (emotional) *prāṇas* throughout the body. It therefore specifically controls the form of rebirth symbolised by the animal kingdom. These Watery *prāṇas* are ubiquitous for the general human population, and are exorcised from the system via the theriomorphic deities.
3. The sewer-like reject *prāṇas* from Splenic centre II, deposited in the Eighth Sphere, produces the conditionings of the hell realms.

In viewing the above we must note that all is mind-conditioned. Therefore the forms of sentience contained as one's *prāṇic* attributes within the body become externalised after one's death. These *saṃskāras* then clothe the individual, effectively becoming the corporeal form. When experienced with those that have generated similar *saṃskāric* tendencies then the conditions purported to the Six Realms manifest. The view, however, is in terms of the belief systems of Buddhism. There exist (astral) scenarios produced by human consciousness that parallel conditionings found physically, but more vibrantly and immediately conditioned by thought.[29] The *preta* and *asura* conditionings pertain to experience in the lower astral sub-planes, and are effectively hellish in nature because of the clothing *saṃskāras* whose vibratory effects must yet wear away. From this perspective the 'god' realms are the higher, exalted astral sub-planes wherein people live out the *karma* of the loving, affectionate *saṃskāras* and those of generosity that were generated. Those in the lower domains, consisting of squalid, murky and foul substance, naturally manifest envy when the brilliance of the higher domains and the residents therein are glimpsed. It is all part of the educative process of *karma* to assist the miscreants to generate better attitudes in the next rebirth.

The Six Realms are representations of the psychic constitution of the human persona, and also correlate to the places of repository

29 See Volume 4, chapter 4, entitled 'The Discriminatory Mind and Dimensionality'.

(*chakras*) wherein *saṃskāras* are stored and experienced. There we have the conditions that produce the Six Realms in the human psyche. The obvious deduction is; if all forms of karmic interrelationships and mental-emotional volitions become *saṃskāras,* they must become the *prāṇas* that circulate within a person's *nāḍīs.* When that individual dies and enters into the Bardo state (Srid-pa'i bardo[30]), he/she then resides in their vital body *(nāḍis),* thus specifically in that portion associated with the major *chakra* that was the onus of expression when incarnate. The *chakras* have not ceased, and now the individual awakens to the potency stored in their petals, the *prāṇas* manifest in the form of the colours and associated visions described in the various 'days' of experience in the *Bardo Thödol.*

What is first observed when meditating upon the Six Realms is the nature of a *maṇḍala* based upon the number six. With respect to the Jinas, their Consorts and their effects upon Nature, we have *maṇḍalas* based upon the number five, of which the five sense-consciousnesses exemplify. The Guardians present the symbolism of the number four, and with the appearance of the Mahābodhisattvas we have the symbolism of the number eight to contemplate. The 5 + 1 Herukas can take a role in terms of the number six in assisting the transformation of the *saṃskāras* pertaining to the Six Realms. They represent the mechanisms whereby the associated colours from the eighth to the fourteenth days can come to be rightly recognised in the Bardo state prior to birth into one of these realms.

A basis to comprehend the meaning of the number six is found in the Sacral centre, a six-petalled lotus. It overlaps the Base of Spine centre, which has four petals. These centres (and numbers) are the foundation for the mode of construction of all the major *chakras.* Avalokiteśvara's sacrificial compassion functions via the integrated *maṇḍala* of the *chakra* system. His 4, 8, and (symbolic) 1,000 arms, represent multiples of the four petals of the Base of Spine centre.

The four arms are expressed in his seated (yogic) position, and for his standing position he bears a halo of arms. There is an inner eight representing the *dharmakāya,* the next 40 signifying the *sambhogakāya,* and the remaining five tiers of 142, 166, 190, 214 and 240 hands the

30 The intermediate state wherein a person is seeking rebirth.

nirmāṇakāya.[31] The mode of moving from the four Base of Spine petals to the symbolic 1,000 petals of the Head lotus happens via the six petals of the Sacral centre.[32] In other words, the six directions of the activity of its petals govern the focus of life's expression. Here then is effected the wheel of birth and death, which is ruled by the field of desire governed by this centre.

The movement is first towards the eight petals of Splenic centre II, as a foundation or preparatory expression for the awakening of the twelve petals of Splenic centre I. The number twelve is double the number of the six petals of the Sacral centre. However, the process first awakens the Inner Round series of minor *chakras,* where their combined number of petals is symbolised by the number of arms of the five *nirmāṇakāya* tiers of the seven tiers of arms (or hands) to Avalokiteśvara's iconic representation.[33]

Much of the symbolism of the Six Realms hinges upon the Sacral centre's method of distributing its *prāṇas* in the six directions possible to it. This centre's main role is as a distributor of *prāṇa,* specifically of the expression of desire, forms of which is the cause for birth into any of the Bardo states. It recirculates the reject *prāṇas* of the two types of above mentioned triplicities into the mainstream circulation for the individual to experience the related *saṃskāras.* Whilst incarnate in a physical body the person can modify these qualities in a positive or negative manner. When disincarnate, however, the individual lives out the expression of any of the major *saṃskāras,* which then become the Bardo state experienced.

Avalokiteśvara represents the principle of compassion, the adjudicating effect of the Lord of *karma* (here the Sambhogakāya Flower), working to rearrange the *karma* of each of the directions

31 See Govinda, *Foundations of Tibetan Mysticism,* 234, from where these numbers are derived.

32 The higher aspects of the symbolism of the 1,000 arms of Avalokiteśvara was explained in Volume 4, chapter 10, under the heading 'Avalokiteśvara and the Sambhogakāya Flower'. This information should be integrated with what is provided here to produce a more complete picture.

33 The symbolism of the number seven can be interpreted in terms of the seven Rays, *chakras* and planes of perception, which these tiers of hands are governed by or administer energies to.

of the dynamo expressed by the Sacral centre, so that there is a way of escape from the *saṃskāric* conditionings that the personal-I experiences in any Bardo level. This represents the method whereby the Sambhogakāya Flower influences the evolution of the personal-I via the related progressive awakening of the *sahasrāra padma,* the 1,000 petalled lotus. It nominally manifests the same number of petals as the arms possessed by Avalokiteśvara as Lord of Compassion because it is the synthesising centre. All happenings below the diaphragm are expressed within its constitution. That below the diaphragm is the field of generation and conversion, and that above is the arena of storage, further refinement and (hopefully) decisive direction.

The *sahasrāra padma* stands at one end of the *chakra* system and is the higher correspondence of the combined ten petals of the Sacral and Base of Spine *chakras.* The entire story of awakening the *chakras* is found in the interrelation between these two centres.

The number 40 of Avalokiteśvara's *sambhogakāya* tier refers to directing groups of the four main Elements from the Head lotus through the *nāḍīs* via the five *prāṇas* of sense-consciousnesses they bear. This movement can be viewed in terms of their *iḍā* and *piṇgalā prāṇas,* or in terms of the eight-armed cross of direction in space. The *sambhogakāya* tier thus represents the subjective, compassionate circulation of these *prāṇas.* The five *nirmāṇakāya* tiers detail the mode of conveyance of these *prāṇas* from the five tiers of petals of the Head lotus, viewed in terms of the five sense-consciousnesses. The purpose of the hands (each bearing a compliment of five *prāṇas* through five fingers) therefore is to transform the base *saṃskāras* conveyed in the *nāḍīs* into the attributes of enlightenment. Representing the fields of compassion, the numbers allotted to these tiers of hands must be interpreted esoterically. Because the representation is symbolic, the numerology can be deciphered by looking to the numbers 42, 66, 90, 14 and 24 (Disregarding therefore the one and two hundreds, which numerologically refer to the demonstration of the energies of Will and Love-Wisdom.) These numbers are the significant numbers related to the organisation of the inner Heart and Throat tiers of petals in the Head lotus, and will be explained in chapter seven. (The number 42, for instance, is immediately cognisant to refer to the energies of the Peaceful Deities.) That chapter will show how these tiers express the energies conveying enlightenment, which each of Avalokiteśvara's hands help to produce.

The number 240 = 12 x 20 of the final tier represents the major petals of the Head lotus, and the five main *prāṇas* processed by them in terms of the four quadrants of space. From them emanate the *prāṇas* from the hands directed to the Solar Plexus centre (the number 2 x 10) and Splenic centre I (the number 12). The postulate here, without writing a thesis on the intricacies of the Inner Round circulation below the diaphragm, is that Avalokiteśvara's compassionate hands work to assist the conversion of aberrant *saṃskāras* generated there into compassionate attributes. As the Sacral centre is the powerhouse and directing centre for these *prāṇas,* so special attention is needed here, namely that of Avalokiteśvara's involvement with the Six Realms.

Avalokiteśvara is the prototype Bodhisattva and embodies the compassion (*bodhicitta*) that Bodhisattvas must garner and express in their various ways. He therefore appears at this stage as a precursor and example for all later Bodhisattvic activity by humanity. He shows what needs to be done concerning the transmutation of base *saṃskāras* (as applicable to the symbolism of the Six Realms) to develop the qualities of the Buddhas that rule each of the realms respectively. His six syllabled mantra, Oṁ Maṇi Padme Hūṁ, intoned by Tibetans to evoke great compassion for the denizens of the Six Realms, also plays its role in that each of the syllables relate to one or other of the Six Realms.

The syllable *Oṁ* is also intoned in meditation to assist in overcoming *saṃskāras* of elated subtle ignorance from the realm of the gods. They are the knowledgeable attributes of mind that people possess, gained from any society's preoccupation with itself. The 'gods' here thus effectively represent the content of the major petals of the *sahasrāra padma,* the major thought forms derived from activities in the world of learning through experience and well-meaning social intercourse. This concerns the process that will allow one to eventually command, in the guise of Avalokiteśvara's white Buddha form, the orderly awakening of the Head lotus with a lute that masters all mantric intonations. Then all light grey reject *prāṇas*[34] will be totally converted or dispelled by the energy at the disposal of the *yogin.* All forms of ignorance are thereby

34 The text states a dull white colour.

converted and eliminated. The white Buddha invokes the deep blue energy of the Dharmadhātu Wisdom of Vairocana to integrate Aetheric energies into the Head lotus.

Note that the body of Vairocana is white whereas his emanation is deep blue, whilst that of Akṣobhya (whose body is deep blue) is white. We can presume an interchangeability of function here. The deep (indigo) blue is the colour of Love-Wisdom *(bodhicitta),* whilst the white (which in reality is iridescent, with the colours of the rainbow implied) expresses the energies of the *dharmakāya* into *saṃsāra.* Vairocana embodies it and projects it via Akṣobhya in the form of *bodhicitta.* Akṣobhya then projects the *bodhicitta* in a form capable of being expressed by those below his exalted realm in the form of the Ray energies veiled by the white colouration.

All of the colours attributed to the denizens of the Six Realms are logically dull in appearance, signifying the low grade energy states of the accompanying *prāṇas.* The assigned colours, however, are general approximations of the associated characteristics depicted.

The dull white (hence greyish) for the general *prāṇas* of the Head lotus at this level of expression implicates the fact that white is a composite of all the other colours of the rainbow (hence *manasic saṃskāras),* whist grey represents the aberrant nature of the *prāṇas.* It should be noted however that the general colour of the intellect is the saffron colour of the robes that Theravada monks wear.[35]

The syllable *ma* assists in overcoming the reject *prāṇas* of envy (said to be of a dull red colouration) from the realm of the quarrelling Titans (the *asuras*), concerning the activity of the twelve-petalled Splenic centre I. This dull red colour signifies the selfish personal will that is generated to obtain things desired, whether possessed by others, or espoused as highly desirable in society, such as enormous wealth. The struggle and strife associated with this realm involves overcoming the sum of the selfish attributes developed by the personal 'self', so that they can either be accepted as part of the serene ego-less pool of *prāṇas* of the Heart lotus, or else be directed via the Throat to the Head centre. A

35 Though flawed, C.W. Leadbeater's, *Man, Visible and Invisible,* (Theosophical Publishing House, Adyar) provides a useful clairvoyant investigation of the meaning of auric colourings.

flaming sword of wisdom and right discriminative knowledge is used to transform *saṃskāras* of envy, of intensified selfishness and jealousy arising from not being able to possess what others have, into their enlightened attributes. As one aspires, so the mind begins to embrace the lofty ideas of the truly enlightened and thus manifest wisdom. Here the *yogin* takes the guise of Avalokiteśvara's green Buddha form, which counters these dull red *prāṇas*. The All-accomplishing Wisdom of Amoghasiddhi is invoked to convert all mind-concepts of the 'self', and its comparisons to the opinions of other 'selves'. All *saṃskāras* are to be converted into enlightenment attributes. Thus the sum total of Earthy *prāṇas* are transmuted and incorporated as the qualities of the 1,000 petalled lotus.

Red is complimentary (and the higher octave) to the green colour associated with the animal world (which is situated on the opposite spoke of the wheel of the Six Realms). Grey-green is the auric colouration for selfishness, the base characteristic of most humans. (Which becomes tinged with red according to the strength of the will developed to obtain what is desired.) Therefore we have the major attributes dealt with by the theriomorphic deities that work to overcome the wrathful propensities of the animal-like *prāṇas* generated through such activity. The green colour of Amoghasiddhi's wisdom then becomes the antidote to this all-pervasive attribute generated by human society.

The syllable *ṇi* is intoned to assist in overcoming the reject *prāṇas* of passions and desires of the human world, given as a general dull blue colour in the text. The Heart centre now becomes the dominant focus in the life of the *yogin* to produce the desirelessness, egolessness, and the spontaneous intrinsic wisdom of the enlightened. All forms of experiences in every realm are thus possible, and it is the only realm wherein enlightenment can be gained to make one a Buddha. This necessitates the evocation of the way of the Heart, from whence emanates *bodhicitta*. Therefore Avalokiteśvara appears here with an alms bowl and a staff, to walk the path of becoming a Buddha. The colour developed is the yellow (the golden emanation of the Heart centre) of Ratnasambhava's Equalising Wisdom, to conquer and transmute all Watery *prāṇas*.

The dull blue colour here is a generic for the type of devotional and aspirational ambition that makes people want to 'reach for the sky' and to claim what is gained for themselves. It therefore implicates their loftier aspirations to accomplish great works and to shine in the world, to overcome glamour-forming tendencies. Great accomplishments in our societies produce the types of prideful display associated with this arm of the wheel of the Six Realms. Pride for example, produces a reddish-orange tinge[36] to the developed *saṃskāras*.

The yellow antidote of Ratnasambhava's wisdom introduces the potency of the Sambhogakāya Flower to overcome the delusional ego-posturing aspects generated by the personal-I. Much *karma* passes before the incarnate ones learn the lessons of dispassion, humbleness and compassion that produce harmonious uplifting attributes in society.

The syllable *pa* is intoned to assist in overcoming the reject *prāṇas* of animal-like propensities, depicted as ignorance and dumbness. This relates to the work of the superimposed eight petalled Splenic centre II. This centre is the powerhouse for the circulation and redirection of all major *prāṇas* generated below the diaphragm, rejecting the non viable ones. Needed *prāṇas* are recycled via the Solar Plexus centre and the *prāṇas* that can be transformed into the way of the Heart are directed upwards to the twelve petalled Splenic centre I. These fear and emotion-driven animal-like propensities are consequently the major *saṃskāras* generated by humanity. Avalokiteśvara thus appears as a blue Buddha with a book in his hand to teach discursive thought and right knowledge of how to overcome all forms of ignorance. All Knowledge Holding deities come into play to assist people to overcome all of these animal-like *saṃskāras* and find the way out of this realm. No Jina attribute is ascribed here (there being Six Realms and only five Jinas) because in reality no rebirth into the animal kingdom is possible, whereas the other aspects of the Six Realms signify zones of general incarnation for humans.[37] This animal realm, however, signifies the general emotional traits generated by people. They are of a grey-green colouration, signifying the underlying selfishness and adaptability to the tribulations of life in *saṃsāra*. When intensified or exaggerated then we have the generation of the qualities that propel one into the *asura* world.

The syllable *(d)me* is intoned to assist the overcoming of reject

36 The reddish colouration increases with the intensity of the pride.

37 For a detailed explanation see my earlier book, *Karma and the Rebirth of Consciousness.*

prāṇas from the avarice and greed-ridden world of the *pretas*. These *prāṇas* are the most deforming attributes in the human psyche. We thus have the characteristics attributed to the *pretas,* distended bellies, small mouths, etc. It is the eight petalled Diaphragm centre's purpose to direct *prāṇas* to the centres above or those below the diaphragm, rejecting all desire-ridden and avaricious *saṃskāras* from entering the region above the diaphragm.

Avalokiteśvara appears as a red Buddha carrying a receptacle full of spiritual food and nourishment to act as an elixir of liberation from the sufferings associated with extensive cupidity, avarice, etc., if they would but properly taste and savour the associated revelations. This elixir counters the dull yellow *prāṇas* said to be associated with this realm.

The yellow colouring is the main energy that ties humans to *saṃsāra* by means of rebirth, being the main colouration governing their kingdom.[38] It is the primary hue conditioning the astral realm into which the deceased is born. The yellow is easily distorted to take on the red-brownish hue of avarice, the grey-greenish hues of deceit, and all other murky colourations of the lower psyche.

The red-orange energy of Amitābha's Discriminative Inner Wisdom is the antidote to these aberrant emotions because clear rational thoughts from the mind must be utilised to understand the nature of the extremities of desire posed in this domain, and to logicise a way of release from addictive desires. This allows the generation of *prāṇas* to produce the qualities of the higher centres. Inevitably the attributes of Mind must be developed to completely master *saṃsāra.*

Finally, we have the seed syllable *Hūṁ,*[39] the prime emanation from the Heart centre to overcome all *saṃsāric* transgressions. It is thus the syllable that signifies the effect of *bodhicitta* in action. Only the strongest compassionate actions, as generated by the *Hūṁ* sound, can help overcome the allurements of the suffering ones ensconced in the hell zones. This word of power helps neutralise the strong emanations of the generated *saṃskāras* of these miserably contorted beings. These

38 The colour of the fourth Ray of Beautifying Harmony overcoming Strife governing this fourth kingdom in Nature.

39 See Govinda, *Foundations of Tibetan Mysticism*, 186-189 for an excellent exposé of this seed syllable's meaning.

zones are the expressions derived from the sewer-like reject *prāṇas* from Splenic centre II, and are deposited into the Eighth Sphere. This process forms part of the mystery of the Inner Round set of minor *chakras*.

Here Avalokiteśvara appears as the king of the *dharma* (*dharmarāja*), an indigo blue Buddha, carrying fire and water in his hands to extinguish or relieve the agonised suffering of those trapped in these realms. The suffering was caused by their hatred for various forms of the livingness of loving life and for the cruelty inflicted upon others whilst incarnate. This blue colouring is that of the deepest Love that works to counter the emanations of the vilest greys, blacks, ruddy reds, and oranges created by those of these realms. Here we have a manifestation of Akṣobhya's Mirror-like Wisdom to counter the evil emanations of the sorcerers and black adepts that find their abodes within the morass of this substance. Enlightened qualities from the centres above the diaphragm must thereby be reflected to those below, whereby these debased *prāṇas* must be transformed into considerate and then compassionate attributes.

The strongest forces (veiled by the blue and carried by the silvery-white radiance of Akṣobhya) must be brought to bear upon the deep greys and blacks of the massed armies of evil intent if there exists any chance for their conversion to the right. The blue of Love imprisons these beings in an energy field they cannot penetrate, as Love is a quality they know not. It sets the boundaries of the hell zones and constitutes a door of release once qualities are generated that approximate the blue hue within the *avīci*. The Hūṁ sound then releases them from their bondage.

The turning of the wheel of the Heart centre (as well as that of Dependent Origination) is effectively expressed in the twelve forms of manifestation carried by the Buddhas of the Six Realms to relieve suffering and to effect the salvation of those ensnared by the lures and illusions of each of the realms.

- In the *god* realms we have a lute and its sounds. The octaves of mantric sound transform the subtleties of the remaining aberrant *saṃskāras* within the Head lotus.
- In the *asura* realm there is spiritual armour and a flaming sword. This armour is needed to protect the liberating one from the psychic emanations from this domain, and the strong *prāṇas* (light) from the

sword are directed towards transforming the *saṃskāras* possessed by the *'asuras'*.

- For *humans* we have an alms bowl and a staff. They must learn to walk the way of a disciple of the *dharma* to assured liberation from *saṃsāra.*
- With respect to the *animal* world we have a book and accompanying speech. The book of wisdom is needed to counter all theriomorphic propensities developed by humans. They must learn to counter animal-like forms of ignorance and dumbness with correct logic.
- For the *preta* domain we have a receptacle containing spiritual food and drink (*amṛta*). The spiritual food represents nourishing energies combined with appropriate teachings needed to assist the transformations of base *saṃskāras,* and to awaken the mind. The *amṛta* then energetically uplifts them up into the more vibrant (heavenly) domains.
- In the *hell* realms the Buddha appears with cleansing fire and nourishing water. The most intense fire is needed to transform the minds of those addicted to dark deeds and sorcery. The nourishing water of truth also helps wash clean the murky substance. Many times must the waters be rinsed through the fabric of *saṃskāras* that have been generated before the residents of this realm can rise above its conditionings. The water also quenches the ferocity of the *iḍā* attribute of the flames of the hot hells, and the fire dries up the murky, Watery disposition of the *piṇgalā* hells.

The Heart centre contains seven sacred petals and five non-sacred ones. The five non-sacred petals are those that receive tainted *prāṇas* associated with the five sense-consciousnesses, which can be contaminated with any of the allurements from the Six Realms.

The god realms represent the expression of the Aetheric Element and the perfection of the smell sense-consciousness wherein the subtlest of perceptions are experienced. The melodic sounds of a lute therefore suffice to awaken them from their revelry.

The human realm awakens the Airy Element and the subtle discriminations of the taste sense-consciousness, that will eventually allow them to experience the bliss of *śūnyatā*. The Airy Element is the conveyor of all the other qualities, hence all represent different aspects of the human conditionings.

The *asuras* embody the critical, analytical attributes of the Fiery Element and the sight sense-consciousness, which makes them envy the things they see but do not possess.

The *pretas* manifest the touch sense-consciousness associated with the Watery Element wherein abuse of the attributes of desire and attachment to phenomenal things can no longer nourish them. They must learn to eat and drink the spiritual food offered to counter their strong desires.

The animals embody the attributes of the Earthy Element of the most concrete aspects of *saṃsāra's* domain. Those therein must develop the hearing sense-consciousness and learn about higher forms of phenomena and knowledge that springs from wisdom's mouth.

Those in the hell states incorporate the worst attributes of all five of these sense-consciousnesses, hence liberation from the state they are found in is most difficult.

As the wheel of the Heart turns through cycle after cycle of purificatory activity so the methods and implements of the Buddhas are used to effectively dispel the aberrant *prāṇas* from the sacred spaces in the Heart. They are either transmuted or the *prāṇas* are recycled to one or other of the *chakras* below the diaphragm. There they reincarnate in the domain of whichever of the Six Realms that is commensurate with their qualities.

The *prāṇas* from the hell realms do not enter the Heart centre, but refined aspects from the other realms can be integrated with its intrinsic *bodhicitta*. The wisdoms of the five Dhyāni Buddhas are generated to help convert *prāṇas* via the specific petal of the Heart that may be the focus of expression at any time.

Pratītyasamutpāda

The twelve links of Dependent Origination (*pratītyasamutpāda*) are depicted as the rim of the wheel of the Six Realms. They are conditioned by the attributes of the twelve signs of the zodiac, via which one is continuously reborn until the Six Realms are conquered through mastery of the respective qualities of each sign. The symbolism of the zodiacal attributes are only hinted at because of the brevity of the images depicted, however the overall pattern of the zodiacal progress is discerned. From the perspective of experiences in *saṃsāra* the concerned wheel is that of the twelve petalled Splenic centre I. (The zodiac of the wheel of the Heart centre deals with the refined and transformed results of the related experiences below the diaphragm.) This astrological view presents the transference of Sacral centre *saṃskāras* (and the impetus of desire) via the turning of the eight spoked wheel of Splenic centre II until they are processed by Splenic centre I before possible inclusion into the Heart centre's circulation.

The symbolism depicted in images of the Wheel of Life (Tib. srid-paḥi ḥkor-lo) contain consistent elements, however various artistic variations do exist. Therefore, Govinda's depiction will be utilised, as it best describes the principles of the twelve stages of Dependent Origination.[40] The wheel itself is normally depicted with four concentric circles of images that summarise the conditionings that afflict the travails of human life in *saṃsāra*. The entire wheel is held by the teeth, hands and feet of Yama, the lord of death and 'king of the law' *(dharmarāja),* a form of Avalokiteśvara (who also holds a mirror in the hell realms, revealing to the miscreants there the truth about themselves). The teeth, hands and feet refer specifically to the three main Elements conditioning *saṃsāra,* the feet Earth, the hands Water, and the head Fire. The wheel therefore signifies the body of Yama. The central sphere consists of three animals holding each other's tails, signifying the three poisons of desire (red cock), hatred, aversion (green snake) and ignorance, delusion (black hog).

The next stage (omitted in Govinda's rendition) is divided into two, with a white half containing humans manifesting virtuous deeds, and a black half with human-like entities signifying various manifestations of forms of evil-doing. Next is the wheel depicting the various images signifying the Six Realms. The outer tier presents images pertaining to the twelve links *(nidāna)* of Dependent Origination.

The central triad of animals also signifies a unity, three in one. From this unity emanates a duality, or yin-yang, the swirling motion that moves the swastika governing evolutionary journeying. The number

40 Govinda, *Foundations of Tibetan Mysticism,* 241-7.

five is also implicated in this three plus two interrelation, signifying the general expression of the sense-consciousnesses to provide the basis for the development of the good and bad deeds generated by humanity. From this activity proceeds the Six Realms, whilst the movement of this wheel is regulated by the proceeds of the twelve *nidānas*.

We start with the ignorance *(avidyā),* or illusion of the concept of 'self' into which one is born, into being real. This is signified by the first sign of the zodiac, Aries the ram, denoting mental beginnings, which sets the entire course of the wheel in motion. This stage is represented as a blind woman trying to find her way in *saṃsāra* with a stick. The mind has not been developed, hence there is much reliance upon blind incentives and instinct supporting activities in the material domain.

Next is depicted the image of a potter, signifying the creation of thought forms, the ideas that clothe the mind with images of what is experienced, producing the volitions to act according to desire-impulses. We therefore have the generation of karmic formations *(saṃskāras)* that keep us bound to cyclic experiences. This stage is signified by the qualities of Taurus the bull, which controls the field of desire, and the substance that clothes the originating thoughts.

Third is the grasping tendencies of a monkey, thus developing elementary consciousness *(vijñāna).* The monkey swings through the branches of the trees in a forest (signifying mental images) grasping for object after object, similar to the initial stages of the development of consciousness. At this stage the *chakras* (the vegetation though which the monkey traverses) begin to awaken, allowing consciousness to form, and later to be refined. Here we have the attributes of Gemini the twins, which rules the *nāḍīs.* The twins are represented by the monkey and the objects in the environment that sustains its activity.

In the fourth stage, the attributes of the thinking principle incarnate properly, whereby consciousness develops the ability to name things by being thoroughly incorporated into the form. We therefore have the phrase 'name and form' *(nāma-rūpa)* attributed for this *nidāna.* The symbolism normally provided is a man in a boat steered by a ferryman. The man signifies the naming function and the journey he is on represents the progress the mind that names things takes. The water signifies the consciousness-stream that takes a new birth every life. The boat then represents the container of the mind and the ferryman the thinking principle (intellect) that steers it. The concept of prevision, of thinking forward by means of the development of the imagination (one of the main factors that distinguishes us from animals, i.e., the monkey of the previous link) is implied. The boat of mind is traversing the currents of *saṃsāra* to get to an objective destination (of the thought). Govinda's rendering is two men in a boat, which signifies the chattering function of the mind which speaks to itself as it names. This stage is expressed by the symbolism of Cancer the crab (a Water sign), which is the sign of incarnation (in this case of consciousness). The crab can traverse the watery environment to reach the shore of every new venture. The monkey associated with the previous link refers to the elementary child-like stage of the ability to think. Mind can now move in its own environment, but must learn to master the Waters.

The fifth *nidāna* develops the ability of consciousness to live in its own house that has six windows, which signifies the six senses *(ṣaḍāyatana),* where the sixth represents the intellect. (Which is the focus of this particular link.) The powers of the mind are now developed and self-consciousness dominates. In the earlier stage a ferryman (extraneous help) was needed to carry the mind to its purpose because it was carried by the Waters, over which the mind had little control. Now, however, the mind is dominant. This is symbolised by the sign Leo the lion, the sign of the powers of the ego, of self-consciousness, of the prideful concepts of the 'I' that rule the material and emotional domain. All of the windows pertaining to the senses are now active. Logically, one would expect the next five links of dependency to have veiled references to the development of the attributes of the five senses. Their existence is not immediately self-evident because of the elementary nature of the intelligent development by those ensconced in *saṃsāra* at that stage. Not yet present are the highly refined and clarified attributes associated with being able to pluck the fruits of the five Jina wisdoms. In terms of the Elements, the order presented is: Earth, Water, Fire, Air and Aether.

The sixth *nidāna* provides us with the symbolism of a pair of lovers. They have made contact *(sparsā),* but are not in full union. The mind (one lover) must yet fully comprehend all of the vicissitudes of the material domain (the other lover) it is infatuated with. There is so much to learn from experiencing the environment wherein one is born.

This stage is symbolised by the sign Virgo the virgin, who governs the entire material domain that is Nature. The associated Element is Earth and the hearing sense-consciousness comes to the fore, because all of the sounds of the material world must be comprehended, for there is much that is dangerous. At this stage the material domain is the focus for all sense contacts.

The seventh of the links concerns the attribute of 'feeling' *(vedanā)* and is symbolised by an arrow piercing the eye of a man. The sense-consciousness developed here is that of touch, contact with objects of sensation through desire, and the Watery Element is thereby developed. Emotional interrelationships of all types are implicated. The emotions are most virulent in the psyche of a normal person, but most people revel in its intoxicating intensities of happiness and sadness. Most of the *karma* that afflicts people is caused by means of their emotions, especially when fused with mind *(kāma-manas)*. This is symbolised by the arrow piercing the man's eye. The emotions cause many forms of blindness as to the nature of the real. The eye gazes upon what it desires and emotionally becomes attached to. This combination causes grief when one discovers that all is impermanent, and nothing that is material, generated by desire, emotional infatuation, or that can be grasped is permanent. Such realisation is governed by the attributes of Libra the balances, which also governs the cyclic outpouring of *karma* (the affliction of the arrow) into *saṃsāra*. The individual progresses from cycle to cycle of emotional expression until eventually the entire Watery domain from whence emotions spring can be mastered. The meditation path is then espoused (a Libran trait) to seek out the cause of the *māyā* (illusion).

Next we have the symbolism of a woman serving a drink to a person, with the attribute being thirst or craving *(tṛṣṇā)*. The thirst here is for more knowledge, comprehension of why, what, wherefore, how, etc. The path of knowledgeable pursuits ensues, necessitating control of all forms of emotional perturbations. The Fiery Element is thereby evoked, fully awakening the sight sense-consciousness. No blinding obfuscating arrow is allowed to remain. The battles between the field of desire, of what one emotionally craves, and the path of knowledgeable pursuits leading to the development of wisdom then manifests. Eventually the way of wisdom must rule, but the path thereto produces much mental-emotional turbulence, trials, tribulation and upheaval in a person's life. (The drunkenness that ensues from drinking too much liquor.) This process is governed by the attributes of Scorpio the scorpion which rules the path of discipleship and uses its sting to kill the objects of desire for things that the mind comprehends to be sources of pain and suffering.

The ninth of the dependent links is shown as a man gathering fruit, and the associated quality is 'clinging' *(upādāna).* (Other depictions reintroduce the monkey with fruit, representing the frivolous monkey-mind now seeking knowledge.) At this stage the path in life becomes divergent. The person may choose to intensify his/her attachments to life, of ambition to obtain more of what is desired; money, material comforts, sexual pleasures, or power over others. Or else the path to liberation from the incessant cycles of rebirth is sought. Either way we have the symbolism of Sagittarius the archer firing arrows. They can be of one-pointed desire and material plane incentives, or else we have arrows of aspiration to lofty ideals. Thus the fruits, the objects of desire or of high aspiration, are grasped and the resultant gain tasted. The Element developed is Air, producing lofty enlightened thoughts, or else the general *prāṇas* of human livingness.

The tenth image presented is that of sexual intercourse, with the associated attribute denoted as 'becoming' *(bhava).* (Other versions present a pregnant woman.) This act signifies the fruition of all of life's processes. One can interpret this in terms of being deeply intoxicated with the pleasures of *saṃsāra* so that nothing else matters; or else yogic ecstasy is achieved wherein the red and white fluids, *iḍā* and *piṇgalā,* wisdom and compassion, are merged in one. Here the attributes of Capricorn the goat are symbolised via the summit or mount of attainment wherein the gain of one's karmic involvement with the material domain is reached. The associated Element is Aether (the synthesis of all the other Elements) and the smell sense-consciousness is developed, wherein the subtlest impressions are obtained.

The eleventh image is that of a woman giving birth *(jātī),* signifying that the gain of life's expression is now recycled. The wheel begins again with the product of the former cycle of accomplishment projected forwards. Past experiences are relived, new impressions gained and the sense-consciousnesses further developed. Upon the enlightenment-path, however, the symbolism relates to the way of the Bodhisattva. After having attained Initiation upon the summit of the mount in Capricorn the Bodhisattva can now teach many young ones (children) coming to receive the beneficence and wisdom offered. The associated sign is Aquarius the water bearer, pouring the Waters of Life to vitalise any new venture. It signifies the free-flowing energies of the compassionate one manifesting beneficent activities. Though often frivolous and shallow, with everything possessed put forward for outward show, the average Aquarian also normally seeks out many new ideas and experiences, thus the various attributes life offers are experienced.

The final *nidāna* is depicted by a man bearing a corpse (signifying death, *maraṇa),* which sums up the significance or final accomplishment of the entire wheel, being maturity and death. Everything material must cease sometime, die and crumble to dust. Those who hang on to transient pursuits must learn this bitter lesson, and pain ensues if they are too attached to the corpse of all their desires and passions. Nothing is real, everything is an illusion, therefore it is best to strive for the verities of a spiritual life, for the liberation of it all. The final sign, Pisces the fishes, is the sign of termination, yet it also signifies bondage, of the union between the two fishes; the material and immaterial, form and Spirit, the Sambhogakāya Flower and the personality. The union allows the available *karma* to be experienced, as well as offering a line of abstraction into the inner realms before rebirth. The entire cycle is then renewed.

The *maṇḍala* of the human life process thus cyclically proceeds until all generated *prāṇas* are fit for the Heart centre's circulation, and another person stands liberated from *saṃsāra*. The bond between the two fishes is then broken.

The Mahābodhisattvas and the Sambhogakāya Flower

The *saṃskāric* qualities that the Wrathful Deities guard against must be appropriately dealt with by humanity. People must be taught what such *saṃskāras* are, their effects, and how not to generate them. We must reckon with the appearance of the eight Mahābodhisattvas and the effect of their work in Nature. The various grades of Bodhisattvas then manifest, to play their roles in the educational program of humanity. All forms of right human relationships, that produce the factor of goodwill and eventually the Will-to-Love, must be encouraged. Society thus gradually evolves for the better, where cooperativeness and the quest for enlightenment replaces competitiveness and separativeness. The world of the Bodhisattvas and Mahābodhisattvas (within Shambhala) will then gradually be revealed to humanity.

As the *maṇḍala* of these Mahābodhisattvas has been explained in the previous volume the reader therefore should refer to that text for detail.[41] This teaching can be integrated with the more recent information concerning the petals of the Sambhogakāya Flower. The correlations are not exact, rather they represent relationships that facilitate the work of the respective Mahābodhisattvas. Also, we saw above that their general effect upon humanity was to stimulate devotion to high ideals, and to provide the background teachings and testings for the Initiation of disciples. The Mahābodhisattvas also work in many different ways to produce the evolution of the kingdom of the Sambhogakāya Flower and its eventual liberation into *śūnyatā*. The work of the *devas* and *karma* are also taken into account.

The *Sacrifice—Love-Wisdom petal,* governed by Akṣobhya-Vajrasattva, mirrors the energies of Vairocana. The Dharmadhātu Wisdom becomes equally directed to the four directions and translated into the qualities of the eight accompanying Bodhisattvas. The *vayū* (wind)[42] is *vyāna*, and the Element is Aether.

The *Love-Wisdom—Sacrifice petal* corresponds to the northern direction of Amoghasiddhi, with the accompanying Bodhisattvas being Vajrapāṇi (north) and Samantabhadra (northwest), and their Consorts are Nṛtyā and Mālā respectively. The *vayū* is *prāṇa*, and the Elements are Air and Earth. Amoghasiddhi's All-Accomplishing Wisdom directs all experiences upwards to realms sublime, after converting them into the qualities utilisable by the enlightened one, or the Sambhogakāya Flower. The gross Earthy defilements must be transmuted into their most subjective Airy counterparts through the sacrificial potency of Love.

41 See Volume 4, chapter 11, entitled 'The Great Bodhisattvas and their Consorts'.

42 The term *vāyu* refers to any of the five Winds or *prāṇas* embodying the qualities of the five Alchemical Elements which course through the *nāḍī* system. They are termed *prāna* (Air), *samāna* (Water), *apāna* (Earth), *udāna* (Fire), and *vyāna* (Aether). Volume 6 will provide further information on these stages of *prānic* vitalisation.

The *Love-Wisdom—Love-Wisdom petal* is identified with the eastern direction of Akṣobhya, thus with the accompanying Bodhisattvas Kśitigarbha (east) and Mañjuśrī (northeast) and their Consorts Lāsyā and Ālokā. The Prāṇa is *udāna,* and the Elements are Fire and Air. Here the Fiery consciousness principle must be converted into the Airy Love-Wisdom normally associated with the eastern direction. Fuelled by the Airy principle the Fiery quality burns at its most intense and transmutes all impurities into the luminescence that is *bodhicitta.* The Airy quality pertains to the love part and the Fiery to the wisdom part of the dual Love-Wisdom aspect. Note that the principal energy that works its transmutative potency via the Sambhogakāya Flower is that from Akṣobhya,[43] therefore this Jina appears twice in this listing.

The *Love-Wisdom—Knowledge petal* is identified with the western direction of Amitābha. The accompanying Bodhisattvas are Avalokiteśvara (west) and Nivaraṇaviṣkambhin (southwest), and their Consorts Gitā and Ghandhā. The *vayū* is *samāna* and the Elements are Water and Fire. Right knowledge and discriminative wisdom must transform all emotional and devotional qualities into their highest forms of aspiration, and the ability to vision the real.

The *Knowledge—Love-Wisdom petal* is identified with the southern direction of Ratnasambhava. The accompanying Bodhisattvas are Ākāśagarbha (south), and Maitreya (southeast), and their Consorts Dhūpā and Puṣpā. The *vayū* is *apāna* and the Elements are Earth and Water. Here all of the gross *saṃsāric* experiences are melded (equalised) in the crucible of the enlightenment experience to produce the philosopher's stone. *Bodhicitta* is the Watery elixir (when viewed in terms of being a universal flux integrating all into the universality of liberation) that is added to the Earthy mineral that represents our *saṃskāras* in the material domain. There right knowledge must be wrought to produce enlightenment.

As the Equalising Wisdom of Ratnasambhava governs the Flower as a unit, so also when manifesting via the Sacrifice and Love-Wisdom pentads it works to integrate all impressions coming from the Head lotus so that they become increasingly more refined and sacrificial on their upward way to the *dharmakāya* experience.

---

43 His Mirror-like Wisdom essentially being an expression of the second Ray of Love-Wisdom.

When this list is integrated with that of the Vidyādhara Consorts, then the picture is more complete. These Consorts represent the *deva* (feminine) principle (the *iḍā nāḍī*) potencies enabling the existence of the *tathāgatagarbha*, whilst the Bodhisattvas represent the masculine (*piṅgalā*) potencies assisting in the general development of this kingdom. The *saṃskāras* converted via the assistance of the Herukas represent the *suṣumṇā nāḍī* stream. What is engendered is the Fiery quality that vitalises, and which will eventually produce the complete enlightenment that the Buddha *gotra* represents. The path to enlightenment concerns the transformation process that will eventually allow *kuṇḍalinī* to flow unimpeded in the *suṣumṇā nāḍī*. This necessitates the transformation of *saṃskāras* by means of the Will and Love-Wisdom that the Mahābodhisattvas embody.

The principle of Love-Wisdom manifests via the eight-spoked wheel of direction in space, whereby the eight Mahābodhisattvas find opportunity to express their service arenas. It signifies the qualities that will be gained through treading the Eight-fold Path and the form of the wisdoms derived from them.

The Mahābodhisattvas are the Lords of compassion working with all aspects and functions of the human condition, with the consciousness-streams of all human units. We saw earlier that they are not just Mind-constructs but also represent seats of power occupied by the Council of Bodhisattvas. As such they have their human representatives. They are Buddhas for all intents and purposes, except that they have not relinquished ties to earth conditionings, as the people of this earth need their ever-active compassionate activity to guide them to liberation. It is a way the Mahābodhisattvas know well, having travelled that path many times. They have travelled to 'the other shore', and know what is 'beyond', and yet remain. In their domain sacrificial Love-Wisdom reigns supreme. Oṁ Svāhā!

4

The Deities of the Bardo Thödol
Part Three:
The Blood-Drinking Herukas and the Mātaraḥ

The eighth stage of the evolutionary process and the Wrathful Deities

The present era of human development can now be analysed, where many people can be found to be transforming undesirable *saṃskāras*. In consciously working to convert forms of sensual, selfish, malicious, and avaricious engagement with *saṃsāra* they begin to tread the Bodhisattva path. On this path they encounter the protectors of the path, the host of Wrathful and theriomorphic Deities. The purpose of these entities is to guard the gates of Initiation and to assist the candidate to convert all defiling potencies into attributes of the white *dharma*. The defilements are generated in the centres below the diaphragm. Their mode of conversion in terms of the deities found from the thirteenth day onward in the *Bardo Thödol* can now be explained.

Stage 8.
The development of unselfish idealism and compassionate action.

This is a natural extension of the loving attitudes of the average person. It refers to the stage in the evolution of humanity where their livelihoods are based around the family unit. First tribal societies became the norm and eventually nations were formed, followed by civilisations that produced the incredible complexities of human life we have today. The development of the mental-emotional lifestyles that are nowadays so prevalent is governed by the unfolding properties of the Knowledge petals of the Sambhogakāya Flowers. When aspirants become interested in overcoming predilection for *saṃsāric* allurements they begin to battle these mental-emotional *saṃskāras* developed via many former lives of emotional activity. The animal-headed deities of the *Bardo Thödol* then manifest at a certain stage in the direct yogic transformation of consciousness. These deities can be collectively viewed as expressions of the (Watery) forces of the Inner Round, when controlled by the Solar Plexus centre. The emotional *saṃskāras* are animal-like because the animal kingdom develops these most elementary emotional attributes. The fearsome emotional potency found in humans, however, is generated by the added intensity of their minds.

Control of these potencies brings the *yogin* into a working relationship with the feminine Wrathful Deities. The highest of these are the eight Mātaraḥ (Tib. Keurima), who transform the mental constructs developed by the eight consciousnesses, and the eight Piśācī (Tib. Phra-men ma) concerned with the transformation of thoughts gained through contact via the sense-consciousnesses with objects. There are also the four animal headed female Gatekeepers[1] of the *maṇḍala*. Concerning them Lauf states that they are:

> The four heralds of the 28 powerful goddesses and also count as members of this group, in which they appear again. But basically they also appear in the death ritual apart from the group as the guardians of the four gates of the maṇḍala.[2]

Finally we have the twenty-eight powerful animal-headed goddesses (Īśvarī), who purify the aggregates of bewildered mental constructs. They produce the development of enlightened activity. When we add the twelve central male and female blood-drinking deities then we have the constitution of the centres below the diaphragm. These control and transform the base *saṃskāras* generated by the *saṃsāric* activities of the

---

1 Lauf calls the four protective deities of the *maṇḍala* of Peaceful Deities 'Guardians', whereas Gyurme calls them 'Gatekeepers'. Similarly the four female deities that guard the four directions of the *maṇḍala* of the Īśvarī are called 'Guardians' by Lauf and 'Gatekeepers' by Gyurme. To prevent confusion I shall term the four protectors of the Peaceful Deities 'Guardians' and their wrathful correspondences (of which there are two groups of four) 'Gatekeepers'.

2 Lauf, 149-50.

many incarnations of personal-I's constituting a consciousness-stream. Thus:

- The *twelve central blood-drinking deities* embody the functioning of the twelve petals of Splenic centre I. This centre forms an integral unity with Splenic centre II, in that certain petals are overlapped.
- The eight *Mātaraḥ* embody the functioning of the eight petals of the Diaphragm centre.
- The eight *Piśācī* embody the functioning of the superimposed Splenic centre II.
- The *four female Gatekeepers* embody the functioning of the four petals of the Base of Spine centre.

The significant symbolism of each grouping of deities can now be discussed in detail.

The twelve blood-drinking deities (Herukas)

Each of the six pairs of central male and female *blood-drinking deities* is said to emanate from 'the central channel branch of the skull, within one's brain, amidst an expanse of light composed of flaming seminal points of rainbow-light'.[3] The order in which they come is:

> Samantabhadhra in the form of Mahottara Heruka. He has three faces: brown, white and red; and six arms: The three right arms brandish a vajra, a khaṭvāṅga, and a small drum, And the left hold a bell, a blood-filled skull, and a noose of entrails. Mahottara Heruka is joyously and indivisibly embraced by Krodheśvarī[4]...
>
> Vairocana in the form of Buddha Heruka. He has three faces: reddish brown, white and red; and six arms: The three right arms brandish a wheel, an axe, and a sword, And the left hold a bell, a ploughshare, and a blood-filled skull. Buddha Heruka is joyously and indivisibly embraced by Buddhakrodheśvarī[5]...
>
> Vajrasattva in the form of Vajra Heruka. He has three faces: dark blue, white and red; and six arms: The three right arms brandish

3 Gyurme Dorje, *The Tibetan Book of the Dead,* 78.

4 Ibid., 78-9.

5 Ibid., 79.

> a vajra, a skull, and an axe, And the left hold a bell, a blood-filled skull, and a ploughshare. Vajra Heruka is joyously and indivisibly embraced by Vajrakrodheśvarī[6]...
>
> Ratnasambhava in the form of Ratna Heruka. He has three faces: dark yellow, white and red; and six arms: The three right arms brandish a jewel, a khaṭvāṅga, and a club, And the left hold a bell, a blood-filled skull, and a trident. Ratna Heruka is joyously and indivisibly embraced by Ratnakrodheśvarī[7]...
>
> Amitābha in the form of Padma Heruka. He has three faces: dark red, white and blue; and six arms: The three right arms brandish a lotus, a khaṭvāṅga, and a mace, And the left hold a bell, a blood-filled skull, and a small drum. Padma Heruka is joyously and indivisibly embraced by Padmakrodheśvarī[8]...
>
> Amoghasiddhi in the form of Karma Heruka. He has three faces: dark green, white and red; and six arms: The three right arms brandish a sword, a khaṭvāṅga, and a mace, And the left hold a bell, a blood-filled skull, and a ploughshare. Karma Heruka is joyously and indivisibly embraced by Karmakrodheśvarī[9]...

Figure 5 is adapted from a similar figure in Volume 3, chapter 3 of this *Treatise on Mind,* which provides the background to this present chapter. It represents the middle path that provides the awakening of the Heart centre. The names of the Wrathful Deities have been placed upon the appropriate spoke of the wheel. The placing of the Herukas is based principally upon the qualities of the respective zodiacal sign that governs the attributes of the spokes of the wheel of Splenic centre I that best suits the Heruka-Krodheśvarī pair.[10] The arrangement can also be viewed in terms of the mode of expression of the seven sacred petals and the five non-sacred petals of the Heart centre. The Consort of the Heruka rules the polar opposite of the sign he governs. As the

6 Ibid.

7 Ibid., 80.

8 Ibid.

9 Ibid.

10 The normal assignment of east to Vajra Heruka, south to Ratna Heruka, etc., based upon the position of their corresponding Dhyāni Buddhas are not applicable here.

petals move from Heruka to Consort, we essentially have the story of what is developed and cleansed in her 'womb'. The related purified *saṃskāra* represents the 'child', or Jina attribute that is growing therein. This is the wisdom quality that the transmuted *saṃskāra* becomes.

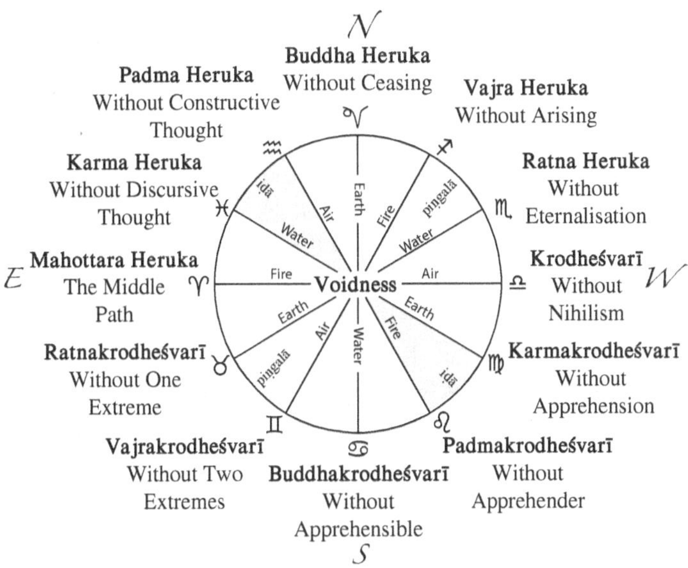

Figure 5: The twelve petalled lotus of Splenic centre I

The attributes given to the rulership of the petals of the various major *chakras* can change over time. Different *maṇḍalic* arrangements come into play according to the stage of development of an individual. Each of the four petals of the Base of Spine centre, for instance, take turns in pointing north, depending upon which of the major Elements is to govern the evolutionary play at any time. This will then affect the orientation of the major petals of the other *chakras*. Generally, the attributions presented in this text relate to the path of discipleship wherein yogic practices are accomplished.

Each of the Herukas are similarly depicted, with three heads of various colourings, four legs and six arms holding different implements, and they are in ecstatic union with their Consorts. When one studies the list we see that generally one of the heads corresponds to the colour of the particular Jina to which it is the wrathful aspect, and the other two heads are red and white. These two colours stand respectfully for the male seminal seed (white) manifesting the masculine attribute of compassion, symbolising the attributes of the *piṅgalā nāḍī,* and the red 'blood' of the woman symbolising her developed wisdom attribute associated with the *iḍā nāḍī* flow. These two *prāṇic* attributes course throughout the entire *maṇḍala* of the wheel. The yab-yum interrelation between Heruka and Consort symbolises the flow of the *kuṇḍalinī* energy along the *suṣumṇā nāḍī,* taken along any axis of the six directions from Consort to partner. This allows the proper processing and integration of the *prāṇas* directed from the groups of six theriomorphic female wrathful entities explained below.

We saw in the last chapter how the Buddha Herukas work in the Head lotus to integrate its *prāṇas* with the Sambhogakāya Flower. In this section we will look to the effect of their forces below the diaphragm. The focus here is upon their Consorts. The petals relegated to the Herukas in Splenic centre I interrelate with associated petals in the Head centre, stimulating their development. These petals represent the main zones of storage of the transformed *prāṇas* from below the diaphragm. The *prāṇas* are received via the petals relegated to the Heruka Consorts, as admixed in the general circulation of Splenic centre I. They are either projected to their corresponding petals in the Head lotus, or else are recycled to Splenic centre II.

In the diagram of the Head lotus (see chapter 7, Figure 19) we see that there are six tiers of minor petals that absorb the *prāṇas* from the six petals of the Sacral centre. They are incorporated into three larger tiers designated Earthy petals. (These *prāṇas* relate to the five sense-consciousnesses plus that of the integrating intellect.) The Head centre then processes them according to its internal organisation. An acorn of nine of these Earthy petals are then incorporated into a synthesising tenth. Here all of the Watery *prāṇas* below the diaphragm are integrated. They absorb the expression of the ten petals of the Solar Plexus centre at any particular time or cycle of activity of Watery *saṃskāras.* In this way the *saṃskāras* that affect consciousness, as generated by the normal life experiences of an individual, get assimilated into the constitution of the Head lotus. With respect to this, it can also be added that the major petals of the Head lotus dealing with the Fiery Element assimilate the *prāṇas* from the Throat centre, and those designated Airy are repositories of the *prāṇas* from the Heart centre.

Mahottara Heruka (an emanation of Samantabhadra) and his Consort Krodheśvarī are orientated along the east-west direction of the wheel (Aries-Libra), as this represents the beginning (the sign Aries the ram) of the turning of the wheel of the Law (Libra the balances) for the entire process. Here then we have the mode of the expression of the regulatory *karma* governing each cycle of activity for all of the Herukas and their Consorts, and in turn, of the entire *maṇḍala* of the Wrathful and theriomorphic deities. Libra also governs the entire meditation process, of the interlude between breaths, and also the cycles of activity. In conjunction with the east-west polarisation of this pair we have the way of the 'middle path' represented, where the stipulation of the Consort's direction of moving from the Heart to the west, and outwards into activity is that it shall be 'without nihilism'. Neither the nihilistic attitude of thinking that *śūnyatā* is the extinction of everything; or of atheistically eschewing the divine in Life, is warranted. A panoply of Peaceful and Wrathful Deities then comes into view.

From the perspective of the *chakras,* it was stated in Volume 3 of this *Treatise on Mind* that the middle path consists of the integral combination of the Heart, Diaphragm, and Splenic centres. This trinity stands midway between the Heart in the Head lotus (its central tier of petals[11]), and the Sacral and Base of Spine centres in the lower part of the body. This makes it the 'middle' in terms of the entire *maṇḍala* of the *nāḍī* system. The focus of this trinity concerns the expression of the *piṇgalā* circulation and the way the second Ray of Love-Wisdom (*bodhicitta*) is *prāṇically* generated. It therefore involves the *chakras* focused upon the generation and expression of this Ray line[12]. When connected to the Head centre we have a group of five *chakras:* the Heart, Diaphragm, Splenic Centre I, Solar Plexus and Sacral centres, representing the qualities of the *piṇgalā* path within the Dharmakāya Way. These *chakras* exemplify the expression of the compassion aspect of the five Dhyāni Bodhisattvas. When the *prāṇas* of these five

11 From this perspective the Solar Plexus in the Head represents the outermost tier of petals to the *sahasrāra padma.*

12 The second, fourth and sixth Rays.

centres have been properly evoked and cleansed of defilements then the experience of *śūnyatā* is possible. The *iḍā* path consists principally of the Ājñā, Throat, Solar Plexus, Splenic centre II and Sacral centres. This path develops great intelligence. The attributes of the Consorts of the Dhyāni Bodhisattvas are evoked here.

The Solar Plexus centre appears in both lists because it is the abdominal brain and effectively is the generator and integrator of all *prāṇas* in terms of the attributes of the desire-mind. The Sacral centre is viewed as the generator of the vital *prāṇas* for both *nāḍīs* that sustain the entire system. When both the *iḍā* and *piṅgalā* paths are integrated and the *prāṇas* are being controlled, then the Dharmakāya way is evident.

The Arian petal designated the *'middle path'* at first relates to the most wilful *saṃskāras* developed by the personal-I. The will must be converted to the Will-to Good for all beings, and then the higher Wills, if the awakening of the above-mentioned *chakras* is to be achieved. It should be understood that the more intense the will utilised the stronger or more problematic the *saṃskāras* generated (e.g., of hatreds, anger, spite), necessitating eventually the generation of an equal counterbalancing force to master them. The generation of the middle path from the perspective of the will is a great challenge. Technically a herculean task, yet it must be accomplished if enlightenment is to be achieved. The conversion of personal will necessitates the practice of calm-abiding (*śamatha*), which produces the middle between extremes; of *saṁsāra* and *śūnyatā*, or between self will and Divine Will. The transformation of passionate *saṃskāras* is obtained via the generation of serene thoughts. This becomes the platform that inevitably allows the highest insights from *dharmakāya* to impress the mind, but the impressions must be held steady in an adamantine embrace of the mind's developed Will-to-Love.

The auric field of the zone of peace must therefore be intensified by means of the developed will, to produce a radiance known as the Clear Mind. This necessitates proper yogic control of the processes incorporated in the entire wheel, as depicted below. Its purpose is to integrate all of the converted *prāṇas* from the Splenic centre into the Heart centre. The process forms the bridge or nexus between *saṁsāra* and *śūnyatā* when the energies of the Throat centre are also rightly utilised.

The brown colour[13] of Mahottara Heruka's body and central face refers to the general colouring of the *prāṇas* of base desire and sensuality, which the Wrathful Deities deal with in the process of converting *saṃskāras*. Esoterically, however, this colour is a fusion of the red, blue and green of the three major Rays, signifying the triune power that turns the entire Wheel of Life.

Plate 8. Mahottara Heruka and Consort

The implements held by the Herukas refer to the *saṃskāras* to be converted in terms of their future compassionate (*piṇgalā*) or wisdom (*iḍā*) quality. The symbols in the right hands of Mahottara (relating

13 The meaning of the alternate smoke colour was earlier explained.

to the mechanism of control of *piṅgalā* attributes of *saṃskāras*) are a *vajra*, a *khaṭvāṅga*, and a *ḍamaru* (drum). The symbols of the left hands (*iḍā* attributes) are a bell, a blood-filled skull, and a noose of entrails. The three implements for each grouping can be viewed in terms of an all-powerful directive Will/Power attribute (*khaṭvāṅga, vajra*), a consciousness-transforming attribute (bell, blood-filled skull), and that relating to governing the expression of attributes of *saṃsāra* (*ḍamaru*, noose of entrails). All forms of *saṃskāras* can then be adequately dealt with, as regulated by the three *guṇas*. Thus all defilements are converted in relation to the major energy qualification by means of the respective enlightened Will (*suṣumṇā*), Love-Wisdom (*piṅgalā*), or enlightened Activity (*iḍā*).

The adamantine power or force of the *dharma,* symbolised by the *vajra,* is used to convert all wilful attributes that lead to or are expressions of dark conjurations into compassionate evocations. The sevenfold attributes of the *khaṭvāṅga* are utilised to convert the mindful consciousness volitions of the will into compassionate thoughts along any of the seven Ray lines. The small drum is utilised to emanate rhythmic mantric sound to shatter wilful attachment to various *saṃsāric* allurements, so that mastery of each type of allurement can be utilised as an aid to conquer others.

The emptiness of phenomena signified by the bell is utilised to awaken consciousness from the dream that *saṃsāra* is the only reality. It produces a wisdom relating to the perception of the existence of higher consciousness-states.[14] The blood-filled skull *(kapāla)* represents the *prāṇa* of the transmuted essence of the defiled mind. It offers the *amṛtā* of revelatory images that overcome the illusions gained through excessive materialistic focus. The 'noose of entrails' (the ensnaring emotions that through attachment to worldly things binds us to incarnation) reinforces the understanding that all attachments to materialistic allurements produce cyclic death-filled transience. One should lasso the truth concerning *saṃsāra* instead, to find the way to liberation into enlightenment's domain. The symbolism of all these functions can be transposed to the other Herukas that hold similar implements.

The polar opposite of the petal embodied by Mahottara Heruka is

---

14 Or consciousness-space, that the clear liberating sound of the bell reaches and clarifies.

that occupied by his Consort Krodheśvarī, designated *'without nihilism'*. Here his Consort overcomes the view of those that are intensely self-focussed in reckoning that there is no further activity after death, that life's judgement allows no continuation of consciousness after the 'I' has died. To a nihilist, considerations of life devoid of such a personal-I are deemed unthinkable and therefore impossible. Being oblivious to the effects of the law of *karma*, wielded by the Libran karmic adjudicators, the emphasis therefore is excessive materialism and all related indulgences. The meditative insights gained when responding to the painful effects of the law of *karma* (the tendency to bemoan one's fate and to despair) cause the ability to master all attributes of life. Such bemoaning is the opposite to that dealt with by Mahottara Heruka, which relates to an over-exemplification of the importance of life, of the powers of the ego and self will over all things.

The entire panoply of karmic agents is controlled by this Libran petal. They are the feminine forces that govern all attributes of Nature so that the gain is eventual enlightenment for all. Responding to the blows of *karma*, human units therefore generate *saṃskāras* of all forms of nihilism and depression concerning the futility of life. They need to be overcome by presenting examples of the livingness of life after death; that death is but an interlude between one state of existence and another. The nature of karmic consequences is then realised, by recognising that something other than a materialistic universe must exist to account for what transpires in the field of consciousness. The nature and manifestation of phenomena can then be properly explained. As Krodheśvarī and her agents embody the sum of the substance from which all phenomena is constituted, so she is eminently capable of guiding all to comprehend this subject. Forms of clairvoyance and intuitional thinking that transcend the boundaries of the 'self' concept can then be engendered, allowing the *prāṇas* generated to become further refined in the *samādhi* associated with the corresponding petal of the Heart centre.

As the great Heruka and Consort embody the totality of the sphere of the *maṇḍala*, the central point and the circumference of the sphere of activity, they are generally not counted in the list of the Peaceful and Wrathful Deities. If counted, we have the 117 deities depicted in the extended list. The *prāṇas* that this pair exemplify are the Fiery-Airy combination, as this is the major energy that circulates in the *nāḍīs* with respect to consciousness. It constitutes the conversion of these *prāṇas* into the consciousness-Void integral to *śūnyatā*. This represents the major energy that drives the wheel of Splenic centre I.

Plate 9. Buddha Heruka and Consort

Vairocana in the form of Buddha Heruka and his Consort Buddhakrodheśvarī are next to be considered in terms of the four arms of the cardinal cross of purposeful direction. He assists in the conversion of the *saṃskāras* associated with the northern petal of the *maṇḍala*, involving the quality designated *'without ceasing'*. The *saṃskāras* qualifying consciousness are thereby to be ceaselessly transformed and transmuted.

The governing sign is Capricorn the goat. Capricorn rules the accumulation of *karma,* and the hard rocky mountain of mind that sustains it, controlling its mode of expression. The summit of the mountain also represents the transfiguration experience whereupon mind is converted to Mind by the Initiate. The quality 'without ceasing' from this perspective represents this continuous transformative process, wherein enlightenment is gained as a consequence of the sum of all form of activity associated with this wheel.

With each turning of the wheel, and milestone passed upon the upward way, consciousness must become increasingly subtler and refined in nature. Thus the person will eventually stand in the Clear Light wherein *śūnyatā* can be experienced. At first such activity is arduous because there are many rough rocks and crags of mind to master, but later the activity becomes effortless and spontaneous. Then the reinforced habit patterns of striving have become so ingrained that one no longer has to think about it. (An example is the ability to walk that people do spontaneously, having forgotten the effort required to learn this ability as a child.) The *prāṇas* engendered are those that come as a consequence of striving to lift all veils of repetitious conscious activity.

The meaning of the reddish-brown colouring of Buddha Heruka's central face is similar to that of the great Heruka. It implies the quality of the will that must be evoked to properly transmute the *saṃskāras* of the many forceful attitudes of mind that people develop. The *prāṇas* of the Earthy Element associated with the entire *saṃsāra* must be converted into Aetheric attributes that betoken the enthronement of the *dharmakāya* as Mind. It was stated that Buddha Heruka's three right arms hold a wheel of the eight directions of space wherein the *dharma* rules, an axe (to chop down the wood of discursive thought), and a sword to rightly discriminate truth from untruth. His left arm holds a bell, a ploughshare (for recycling the seeds of the transformed *saṃskāras*), and a *kapāla*.

Buddhakrodheśvarī's function in the human body is to transform murky, Watery *saṃskāras* so that they can be incorporated into the petal designated *'without apprehensible'*. These *saṃskāras* are the sum of people's identification with phenomena they take to be the real. The *saṃskāras* are not apprehensible in this way because they are illusional. Inevitably people will come to know the true nature of all phenomena, that there is nothing to be apprehended other than change itself. The *prāṇas* that result from contact with the ephemeral are channelled to the corresponding petal of the Heart lotus, denoted 'discerning the real'. They then become the base purpose of what ultimately becomes the experience of Thusness ascertained in consciousness. The sign Cancer ruling this petal refers to the birthing process of all that is to be apprehended. Buddhakrodheśvarī therefore represents the process of reorientation within the depths of *saṃsāra* that allows the transformation of the related *saṃskāras* so that the non-apprehendable (Void of things) will be experienced. We can see that the road from the deep recesses of *saṃsāra* (Cancer) to the attainment of great heights of revelation (Capricorn) must be trod before this is possible. The entire field of consciousness is consequently governed by the Buddha Heruka and his Consort. They control the entire treading of the path of Initiation into the mysteries of being/non-being from the greatest depths of *saṃsāric* activity to great mountainous heights of revelation (Capricorn). The sum of the desire-mind and the world of phenomena is thereby mastered, becoming a vehicle for gaining the *dharmakāya* vision.

Buddhakrodheśvarī's role, therefore, is to organise the substance of the experiences that are continually reborn via Cancer so that it is possible to find one's way out of the depths of the materialism that abounds all around.

The two pairs of Herukas and Consorts so far discussed constitute the major *cardinal cross* attribute of the Splenic centre I *maṇḍala*. The Great Heruka and Consort here represent the feminine,[15] serenely receptive east-west arm of this cross, which is impregnated with the dynamic masculine down-up driving energy of Buddha Heruka and

---

15 We should note here that the *chakras* below the diaphragm are feminine with respect to the Head lotus. This horizontal line of the *maṇḍala* represents the dividing line of the diaphragm separating the upper and lower spheres of attainment. It must be penetrated by the high impressions associated with Vairocana before any transformations of *saṃskāras* are possible. Also below the diaphragm Mahottara Heruka and Consort represent the functioning of the Splenic centre as a unit, but the focus is upon the feminine, as all happens within the domain of *saṃsāra*.

Consort. For this reason Buddha Heruka manifests at the centre of the *maṇḍala* of the Herukas. As one travels thus via the petals incorporating the attributes of the eight intermediate positions of the wheel all the forms of activity are instigated that transform the *saṃskāras* of the five sense-consciousnesses. The sense-consciousnesses are specifically objects of transformation into Jina qualities by the Herukas. Incoming *prāṇas* are incorporated in the petals governed by the Consorts, and are transformed therein according to consciousness-directives from the Heruka. The transformed *prāṇas* then flow to the petals governed by the respective Heruka and are then directed to the Heart or Throat centres above the diaphragm.

The *prāṇas* of the four main Elements governing *saṃsāra* are the focus of the activities of the remaining Herukas and Consorts. These *prāṇas* manifest in the form of an *iḍā* and *piṇgalā* stream. The *iḍā* stream is the effect of the work of Padma and Karma Herukas and their Consorts, whilst the *piṇgalā* stream is an expression of the work of Vajra and Ratna Herukas and their Consorts. This is by virtue of the fact that Padma and Karma Herukas embody the expression of the Elements Fire and Earth (which are *iḍā*) of their respective Jinas. Similarly, Vajra and Ratna Herukas embody the expression of Air and Water, which are *piṇgalā* in nature. From this perspective Mahottara and Buddha Herukas convey the expression of *suṣumṇā* Fires. For the major evolutionary period a mutable cross is formed by the other four Herukas, with *prāṇas* bearing *iḍā* qualities mainly flowing. Upon the path of Initiation it manifests in the form of a fixed cross through the generation of mainly *piṇgalā prāṇas*. Within each of these main streams of *prāṇic* flow is an *iḍā* and *piṇgalā* expression for the individual petals.

The right hands of the Herukas direct the *prāṇas* upwards to either the Heart or Throat centres. The left hands assist the Consorts in transforming *prāṇas*. The top right hand of each Heruka carries the emblem of the respective Heruka's Jina family. The five remaining hands therefore embody the process of the conversion of the *saṃskāras* of the five sense-consciousnesses for the particular Element conveyed by the Jina family to which the Heruka belongs. The associated information is tabulated below, as derived from Gyurme's account. Other accounts and their thangkas may differ from this arrangement, but shall not be entertained herein. The lists presented are in descending order from

the two remaining right hands, embodying the processing of Aetheric and Airy *saṃskāras,* followed by the three left hands, governing the processing of the three worlds of human livingness, the Fiery, Watery and Earthy *saṃskāras.* The ordering therefore is in terms of mastering the smell, taste, sight, touch and hearing sense-consciousnesses.

	Buddha Heruka	**Vajra Heruka**	**Padma Heruka**	**Ratna Heruka**	**Karma Heruka**
	Aether	Air	Fire	Water	Earth
Emblem	wheel	*vajra*	lotus	jewel	sword*
Aether	axe	*kapāla*	*khaṭvāṅga*	*khaṭvāṅga*	*khaṭvāṅga*
Air	sword	axe	mace	mace	mace
Fire	bell	bell	bell	bell	sword
Water	ploughshare	*kapāla*	*kapāla*	*kapāla*	*khaṭvāṅga*
Earth	*kapāla*	ploughshare	drum	trident	mace

Table 1. The Herukas, Elements and implements

* Normally the emblem for Amoghasiddhi is a *viśvavajra.*

Buddha Heruka conveys the most refined Aetheric *prāṇas* of the system. He absorbs all of the consequences of the conversion process from the activities of all the other Herukas and their Consorts. Consequently, his main implement and emblem is the *wheel* of the *dharma,* of conscious direction in space, which can channel these *prāṇas* in terms of all eight directions. They are projected to and from the higher *chakras,* and he integrates all *prāṇas* into the *maṇḍala* of the Herukas. The five remaining hands hold in order, an axe, sword, bell, ploughshare and a *kapāla.*

- His right middle hand holds the *axe,* which is used to cut the heads of enlightened perceptions from the general stream of the most subtle forms of discursive thoughts or from those that still retain concepts of an 'I'.

- The *sword* is used as a focussing instrument to project the Rays of light throughout the *nāḍīs* so as to transform the most truculent *saṃskāras* into the radiance of Mind.
- The *bell* is used to empty the mind of erroneous conceptual ideas.
- The *ploughshare* is used to furrow the *nāḍīs* so the *prāṇas* can freely flow without impediment. We are reminded that for the most part of human interrelations these *prāṇas* are Watery in nature and must be converted into their Airy correspondence (through the esoteric attributes of the sword) if they are to be integrated into the Heart centre.
- The *kapāla* reaps all the most refined *prāṇas* obtained through all aspects of human relationships in the material domain.

Plate 10. Vajra Heruka and Consort

Akṣobhya in the form of *Vajra Heruka* has dark blue, white, and red faces. (The dark blue being Akṣobhya's colour.) The 'three right arms brandish a *vajra,* a skull, and an axe', whilst those of his left hands 'hold a bell, a blood-filled skull, and a ploughshare'. The *saṃskāras* transformed are those of an Airy-Fiery nature.

Vajra Heruka is assigned the quality designated *'without arising'*. The one-pointed arrows of rightly completed thought of the *dharma* directed towards the targets of enlightenment and liberation (governed by the sign Sagittarius the archer) quickly eliminate illusional and glamoured forms of thinking so that they do not arise. Thus the *saṃskāras* mastered are those that come as a consequence of lifetimes of wrongly directed thoughts in any arena of activity in the three worlds of human livingness. The developed will is utilised to prevent such qualities from arising by their appropriate conversion, rather than mere suppression. What 'does not arise' here are the attributes of mind that bear materialistic *saṃskāras.* They have been converted into the *piṅgalā* attributes of *bodhicitta* by the time they are ready to be utilised by Vajra Heruka. These *prāṇas* can then be directed to the corresponding petal of the Heart lotus ('error free thusness'[16]). The *prāṇas* engendered therefore produce the Voidness revealed by the middle path. This is the gain of the cessation of attributes of mind. From another perspective the Void is revealed by eliminating the veils of substance and concepts to each point of the wheel of *saṁsāra.*

Vajrakrodheśvarī converts Fiery-Airy *saṃskāras* associated with the quality *'without two extremes'*. The position of the *maṇḍala* here, signified by Gemini the twins, refers to blending the qualities of *iḍā* and *piṅgalā* by means of the techniques associated with *śamatha* (calm abiding meditation). The resultant gain can then be absorbed into the corresponding petal of the Heart lotus. The types of *saṃskāras* created in relation to the various forms of *māyā* must be integrated in this way in the Temple of Life (which the sign Gemini symbolises). The two extremes can also relate to the *saṃsāra-śūnyatā* duality. The middle path is then the nexus uniting the two into a oneness of enlightenment. Here there is neither forms of nihilism (indicated by the term 'Void')

16 See the figure of the Heart centre in Volume 3, chapter 2 of this *Treatise on Mind* for these corresponding petals.

or forms of attachment to transient, ephemeral, corruptible things, ideas, or idealisms, associated with *saṃsāra*. *Prāṇically* it refers to integrating the energies from the corresponding petal of the Heart centre to help purify the Airy *saṃskāras* flowing to this petal. The admixture rejects the aberrant *saṃskāras* for recycling and projects the remainder to her Consort.

The emblem of this Heruka is the *vajra*. It shows that the objective for the general flow of the Airy *prāṇas*, of which Vajra Heruka is the custodian, is to awaken the wisdoms and immutable power of the Jinas through all the conversions of *saṃskāras* that are carried out in the *nāḍīs*. The refined discernments of the taste sense-consciousness are consequently developed.

- The right middle hand conveying Aetheric *prāṇas* holds a *kapāla*, to contain all of the transformed *prāṇas* garnered by the *yogin*. These are the most refined *prāṇas* contained in the *nāḍīs* and are directed to Buddha Heruka to be channelled to the centres above the diaphragm.
- The *axe* separates the most desirable discernments from those to be recycled and converted.
- The *bell* rings out the notes to clarify all *prāṇas* from their *manasic* dross, so that only the most refined thoughts are reaped. They lead eventually to considerations of emptiness.
- The *kapāla* contains the most refined Watery *prāṇas* reaped from the conversions carried out in this domain by the other Herukas and their Consorts so that they can be directed to the Heart centre.
- The *ploughshare* furrows the Earthy Element so that all materialistic *saṃskāras* can be loosened preparatory to being refined. Between Buddha and Vajra Herukas we see that all of the most corporeal or murky *saṃskāras* can be made to flow and be directed to the arenas of conversion.

Amitābha in the form of *Padma Heruka* has dark red, white and blue faces. He brandishes a lotus, a *khaṭvāṅga*, and a mace in his right hands, and a bell, *kapāla* and drum in his left hands. He assists in converting the Fiery *saṃskāras* that are *'without constructive thought'*. This concerns transmuting the *saṃskāras* representing too much self-focussed and empirical thinking. The production of many little incessantly flighty (Airy) thoughts that come and go keep the mind busy with streams of shallow ideals and petty ideas. All types of Aquarian shallow, superficial, lazy thoughts that only partially ascertain truth must be overcome. One must learn to quieten the mind for it to become more expansive and embracive of enlightening ideas. Mastering these *saṃskāras* necessitate overcoming animal-like mental activity. The mind must be sensitively focussed, farsighted, to seek out the heart of truth, if comprehension of the *dharma* is to be deepened. Padma Heruka then sends the general *iḍā prāṇas* to the Heart or Throat centres and thence the Head lotus.

Plate 11. Padma Heruka and Consort

The lotus is Amitābha's emblem and here symbolises Padma Heruka's ability to control the progression of *manasic prāṇas* in all *chakras* wherein elements of mind are expressed. Every petal of the *chakras* are utilised in the process of refinement of these *manasic saṃskāras*. Padma Heruka deals specifically with the *sight* sense-consciousness, hence with all of the main attributes of mind and their conversion into enlightened perception.

Padma Heruka's Consort, Padmakrodheśvarī, governs the quality *'without apprehender'* that relates to continuously overcoming apprehending phenomena as real by identifying with the 'self' concept. The sign Leo the lion, Padmakrodheśvarī's position on this wheel, represents the powers of the self-conscious individual, of self-identity. The *saṃskāras* to be transmuted concern the elimination of concepts wherein one places oneself at the centre of one's universe, within one's entire mental emotional apparatus and not just conceptually. The instinct of self-assertion must be transmuted into a Will-to Good for all. The leonine concept of 'self', of being the centre of one's self created universe, must be converted to the Aquarian *saṃskāras* of the group consciousness that is the basis to the Bodhisattva path. This process of transforming the basis to all mentalistic activity of 'self' develops the *prāṇas* directed from this petal to its correspondence in the Heart lotus.

- All elements of mind are involved in this conversion process, so it is fitting that the (Aetheric) implement wielded is the *khaṭvāṅga,* which expresses power over the sum of *saṃsāra.* This also applies to Ratna and Karma Herukas, because together they convert all *saṃskāras* of body, speech and mind of the three-fold personality.
- The *mace* is in the form of a heavy club used to bludgeon the attributes of the defilements of mind so that they no longer arise. It helps produce mastery of the entire process of thought-form construction. It must be used with effectiveness to control the unruly *saṃskāras* in each flower so that they can no longer manifest. Preceding the *khaṭvāṅga,* it represents the force of the will of mind that when rightly utilised ensures complete control of all activities in *saṃsāra.* The gain is the power wielded by the *khaṭvāṅga.* The mace pounds the substance of gross *saṃskāras* to produce the subtle

discernments associated with the taste sense-consciousness that are conveyed as the Airy currents of *manas*. The mace is similarly used by Padma's two brothers that help govern the three-fold personality.

- The *bell (ghaṇṭā)* governs the Fiery attribute of *manas* (the sight sense-consciousness). It is similarly held by the top left hands of all the Herukas, except Karma Heruka, who holds a sword. The reason for holding this bell in this most *manasic* of positions is that all attributes of mind must be subdued so that the voice of silence can be heard conveying the ear-whispered truths emanating from the domain of Mind. Eventually the resonance of Emptiness must be realised via mastery of the feminine principle that the bell represents. Wisdom is the outcome.
- The *kapāla* is held in the middle left hand conveying the Watery attribute of *manas*. It thereby collects the gain of the transformed *kāma-manasic saṃskāras* and further refines them before they can be directed to the higher *chakras* via the general *iḍā* flow, of which Padma Heruka is the custodian.
- A small *drum* beats out the sounds of submission of all the *saṃskāras* generated through material plane contact and experience. The mantric sound it intones must be amplified by this means to overcome the dullness of hearing and numbed consciousness of those incarnate. Eventually the clear sound of the bell will be heard that enables the hearing sense-consciousness to perceive Voidness.

Ratnasambhava in the form of *Ratna Heruka* has dark yellow, white, and red faces. His three right arms brandish a jewel, a *khaṭvāṅga* and a club. His left ones wield a bell, a blood-filled skull and a trident. His emblem is the jewel that governs the wish-fulfilling desires of people. (Or else it relates to the adamantine diamond-Mind of the enlightened.) The Element concerned is Water that governs the evolution of the taste sense-consciousness. Ratna Heruka assists in the conversion of Watery *saṃskāras* into the attributes of *bodhicitta* that can be absorbed into the Heart centre. This then develops the quality designated *'without eternalisation'*, which negates the beliefs of those that look towards eternal life in a heaven (or in an *ātman* state) as the supreme reward of their activities when following the dictates of religious scriptures.

The *saṃskāras* overcoming all types of fanaticism are developed. Wherever misaligned intensities arise in the body of emotions, mind, or any other arena of life, they must be controlled and transformed if one is to walk the middle way to enlightenment. Thus people are tested because the (Watery) emotions are the most difficult attributes of life to control, especially when reinforced by religious dogma. The sign Scorpio associated with this position governs the various tests upon the path to Initiation. The *prāṇas* obtained by conquering misplaced religious idealism are directed in the corresponding petal of the Heart lotus ('not otherwise thusness'). The adamantine jewel of non-discursive reason in all of the corrected facets of the mind is the reward.

Plate 12. Ratna Heruka and Consort

Ratnakrodheśvarī converts the Earthy-Watery *saṃskāras* associated with the quality *'without one extreme'*, which refers to extremisms and fanaticisms in each field of desire. The qualities of the sign Taurus the bull is implicated here, who governs all attributes of desire, and the home environment of comfortable attitudes of mind. Clearly one on the road to enlightenment must control the *saṃskāras* generated by such activity so that no mental emotional extremes of attachment to *saṃsāric* allurements are possible. The Voidness generated through this form of action is what remains when desire is conquered and eliminated.

- The Aetheric hand wields a *khaṭvāṅga,* and has the same significance as that wielded by Padma Heruka, but in this case the emphasis is in the generation of *piṇgalā prāṇas* that can be absorbed into the Heart centre via the cleansing of Watery attributes.
- The *mace* and *bell* held by the Airy and Fiery hands have similar functions to that explained with respect to Padma Heruka, but here the focus is upon mastering of the Watery Element, especially with respect to the development of the minor *siddhis,* and conquering all forms of emotionalism. They must come totally under the control of the *yogin* by awakening the pathways to the Heart centre. Ratnasambhava's Equalising Wisdom must eventually reign supreme over any extremist tendency.
- The *kapāla* held by Ratna Heruka with the Watery hand has a similar significance as explained with respect to Vajra and Padma Herukas. Ratna's *kapāla* however is the supreme container for these Watery *prāṇas,* thus most of the work done to convert their forms of emotional extremism happens under his auspices. One should comprehend the extreme difficulty here because of humanity's intense polarisation in their emotional and desire bodies.
- The *trident* held by Ratna Heruka signifies the ability to wield the minor *siddhis* when the triune energies of the central spinal column are mastered, once the Waters are controlled by the influx of *prāṇas* from the Heart. It is the prime implement used upon the path of Initiation to convert turbulent Watery *saṃskāras* into their pacified, equanimous, serene counterparts.[17]

---

17 This is also the significance of Neptune's trident, the God of the Waters in Greek Mythology.

Plate 13. Karma Heruka and Consort

Amoghasiddhi in the form of *Karma Heruka* has dark green, white, and red faces. His right hands hold a sword, a *khaṭvāṅga* and a mace. The left hands wield a bell, a blood-filled skull and a ploughshare. The Earthy Element and the hearing sense-consciousness is mastered. He embodies the Piscean petal of Splenic centre I, designated *'without discursive thought'*. Such thought involves moving from topic to topic in a rambling manner with relatively little analytical reasoning. The various forms of low-grade psychic or mediumistic tendencies are often the result. (Which are governed by the sign Pisces the fishes.) Often then there is an inability to hold any thought for too long, with no proper analysis of the subject at hand; consequently the mind is influenced by any thoughts or impressions that may happen to be in the psychic environment. Consciousness incorporates them shallowly and emotionally, producing bonded activity. The bonding is to the 'self' concept, material things, or to images desired, based upon the type of selfishness that the emotions produce.

The *saṃskāras* that must die therefore concern the forms of bondage that the personal-I is prone to. Thoughts must be unyoked from all types of concretised concepts and desires. Symbolically this concerns moving out of the water to dry land, and into the vitalising rays of the spiritual sun. Truth can then be discerned for what it is. Consequently, Karma Heruka produces the termination of the cycles of material plane activity. The *prāṇas* directed to the Heart or Throat centres are those that come as a consequence of striving to achieve higher, abstract, enlightened thought.

His Consort Karmakrodheśvarī assists in converting the Earthy-Watery *saṃskāras* involving the quality designated *'without apprehension'* as part of the major *iḍā nāḍī* stream. This concerns the faculties of mind that allow one to perceive things, and which also produce an anticipation, anxiety, or fear of things to come, especially as the meaning of many aspects of *saṃsāra* are comprehended or grasped. The *saṃskāras* of anticipation, anxiety, wrong comprehension (philosophically, religiously or scientifically) and delusional identification with things material and subjective are transmuted here. Whatever the mind deems essential in life, but in fact is transient, must be comprehended without fearful apprehension of what may come in the future. An unwavering acceptance of the dictates of *karma* through the development of an enlightened perception must take its place. When the *saṃskāras* of apprehensiveness are converted, the *prāṇas* are conveyed by this petal and must be expressed in each new undertaking. The associated petal is governed by Virgo the virgin, being the Earthy sign that gives birth to new ideas and initiatory undertakings. This prepares disciples to turn their consciousness away from materialistic incentives and towards enlightenment. All feminine forces governing the material domain can then be mastered.

Mastery of Earthy *prāṇas,* that are generated through physical plane living, need application of the strongest willpower to overcome. The implements in Karma Heruka's hands reflect this need.

- Instead of the bell wielded by all the other Herukas for the Fiery right hand (signifying the mastery of the sight sense-consciousness), Karma Heruka wields a *sword,* so that Rays of light can be projected via this focussing tool, to convert dark *saṃskāras* of mind. Right discriminatory effort is also needed to cut away erroneous beliefs and wrong discursive thoughts.

- The *khaṭvāṅga* wielded by the Watery hand overcomes desire and emotional *saṃskāras* generated through physical plane livingness. The *khaṭvāṅga* projects the forces from all of the planes of perception to overcome the desire-mind propensities of the body, speech and mind.
- The *mace* held in his Earthy hand is used to pummel the hardest of the material *saṃskāras* so that even the most dull of hearing have a chance to receive impressions from the higher domains.
- The left hands hold a *bell* to ring out the sounds of the service work to be done, so that enlightenment can come, a *kapāla*, to drink the Blood of Love that will help to bring Emptiness to all, from the *saṃsāric* mire that they are addicted to. Also, a *ploughshare*, to furrow the earth's fertile soil, so that the man-plants can be sown, to grow healthy and tall.

The eight Mātaraḥ

The *eight Mātaraḥ* (Tib. Keurima) are said to be the embodiments 'of the [eight] classes [of consciousness]'. These classes relate to the eight petals of the *Diaphragm centre.*

> Amidst an expanse of light in the eastern channel branch of one's skull,
>
> [Stands] Gaurī, white in colour, holding a human corpse cudgel and a skull;
>
> Amidst an expanse of light in the southern channel branch of one's skull,
>
> [Stands] Caurī, yellow in colour, shooting an arrow from a bow;
>
> Amidst an expanse of light in the western channel branch of one's skull,
>
> [Stands] Pramohā, red in colour, holding a crocodile victory-banner;
>
> Amidst an expanse of light in the northern channel branch of one's skull,
>
> [Stands] Vetālī black in colour, holding a vajra and a blood-filled skull;
>
> Amidst an expanse of light in the south-eastern channel branch of one's skull,

[Stands] Pukkasī, red-yellow in colour, clutching and devouring entrails;

Amidst an expanse of light in the south-western channel branch of one's skull,

[Stands] Ghasmarī, green-black in colour, stirring a blood-filled skull with a vajra;

Amidst an expanse of light in the north-western channel branch of one's skull,

[Stands] Caṇḍālī, pale-yellow in colour, [clutching] a human corpse and eating its heart;

Amidst an expanse of light in the north-eastern channel branch of one's skull,

[Stands] Śmaśānī, blue-black in colour, tearing apart the head and body of a bloated corpse.[18]

The eight consciousnesses can be listed as the *ālayavijñāna, kliṣṭamanas,* the intellect, and then the five sense-consciousnesses. We are not told in the text to which class of consciousness each of these eight Mātaraḥ relate. We therefore have to draw our own conclusions, taking the directions of *prāṇic* flow of the Mātaraḥ as a guide. I had presented an esoteric listing of the directions of space to which these eight consciousnesses are assigned, as presented in Volume 4, chapter 9 of this treatise. This listing refers to the overall *prāṇic* circulation in the body. This differs from that presented in conventional accounts, such as the list of the 'spokes of the heart channel-wheel' given by Geshe Kelsang Gyatso.[19] I shall utilise the account of the directions he has assigned because the focus here is upon the Heart's circulation, and the attributes of the Mātaraḥ follow this assignment. The information has been adapted in the following table to facilitate a better understanding of the functions of the Mātaraḥ.

---

18 Gyurme Dorje, 81-82.

19 Explained in Volume 4 of this *Treatise on Mind,* 329-330. See Geshe Kelsang Gyatso, *Clear Light of Bliss, A Commentary to the Practice of Mahāmūdra in Vajrayana Buddhism* (Wisdom Publications, Boston, 1982), 22-23.

Direction	Name of spoke	Consciousness	Mātaraḥ
east	the triple circle	*ālayavijñāna*	Gaurī
south	the desirous	*kliṣṭamanas*	Caurī
west	the householder	intellect	Pramohā
north	the fiery	sight	Vetālī
southeast	channel of form	hearing	Pukkasī
southwest	channel of smell	smell	Ghasmarī
northwest	channel of taste	taste	Caṇḍālī
northeast	channel of touch	touch	Śmaśānī

Table 2. The eight winds and the Mātaraḥ

Figure 6 illustrates the Diaphragm centre, into which the Mātaraḥ have been incorporated.[20]

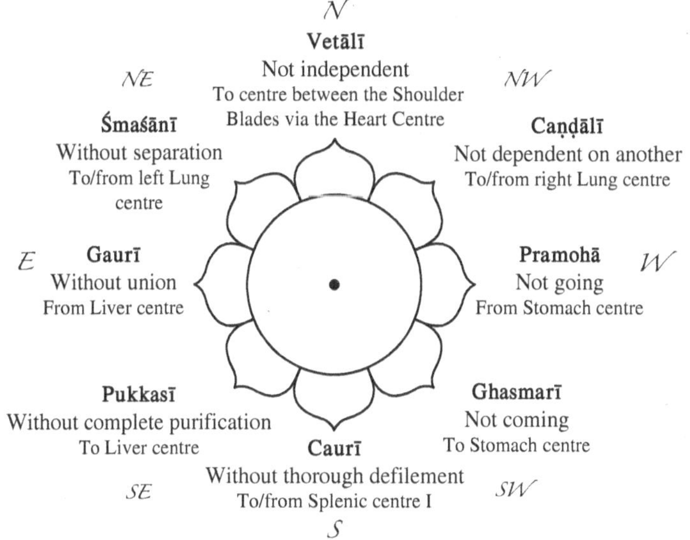

Figure 6. The Diaphragm centre and the eight Mātaraḥ

20 This figure is adapted from two figures on the Diaphragm centre in Volume 3, chapter 3. Note that all petals both receive and transmit *prāṇas*.

I will briefly explain the significance of the colours assigned to the Mātaraḥ. Firstly, it shall be noted that the colour black is inadmissible for any practitioner of the white *dharma*. Only followers of the left hand path manifest the characteristics of extreme hatred, etc., as indicated by this colour. The proper colour is the dark blue (indigo) of the energy of Love-Wisdom.

Lauf states, using the term Keurima for Mātaraḥ:

> The Keurima are called "Wisdom-Ḍākinīs of the eight kinds of awareness" (T. rNam-shes brgyad-kyi ye-shes mkha'-'gro bzhi). These Ḍākinīs are also emanations from the cosmologically oriented portions of the head and are divided into two groups, that of the "inner four Ḍākinīs" (T. Nang-gi mkha'-'gro bzhi), of the cardinal directions with pure colors, and that of the "outer four Ḍākinīs" (T. Phyi-yi mkha'-'gro bzhi), of the intermediate directions with mixed colors. Once again the head is pictured as an eight-petalled lotus.[21]

If we take the black to represent deep blue, as attributed to the quality of Akṣobhya, and the colours white, yellow and red to that of the colours of the related Jinas, then the omitted colour is green. The qualities of Amoghasiddhi are here implied, who then takes the central position of the *maṇḍala* of the Mātaraḥ. This means that their prime objective is to awaken the potency of his All-accomplishing Wisdom. The methodology requires mastering the Element Earth, whilst the other potencies of the Jinas are subsidiaries. We see, therefore, that the *saṃskāras* gained from the outward focus upon the material plane are principally the objects of transformation by the actions of the Mātaraḥ.

From now on all of the deities to be discussed are feminine, as are the Mātaraḥ, whilst the rest are also theriomorphic. (The exception being Vajrakīla Heruka, who will be explained in chapter 6.) The Mātaraḥ take the form of *yoginīs*. This immediately implies that they stand above the others, and in terms of the *nāḍīs* we have the role of the Diaphragm centre, which is situated between the centres above the diaphragm and those below. Hence it conveys characteristics from both groups of *chakras*. The Mātaraḥ are effectively mediators between the Consorts so far explained and the theriomorphic forces. The Diaphragm centre

21 Lauf, 147.

forms a triad with a minor centre situated between the shoulder blades and Splenic centre I. It represents the middle point or 'Son' between them, whilst Splenic centre I is the activity aspect of this triad. These *chakras* are concerned with *prāṇic* vitalisation of the entire bodily nature via the process of breathing. The general colour of the *prāṇas* conveyed is golden. This work also incorporates two minor centres situated at the breasts (the Lung centres). The qualities of these five minor *chakras* symbolise the inbreathing of the five *prāṇas*. The Heart centre is the central animating dynamo of this pentad. It anchors the (Monadic) energy of Life that integrates all factors of the form into a unity of conscious activity. With the in and outbreathing of *prāṇas* of the individual it incorporates that Life with a unique *prāṇic* colouring *(jīva)* for that individual. The *jīva* (the energy signifying the vital 'life' of a being) is then distributed by means of the activity of the five above mentioned minor centres.

It should be noted that the eight petalled Diaphragm centre can veil the activity of a Heart centre for the average individual, as it transmits the *prāṇas* generated below the diaphragm, which are mainly of a Watery nature, to and from the Heart. The Buddhist perspective given in the Tantras, such as that quoted in Gyatso's *Clear Light of Bliss*, where it is asserted the Heart Centre has eight petals, can be considered correct from this perspective.

Gaurī, the *eastern* direction (progressing inwards to the Heart of Life), is depicted holding a human corpse cudgel and a *kapāla*. The name given by Gyatso for the direction of this spoke of the *chakra* is 'triple circle', and was said to relate to the *ālayavijñāna*, the store consciousness to the three levels of the domain of the abstract Mind. It is also said to relate to 'the earth element'. I shall take this statement to refer here to the natural ground of the eight consciousnesses. This petal of the Diaphragm centre was designated as *'without union'* in Volume 3. From the perspective of the Diaphragm centre this eastern direction concerns the *piṇgalā prāṇas* that have been refined in the Liver centre and are in the process of being directed to the Heart centre. The Heart centre represents the place of anchorage of the *piṇgalā nāḍī*. As everything is intrinsically Void, this petal derives that characteristic from the most refined *saṃskāras* from the Liver centre so that they can be directed to the Heart. They enter into the Diaphragm centre and receive their final refinement into the attributes of *bodhicitta* (the Heart's emanation) or else they are to be recycled via Splenic centre I. If so they help to purify some of the base *prāṇas* of the Inner Round minor *chakras*. For these *chakras* the incoming energies manifest in the form of the *ālayavijñāna*. (Similarly for those entering the right Lung centre.) The objective is to cause the cleansing or transmutation of the more base, animal-like *saṃskāras* (emotions, desires, and materialistic aspirations) generated in these centres. There consequently can be no union with them until all defilements have been thoroughly dispelled.

If the energies from the Liver centre find their way to the Heart centre (via the northern petal) then the attributes of *bodhicitta* are manifest and thus there is no need for 'union' as the *prāṇas* have been made Void. If deflected to the right Lung centre (the northwest direction) then they produce the *piṇgalā* circulation for the minor centres above the diaphragm, to eventually play a role in the Ājñā centre and the development of the minor *siddhis*.

If enlightenment is to ensue, all of the aberrant *manasic* attributes of the *ālayavijñāna* environment must be transformed into the form of

Gaurī

Caurī

Plate 14. The Mātaraḥ Gaurī and Caurī

the energy (*bodhicitta*) that sustains the Heart centre. Concerning this 'environment' with respect to the *ālayavijñāna,* there is the dual aspect of mind to consider, the abstract Mind and that which is concreted. The abstract Mind also includes the son of Mind (the domain of the Sambhogakāya Flower). These three represent an interpretation of 'the triple circle' of Gyatso's list. It concerns the interrelation between the major aspects of mind/Mind so that consciousness can evolve in a progressive manner. Another interpretation is that it refers to the three main tiers of petals to the Head lotus. A more obvious interpretation of this 'triple circle', however, is that it represents the arena of interrelation between the three principle channels, *iḍā, piṇgalā* and *suṣumṇā.*[22] When properly integrated then the raising of *kuṇḍalinī* is possible. It can also refer to the movement of *prāṇas* downwards from the Diaphragm centre via Splenic centre I (to transform the attributes garnered through sense-perception and that develop the mind); northwards to abstraction (the Heart centre); or outwards to empower the *piṇgalā* stream (the right Lung centre) of the minor centres, which en-Souls their activity. For these reasons Gaurī is the only Mātaraḥ effectively possessing or holding three symbolic representations, where a human corpse (*iḍā nāḍi*) doubles as a cudgel (*suṣumṇā*) and the *kapāla* is the *piṇgalā nāḍi.*

The general reference above to the phrase 'channel branch of one's skull' refers to the subsidiary *nāḍīs* emanating from this central triad of *nāḍīs.* The 'human corpse' Gaurī holds relates to the attributes of the concrete mind (*iḍā nāḍi*) that must be cudgelled into subservience by the activities of the *yogin* or *yoginī* taking Gaurī's guise, utilising *suṣumṇā* attributes if they are to serve the way of the awakening Heart centre. The cudgel represents the type of force that must be brought to bear by the meditator upon transforming the erroneous qualities of mind presented. The *kapāla* signifies the death of all forms of concretions of mind and their refined abstraction into the pure blissful elements of consciousness (the *piṇgalā nāḍi).* Base manasic *saṃskāras* are replaced with the Clear Light of the abstract natural state of Mind. This sets the stage for the work of all of the remaining Mātaraḥ, who deal with the various attributes of the 'corpse' of one's desires, allurements,

22 They can also be viewed in terms of the white, red and blue channels of body, speech and mind of Gyatso's account. (*Clear Light of Bliss,* 23.)

attachments to concepts and erroneous ideas, etc., as per their rulership of one of the eight consciousnesses.

It should be emphasised that this analysis of the Wrathful Deities concerns the transformation of the *prāṇas* of consciousness in the *chakras* below the diaphragm, from which the attributes of the *ālayavijñāna* environment are drawn and refined into enlightened characteristics. This eastern direction also governs the way the transformed *prāṇas* of the *maṇḍala* of the Diaphragm centre are brought to the Heart. At this level of expression the Heart centre embodies the abilities of the Sambhogakāya Flower (the 'son of Mind') to transform consciousness. The main intent of the *yogin* therefore at this stage is to awaken to the *ālayavijñāna* form of enlightenment via the mastery of the attributes associated with the Wrathful Deities.

The Wrathful Deities thus represent a visualisation technique assisting the transformation of consciousness to produce the desired outcome. Unfortunately, the background *maṇḍala* of the entire Inner Round system of *chakras* upon which this presentation of minor *chakras* is based cannot yet be revealed. However, enough is presented to indicate the functioning of the more important ones below the diaphragm for the astute practitioner to find the teachings presented particularly useful, if enlightenment is the goal. Figure 7 illustrates the general schema of the *chakras* and *nāḍīs* found below the diaphragm.[23]

Caurī governing the *southern* direction, downwards into manifestation, shoots an arrow from a bow. This channel is entitled 'the desirous', which refers to *kliṣṭamanas,* the defiled mind. This direction involves interaction with the sum of the substance of *saṃsāra.* This petal therefore expresses the main *nāḍī* that connects to Splenic centre I[24] and integrates the sum of the energies associated with *prāṇic* flow below the diaphragm, which are consistently Watery. Here is expressed the *karma*-forming *saṃskāras* to be dealt with at any moment of one's life, that would spiritually defile if not properly cleansed. By the time such energies are directed upwards via the Diaphragm centre most of

23 The figure is not precise, but provides sufficient detail for the interpretation of the *Bardo Thödol.*

24 The dual Splenic centre acts as a type of sewer in the *nāḍīs*, transforming or cycling out of the body as much as possible of the natural defilements (of mind).

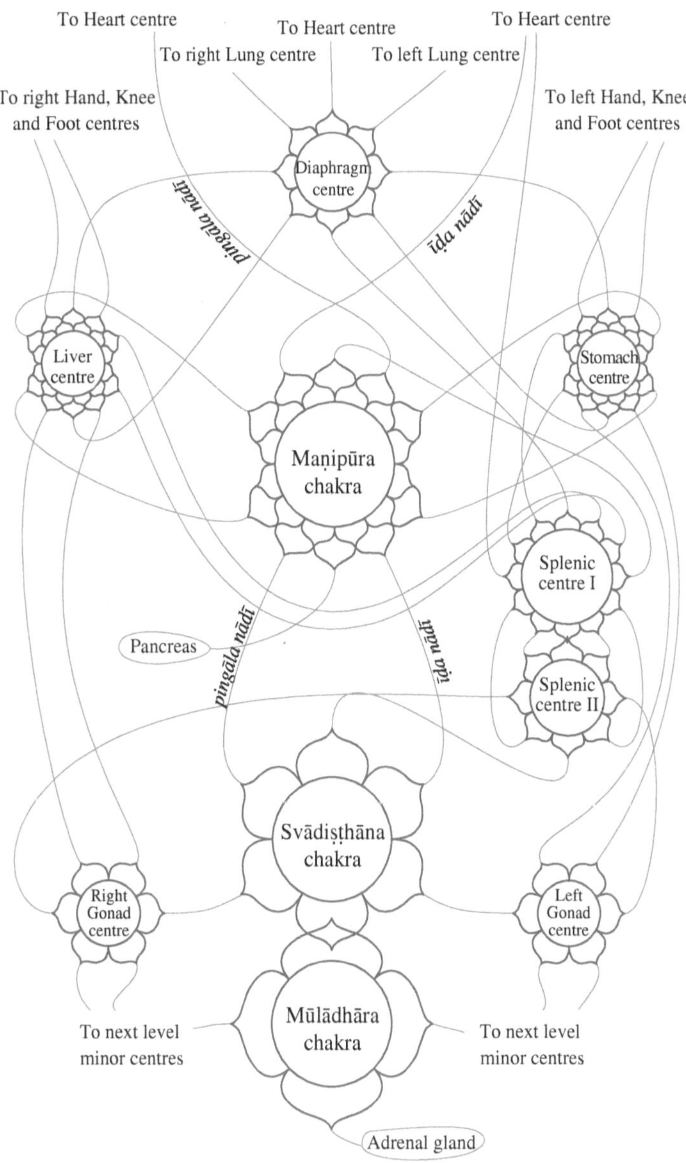

Figure 7. The *chakras* below the diaphragm

their grosser qualities have been purified, hence the *prāṇas* found at this petal are designated *'without thorough defilement'.*

The arrows shot from Caurī's bow are of aspiration, inspiration and high ideals that aim to transform base characteristics by directing the thoughts of mind to loftier targets. The arrows fly from the southern direction (the lower centres) upwards to the Heart centre.

Pramohā holds a crocodile victory-banner in the *western* direction of outwards interrelation of service with humanity. The quality designated is *'not going'*, and the channel depicted is 'the householder'. The reference here is to the householder of the mind, the intellect that coordinates and integrates the expression of the five sense-consciousnesses. We thus have the thinking capacity that enables humans to properly interrelate with each other to create the sum of the activity in our societies. The crocodile is an animal that lives both in the water and on dry land, so we see that the *saṃskāras* of the desire-mind have to be effectively dealt with here, until one can joyously hold up the victory banner of their mastery. In the iconography a Makara is depicted instead of a crocodile.[25]

For all *chakras* there is always a coming and going of *prāṇas.* However, all except for the Heart and Diaphragm centres act as processing centres for the *prāṇas* and contribute their own evolved characteristics. The Heart centre is the central of the major *chakras* and is the repository of *śūnyatā,* which does not posses such characteristics, but *bodhicitta* is its emanation. This energy is utilised to cleanse defilements in the other centres. The Diaphragm centre is the central of the minor centres and effectively acts as a type of pump cycling *prāṇas* from the centres above and below the diaphragm. The Diaphragm centre thus works to redirect admixed *prāṇas* to their appropriate destinations according to their attributes, going upwards if they pertain to the real

25 A Makara is a half animal half fish mythical aquatic figure, and is an auspicious symbol of the life-giving source, the Element Water. The meaning of this mystical term is 'the crocodile', an early version of the sign Capricorn, and concerns the fusion of the Watery Element with that of the mind. Hence it concerns the evolution of the desire-mind, and also with all aspects of magical invocations wherein the Watery aspect is invoked or to be controlled. In the ritual dagger *(phur ba)* the three-pronged blades and serpents are seen being emitted from the mouth of a Makara. Similarly the four outer prongs of the *vajra* are formed from the *prāṇas* pouring out of the mouth of Makara. Another representation is as a goat-fish.

(the awakening of higher perceptions), or downwards if the *saṃskāras* are *saṃsārically* inclined. The *prāṇas* not capable of being absorbed by the centres above the diaphragm are rejected and cycled back to the centres below the diaphragm, and are greyish in colour. Many who strive for high attainment may suffer serious discomfort in this centre because of these greyish energies. However, because the Diaphragm centre is the median between extremes there is no contribution to this *prāṇic* flow of its own characteristics. There is literally no coming or going of its own intrinsic quality.

The western position attributed to this eight-spoked wheel projects incoming *iḍā prāṇas* from the Stomach centre towards the left Lung centre (Śmaśānī) to feed the *iḍā* circulation above the diaphragm. *Manasic prāṇas* are flowing *in* from this direction, rather than going outwards (as would be expected for the western direction) hence the designation is 'not going'. In this case the field of service is the upwards direction to the Throat centre. The energies from the centres above the diaphragm are projected to those below. They are viewed as the direction west, from the point of view of stimulating intellectual activity that educate humanity. If the energies reach the Sacral centre, then the direction south is represented.

The Solar Plexus centre becomes the place of admixing of the *prāṇas* of all such activity, of the flow of energies from the right and left Lung centres via the Liver and Stomach centres. Desire-mind dispositions are thereby generated. The Mind, however, ultimately must rule the entire proclivity of emotional activity. Such activity must be converted to wisdom and not forcefully suppressed. The *manasic* energy producing such control below the diaphragm comes from Pramohā's assignment, assisted by the directives from the Throat and Heart centres working in unison. Pramohā's victory banner symbolises mastery over this process and therefore of the triumph over all the mental-emotional thoughts generated via the lower centres. The major battles concerning the generation of enlightenment-attributes by mastering the attributes of mind (governed by the Throat centre-Stomach centre combination) are all fought to produce this triumph. Final victory is assured when Pramohā successfully rejects all unwanted egotistical, selfish and prideful *prāṇas* from flowing to the higher centres.

The western direction occupied by Pramohā expresses the way that the *prāṇas* representing 'the field of service' come to it for admixing and their further projection. The energies then proceed to the centres associated with any of the spokes of the wheel that represent the continuation of their natural flow. The Diaphragm centre sorts out where the various categories of *prāṇas* should go.

We can see from Figure 6 that Pramohā and Ghasmarī work as a functional team (representing the energies going to and from the Stomach centre) with respect to the *prāṇas* coming from the Throat centre via the left Lung centre. Similarly, Gaurī and Pukkasī work as a functioning pair anchoring the *piṇgalā prāṇas* of the Liver centre via which the Heart centre comes to influence Solar Plexus centre activities.

The mind/Mind works to transform *saṃskāras* with the help of the energies from the Heart centre. All processes are enacted in the mind, thus it is here where final victory must be achieved. The battle of transformation may be fierce and often necessitates the wrath of all the *ḍākinīs* involved. The force of this transformative process can often be pronouncedly felt in the Diaphragm centre because of the interrelation of the two energy streams from below and above the diaphragm that happens here.[26] Once victory has been achieved then the expanse of the accomplished Mind can fly in the winds (the Airy Element) of enlightened consoiousness signified by the banner Pramohā holds.

The effect of premature or undue stimulation from either the Throat or Heart centres for either the western or eastern directions in the case of normal egotistical and/or selfish individuals could unduly further stimulate negative sensations in the Diaphragm centre. (Though they may manifest on a subtler, more veiled, and potent scale.) This is not desirable. We can see, therefore, the need for the gradual transformation of base *saṃskāras* before the invocation of unduly strong energies are yogically permissible. Such energisation will come when the attributes of the Solar Plexus centre have been sufficiently purified, allowing the most refined aspects of the emotions to dominate. (Such as devotion, loving disposition and aspiration, all of which will come to be further refined into the potency of *bodhicitta).* The Watery flow of the Solar

---

26 The conversion process may last for years. Practitioners may also experience unpleasant energies in other centres.

Plexus have then been transformed into what can be considered an Airy aspiration. The Solar Plexus must therefore eventually be completely submissive to the Heart centre's influx. Then the development of *siddhis* are possible without producing disastrous consequences.

Pramohā

Vetālī

Plate 15. The Mātaraḥ Pramohā and Vetālī

The crossing over of characteristics between the petals of the Diaphragm centre makes this section on the Mātaraḥ difficult to properly describe, because much depends upon time considerations, i.e., as to where upon the path of Initiation the individual stands.

In the *northern* direction (of upwards to divinity) *Vetālī*, said to be black in colour (esoterically indigo blue), holds a *vajra* and a *kapāla*. Here this direction leads upwards to the Heart centre, and then with respect to *prāṇic* circulation, to the centre between the Shoulder Blades. Vetālī is *'not independent'* from the activities of these two centres. This upward focus produces an integration with all that is real. Following this path to the Head centre produces enlightenment, which allows one to contemplatively become, omnipresently aware. It is dependent upon all of the process and forces that are moving north.

This petal of the Diaphragm centre brings into play the inbreathing of the energies from the enlightened realms (the domain of the

Sambhogakāya Flower) that will produce transformation of gross *prāṇas* in the centres below the diaphragm. Unification with the all, both with the 'below' and 'up or beyond' can then occur, to demonstrate oneness. It facilitates the absorption of the rivulets of consciousness into the ocean of being/non-being.

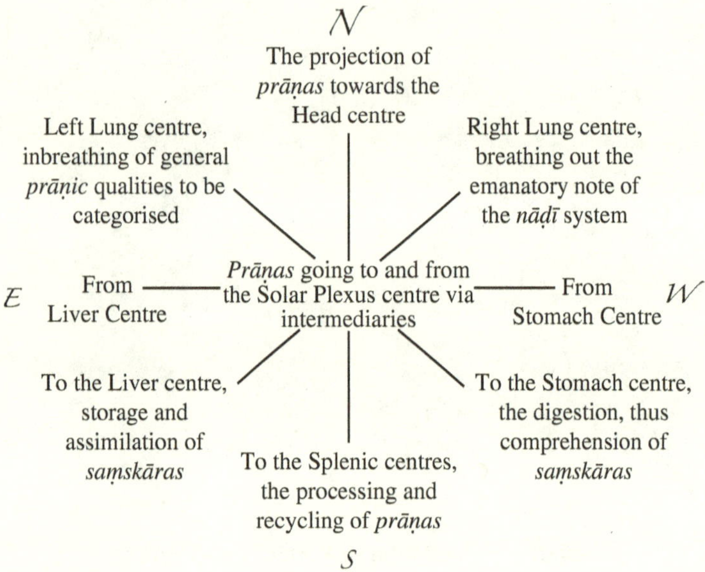

Figure 8. The Diaphragm centre as a distributor of energies

The associated channel is given as 'the fiery'. As the five sense consciousnesses are yet to be assigned, so we find, through a process of deduction in relation to the other four, that this channel refers to the Fiery qualities developed by the eye consciousness; the sense of sight, which helps to establish the images utilised by the mind. It also assists the eye's sense of direction, giving it orientation in space.

The *vajra* embodies the sum of the attributes of the five Jinas, which are evoked here through right visualisation techniques, if all base *saṃskāras* are to be appropriately battled and the resultant transmutations directed north. What remains in the *kapāla* worthy for drinking by the *yogin* will then be the elixir of the Clear Light (the abstract Mind).

Cleansing, transformative *prāṇas* from the Heart centre need to be invoked by the yogic process of transforming *saṃskāras,* allowing the visualising process ('sight') to direct the *prāṇas* to where they are needed. Coupled with visualisation is the need to regulate breath, which is accomplished via the extension of the *nāḍī* through the Heart centre to the centre between the shoulder blades. This centre is literally the powerhouse of the entire breathing process, of which two tiny *chakras* in the nostrils are extensions. This extension of the northern direction of the *prāṇas* of the Diaphragm centre also implicates the activity of the Throat centre, which directs the attributes of mind that control the 'breath' *(prāṇa)* to be expressed at any time. The Shoulder Blade centre also expels reject Airy *prāṇas,* directed thereto by the fierce attributes of Vetālī, who separates often very subtle aberrant *prāṇas* from vibrant ones. This centre, the Diaphragm centre and the Splenic centre thus work as a triangle of minor centres concerned with the assimilation and processing of the Airy characteristics of *prāṇas.*

In the *southeast* direction (of 'expression') denoted *'without complete purification'* in Figure 6 we have Pukkasī, 'clutching and devouring entrails'. Pukkasī directs vitalising and transforming *prāṇas* to the Liver centre, which assimilates and stores the Watery emotional and desire attributes that are symbolised by the entrails she clutches. The

Pukkasī

Ghasmarī

Plate 16. The Mātaraḥ Pukkasī and Ghasmarī

concept of devouring them implicates their transformation into useful *prāṇas* that vitalise rather than debase consciousness.

The Watery *piṅgalā prāṇas* are generated in the intestinal area wherein desirous thoughts are digested. They then enter the Liver centre where they are stored until needed. When the most refined of these *prāṇas* are directed upwards they are often expressed in the Diaphragm centre in a form that needs further purification. They then find their way to the Splenic centre for further refinement. If they pass the grade they flow to the left Lung centre.

For most people impressions from the higher centres generally become completely swamped by the desire-mind filled life of the normal day-to-day experiences. The experiences of what is pleasurable generally reinforce desire for further intoxicating stimulants. Such *prāṇas* are recycled through the lower centres and will inevitably produce sickness and diseases through lack of empathy with the evolutionary push of the entire organism. When *prāṇas* from the Heart centre are evoked they will project diseased *saṃskāras* to the surface to be progressively cleansed. The work of Pukkasī then comes to the fore, as she embodies the wrath needed to help effect the necessary transformations, and to reject those not suitable for circulation in the higher centres. Eventually *bodhicitta* is developed through transformation of basic desire directed thoughts into higher aspirational ideas and revelations.

As long as there is desire-driven contact with the material world those that live in it cannot completely purify the resultant *manasic saṃskāras*. Many bitter experiences must be digested and assimilated before it becomes clear as to the need to travel the Bodhisattva path, by rightly understanding everyone's true needs.

The 'channel of form' is assigned to the southeast, which relates to the sense of hearing, necessitating sounds created by the interaction between forms. The entrails that Pukkasī is depicted 'clutching and devouring' represent the most displeasing aspect of the dense form. They symbolise gross physical appetites that are normally the first to be discarded by the enlightenment bound *yogin*. The functioning of all organs that create unwholesome *saṃskāras* are thereby appropriately consumed and transformed into enlightenment-attributes. For this reason, of all of the actions of the Mātaraḥ, the eating of entrails best depicts the nature of the hearing sense-consciousness. Much of the idle gossip, vile invectives, deceitful information, slander etc., that people hear is likened to the substance needing such transformation.

In the *southwest* direction (of 'understanding') regulating the *prāṇas* directed to the Stomach centre we have Ghasmarī, stirring a blood-filled *kapāla* with a *vajra*. The assigned attribute is *'not coming'*. Here the *vajra* resonates the energies of the Jinas into the fields of lower mental cognition governed by this centre, to produce the transformations of normal thought processes. They are 'stirred' and thoroughly admixed with enlightenment-producing resonances. The interaction between these clean potencies and the *saṃskāras* of mundane, normal, self-centred thoughts actively produces their transformation into the elixir of enlightenment.

Prāṇas are assimilated into consciousness after the Inner Round circulation has digested raw experiences. It produces a base quality that sustains the now, of what may be considered the elementary *manasic* comprehension for any *saṃsāric* cycle of expression. The stirring of consciousness to produce *saṃskāras* of knowledgeable things expresses a function of the Stomach centre. This centre is the store of *iḍā prāṇas* from below the diaphragm. From this perspective there is nothing in this direction that ultimately is 'coming' once the mind has been mastered. Until then, thoughts *(prāṇas)* are coming and going and the *prāṇic* field is continually being modified in terms of the way that consciousness changes at any time. The *prāṇas* dealt with are pronouncedly *manasic,* 'left hand' *(iḍā),* associated with the eye of knowledge and intellectual pursuits. They represent the most materialistic, concrete knowledge based, and often bigoted, critical, and reactionary attitudes of mind possessed by the individual. All forms of critical assertions and hatreds are processed in this centre. Consequently they are most difficult for most to properly transform. Thus Ghasmarī presides over all battlefields that produce such transformations in the lower centres along the way to enlightenment.

Vetālī, who embodies the sight sense-consciousness, and who also holds a *vajra* and *kapāla,* visualises the nature of these *prāṇas* and their transformations, and directs the gain to the higher centres. Ghasmarī, on the other hand, brings what is visualised into active manifestation and *stirs* the proceeds with a *vajra* to produce positive results.

The 'channel of smell' is attributed to this direction, the subtlest of the senses, capable of lifting our thoughts to their loftiest expression of comprehension concerning the true nature of the transience of *saṃsāra*. The 'smell' that is expressed here, however, is that of the lower perceptions, more akin to animal cunning, rather than the highly refined perceptions of the enlightened Mind. The function of Ghasmarī is to stimulate the container *(chakra)* of base awareness, so that the prevailing thoughts can be converted into their enlightened attributes. This is a most difficult task, thus the full force and significance of a *vajra* is needed. Many are the strong mental-emotions to be converted along all five sense-consciousnesses (synthesised by the sense of smell). The appellation 'not coming' here also refers to the difficulty of the energy from the Heart centre to positively stimulate the activity of this centre. They are not seen there until the path to enlightenment is trod.

The *northwest* direction manifests the cleansing mantra of emanatory good will to all. Here we have Caṇḍālī clutching 'a human corpse and eating its heart'. She manifests the form of action given as *'not dependent on another'*. The *prāṇas* from this petal are directed to the right Lung centre where they are incorporated, and are also breathed out into the *piṇgalā prāṇic* circulation, where the Heart centre is the focus. This energy is immediately absorbed in the *chakras* concerned because the innate act of discernment of the Diaphragm centre has already eliminated all dross (forms of *saṃskāras* that are not capable of being utilised by the higher centres). In this way the *prāṇas* are not dependent upon any further processing, they will simply flow according to their inherent *piṇgalā* conditioning. The statement 'not dependent on another' has a reference to the interdependence of all lives in our universe. All are interdependent and automatically assist the other, however each unit is self-reliant and self-contained, whilst in *śūnyatā* they are not dependent. *Iḍā prāṇas* represent the attributes of consciousness relating to concepts of an 'I', thus dependency, whereas *piṇgalā prāṇas* relate to the development of concepts of 'self-lessness' (hence non-dependency). The *piṇgalā* stream manifests an integrating attribute, of oneness. The quality of 'without separation' on the other hand is attributed to the left Lung centre, because being part of the *iḍā nāḍī* system its *manasic* attribute demonstrates the natural separativeness of the mind, however by the time these *iḍā prāṇas* reach this centre the discriminative and separative functions have been transformed into pure ideation. Separativeness has been vanquished.

A function of the Diaphragm centre is to admix *prāṇas* so as to convert the *iḍā* type of *prāṇas* from the Stomach centre into their more *piṇgalā* qualities that are receptive to the right Lung centre. Similarly *prāṇas* from the Liver centre become more *iḍā*. This is a consequence of the energies from Gaurī (from the Liver centre) and Pramohā (from the Stomach centre) meeting at the centre of the *chakra*. The purpose is to equilibrate all experiences as much as possible with the energy of *bodhicitta* from the Heart centre. Essentially, as the *prāṇas* cross over from below the diaphragm to above it, they also partially cross over attributes. The purpose is to strengthen attributes in any line of development (*iḍā* or *piṇgalā*) that may be weak because not formerly developed in that stream. For complete enlightenment to ensue, all qualities developed must be fully mastered, producing no inherent weakness in any *prāṇic* stream.

The qualities attributed to each of these *prāṇic* directions are thus not what one who cursorily interprets the *prāṇic* flow would normally expect. For instance, what is expected from the southwest direction (Ghasmarī) is that there is a flow of *iḍā prāṇas* from the Stomach centre to the left Lung centre. This may indeed be so for normal development, but they come to be stripped of the characteristics normally associated with them in yogins because of a purifying stream of *piṇgalā prāṇas* from the Heart centre. The purpose of the stream from the Heart centre is to eventually produce the Void Elements from the five-sense consciousnesses. We can therefore see that very little flow will come to this direction except at a very advanced stage of development, as most *prāṇas* will simply be returned to be reprocessed below the diaphragm until the required purity has been achieved.

The orientation in Figure 7 is a downwards motion of vitalising *prāṇas* from the Lung centres to the Liver and Stomach centres. The *prāṇas* coming from the Liver and Stomach centres are the most refined that these centres can produce. They admix in the Diaphragm centre before being either rejected and thus flow to Splenic centre I, or else they find their way to the right and left Lung centre circulations. This circulation indicates the mode of flow for those working to transmute *saṃskāras*. This is accomplished yogically by means of breathing practices (psychic breath) in conjunction with correct visualisation techniques. Such techniques are normally presented as the most esoteric or important part of the practice and generally have accompanying mantras. For average humanity one would expect a strong flow of Watery *prāṇas* coming from the Stomach and Liver centres, in which case they would come from the southwest and southeast directions, and not the west and the east, thus the appellations 'not coming' would be assigned to the west and 'not going' to the southwest. Similarly the positions of 'without union' and 'without complete purification' would change positions. This is consistent with the change of the orientation of the arms of a mutable cross.

Liberation in the northwest direction (Caṇḍālī) comes through non dependency upon others because enlightenment proceeds through mastery of one's own *saṃskāras.* The concept of good will incorporates the most refined qualities one possesses to be directed to another. It is a process that eventually produces an integral union of one with the all, as good will morphs into the Will-of-Love. The evolved quality thus automatically identifies with all that is. Being the real, truth (enlightenment) exists of its own accord, it does not depend upon other things. It however adapts its expression in response to the qualities manifested by others to properly feed them what they

Caṇḍālī

Śmaśānī

Plate 17. The Mātaraḥ Caṇḍālī and Śmaśānī

require. The emanatory quality of truth is thus a note of recognition that instantaneously feeds the all with the qualities integral to it. *Bodhicitta* is the source, skilful means is the method of delivery.

The 'channel of taste', which produces subtle discernments and refinements of consciousness, is attributed to this direction. In this case it develops the way of the Heart, whose *prāṇas* it consumes when *iḍā prāṇas* (the foundation of wisdom) are integrated with those from the dominant *piṅgalā* stream (the development of compassion). The human corpse that is clutched then represents the *saṃskāric* products of the sense-consciousnesses from which the Life-essences of transmuted awareness have been extracted. The remainder, that is not nourished, consequently dies. All that remains from living the corpse-like cycles of experience in the Six Realms is the heart (transcendental consciousness) that is being consumed. All other attributes of this corpse have been rejected as unworthy for the mechanism of expressing the *bodhicitta* that the heart conveys.

Finally, in the *northeast* direction signifying *'union',* characterised by the quality *'without separation'* we have Śmaśānī, tearing apart the head and body of a bloated corpse. The bloated nature of this corpse implies the sicknesses and death-dealing aspects of such qualities as pride and ego-building attitudes of mind. These are some of the most difficult *saṃskāras* to master and transmute, therefore literally the corpse of the egoistic attributes of the personal-I must be 'torn apart' to find any value therein. The use of the fingers (touch) allows Śmaśānī to tear apart this corpse to see if there is anything life-sustaining or nourishing therein. Touch enables the person to definitely validate the reality of any physical object. It facilitates a most minute analysis of whatever is perceptible, that it is not merely a mirage. The touch sense-consciousness attributed to this direction specifically relates however to the demonstration of the Watery Element, where one can emotionally touch other's emotional sensitivities, feelings, etc.

In relation to the term *'without separation'* the left Lung centre technically 'breathes in' the *prāṇas* from the external environment so that they can be made integral to the *nāḍī* system, to which there is 'no separation'. The right Lung centre[27] on the other hand technically

27 The left and right Lung centres can also be termed left and right Breast centres, signifying where they are situated.

directs *prāṇas* (wisdom, consciousness-attributes) to outside of the body, integrating them into the vaster *maṇḍala* of the complete body of expression of which it is a part.

In general the right Lung centre directs overall *piṇgalā* qualities via the Heart centre to the Head centre so that they can be categorised and utilised for decision making and for forming ideas. The left Lung centre is mainly concerned with channelling *manasic* directives to and from the Throat, Head and lower centres so that the mind can control all thinking and bodily activities. There is, however, a general overlapping of function between both of the Lung centres. Together they process the refined attributes of *kāma-manas* (desire-mind), where the focus of the left Lung is the *manasic* portion and the right Lung the *kāma* aspect. The method of integration of all *prāṇas* to and from the Head lotus happens via the two lobes of the Ājñā centre.

Effectively the left Lung centre breathes in *iḍā prāṇas* from the Stomach centre and directs them to the Throat centre after they have been modified with more *piṇgalā* qualities. When the related *prāṇas* are focussed via consciousness in this northeast manner then there is no separation between the Stomach and left Lung centres via the orientation to both the Throat and Heart centres. The *iḍā-piṇgalā prāṇas* can then flow from the northeast petal to the southwest petal to assist in the conversion of Stomach centre attributes. These attributes then enter the Splenic centre circulation, where the worst aspects of one's mental-emotions can be washed clean. When one is consciously upon the path to enlightenment all of the lower centres will thereby inevitably come under the domination of the impulses from the Heart. A communality or unity of purpose is produced through engendering the factor of *bodhicitta* throughout the diversity of forces associated with the lower centres.

In summary, the pentad of minor *chakras* that are an expression of 'the golden triangle' and are centrally integrated by the Heart centre can now be tabled. The Heart centre integrates the *prāṇas* absorbed into the system via food and from the air with the Life stream from the Monad (via the Sambhogakāya Flower), which then becomes *jīva,* the individual Life force. The *jīva* is then conveyed via these five centres into the rest of the body. The Heart centre also conveys the energy that transmutes the *saṃskāras* generated via *saṃsāric* activity. The five centres are listed according to the type of Element conveyed. Each Element has its corresponding sense-consciousness. Two lists of these *chakras* are presented. The first relates to the *prāṇic* circulation for normal human activity, the second relates to the path of Initiation, where the individual is consciously working upon the refinement of *saṃskāras*.

Element	Sense	Normal activity	For the Initiate
Aether	Smell	Shoulder Blade centre	Shoulder Blade centre
Air	Taste	Right Lung centre	Diaphragm centre
Fire	Sight	Left Lung centre	Splenic centre I
Water	Touch	Diaphragm centre	Right Lung centre
Earth	Hearing	Splenic centre I	Left Lung centre

Table 3. The *chakras* governing *prāṇic* circulation

The cross over from the *prāṇic* circulation governing normal evolution and that associated with the path of aspiration is a process that takes some time to achieve. It therefore makes it difficult to properly explain the nature of the *prāṇic* flow between *chakras*. The focus in this text consequently is upon those who are consciously working to transform *saṃskāras* with view to eventual enlightenment. They have turned about in their seat of consciousness and the nature of the *prāṇic* flow reflects this. For them the theriomorphic deities that will be described in the next chapter become forces to be reckoned with.

5

The Deities of the Bardo Thödol
Part Four:
The Wrathful Deities below the Diaphragm

The eight Piśācī

This chapter shall continue with consideration of the eighth stage of the evolutionary process. (The development of unselfish idealism and compassionate action.) The sum of the theriomorphic deities can now be considered in the context of how they govern the general course of transforming *saṃskāras.* The focus is upon the centres below the diaphragm. Having explained the functions of the Diaphragm centre and Splenic centre I, the next centre needing explication is *Splenic centre II,* whose petals are embodied by the transformative qualities of the eight Piśācī,[1] who are said to be the embodiments 'of the [eight] sensory objects'.[2] Gyurme states:

> Amidst an expanse of light in the outer eastern channel branch of one's skull,
> [Stands] lion-headed Siṃhamukhī, brown-black in colour, carrying a corpse in her mouth;
> Amidst an expanse of light in the outer southern channel branch of one's skull,
> [Stands] tiger-headed Vyāghrīmukhī, red in colour, with her two arms crossed;
> Amidst an expanse of light in the outer western channel branch of one's skull,

1 Tib: Phra-men-ma.

2 Gyurme Dorje, *The Tibetan Book of the Dead,* 82-83.

> [Stands] fox-headed Śṛgālamukhī, black in colour, eating entrails;
> Amidst an expanse of light in the outer northern channel branch of one's skull,
> [Stands] wolf-headed Śvānamukhī, blue-black in colour, tearing apart a bloated corpse;
> Amidst an expanse of light in the outer south-eastern channel branch of one's skull,
> [Stands] vulture-headed Gṛdhramukhī, white-yellow in colour, carrying a human corpse draped over her shoulder;
> Amidst an expanse of light in the outer south-western channel branch of one's skull,
> [Stands] kite-headed Kaṅkamukhī, red-black in colour, carrying a large human corpse;
> Amidst an expanse of light in the outer north-western channel branch of one's skull,
> [Stands] crow-headed Kākamukhī, black in colour, brandishing a skull and a sword;
> Amidst an expanse of light in the outer north-eastern channel branch of one's skull,
> [Stands] owl-headed Ulūkamukhī, dark blue in colour, holding a vajra.[3]

These *ḍākinīs* are significant because of the major transformative battles that occur in *Splenic centre II.* This centre acts as a sewer system in the body, where the recirculation, conversion or elimination of *prāṇas* occurs. Background information allowing the correlation of the petals of this centre with the qualities of the eight Piśācī was given in Volume 3 of this *Treatise on Mind.* The focus of the Piśācī is upon the *skandhas,* limiting the concept of their expression in terms of the base elemental *substance* incorporated into the forms of the various aspects of consciousness that are conveyed as the *saṃskāras.*

The eight sensory objects refer to the objects contacted by means of the eight consciousnesses whereby they gain information. The various sensory objects thus relate to the method of deriving the base of all consciousness *(ālayavijñāna),* the dissonant mental-emotions *(kliṣṭamanas),* general thoughts, sights, objects of taste, sounds, smells, and physical objects. In reality all that we perceive generates various types of *prāṇas* that modify consciousness, and with which

3 Gyurme Dorje, 82-83.

consciousness functions. Splenic centre II integrates all of the *prāṇas* obtained through sensory contact, rejecting those that the system no longer finds viable, and directs the remainder to Splenic centre I.

The process therefore concerns converting the major *prāṇas* developed by the average person whilst living and working in everyday society. Consequently, all of the Piśācī and Īśvarī subsequently dealt with from now on are involved in this process. The overriding quality generated is that of the feminine *iḍā nāḍī.* These *prāṇas* are difficult for the disciple to transform into masculinely polarised enlightenment-attributes (the *piṇgalā* stream synthesised in the Heart centre) because the mental-emotions are so ubiquitous. Generating the attributes of Love-Wisdom, based upon cool clear logic, is difficult as most people find it hard to imagine what life would be like without their emotions.

The theriomorphic attributes of these *ḍākinīs* inform us that their focus is with the major Watery *prāṇas* that are engendered (therefore they are animal-like) and circulated in the Inner Round system of *chakras.* They are centrally processed by the Solar Plexus centre. The deities of Splenic centre I and the Diaphragm centre integrate the energies of the Heart centre with the animal-like *prāṇas.* The remaining sets of theriomorphic deities deal exclusively with the transformation of Watery *prāṇas* into their higher more (human) Fiery attributes.

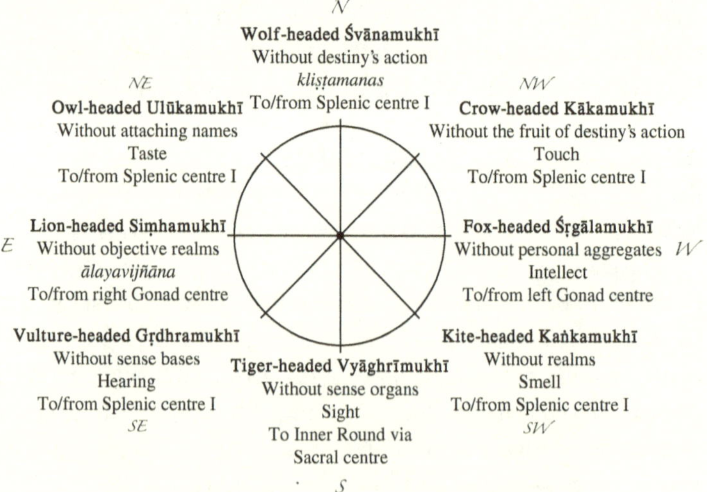

Figure 9. Splenic centre II and the eight Piśācī

In analysing the general mode of activity of Splenic centre II we find that it manifests principally in terms of two arcs of expression. The northern arc (channelling the *prāṇas* of touch, *kliṣṭamanas* and taste) represents the processing of Watery *prāṇas* to and from Splenic centre I. The southern arc represents the processing of Earthy *prāṇas* to and from Splenic centre I, plus the energising of the entire Inner Round of the 49 small *chakras* (via the sense of sight).

The central east-west line relates to the circulation of all *prāṇas* to and from the (next level up) minor centres via the Gonad centres. The cumulative *prāṇas* from these centres also represent the Fiery input for Splenic centre II (interpreted in terms of their Earthy and Watery attributes). From this perspective they represent the sum of what might be considered its *manasic* environment.

In the *eastern* direction we have the lion-headed Siṃhamukhī carrying a human corpse in her mouth. Lions, depicted as basking in the sun, symbolise the quality of the illumination that the sun brings. Such illumination normally represents the *ālayavijñāna* environment, however here the interpretation is from the point of view of the *prāṇic* direction to the right Gonad centre. The Gonad centres and their relation to the Sacral and Base of Spine centres represent the storehouse of mind for the *prāṇas* at this predominantly Earthy-Watery level of expression. Note that in terms of *prāṇic* circulation Splenic centre I deals mainly with the Fiery-Airy attribute of the Watery-Earthy circulation below the diaphragm, Splenic centre II with Earthy-Watery *prāṇas* fanned by their Fiery aspect. Effectively the concern here is with the genesis of mind, whilst the 'sun' under whose light this lion basks is that of the Sacral centre, which is the source of *prāṇic* vitality for all minor *chakras* and those of the Inner Round. It acts as a distributor for all *prāṇas* in the body. It thus mainly acts as an energy distributor, which in the average person relates to the expression of desire, physical attraction and vitality. The corpse that Siṃhamukhī carries represents the sum of the above attributes, which apart from vitality, act as a dead weight to a perspective *yogin*.

The *ālayavijñāna*-mind attribute dealt with in the east-west orientation of this *chakra* concerns the tiny units of sentience associated with the 49 small *chakras* of the Inner Round, plus that of the Earthy circulation of *prāṇas* in the body. The reason why the term 'sewer system' has been used to describe Splenic centre II is because its main purpose is to wash away the major Earthy defilements and impediments so that the cleansed *prāṇas* can flow to the higher centres.

The sensory object here[4] is that of the *manasic* substance of the *ālayavijñāna*. The objective is to cleanse the Earthy aspects from the desire-mind (the 'human corpse') so that thought becomes more Fiery. The quality attributed to this direction in Volume 3 is '*without objective realms*'.[5] These realms are the dimensions of perception that manifest from top down in the form of various layers of increasingly dense substance into which consciousness sinks through attachment to grosser, duller, and exaggerated forms of mental-emotional behaviour and attitudes. These levels of perception allow aspects of consciousness to be classified. We thus have the concrete and desire-minds constituting aspects of the formed *(rūpa)* realms, whilst the formless realms are viewed in terms of the subdivisions of the *(arūpa)* abstract Mind. There is also the state of pure desire denoted as *kāmaloka*. With respect to this circulation the *arūpa* realms are represented by the energies from the Heart and Head centres. The transmutation of all *prāṇas* found below the diaphragm into enlightenment-attributes results in their elevation to the *arūpa* level of the Heart centre. The rectified wheel that is turned produces the elimination of 'objective realms'. The centres below the diaphragm will then no longer exist for the individual as places of normal residence. Eventually the substance of the *ālayavijñāna* environment will be mastered by transforming all base Watery *saṃskāras* into their Fiery correspondences.

All of the *prāṇas* channelled by Splenic centre II are of an Earthy-Watery mix, however, the general cleansing Watery-Fiery *prāṇic* flow from all minor *chakras* below the diaphragm coupled with that of Splenic centre I are admixed in this eastern gate wielded by Siṃhamukhī. This energy works to purify the *piṅgalā* attributes developed by the Earthy

4 One must view these 'sensory objects' as internalised attributes of consciousness if they are to be dealt with yogically.

5 These assignments are derived from the Tantra *'Great Gates of Diamond Liberation'* explained in Volume 3, chapter 3, and relate to the enlightened attributes developed through transformation of the base characteristics of the associated petals of the *chakra*.

circulation of the minor *chakras*. Similarly the western petal of the fixed cross aspect of Splenic centre II works to cleanse the *iḍā* stream from the minor and small Inner Round *chakras*. Such a purifying flow is natural for advanced people who are no longer predominantly focussed upon their physical bodies, but rather upon mental pursuits. One seeking liberation must, however, inevitably utilise the evolved will to project the *arūpa* consideration through this Splenic centre II flow.

The tiger-headed Vyāghrīmukhī standing with two arms crossed is found in the *southern* direction. The sensory object here is the object of sight. From this perspective the sense of sight perceives all material objects and integrates them into a panoramic vision. The specific Element channelled by this petal is Earth-Fire. The tiger symbolically lurks in the jungles of the mind where the attributes of the defiled mind, the animal-like mental-emotions, hide. In this case, the 'jungle' represents the forces of all the small Inner Round *chakras* of the *nāḍī* system wherein the emotional and desire attributes are generated. The objective of the tiger is to seek out and prey upon all such *prāṇas* and to elevate them to the higher domains by consuming (and hence transforming) them. The hands (the extension of the arms) are normally used as manipulative or grasping tools to obtain the object of desire, but are here crossed, signifying the demonstration of proper control over all forms of desire. They are crossed over the chest cavity to signify the ability to prevent any of these defilements affecting the higher centres. Also implied is the symbol of the mutable cross, of repeated cyclic activity, thus of the recycling of *prāṇas* until they are thoroughly cleansed of the aspects of one's Earthy-Watery constitution.

The direction south channels *prāṇas* to the physical body, and the quality attributed is *'without sense organs'*. The sense-organs are the externalisation of the small *chakras* that this southern direction administers to.[6] (This work is effected via the Sacral and Base of Spine centres, whose energies are also utilised, which also accounts for the fierce potency of the tiger symbolism.) The entire material form is consequently integrated into a unity of *prāṇic* expression by means of these organs. Obviously no interrelation with the material world

6 The organs of the physical body are the automatic reflexes of whatever energies manifest through the *chakras* that embody their functions.

Siṃhamukhī

Vyāghrīmukhī

Śṛgālamukhī

Śvānamukhī

Plate 18. The Piśācī Siṃhamukhī, Vyāghrīmukhī, Śṛgālamukhī and Śvānamukhī

can occur without these organs, and no opportunity for experiential growth. Depending upon the nature of the *prāṇas* involved, the cleansing of *karma* often produces sickness. Watery *prāṇas,* for example, generally contain many Earthy defilements that produce ill health when externalised in an organ. Health manifests when gross *prāṇic* defilements are eliminated.

When the physical body is no longer the onus of attention then *siddhis* can awaken through complete control of the subjective or subtle internal sense organs *(chakras).* Once the *siddhis* are awakened then the external sense organs cease to be factors of consideration. In an enlightened being the sense organs still exist, but their activity is supplementary to the *chakras* that are consciously utilised, rather than unconsciously. They act as instruments of pure cognition and allow contact without attachment to the objects of *saṃsāra.* Effectively then there is nothing (new) that is apprehended by means of the senses, as the 'solidity' of things becomes non-substantial, ephemeral, unreal. This is an effect of the entire path of the cleansing, transformation, and transmutation of *saṃskāras,* which begins in this southern direction.

In the *western* direction of outwards to the field of service we find the fox-headed Śṛgālamukhī eating entrails. The sensory object is the object of the mind's perceptions sought after by the wily fox. We therefore have the functioning of the intellect, 'eating' the substance of thoughts (the expressions of the five sense-consciousnesses). Despite its cunning, the fox is depicted consuming the most Watery aspects of *saṃsāra* rather than the fleshy nutritious part. The fox's natural cunning, however, represents the 'sensory object' of intelligent thoughts (or mind) of the individual, whereas eating entrails signifies the fusion of that mind with emotions and desire, thus the demonstration of the desire-mind *(kāma-manas)* that most are ensconced in. Here the Fiery-Earthy Element is exemplified, and when integrated with this field of desire, then we get the worst, most entrenched *saṃskāras* to be converted.

The domain of service here, of desire mentalistically appropriated, is the *iḍā nāḍī* for this Earthy circulation directed via the left Gonad centre. The substance aspect *(skandhas)* of the *saṃskāras* are exemplified as desire is conditioned by sense contact with phenomena and directed by feeling perceptions. This is part of the circulation governed by the

Sacral and Base of Spine centres. Inevitably, however, the circulation of *prāṇas* from all the minor centres are directed to the Solar Plexus centre, the central universal store for all *prāṇic* circulation below the diaphragm. The Solar Plexus then sorts out the *prāṇas* and directs them to their respective centre of consciousness-volition.

The quality attributed to this direction is designated *'without personal aggregates'*. In this direction we see that the *skandhas* ('personal aggregates') tend to be accumulated through desirous perception. The *yogin's* task therefore is to completely counter this activity so that such accumulation is not possible. The transformative work of Splenic centre II in this petal is to strip from these *saṃskāras* as many adverse qualities as possible before directing them to the left Gonad for general circulation in the *nāḍīs*. Here the cleverness of the fox comes to the fore to endeavour how best to achieve this goal. The primary battles of converting base *saṃskāras* of 'personal aggregates' into attributes of desirelessness happen here. Refined *prāṇas* can also be directed to Splenic centre I with view of them being acceptable for circulation in the centres above the diaphragm.

The transformation of the Earthy-Watery *skandhas* upon the path to enlightenment inevitably evokes the All-accomplishing Wisdom of Amoghasiddhi. All eight qualities attributed to the petals of Splenic centre II describe the processes needed to effect this transformation. The base characteristics of the related *saṃskāras* must be converted into the most refined aspects of the eight consciousnesses. In this western petal they are infused with the Fiery fox-like characteristics of consciousness, allowing comprehension of the way negative attributes of desire affect decision making. Plans can then be made to counter the development of such attributes.

In the *northern* direction is found the wolf-headed Śvānamukhī tearing apart a bloated corpse. The sensory object concerns 'the desirous' *(kliṣṭamanas)*, which here represents the most refined Watery-Earthy *prāṇas* developed through Splenic centre II activity northward to Splenic centre I. For that centre the *prāṇas* coming to it from its lower companion represents the most Earthy attributes it must process. We saw by the treatment of the eastern and western directions that Splenic centre II mainly processes *prāṇas* governing the field of desire as expressed by the Gonad and Sacral centres. As the more coarse attributes *(skandhas)* of the Earthy Element are washed away to produce a refinement of aspects of desire, coupled with increased *manasic* aptitude (creativity), so then the attributes of *kliṣṭamanas* (the 'defiled mind') are generated. This is signified by the activities of the wolf, a very sociable animal, who generally works as part of a pack to hunt its prey (the objects of desire). The inference is that the prey must be herded by various factors coherently influencing each other if the object of desire is to be satiated. The logical mind (the pack of wolves) must be developed to produce the best outcome. Each wolf represents an individual thought-stream, part of a grouping of multiple perspectives that collectively produce the image of what is desired. Rash, impulsive behaviour for the desirous is superseded by thoughtful acquisition. The Watery-mind *(kliṣṭamanas)* is thus established.

As the general idea pool of the mind is developed, the resultant logic can tear apart the corpse of illogical concepts associated with *saṃsāra*. (The sum of the images that bloat the corpse of all illusional thoughts.) The purpose of Śvānamukhī then is to help annul the bloated forms of desire-mind attachments to *saṃsāra*. All *karma* is the effect of the substance of mind that must eventually be directed towards properly examining the corpse of what was once considered real by the eye-consciousness. This prey represents the *saṃskāras* from many minor centres.

The quality attributed to this direction is designated *'without destiny's action'*, which refers to that which does not produce *karma*. At first there is the propensity of strong desire to produce all types of karmic bondage. It is difficult to break these attachments, yet the enlightenment-bound *yogin/yoginī* must succeed in annulling every form of *karma*-producing activity as the path northwards is trodden. The *manasic* impetus from the Throat centre to control all activities of desire as focussed by the eye is invoked via this petal. The eye directs the expressions of *karmic* volition right through to the southern direction wielded by Vyāghrīmukhī so that all the *prāṇas* from the Inner Round can be incorporated. The *prāṇas* evoked are utilised by the mind to produce a new seed thought for a future action. The energy of desire is generated in the lower centres and incorporated by the directives of the eye. The integrated Earthy-Watery attributes of the most Fiery *prāṇas* generated that Splenic centre II is capable of channelling are then directed northwards to produce the constant refinement and transmutation of *saṃskāric* expression.

The elimination of 'destiny's action' concerns the manifold incidents that *karmically* propel the person to climb the mountain of achievement for whatever is the focal point of aspiration, such as the perfection of a particular *saṃskāric* attribute. The focus via this petal thus aims to achieve whatever the purpose the mind wishes to fulfil in terms of the transformation of *saṃskāras*. Eventually the forms of *karma* that attach consciousness to *saṃsāra* will be an annulled. The generation of the related *saṃskāras* therefore ceases, either through transformation and direction upwards to the Heart centre, or else projection out of the system altogether by preventing their attributes from occurring.

The fixed cross positions of the eight-armed wheel of direction in space deal with the main *prāṇic* orientations of Splenic centre II. The intermediate mutable cross positions of the four deities below deal with the *iḍā* and *piṅgalā* expression of *prāṇas* of the desirous attributes gained via the sense-consciousnesses (apart from sight, which is directed via the north-south direction). The southeast-northwest expresses the *iḍā* line to and from Splenic centre I and the northeast-southwest line the Airy-Aetheric *piṅgalā* line to and from Splenic centre I. This interrelation allows a thorough and rapid sorting out of all *prāṇas* to be processed by the combined Splenic centres, for many are the aspects of desire and emotion generated by most people all of the time. The *prāṇas* directed from Splenic centre I to Splenic centre II via this mutable cross represent what is rejected, needing further processing, hence do not need to be further explained here.

In the *southeast* direction of 'expression' is found the vulture-headed Gṛdhramukhī carrying a human corpse draped over her shoulder. The sensory object here is the object of sound impacts. The vulture is the prime emissary of the 'sky burial' practiced in Tibet, where human corpses are cut up and left for these birds to consume. The concept of sound impacts here presumably relates to the noisy scene at feeding times for these birds. As previously stated hearing is the most limited of senses because sound is the result of clashing together of physical objects. These sounds are related to the death of phenomena. Esoterically, they relate to the rather coarse Earthy *prāṇas* circulating through the *nāḍīs* of the practitioner. This physicality is symbolised by the weight of the corpse that Gṛdhramukhī carries over her shoulder for later consumption (processing). Within the overall context of the Earthy *prāṇas* Gṛdhramukhī processes a subsidiary hue of a Watery expression of base desire, lust and general sexuality to and from the Gonad centres and the Inner Round. The author of the *Bardo Thödol* implies that such activity relates to the transience of carrion feeders consuming cut up corpses. This entire activity is a dead weight upon the *yogin's* shoulders.

The quality attributed to this direction is designated *'without sense bases'*. These sense bases are the fields of activity for the senses where sensory input is categorised by the mind. This includes all types of relationships with the material world and with human beings, wherein people develop their minds. This is the outcome of the field of desire which produces attachment, as controlled by the qualities of the Sacral centre. The Sacral centre absorbs the *prāṇas* derived from all forms of contact with the external environment from the output of the individual's desire body. Here we find the myriad sounds and clashing noises of civilisation and those of human speech that impact upon the individual. Many are the emotional responses, desirous articulations, and tendencies for base *saṃskāras* to be generated. The *yogin* must overcome the propensity to be attached to activity that intensifies attachment to the objects of the senses. The entire material world, including that which produces pleasure, is transient and such transience must be eschewed as objects of fulfilment to eliminate reliance on the sense bases.

The effect of the sense bases being grounded through desire are increasingly accentuated, causing the painful outcome of desire-attachment to be so thoroughly comprehended that inevitably aversion to these bases manifests. Eventually one learns to detach consciousness from the expressions of the senses, and to transmute the coarse desires and self-oriented emotional concepts of sexuality (the 'human corpse' of that which causes cyclic rebirth) into selfless Love for all. The effortless sound of the *dharma* will then be heard and the carrion for Gṛdhramukhī to consume eliminated.

In the *southwest* direction of 'understanding' we have the kite-headed Kaṅkamukhī carrying a large human corpse. Kites are medium sized birds of prey that typically have a forked tail, often found soaring in updrafts of air. Such flight provides ability to view a vast panorama of the plains (*saṃāra*) below. Their forked tail indicates that such vision incorporates both the *iḍā* and *piṇgalā nāḍī* streams. However, this kite is lumbered by the weight of the *saṃskāric* qualities of the corpse it carries.

The sensory object refers to the perfumes, etc., that cause olfactory stimulus. This relates to the way substance of the highest Element (Aether) is integrated into the qualities of the corpse. We must view Aether here within the context of it being an expression of the Earthy Element. It therefore relates to the smells of the physical domain and its etheric counterpart. Rather than the liberating stimulus to mind that would normally be expected with this sense we have its debasement. The concern of this encumbered bird here is the purification of the most onerous, material aspects of the *piṇgalā nāḍī* so that eventually full flight is possible without the 'corpse'. (Its 'smell' will then no longer be discernible.) The object is to refine the *piṇgalā prāṇas* derived from the Gonad centres and Inner Round so that they become more Airy and hence suitable for incorporation into Splenic centre I. Concrete desire must be transformed via the elements of the thought processes into loving aspiration. The burden of the corpse carried by this bird represents the generation of Earthy desire-mind *saṃskāras*. A more Watery *prāṇa* is processed than as in the case of Gṛhramukhī, and with the introduction of the Fiery Element the objective is to 'evaporate' the Earthy-Watery expression to make it more Airy (hence the sense of 'smell'). In this way a subtler comprehension of the nature and consequences of desire is produced than can be gained by the *iḍā* stream. In this petal the attributes of aspiration to noble ideals are developed that eventually lifts one above the factor of desire.

The quality attributed to this direction is denoted '*without realms*'. That which has no boundaries with respect to containing *prāṇas* is consistent with the expression of the sense of smell. All can be accounted for, stored and expressed via this highest sense faculty. The concept of 'realms' implies the dynamics of the Six Realms and the various ways of experiencing all aspects of *karma*. It is also concerned with the sewer-like elimination of *prāṇas* to the Eighth Sphere, as explained earlier. That which produces the conditioning 'without realms' therefore eventually allows one to escape the cycle of rebirth into any of the Six Realms. The methodology relates to the generation of *piṅgalā prāṇas* that lead inevitably to the Heart centre, hence to the experience of *śūnyatā*. Because all interrelationships generated in these Realms are to be experienced, so the corpse carried by this *ḍākinī* is large and the task of conversion enormous. Nevertheless, the process must begin sometime, which is the role Kaṅkamukī plays as she lifts her burden into the air, to Splenic centre I.

In the *northeast* direction of 'unity' there is the owl-headed Ulūkamukhī holding a *vajra*. The owl is generally viewed as symbolising a wise being because of its ability to see in the dark where it hunts its prey. The darkness represents the blindness of ignorance, the first spoke and driving force of the twelve-spoked wheel of interdependence (*pratītyasamutpāda*). Literally implicated here is that the owl is what overcomes the blindness of ignorance. The force of the *vajra* is used to draw the elements of wisdom from out of the darkness. Whatever wisdom can be found then represents the owl's prey, or conversely it works to eliminate attributes that prevent such attainment.

The sensory object here is that of the food one eats. The sense of taste esoterically relates to the *skandhas* of the Element Air. Here, however, the most material aspect of the taste sense-consciousness is experienced, associated with physical plane sensations and related knowledgeable attributes. They are tasted, some are savoured and others are rejected as vile tasting, even poisonous. Many types of 'foods' are tried until eventually forms of *prāṇas* (foods) that do not serve to nourish the spiritual life are eschewed. The most loving attributes of the Inner Round and Gonad centre *prāṇas* are processed by the owl so that they can be projected to Splenic centre I in the form of *piṅgalā prāṇas*.

We have moved from a primarily Earthy and desire based scenario associated with the southern petals to a Watery-Airy emotional based scenario for the two northern petals of the mutable cross under consideration. Within this context, Ulūkamukhī directs the subsidiary Airy-Watery *prāṇas* of the fundamental Earthy Element processed by this centre. They must be cleansed of defilements by means of the powers of the *vajra* with view of them eventually being directed to the Heart centre. The Airy component implies that already they are the

Gṛdhramukhī

Kaṅkamukhī

Ulūkamukhī

Kākamukhī

Plate 19. The Piśācī Gṛdhramukhī, Kaṅkamukhī, Ulūkamukhī and Kākamukhī

most refined that Splenic centre II is capable of expressing, but they must be further processed if they are to pass through the tests that will be applied by the Mātaraḥ on the way to the Heart centre.

The quality given to this direction is the attribute '*without attaching names to objective realms*'. That which attaches names is the mind when it organises itself to know things. One must therefore first observe the functioning of the mind if all knowable things are to be brought into its ken. Ultimately then the form of *prāṇic* vitalisation can be generated that eliminates identity with phenomenal forms (attaching names) by overcoming the directives of the discursive mind. Very little if any substance then needs processing by this centre. All *prāṇas* have been converted into the attributes of the non-discursive Mind. The path to the Heart centre inevitably produces the experience of unification and of oneness preparatory to the experience of the Void, wherein such concepts as 'names' becomes meaningless. The input from the Throat centre is also needed at first because if the wayward emotions are to be pacified the force of the regulatory mind must be invoked to control them. The pacified, cleansed *prāṇas* can then be directed to Splenic centre I, wherein the energy from the Heart centre can thoroughly purify them. The occupancy of Splenic centre II will then be freed from the qualities of self-identification, which identifies things in relation to the concept of an 'I'. As this happens the attributes of *bodhicitta* are generated. The densest, most concreted Earthy *prāṇas* are eliminated by this washing process. The *vajra* held allows some of the most intense energies from the higher realms to be brought to bear to thoroughly produce this process.

In the *northwest* direction of emanatory positive expressiveness ('good will'), we have the crow-headed Kākamukhī brandishing a skull and a sword. The crow has black feathers, a strong beak used for scavenging food, and a raucous voice. What is emphasised here by the enlightened codifier of the symbolism of this text concerns mastery of the material conditionings of *saṃsāra* by means of the development of the attributes of Mind via the *iḍā nāḍī*. The symbolic crow has prevailed over the environment it resides in, as is consistent for one embodying the qualities of this northwest direction. Therefore the crow carries a skull, signifying the rulership of the process of birth and death that comes as a consequence of the evolution of *manas*. The accompanying sword of right discrimination allows it to sever ties to limiting *saṃskāras*.

The sensory object here is that which can be touched, causing the awareness of physical objects. Watery, desirous responses are evoked through the experience of sense contact. Inevitably, the mind must be developed to comprehend the objects of contact before *saṃskāras* can be converted into knowledgeable attributes and directed to Splenic centre I.

The quality attributed to this direction is designated '*without the fruit of destiny's action*'. This fruit concerns everything that can be gained by consciousness through the expression of *karma*. The death-like mental-emotions processed generally produce desire for further intoxicating experiences, the gathering of further bits of information by the scavenging crow. Much must be gleaned from *saṃsāra's* turmoil, with its death-like attributes, symbolised by the skull that is held. This skull also indicates the way to the Head lotus that this path offers, once the sword of right discrimination is utilised and death-like *saṃskāras* (the materialistic 'fruit of destiny's action') no longer rule. A different fruit comes to view, that concerning liberation from it all.

The qualities symbolised by the two groups of Piśācī can now be summarised.

- The deities of the fixed cross directions have mammalian heads, whilst those of the mutable cross are bird-headed.
- All are carnivorous hunters, except the vulture (a carrion feeder) and the crow (a scavenger).
- The animal-headed deities anchor the objects of the senses firmly in the bodily form. They stalk the prey of one's desires, physical appetites and lust.
- The bird-headed deities symbolise the attributes of fleeting sensuality, short-lived desires and flights of fancy.
- The lion symbolises the generation of the *saṃskāras* of pride, the ego, basking in the sun of one's accomplishments.
- The tiger symbolises obtaining the things desired by stealth, powerfully foraging in the shadows of the jungles of *saṃsāra*.

- The fox obtains its prey through cunning, implying also the *saṃskāras* of trickery and thievery.
- The wolf demonstrates the (emotional) intelligence of the group or society one is part of. It implies the voracious garnering of objects desired by the communality of the group for its own pleasure, consumption, or amusement.
- The vulture is a carrion feeder, being sustained by the offal of other's opinions and the leftovers of the life process.
- The kite can find prey from great heights, then will swoop to obtain the fancy that was observed or imagined.
- The owl works in the dark night of *saṃsāra* to obtain its desired sustenance.
- The crow scavenges for all types of foods (ideas) and leftovers discarded by others. This produces a form of superficiality in all undertakings.

The four female Gatekeepers

The *four female Gatekeepers* are 'pristine cognition in emanational form'. They are part of the visions shown on the thirteenth day of the Bardo experience.

> In the channel branch at the eastern gate of the skull, within one's brain,
> Is horse-headed [Aṅkuśā], white in colour, carrying an iron hook and a skull.
> In the channel branch at the southern gate of the skull, within one's brain,
> Is sow-headed [Pāśā], yellow in colour, holding a noose and a skull.
> In the channel branch at the western gate of the skull, within one's brain,
> Is lion-headed [Sphoṭā], red in colour, holding an iron chain and a skull.
> In the channel branch at the northern gate of the skull, within one's brain,
> Is snake-headed [Ghaṇṭā], green in colour, holding a bell and a skull.[7]

The name 'pristine' signifies that they are expressions of the four petals of the foundational, primal centre, the Base of Spine (*mūlādhāra)*

7 Gyurme Dorje, 84.

chakra. The Base of Spine generates the simplest of the form-building *prāṇas,* from which all other *prāṇas* stem. They become increasingly qualified with many overlays of *saṃskāric* hues as we move up the spinal column. This centre channels the 'cognitions' or sentience (basic instincts) of the four primary kingdoms in Nature, the mineral, plant, animal, and human.[8] Pristine cognition also relates to the primordial nature of these energies as unchanged by mind, the essence of these qualities. Thus they are the initial gates to entering the *maṇḍala* of the human etheric body and all lower *chakras.*

All the Gatekeepers hold skulls *(kapalās)* representing the cognitions, reservoirs of one or other of the four *prāṇas* embodying the qualities of an associated kingdom. The sentience of all lives embodying the conditionings of *saṃsāra* are the basis for the transient cycles of coming and going of the *prāṇas* from each kingdom. Their significance is quite important as the Base of Spine supports the activities of all other *chakras.* Together the petals wield the expression of the primeval energy *(kuṇḍalinī)* and are responsible for the processes of vivifying the *maṇḍalas* of each kingdom with the Fires of Life. The instigation of the forms of group *karma* associated with these kingdoms therefore starts with them.

The white horse-headed Aṅkuśā, who carries an iron hook and a skull, guards the *eastern* gate or petal of this centre. The horse is the animal most closely allied to humans, whose consciousness rides the horse and directs it to where desired. The 'iron hook' concerns the aptitude of people to hook in all forms of *karma* that condition their empirical experiences. Eventually subtler forms of experiences are hooked producing a consequent drive to liberation. Alternatively, the hook can be considered to pull out undesirable *saṃskāras.*

The horse's head is also a symbol of Hayagrīva, the wrathful emanation of Avalokiteśvara, representing the compassion of all Bodhisattvas. The symbolism effectively implies that all of the animal-like *prāṇas* (i.e., those generated below the diaphragm) are controlled by Hayagrīva, for which the exceptional compassion of the 'downward looking one' applies.[9]

---

8 These kingdoms are here catalogued in the esoteric and not in terms of the scientific view.

9 For this reason also Hayagrīva often appears at the top of the ritual dagger (phur ba) instead of the half *dorje.*

Avalokiteśvara takes an animal form with respect to this because of the need to tame all of these animal-like forces when disguised as one of them. Also, a function of the human kingdom is to compassionately serve the lesser kingdoms via the animal bodies into which they incarnate. This is the basis for the eventual generation of the quality of Love-Wisdom associated with this eastern direction. Lauf thus states that this Gatekeeper teaches the quality of 'boundless compassion'.[10]

The Element expressed to be refined is Air. The white colour represents the qualities of the Dharmadhātu Wisdom of Vairocana, which is the objective of the human kingdom to express. As the other colours of these Gatekeepers are yellow, red, and green so by deduction we can presume that the indigo blue colour of Akṣobhya, representing his Mirror-like Wisdom, stands in the centre of this *maṇḍala*. Blue, therefore, is the primary quality of these colours. All must inevitably come to express the Airy quality of the Void *(śūnyatā)* that Akṣobhya represents—all kingdoms therefore are intrinsically 'empty'.

The *northern* gate or petal of this centre is guarded by the yellow sow-headed Pāśā, who carries a noose and a skull. Of all the members of the animal kingdom that could be used to symbolise the qualities of the plant kingdom at this basic level, perhaps pigs are better than most, as they are much involved with dirt. The sow digs in the earth with its snout looking for roots and other nutrients to eat. This symbolism therefore has a reference to the plant kingdom, which grows in the earth, similarly looking for nutrients.

A noose lassoes all forms of desirable qualities, *saṃskāras* and *karma*. It is really a form of a swastika, implying a free flowing and mutability of energies, with two arms enclosed, implying the ensnaring or capturing of energies. The symbol is depicted thus:

This indicates the prime function of the plant kingdom, which is to capture sunlight, and then convey these captured *prāṇas* of light to the animal kingdom as their food. From this function we can extrapolate this

10 Lauf, 150.

Aṅkuśā

Pāśā

Sphoṭā

Ghaṇṭā

Plate 20. The four female Gatekeepers

Gatekeeper's quality of 'boundless kindness'.[11] The Element is Water, also signified by the yellow colouring associated with Ratnasambhava.

This petal overlaps with the base petal of the Sacral centre (Bhujanā), hence is a place of the generation of the *nāḍī* system (coupled to the Knee and Lung centres). When myriads of nooses ('ankh-ties') depicted above are joined together then the basis for the channels *(nāḍīs)* through which *prāṇas* can flow is established.

The red lion-headed Sphoṭā, who carries *'an iron chain and a skull'*, guards the *western* gate or petal of this centre. We now have the complete attributes of the animal kingdom represented in the king of the beasts. The iron chain indicates that they are bound by links of interrelationships, group *karma*, and basic instincts, from which they cannot escape. With respect to humans the chain signifies the many misdeeds, *saṃskāras,* and *karma* that enchain them. They effectively must break the chain—link by link—to be freed from its influence. It is not sufficient to cut it merely in one place because many links (of *karma*) go to make the complete construction. Once the links are broken then the person experiences the 'boundless sympathetic joy'[12] that this Gatekeeper teaches. The joy comes from the resultant freedom, and the sympathy is to those still chained. The links can also be viewed in terms of the established *nāḍī* system through which *prāṇas (saṃskāras)* wielding this karmic force flow. The Element is Fire, an expression of the red colour associated with Amitābha.

Finally, the green snake-headed Ghaṇṭā, who carries *'a bell and a skull',* guards the *southern* gate or petal of this centre. The snake is most closely associated with the earth, or mineral kingdom, upon which it slithers. The bell indicates all of the sounds that control the emanation of the elementary lives associated with this kingdom. Representing the substance from which *saṃsāra* is constructed, and ultimately the wisdom ('serpent power') that comes from its mastery, this Gatekeeper may teach 'infinite equanimity'.[13] The Element is that of the Earth, associated with the green colour of Amoghasiddhi.[14]

---

11 Ibid.

12 Ibid.

13 Ibid.

14 Note that Amoghasiddhi is assigned to the northern position when representing the development of wisdom by humans, and south with respect to the phenomena of Nature.

The northern and eastern directions of Aṇkuśā and Pāśā is what allows them to 'draw us forward, Obstructing the entrance of confusion to the four types of birth, and opening the doors to the four rites of pure enlightened activity' (producing the liberation of *kuṇḍalinī).*[15] The 'entrances through the four types of birth' that these Gatekeepers can help to obstruct also relate to the qualities derived from the four petals (gates) of the Base of Spine centre. These are 'birth from a womb', referring to birth in the human kingdom; 'birth from an egg', to birth in the animal kingdom; 'birth from heat and moisture' to the mineral kingdom; and finally, 'miraculous birth', associated with the plant kingdom (the *chakras).*[16] The western and southern directions occupied by Sphoṭā and Ghaṇṭā causes them to 'support us from behind' with their animal-like and Earthy *prāṇas.*[17]

The twenty-eight animal-headed female goddesses

The *twenty-eight animal-headed female goddesses* (Īśvarī) can now be analysed. They are subdivided into five groups, with four groups of six deities each and one of four deities. All these numbers are of importance. First we must look to the process of transforming the five sense-consciousnesses into the five *prajñās* of the Jinas. The Īśvarī are *śaktis,* feminine psychic powers or forces, which the prospective *yogin* or *yoginī* must rightly control. Each of the five groups deals with one or other of the *prāṇas* of the five Elements. We come now to the domain of the Solar Plexus centre, which is arranged in two groups of five petals, so it can properly assimilate and process the Watery *prāṇas* of the *iḍā* and *piṇgalā nāḍīs.* We have:

1. The four female Gatekeepers enacting *emanational rites* govern the petals of the in and outgoing *iḍā* and *piṇgalā nāḍīs* to and from the Solar Plexus centre (*maṇipūra chakra).* This arrangement utilises four of the ten petals of the Solar Plexus centre. Their control is of the most refined Fiery-Airy-Watery *prāṇas* the Solar Plexus is

15 Gyurme, 84.

16 These quotes are from Dudjom Rinpoche, Jikdrel Yeshe Dorje, *The Nyingma School of Tibetan Buddhism,* (Wisdom, Boston, 1991), page 132 of Section Two.

17 Guyrme, 84.

capable of expressing. This leaves six petals free. The associated Jina is Vairocana, therefore the sense-consciousness associated is smell.

2. The six 'Queens of Yoga' enacting the *rites of pacification* (the east) governing the remaining six petals of the Solar Plexus centre. These petals control the main body of the Watery-Fiery-Earthy emotional *prāṇas* of the Solar Plexus. The associated Jina is Akṣobhya, with the sense-consciousness being taste.
3. The six 'Queens of Yoga' enacting the *rites of subjugation* (the west) embody the functions of the left Gonad centre. This centre is a six-petalled lotus. These petals control the Earthy-Fiery form-building *prāṇas*. The associated Jina is Amitābha, with the sense-consciousness being sight.
4. The six 'Queens of Yoga' enacting the *rites of enrichment* (the south) embody the functions of the six-petalled right Gonad centre. This centre controls the Earthy-Watery desire grounding *prāṇas*. The associated Jina is Ratnasambhava, with the associated sense-consciousness being touch.
5. The six 'Queens of Yoga' enacting the *rites of wrath* (the north) embody the functions of the Sacral centre. The six petals of the Sacral centre control the Earthy-Watery-Fiery desirous sensation-seeking *prāṇas* causing attachment, as well as general bodily vitalisation. The associated Jina is Amoghasiddhi, with the associated sense-consciousness being hearing.

The process related to the transformation of the *saṃskāras* of all these petals so that the resultant *prāṇas* can be accommodated by the Heart centre is explained in Volume 3 of this *Treatise on Mind*. Cross-referencing shall therefore be carried out between the quality of a Wrathful Deity in the *Bardo Thödol* to a specific petal as is described there.

The four female Gatekeepers enacting emanational rites

These *Gatekeepers* embody the two ingoing and the two outgoing petals of the Solar Plexus to the *iḍā* and *piṅgalā nāḍīs*. The two top petals are oriented towards the Heart centre and the bottom two petals to the Sacral centre. The *iḍā* and *piṅgalā nāḍīs* are part of the primary triad that runs up the spinal cord to vivify the Head lotus through, at first, its outermost tier of petals.[18] The *nāḍī* that awakens the Heart centre conveys the most refined energies from the Solar Plexus centre, whilst the *prāṇas* from the Sacral centre convey desire attributes that feed the activities of all the minor centres that interrelate with the Solar Plexus at any time. The focus of the Watery-Earthy Sacral centre is desire for sensation and sense-contact with the material domain. The energies from the Heart or Sacral centres can be integrated in the Solar Plexus centre to incorporate all the minor centres. The Solar Plexus centre acts as a type of crucible or retort to process all their energies. A swastika of energies thereby moves in the centre of the Solar Plexus centre admixing all energies and refining them according to the quality of desire/emotions of the *saṃskāras* conveyed by consciousness at any time. The various gradations of energies find their sink in one or other of its petals, which then direct the *prāṇas* to their appropriate destinations. In general, all *chakras* function this way.

The 'emanational rites' demonstrated by these Gatekeepers are expressed in lieu of the 'pristine cognition in emanational form' attributed to the Gatekeepers explained above. The Gatekeepers of 'emanational rites' enact the rites to express or manifest the *saṃskāras* of cognitions that are not pristine, thus they are much more active than the earlier four. Gyurme states:

> At the [outer] eastern gate of one's skull is Vajrā [Mahākālī],
> White, cuckoo-headed, and holding an iron hook;
> At the [outer] southern gate of one's skull is Vajrā [Mahāchāgalā],
> Yellow, goat-headed, and holding a noose;
> At the [outer] western gate of one's skull is Vajrā [Mahākumbhakarṇī],
> Red, lion-headed, and holding an iron chain;
> And at the [outer] northern gate of one's skull is Vajrā [Lambodarā],
> Dark green, snake-headed, and holding a bell;
> O you, the four female gatekeepers, Queens [of Yoga] who enact the emanational rites,
> Perform the rites which obstruct the doors [leading] to [mundane] rebirth from the intermediate state![19]

18 Which has earlier been depicted to constitute the Solar Plexus in the Head.

19 Gyurme, 86-87.

This group of theriomorphic entities embodies the functions of Vairocana with respect to the remaining groups of the Īśvarī. By collecting the most refined, abstracted *prāṇas* from the four groups, they receive *prāṇas* from the Heart centre and integrate them into the general circulation below the diaphragm. Similarly, they receive the most refined Sacral centre energies being expressed at any time and appropriately process them with respect to what is needed for the Inner Round group of *chakras*.

When the colours of all the Īśvarī are observed (white, yellow, red and dark green), then once again we see that the dark blue of Akṣobhya is omitted. This means that the quality of Love-Wisdom *(bodhicitta)* is what must be developed by the individual consciousness with the help of the activity of the theriomorphic forces. This is the object of the alchemical processes associated with all of the centres concerned. *Bodhicitta* must be wrought through the crucible of experience, and all Wrathful Deities, male or female, exist to help accomplish this. The blue is the gain of all of life's processes.

The four Gatekeepers of Emanational Rites control the expression of the Watery *prāṇas* below the diaphragm. With respect to the north-south orientation, they either move towards the Head centre or towards the Base of Spine centre. The concern here, however, is with the expression and conversion of those *saṃskāras* that will eventually produce attainment of the second Initiation by the individual—signifying the mastery of the Waters. This incorporates all of the elementary stages that develop good will and the Will-to-Love, thus the generation of devotion and aspiration to high ideals that produce the Bodhisattva path. These four deities therefore hold the keys to the development of the lower *siddhis,* and guard the secrets of these powers. The six 'Queens of Yoga' concerned with the *rites of pacification* who embody the remaining petals of this *chakra* govern the horizontal east-west direction of the *prāṇic* flow of the Solar Plexus centre. Their purpose then concerns the major transformative battles that happen there.

Vajrā Mahākālī and Vajrā Mahākumbhakarṇī occupy the northern orientation of the *iḍā* and *piṅgalā nāḍīs* to and from the Solar Plexus centre, whilst Vajrā Mahāchāgalā and Vajrā Lambodarā occupy the southern direction.

Vajrā Mahākālī, white, cuckoo-headed and holding an iron hook, embodies the functions of the *piṇgalā nāḍī* that directs Airy *prāṇas* to and from the Heart centre, expressed by the quality of the *eastern* orientation of the north.[20] The symbolism of the northern direction relates to the attainment of the second Initiation, which necessitates direct input of energy from the Heart centre. These *prāṇas* are symbolised by the bird's head because a bird can take flight in the air. The hook is used to hook out all *saṃskāras* that are incapable of being expressed by the Heart centre, or which would pervert the purity of its compassionate expression. It therefore purifies the *prāṇas* that must flow to this centre. The cuckoo with its ability to sing its familiar cuck-oo sound (sometimes considered to be a warning) symbolises the sound of the beating Heart. It is also a parasitical animal that lays its eggs in other birds' nests and leaves the host birds to incubate and rear its young. This can refer to the Heart centre's function of laying seeds of compassion in the Solar Plexus centre, and therefore the entire Inner Round, so that all attributes eventually develop into enlightenment-principles.

In the *western* orientation of the northern direction the Fiery Element must be generated to control the Waters, thus the energies of the Throat centre are appropriately invoked to engender attainment of the first Initiation. Control of these *saṃskāras* signifies mastery of the Element Earth. Here the red lion-headed Vajrā Mahākumbhakarṇī manifests holding an iron chain, symbolising the *prāṇas* to be channelled by the *iḍā nāḍī* to and from the Throat centre.[21] These *prāṇas* are often of a Fiery-Watery disposition, the iron chain indicates that the *saṃskāras* chain one to *saṃsāra*. A strong chain can also be used to pull one free from such attachments. The lion depicts that which is the king of the *saṃsāric* jungle (*manas*), the attributes of which can be controlled with the help of this Gatekeeper.

The next two deities embody the functions of the *iḍā* and *piṇgalā nāḍīs* to and from the Sacral centre. They deal specifically with the

---

20 Though situated on the Airy northwest arm of the Solar Plexus centre the *nāḍī* crosses over at the diaphragm to enter the southeast (Gemini) petal of the Heart centre.

21 The *nāḍī* begins at a northeast petal of the Solar Plexus centre and crosses over at the diaphragm to enter the southwest Leonine petal of the Heart centre on its way to the Throat centre. The appellations 'western', 'eastern', etc., for these *nāḍīs* therefore relates to their orientation rather than actual placement in the Solar Plexus centre.

Vajrā Mahākālī

Vajrā Mahākumbhakarṇī

Vajrā Mahāchāgalā

Vajrā Lambodarā

Plate 21. The four Gatekeepers of Emanational Rites

factors of desire, sensuality, and the emotional vitality that allow one to cope with all forms of interrelationships. These factors also cause the procreation of the species.

In the *southern* direction the entry into the path of discipleship happens wherein aspects of yogic aspiration to master the emotional and desire elements are seriously contemplated. One's resources are evoked to overcome all types of attachment to transient objects of form, material comforts, and money. *Karma* and the relation of physical plane law to spiritual law must be comprehended. Everything related to the sexual function is a particular focus. This produces all the problems of concepts of celibacy verses forms of sex magic. Thus the foundation for eventually taking the first Initiation is laid through the generation of the path of aspiration. This orientation away from the mundane world of sense-perception and towards enlightenment allows the path of yoga to be practiced, with view to eventually gain the fruits of *raja yoga.*[22] The pledge is then made to follow the Bodhisattva vows. Such vows may not necessarily be outwardly spoken, rather they are an inner emanation from the Heart centre that motivates the practitioner to manifest unending compassion in all he/she does. This process involves the generation of the Will-to-Love, wherein all aspects of the emotions and desire must be understood and mastered.

The yellow goat-headed Vajrā Mahāchāgalā holding a noose has a southwest orientation and demonstrates the function of the *iḍā nāḍī* to and from the Sacral centre. The goat forages all kinds of experiences in *saṃsāra* that are appealing or nourishing to it. At first they are of a predominantly Watery and materialistic disposition. The goat stubbornly adheres to its foraging (consciousness-development) activities, but is quite capable of climbing the mountain of altruistic heights (the Initiation path) when it sees the need. In this way the goat generates the *iḍā* quality through the development of the attributes of mind that unite with the Watery dispensation of the Solar Plexus centre. *Kāma-manas* (desire or emotional-mind) thereby becomes the major attribute of this centre.

The noose lassos the types of *saṃskāras* that will develop into higher, more loving attributes that lay the foundation for later expression of *bodhicitta*. It can also lasso all elements of desire. The goat manifests

22 Kingly yoga, incorporating the lower Tantras: *kriyātantra, caryātantra, and yogatantra.*

a strong wilful determination to obtain whatever desire is aroused,[23] demonstrating also the strong self will of the Solar Plexus centre. The attributes of the Solar Plexus are also found in the manifestation of all selfish qualities, signified by the many forms of vegetation which the goat seeks. It is able to live in the harshest terrains (of *saṃsāra*) within which it can eek out a living. In many ways, therefore, the goat symbolises the generalised attributes of the Solar Plexus centre itself. (The mountainous view from the perspective of Sacral centre activity.) Once the focus is upon the vision of what the mountain veils and great determination is developed, self will becomes the Will-to Good upon the yogic trail of austerities, so all emotions can be dried from their Watery base. The goat exemplifies the basic attributes of a *yogin,* in which case the goat's will has been turned around in order to master the entire processes and principles of desire. The mountain symbolises travelling up the entire *nāḍī* system, both *iḍā* and *piṇgalā* to the Head lotus.

It should be noted that when the energy from the Heart centre starts to influence the Solar Plexus centre, to produce loving emotions, compassionate ideals and aspiration, the southern assignments change. The serpent (Lambodarā) then bears the *iḍā nāḍī* (preparatory to the awakening of *kuṇḍalinī)* and the goat (Mahāchāgalā) seeks the *piṇgalā,* which is found at the mountaintop. The colourations assigned to the goat and the snake reflect this transition, where the green of the snake is that of Amoghasiddhi's All-accomplishing Wisdom, which represents the mastery of *iḍā* attributes (of the Base of Spine centre). The goat's yellow colour is that of Ratnasambhava's Equalising Wisdom, which represents the mastery of *piṇgalā* attributes (mastery of the attributes of the Sacral centre). This changeability is consistent with the vacillating nature of the Solar Plexus centre, which controls the dispensation of the fickle emotions. The Watery substance is instantly coloured by the input of *manas* or desire to produce the emotional-mind and desire-mind. All these aspects must be totally controlled by the enlightenment-bound one.

The goat therefore represents the energies of the mind/Mind needed to control the entire field of the emotions (the Waters) to produce harmony where there was once strife. The snake evokes the general *prāṇic*

---

23 This willful attribute associated with both the goat and the Solar Plexus centre is the major reason why this animal was chosen to represent this particular petal of this *chakra.*

dispensation of the body so that the Earthy Element can be mastered. The lion will then project a *piṅgalā* form of *iḍā* to the Heart centre and the cuckoo an *iḍā* form of *piṅgalā*. The sun drenched environment of the basking lion symbolises the *piṅgalā* attributes of energies from the Heart. The cuckoo's song is an *iḍā* attribute.

The dark green snake-headed Vajrā Lambodarā generally conveys *piṅgalā prāṇas* of desire directed to and from the Sacral centre (a southeast orientation). These are of an Earthy nature generated in the lower centres through attachment to all types of material and desirous possessions. This is symbolised by the serpentine motion of the snake as it moves upon the ground. Indeed, this motion symbolises the way of movement of all *prāṇas*, the most basic types of which are conveyed to the Solar Plexus centre from this direction. (From here the direction north is aspired to, as one stands at the lowest point of materialistic activity and must look up from there.) The worst of the *saṃskāras* of attachment must be shattered by means of the sounds of the bell held by this deity.

Upon the path to enlightenment the bell is used as a prime ritual tool to call forth the transmutative mantric sounds of emptiness. After the Waters have been mastered, this sends the note for the generation of the serpent power *(kuṇḍalinī)*, thus the proper yogic ascent of the Fires up the spinal column to liberate the *yogin* via awakening of all the petals of the Head lotus.

The term *vajra* precedes each of these *ḍākinī's* names, indicating that the *nāḍīs* can convey the adamantine *prāṇas* of accomplishment *(siddhis)* once right meditative techniques have been mastered. The main objective of the *Bardo Thödol* is to elucidate for *yogins* and *yoginīs* the means to develop this meditative potency. We see that the major *prāṇas* in the system are collectively generated in a fivefold subdivision via the *iḍā* and *piṅgalā nāḍī* flow, when taking the Gatekeepers as a unit. These Gatekeepers fiercely guard the nature of the *siddhis* developed, carefully eliminating any disposition that may produce left-hand (dark brotherhood) aspects. This is particularly relevant if *kuṇḍalinī* is to be activated. The power of the *vajra* then manifests in the lower centres, because they have come under the control of the *prajñās* of the Jinas flowing in via the Heart centre.

The summation of these directions with respect to the types of *siddhis* represented can be briefly revealed:

- *North*: Battle with the field of desire. *Siddhi*: mastery of the basic energy distribution of the body, thus everything symbolised by the term 'sex' (*prāṇic* vitalisation), and also the power to heal psychically.
- *South*: Battle with the generation of the will. *Siddhi*: the ability to master yogic austerities.
- *West*: Battle over the sum of the Waters. *Siddhi*: development of psychic powers such as clairvoyance, clairaudience.
- *East*: Battle over subtle obscurations to the freedoms of consciousness. *Siddhi*: development of creative Idealism, direct yogic cognition, intuition, the faculties of Mind.

Practitioners should honestly discern the level of attainment they presently are at concerning the liberation (Initiation) process. Far too many focus upon the highest yoga stage (*anuttarayogatantra*) when they are effectively just beginners on the path, still working to control their emotional thinking. Thus their concern should be upon mastering the attributes associated with *caryātantra*, or thereabouts. One will not progress very far on the path through egoistical focus upon too high a gradient on the mount they have to climb when they are ill-equipped to do so. Only a tiny handful of the most advanced of the thousands of prospective *yogins* can master Initiation testings required for the highest yoga Tantra. All have the capacity, but generally a number of lives are needed. Slow and steady goes the path to enlightenment. One effectively masters one type of *saṃskāra* at a time. The complexity of the teachings in the *Bardo Thödol* indicates why.

Having set the stage for the goal of the lower Initiations as veiled by the functions of these four Gatekeepers, the attributes of the remaining Īśvarī can now be analysed. They deal with the actual process associated with mastering the necessary *saṃskāras*. Each *ḍākinī* deals with the conversion process of a particular type of *saṃskāra,* as symbolised by the petal governed. This alchemical process signifies the stages of yogic accomplishment within the alembics, spiritual retorts and distillation units that these *chakras* and the accompanying *nāḍīs* riding up the spinal column signify. *Wrath* is the initial head-on meeting of the aberrant forces needing transforming, to be later transmuted.

Subjugation is the cycling and recycling of the enriched qualities in the retorts of the *chakras* until the required grade of perfection is reached. *Enrichment* is the final purification and intensification of the required qualities. *Pacification* is the mastery of the enriched essence so that it can be utilised to produce whatever purpose is desired. Finally we have *initiation,* the attainment of the philosopher's stone that produces liberation from attributes of *saṃsāra,* thus gaining the *siddhis* that this 'stone' bequeaths.

This process of conversion of *saṃskāras* in the list of the Īśvarī shall be dealt with in the proper reversed order, starting with the rites of wrath. This is the beginning of the Fiery conversion of the base substance (the mercurial mental-emotions) that eventually becomes the alchemical gold.

The six 'Queens of Yoga' manifesting the rites of wrath

These 'Queens of Yoga' governing the *northern* direction embody the functions of the Sacral centre. The wrath here is directed at the most powerful desires, sensual, sexual energies and urges, as well as those of personal vigour and martial qualities. The most fierce energies the *yogin* can muster are therefore utilised to trample upon the arousal of these *saṃskāras.* The fearsome Wrathful Deities utilised to master these qualities come under the auspices of Amoghasiddhi and his All-accomplishing Wisdom. (The northern direction.) Here lies the powerhouse governing all later awakening of the *siddhis* by the accomplished *siddha.* Gyurme translates the relevant passage as:

> In the minor channels of the northern outer courtyard of one's skull,
> [Stand] the six Queens of Yoga who enact the rites of wrath:
> Wolf-headed Vāyudevī, bluish green, and brandishing an ensign;
> Ibex-headed Agnāyī, reddish green, and holding a firebrand;
> Sow-headed Varāhī, blackish green, and holding a noose of fangs;
> Crow-headed Cāmuṇḍī, reddish green, and holding an infant human corpse;
> Elephant-headed Bhujanā, blackish green, and holding a bloated corpse.
> And snake-headed Varuṇānī, bluish green, and holding a noose of snakes;
> O you, the six yoginī from the north, who enact the rites of wrath,

> Perform the rites which utterly destroy the confused perceptions of the intermediate state![24]

The *maṇḍala* of the Sacral centre is based on an interlaced hexagram. The hexagram demonstrates a northern (masculine) or Will triad that is concerned with the upward aspiration towards knowledge and liberation, and a southern, feminine triad concerned with the creative processes and the concretion of energies. The points of the triangles manifest the general triplicity of Will, *manasic* input, and activity. These interrelated triads are represented by the qualities of a Buddha in *yab-yum*, with the upward pointing triad represented by the Buddha and the downward pointing triad representative of the feminine Consort.

All *prāṇas* that vitalise the form are admixed with the Earthy Fires from the Base of Spine centre and those from the Gonad centres to build the health aura of the individual. We also have the initial processing of all forms of sense contacts, thus the input to the five sense-consciousnesses, producing all of the basic life processes, the *dharma,* and the series of *karmic* factors. The process of the externalisation of desire and of contact with the phenomena that one is attracted to produces that attractive magnetism that people relate to as their sexual impulses. Their drive for the propagation of the species is also stimulated. The basic instincts thus come to the fore, denoted as self-preservation of the individual, of sex, the group or herd instinct that causes people to live as part of communities, that of the self-assertion of the personality, and the instinct towards knowledge (producing the drive for continuous sensory input).

This centre is concerned with the *prāṇic* vitalisation of the body. It is essentially the dynamo that circulates *prāṇas* throughout the *nāḍīs,* from whence the vital health of the gross form is derived. The *yogin* must positively master its expression and drive the generated *prāṇas* upward for the empowerment of the various *siddhis* mentioned with respect to the *maṇipūra chakra.*

There are also six *bīja* characteristics, one for each petal, as described in Volume 2 of this *Treatise on Mind,* and summarised in Figure 10 (which was taken from that volume). The listing from the

24 Gyurme, 86.

Bardo Thödol shall be interrelated with the *bīja* characteristics. In the list there are pairs of animals and birds, followed by an animal and a snake. The birds represent the Airy qualities of the general *prāṇic* circulation, therefore they are the *prāṇas* that take flight upwards to the higher centres. The animals are earth dwelling entities, that either forage or seek out prey, of which the *prāṇas* of these major *nāḍīs* are constituted. This arrangement is correct with respect to the layout of the Sacral centre, as four petals are directly concerned with the generation and projection of *iḍā* and *piṅgalā nāḍīs,* leaving two with different functions.

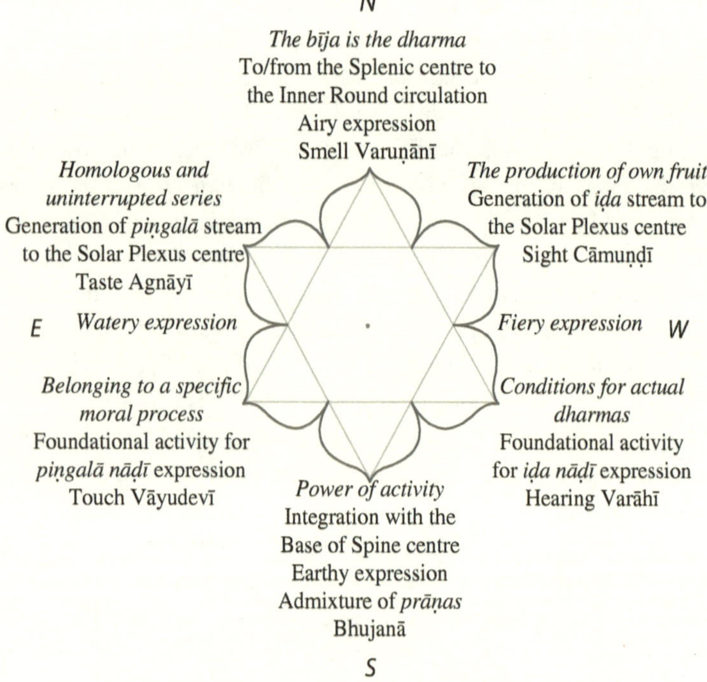

Figure 10. The Īśvarī of Wrath and the Sacral centre

Assigning *saṃskāric* qualities to the Īśvarī, or any other group of deities, is a little more complex than one would imagine at first because there are literally five levels of *saṃskāras* that need to be described for any direction.

1. That related to the most base or sensual individual, where only the dimmest concept of the need to master these qualities exists, except for purposes of self-glorification. Much *karma* is generated at this level. The Element represented is Earth.
2. That associated with average emotionally polarised people where selfish absorption is the norm. Eventually the inevitable generation of good will produces the path of aspiration in some, and religious devotion in the masses. Religious teachings then train these people to work upon their basic unruly *saṃskāras*. The Element represented is Water.
3. The more mentally polarised intelligentsia, the logical thinkers amongst humanity. A sharp divide develops amongst people at this point. First we have those who espouse entrenched materialism, competitiveness and self-centred activities. Next there are those that comprehend the illusionality of all phenomena and begin to seriously seek answers as to its meaning. Answers then come in the *dharma* they find, or else in altruistic philosophy. The ability to master *saṃskāras* is greatly facilitated by this group because they can bring clear *manasic* impetus to the task. The Element represented is Fire.
4. Those who have comprehended the solution to life's quest via the intuition, logical deduction, and by the teachings and examples offered by others. They manifest forms of (yogic) practice that lead to the necessary mastery and transformation of *saṃskāras* because they have been initiated into a valid methodology of release from the bonds of *saṃsāra*. The Element represented is Air.
5. Those who have attained life's goal and need no longer seek. They are the enlightened ones amongst us. The Element represented is Aether.

Of these five groups our analysis can avoid the first and last, and therefore concentrate on the types of *saṃskāras* that the middle three groups deal with, because they are the ones actively seeking their control one way or other. However, to avoid pedantry by making separate listings for each of the three groups (which would be difficult because of much overlapping of qualities), we can treat them as a generalised unit, leaving the practitioner to make the distinctions if desired when analysing their own level of *saṃskāric* cleansing. The Sacral centre is vital for this transformation work because the basic energies needed for accomplishment are drawn from here.

With respect to the six 'Queens of Yoga' manifesting the rites of wrath, it should be remembered that they are generally concerned with the transformation of the most aberrant *saṃskāras* in the body. The stronger the *saṃskāra* the more potent the wrath (energy) needed to deal with it. It generally takes considerable time to effectively transform most *saṃskāras* into wisdom attributes because they have been developed over many lives of activity. The task is not easy, and many subjective and overt tactics are needed to counter their effects. The most obstinate desire-forms inevitably must be forcefully dealt with. They must never be suppressed, sidestepped, or converted into another troublesome beast, needing later wrathful activity to counter. Disciples and *yogins* must work with their own wearisome psychology until victory is eventually achieved, producing a tranquil ocean of illumination.

This group of *ḍākinīs* dealing with the 'rites of wrath' is greenish in colour, signifying that their concern is with the effects of the general *karma* and *saṃskāras* of the Earthy Element. Ultimately such activity comes under the auspices of Amoghasiddhi. The mastery of these *saṃskāras* represents the basis to the attainment of his All-accomplishing Wisdom.

The Sacral centre as an eight-armed cross

Though there are six petals to the Sacral centre they can be arranged in the orientations of the eight-armed cross of direction in space. (This cross incorporates the interrelation between the fixed and mutable crosses.) This allows resonance with all of the other groups of eight so far mentioned (such as the eight Mahābodhisattvas) wherewith they can affect Sacral centre activities via their relationship with the associated direction wherein they stand.

The *fixed cross* aspect for this *chakra*, signifying the major energy direction, can be viewed when the northern and southern petals are as normal, but the eastern and western directions are each considered as a unity of two petals.

For the *northern* direction of upwards to the liberated realms, we find that these 'realms' are viewed in terms of the refined *prāṇas* of Splenic centre I, where the *prāṇas* are processed with view of whether they can be directed towards the *chakras* above the diaphragm. This direction incorporates the *prāṇas* of the upward pointing triad of petals, with the base being the two petals that are the foundation for the generation of the *iḍā* and *piṇgalā nāḍīs,* plus the northernmost petal titled '*bīja* is the *dharma*'.

This and the other statements concerning the nature of *bījas* presented in the six petals of the Sacral centre are derived from Swati Ganguli, *Treatise on Thirty verses on Mere-Consciousness.* They were explained in detail earlier in Volume 2, chapter 4, hence they are only listed here, as the reader can refer to the previous information for detail.

> (i) the *bījas* are momentary (*kṣaṇika).* They are the *dharmas* which perish immediately after birth which possess a power of activity,
>
> (ii) *bīja* is the *dharma* which is simultaneously and actually connected with its fruit,
>
> (iii) the *bījas* continue in a homogeneous and uninterrupted series until the final stage of the Holy Path of ascetic practices is attained,
>
> (iv) the *bījas* belong to a specific kind of moral species which means they must possess the capacity to produce actual *dharmas*—good, bad or non-defiled, which have perfumed and created them,
>
> (v) the *bījas* depend on a group of conditions to realize their capacity to produce an actual *dharma,* and
>
> (vi) each *bīja* leads to the production of its own fruit. A *bīja* of *citta* leads to the manifestation of *citta* and a *bīja* of *rūpa* leads to the manifestation of *rūpa.*[25]

The energies of the upward pointing triad represent the natural expression of the Sacral centre, relatively unadulterated by the sway of other forces. The rejected Earthy *prāṇas* from the Splenic centres are directed to this northern petal for reprocessing. Also, the Airy

---

25 Swati Ganguli, (trans.) *Treatise on Thirty verses on Mere-Consciousness. A critical English translation of Hsüan-Tsang's Chinese version of the Vijñaptimātratārimśikā with notes from Dharmapāla's commentary in Chinese,* (Motilal Barnasidass, Delhi, 1992), 40-41.

saṃskāras generated in the Sacral centre (representing the basic *prāṇic* vitality of the system) are directed thereto to be included into the general circulation of the entire body's *nāḍī* system via the Splenic centres.[26] 'The dharma' associated with the *bīja* quality conveys the qualities of the major *prāṇic* flow apart from the central *iḍā* and *piṇgalā nāḍī* (which flow up the spinal column). It is that which comes to and from Splenic centre II. All the general *dharmas* (factors of existence re attributes of mind) generated through physical plane interactions with others in the field of normal human relationships are processed in the spheres of sensory activity associated with the minor *chakras.*

The bluish green snake-headed Varuṇānī, who holds a noose of snakes, embodies this process. The noose of snakes represents the *prāṇas* of all of the volatile little maggots and serpents of desire and emotionality channelled through the Splenic centres, and the next level of Inner Round circulation. They may also be directed into the Eighth Sphere. Eventually these 'maggots' are transformed into various *siddhis* by means of *kuṇḍalinī,* the awakened 'serpent power'.

In this direction the structures in consciousness are built, and eventually the discipline is developed that will allow one to overcome the hydras of sex, money, and material comforts. The way to take the first Initiation can thereby be found. Obviously many battles must be fought upon the transformatory path (associated with Splenic centre activity) before such mastery of physical plane urges and appetites are possible.

The *eastern* direction is represented by the pair of *piṇgalā* petals that lay the foundation for the entire *piṇgalā* circulation in the body. They express and integrate the emotions with desire, representing therefore the most important qualities normally channelled by this *chakra,* especially in the field of human sexual relationships. The intensity of this combination is experienced by most people, especially in their juvenile years, therefore needs no further description. Sensationalised euphoria and wild emotional reactions are typical of the types of sensations that may be engendered, and require a strict moral code to control them.

The *western* direction adds the potency of *manas* (the *iḍā nāḍī* flow) to the Watery expression. It thus generates desire-mind in its inceptive stages, producing attractions, infatuations, allurements with

26 The Airy energy is then utilised to process the incoming Earthy *prāṇas.*

objects of the senses, and passionate images in the mind via the pair of petals expressing this direction. The qualities of mind are increasingly developed as energies rise up the spinal column, however, they are strongly affiliated with what people desire for themselves.

The *southern* direction integrates all of the energies of the Sacral centre with those of the Base of Spine centre to empower all forms of physical plane actions, those of a martial nature, with sexual relations, the engendering of brute force to overcome all forms of obstacles. It produces a sustained power to achieve, plus physical courage, as well as a strong burning desire for whatever the emotions latch on to. There can also be a strong animal vitality or personal magnetism developed, often accompanied with an undue focus upon physical health and bodily dexterity. The entire field of desire via the two Gonad centres comes into play here.

The overlapping between this southern petal and the northernmost petal of the Base of Spine centre is quite important because it is the place where *kuṇḍalinī* is generated. It is the zone of expression wherein the *nāḍī* system is built, therefore it represents the means whereby the entire body first comes to be energised with all of its basic *prāṇas*. Consequently, the Element associated is Earth.

This direction is symbolised by blackish green elephant-headed Bhujanā who holds a bloated human corpse, with the *bīja* quality being 'power of activity'. The elephant is a strong sure footed quadruped, whose legs stand like pillars upon the earth. It thus aptly symbolises the strong interrelation of the Sacral centre with the four petals of the Base of Spine centre. Each one of these pillars represents the qualities of the four Elements and kingdoms associated with these petals. This powerful animal supports the weight of the manifest *nāḍī* system, allowing the qualities of the four ethers to be expressed. The four feet of Bhujanā also represent the integration of the field of desire via the two Gonad centres with the interlaced Base and Sacral centres.

Each of the planes of perception manifest as a septenary, e.g., the mental consists of four concreted and three abstracted sub-planes. The physical plane is the mirror-image of the mental plane, therefore there are three concreted sub-planes—our three corporeal spheres (dense, liquid and airy), plus four abstracted, etheric sub-planes wherein resides the *nāḍīs*. Through these *nāḍīs* pour the *prāṇas* of the Fires of mind *(manas),* which integrate with the qualities of the other Elements to produce the various *saṃskāras* that condition us. They bring the expression of consciousness to the foundation that the material domain and the lesser kingdoms of Nature have supplied. Humanity are the consciousness-bearers. The fixed cross aspect of the Sacral centre also has a direct receptivity to these four etheric sub-planes. Thus the southern petal incorporates the *prāṇas* associated with the fourth ether, this is the level of the *chakras* below the diaphragm and the Inner Round. The western pair of petals generates *iḍā prāṇas* to the third ether, wherein is found the Throat centre. The eastern pair generates *piṇgalā prāṇas* to the second ether, wherein is found the Heart centre. Finally, the northern petal denoted 'the *bīja* is the *dharma*' to the qualities of the first (subtlest) ether that allows abstraction of all *manasic saṃskāras* into the Head lotus.

The bloated human corpse implies that in this integration we have the foundation of the forms of activity for the generation of all the death-like *saṃskāras* of the entire corporeal body. Essentially they are the selfish, sensual, and war-mongering activities of humans, all of which are death-like because illusional. This is possible because all the *chakras* stem from or rest upon this fundamental base integration. This base petal consequently manifests in a different way to the other petals. It is a place of admixing of base *prāṇas* rather than a zone of generation of *saṃskāras,* once the basic animal-man stage of evolution has been passed. It performs a function similar to the sixth sense-consciousnesses (the intellect) at this primary level of expression.

With respect to the *mutable cross* associated with this *chakra* the major forms of activity manifest via the remaining four petals. They are concerned with the generation and crossover of *iḍā* and *piṇgalā prāṇas* to the Solar Plexus centre. It therefore represents the foundation for the entire flow of *prāṇas* along the spinal column. Once absorbed in the Solar Plexus centre they are mixed with the *prāṇas* coming from the Stomach and Liver centres. As the Sacral centre spins so it sorts out the internal energies. Some of the *piṇgalā*-like *prāṇas* are more *iḍā*-like in terms of the Solar Plexus expression and move towards the *iḍā* stream for processing. They then become part of the left hand stream wherein the attributes of intelligence are expressed. The others stay in the *piṅgalā* stream and continue in the right hand flow, becoming the basis for the eventual development of good will and Love. The commingling of *prāṇas* in the centre implicates the often volatile and turbulent nature of people's emotions.

It should be noted that none of the four entities associated with this mutable cross aspect of the Sacral centre, except maybe Varāhī, bear clearly definable *iḍā* or *piṅgalā* characteristics. There is thus a mixed symbolism between the animal head and what the theriomorphic entity carries. This is because at this most elementary level of consciousness the principle of desire, animal passion, and forceful impulses are developed, blurring the attributes of consciousness. These four petals generate desire impulses that help empower the emotional attributes and *manasic* capacity of the Solar Plexus centre to produce *kāma-manas* (desire-mind). The north-south orientation of the mutable cross deals specifically with material plane living.

First, the two northern petals that directly channel energies to and from the Solar Plexus centre should be noted. These energies feed all attributes of people's materialistic lifestyles; their desire for plush houses, physical possessions, plus all emotional drives producing attachment to phenomena. The nature of such attraction is well known, and the *saṃskāras* become deeply entrenched. Our main emphasis here, however, is not upon these qualities, but rather with the theme of their mastery, thus of Initiation. The movement of *prāṇas* in this direction eventually produces the foundation for testings associated with the first Initiation. In these petals, therefore, the focus is upon the eventual mastery of the hydra associated with desire for material comforts. This refers to all aspects of excessive involvement within the home environment and living styles in the society within which one lives. The desire for a rich and comfortable lifestyle clashes with the type of (mental) austerities required for yogic accomplishment. The resources one possesses in life must therefore manifest a proper utilitarian function, where they assist one's endeavours to serve humanity. An excessive and exorbitant amount of things possessed is normally deadly to the quest for enlightenment. The tests concerning the right use of money (a form of material energy) are met when endeavouring to master the *saṃskāras* of all four petals of the east-west interrelation. Those concerning the sex impulse necessitate mastering the *saṃskāras* generated in the bottom pair of petals that integrate the Gonad and Base centres.

The northeast petal (of 'unity') directs the general *piṅgalā* stream to the Solar Plexus centre. Its function is controlled by the reddish green ibex-headed Agnāyī, who holds a firebrand. The *bīja* is denoted 'homologous and uninterrupted series'. This series represents the continuous flow of *prāṇas* generated through normal Sacral activity, which becomes the basis for the entire *piṅgalā* flow. A firebrand is a piece of burning wood or stick (thus can symbolise a *nāḍī)* that can be used as a torch or a weapon. The Fiery nature of the firebrand would normally signify the *prāṇas* that flow through the *iḍā nāḍī,* because this is the Element conveyed by that *nāḍī.* However, here it is subservient to the main *prāṇic* qualification represented by the ibex. Thus *manasic* qualities are generated whilst grazing in the rough terrain and craggy places of *saṃsāra.* Being a wild goat (rather than a carnivore) the ibex embodies the general more peaceful *piṅgalā*-like

Varuṇānī

Bhujanā

Plate 22. The Īśvarī of Wrath; Varuṇānī and Bhujanā

Agnāyī
With Trident - should be a Firebrand

Cāmuṇḍī

Vāyudevī

Varāhī
With Firebrand - should be a Noose of Fangs

Plate 23. The Īśvarī of Wrath; Agnāyī, Cāmuṇḍī, Vāyudevī and Varāhī

desire impulses of the Sacral centre. The 'uninterrupted series' of *saṃskāras* can then flow to the Solar Plexus centre. The *piṇgalā-iḍā* stream that is generated carries with it *saṃskāras* that like a firebrand illumines the way ahead with desire-mind upon the fields and rough, craggy terrains of *saṃsāra*.

The *northwest* petal generates the *iḍā nāḍī* projected to the Solar Plexus centre, governed by the reddish-green crow-headed Cāmuṇḍī, who holds an infant human corpse. The generation of the self will that can ravage all forms of life upon the planet (thus the human corpse) for one's own gain occurs here. (Later upon the path this quality must be converted to goodwill.) The corpse is an infant because the *iḍā* characteristics are still in their inception stage. (The arena of desire impulses of all types does not favour the development of strong mental proclivities.) The *bīja* characteristic is denoted 'production of its own fruit'. The characteristics of 'fruit' are denoted here, as compared to a simple homologous series for the *piṇgalā* petal, because the manasic development associated with the *iḍā nāḍī* produces many fruits (ideas) of what is desired. The hardships of life in the physical domain (the *prāṇas* of which are assimilated by this centre) produce the development of all the sense-consciousnesses needed for basic survival in a very competitive, often violent and dangerous world. The *piṇgalā prāṇas* on the other hand are generally generated through the more sedate lifestyle of a home environment in a rural or urban setting, fuelling more loving characteristics.

The crow is a scavenger (here symbolically) of the mind, scavenging bits of information from various sources in *saṃsāra*. This is consistent with the development and expression of the 'left hand' *iḍā* stream (which conveys all the attributes generated by mind). The infant human corpse indicates the fact that this stream channels the more elemental, basic, concreted *prāṇas* (formative child-like *saṃskāras*) compared to the more sophisticated emotional, affectionate, and then loving *prāṇas* of the 'right hand' *piṇgalā* stream. The *piṇgalā* stream leads to the development of wisdom *(prajñā)*, whereas the *iḍā* stream produces the modifications of mind, of much knowledge (*jñāna*).

The southern pair of petals deal with the generation of Sacral *prāṇas* proper, which lay the foundation for the eventual expression of the *iḍā* and *piṅgalā nāḍīs* throughout the *nāḍī* system. (This pair of petals also interrelates with the left and right Gonad centres, which are minor centres concerned with the reproductive function.) All attributes of the desire function are generated here, especially the entire whirlpool of emotions and human antics concerning the sex appeal. The types of sexual violence, strong physical urges, jealousy, sexual magic, predatory activities, etc., come as a consequence of the more base expression of this attractiveness. Then there are the more violent masculine predilections to martial arts, physical violence, waging war, brutish aggression. An adrenalin rush that comes through fear, as the adrenal glands are the externalisations of this *chakra,* generally accompanies these Sacral centre functions. Concepts of 'the body beautiful' that allure both men and women are generated where excessive focus upon the prowess of the form is indulged in. Inevitably, we have all of the social mores garnered around the sexual function in society. The general flavouring of this pair of petals represents the generation of the elementary Fires for the Sacral centre. The tests upon the path in this direction thus involve the processes that eventually produce mastery over one's sexual urges and desires. Suppression is not the answer, but rather control over strong *saṃskāras* developed over many lifetimes.

The petal associated with the *southeast* direction ('expression') concerns the foundational activity for the *piṅgalā nāḍī* via sexual interrelationships, which produce all of the basic emotions related to the love, devotion and affection that is the mainstay of this *nāḍī* stream. Here we find the role of the bluish green wolf-headed Vāyudevī who brandishes an ensign. The *bīja* characteristic is denoted 'belonging to a specific moral process', which evolves through experiences that produce such understanding through developing loving sexual relationships.

The wolf is a noble and very intelligent animal that generally hunts in packs. This speaks of the type of social organisation and group cooperation characterising the best of human activity, thus is consistent with the type of quality to be expressed by the *piṅgalā* stream. This animal was presented previously in the form of Śvānamukhī, in relation to which it was stated in part that the 'wolf demonstrates the (emotional) intelligence of the group or society one is part of. It implies the voracious garnering of objects desired by the communality of the group for its own pleasure, consumption, or amusement'. In the context of this Sacral petal therefore, we have all of the implications garnered by the sexual function as a consequence of people existing within communities, tribes and families. Many different types of *saṃskāras* have evolved which individuals must later effectively deal with, and as they do so they develop specific moral processes in their societies, within relationships, and individually, to assign what is sexually permissible or not.

The ensign this deity carries would be inscribed with the insignia characterising this general *piṇgalā nāḍī.* The insignia is however an emblem of a particular thing, signifying the development of mental *(iḍā)* characteristics that can analyse and project forward its qualities. It thus assists with the formation of the basic attributes of the *piṇgalā* stream in its early formative, *iḍā,* period.

The *southwest* direction of this swastika of energies, ('understanding'), is represented by the blackish green sow-headed Varāhī holding a noose of fangs. The *bīja* characteristic is denoted 'conditions for actual *dharmas*'.[27] The *dharmas* here represent all of the mentalistic understandings concerning the nature of things, as consistent with the symbolism of the western direction. The sow forages in the dirt and mud for sustenance, similarly to those humans travelling upon this *iḍā* path, who are addicted to the alluring fragments of information and fleeting moments of pleasure found within the muddy fields of *saṃsāra.* The 'noose of fangs' indicates the process of the mastery of all snarling, biting, and vicious attributes found in many human interrelationships. We all know of the many forms of cruelty and nastiness that humans are capable of inflicting upon others in our societies. The fangs also signify the 'sedimentation' of the rejected *prāṇas* from the Splenic centre II activity that must be re-experienced and eventually converted, because of painful repercussions, into compassionate considerations.

The symbolism of the sow earlier dealt with concerned the 'sow-headed Pāśā, who carries a noose and a skull'. It was stated: 'Of all the members of the animal kingdom that could be used to symbolise the qualities of the plant kingdom at this basic level, perhaps pigs are

---

27 See Theodore Stcherbatsky, *The Central Conception of Buddhism,* (Motilal Baranasidass, Delhi, 1994), 74-75, for a summary of the properties of these 'factors of existence'.

better than most, as they are much involved with dirt'. With respect to the Sacral centre, the plant kingdom represents the *chakra* and *nāḍī* system, whilst the dirt represents the physical plane activities that are the focus of expression at this level, with which the 'sow-individual' develops basic *saṃskāric* experiences, 'actual *dharmas*'.

Within the Sacral centre activity, five of the petals have a direct relation to the expression of the five sense-consciousnesses.

a. The snake-headed Varuṇānī, who holds a noose of snakes, develops the qualities of the head of this pentad. The sense-consciousness developed therefore is that of smell, and the Element is an Aetheric version of Earth. (Which lays the foundation for the awakening of *kuṇḍalinī,* the 'serpent power'.) The Aetheric Element at this stage is effectively non existent, instead we have the general conveyor of the mix of all the *prāṇas* to and from Splenic centre II.

b. The ibex-headed Agnāyī, who holds a firebrand, develops the attributes of the right hand of this pentad, the taste sense-consciousness, with the associated Element being the Airy aspect of Earth.

c. The crow-headed Cāmuṇḍī, who holds an infant human corpse, develops the attributes of the left hand of this pentad, the sight sense-consciousness, with the associated Element being a Fiery aspect of Earth.

d. The wolf-headed Vāyudevī, who brandishes an ensign, manifests the qualities of the right leg of the pentagram, thus the touch sense-consciousness, and the Watery aspect of Earth.

e. The sow-headed Varāhī, holding a noose of fangs, embodies the function of the left leg of the pentad, thus the generation of the *saṃskāras* of the hearing sense-consciousness, the Element being an Earthy generation of Fire.

The innate products of the evolutionary process that are the foundation of most of our activities, the *five instincts,* can also be considered to be expressions of this *chakra.*

The southern petal expresses the *saṃskāras* of the instinct of self-preservation, overcoming an innate fear of death. It is effectively an expression of the Base of Spine centre because one's most basic need is to preserve the viability of the entire human body so that all which is experienced as one's life progresses can be assimilated. The conquest of this fear produces eventual immortality (of consciousness).

The instinct of self-assertion causes the establishment of a concept of individuality, egotism, of separativeness from all other similar entities. Its expression is fostered via the northernmost petal of this *chakra*. It countermands a fear of failure of any of life's tasks or directives and produces many of the forms of aggressiveness found at this early stage of human development. It must eventually be overcome by generating the Will-to-Love.

The group or herd instinct, which comes as a consequence of an innate fear of loneliness, is fostered in the eastern pair of petals. People thus gather together in communities, where they build social and family ties, and amass a large amount of resources to which they become very attached. It produces all of the complexities of normal life, involving social standing, societal structure, and materialistic focus. Its mastery will eventually produce that awareness known to Bodhisattvas, where consciousness is shared by the entire *maṇḍala* which they embody.

The instinct towards knowledge, to gain the objective of the entire evolutionary urge, overcoming the fear of ignorance, is an expression of the western pair of petals. Its mastery will produce enlightenment.

The sexual instinct, countermanding the sense of the fear of isolation, is an expression of the combined petals of the Sacral centre. It is therefore fundamental to this *chakra*. The mastery of this fear will produce eventual yogic fusion with all *prajñās* (psycho-spiritual forces) in the body.

Effectively, the main *chakras* exist to overcome and transmute the innate effect of these instincts. Thus the Base of Spine-Head centre interrelation deals directly with the instinct of self-preservation. The instinct of the self-assertion of the individual is a Solar Plexus development. The group or herd instinct is a function of the Heart centre to address. The instinct towards knowledge helps kindle the activity of the Fiery petals of the Throat centre. The sexual instinct is controlled through mastery of Sacral centre interrelationships. The Ājñā centre coordinates the interrelation between the *prāṇas* of all these instincts. The Head centre integrates them all and produces the directives to transmute their effects into enlightened proclivities.

The general interrelation between the Sacral and Solar Plexus centres and the nature of the *prāṇic* circulation in the body can be summarised in the way that the wheels of these centres turn. As the relative petals align so energy flows from one to the other. This allows the *bījas* of the Solar Plexus to activate the petals of the Sacral centre in turn. *Saṃsāric* activity continues until the liberating way to the Heart centre is found. From the perspective of consciousness, it is a spiral stairway of beauteous revelation producing eventual bliss.

We see from the above that the theriomorphic deities are personifications of all the major and the most important minor *chakras* below the diaphragm. If we omit the twelve blood drinking deities, who embody the twelve petals of Splenic centre I (which stands as the Heart centre for this circulation below the diaphragm), then we get 48 petals altogether. There are twenty petals for the eight Mātaraḥ, the eight Piśācī and the four female Gatekeepers, plus the twenty-eight powerful animal-headed goddesses. The number 48 equals one half of the number 96, the number of secondary petals to all major *chakras*. These petals are specifically responsible for the processing of Watery *prāṇas*. This number also signifies the number of petals to any one of the two lobes of the Ājñā centre. Each lobe consists of 48 petals, allowing the right lobe to adequately convey all *piṇgalā nāḍīs* and the left lobe to similarly convey all *iḍā nāḍīs*. This *chakra* can thus function as the Third Eye with respect to the activity of the major and minor centres in the body. It can consequently direct the minor *siddhis* when they are finally generated upon the yogic path.

The six 'Queens of Yoga' who enact the rites of subjugation

The *rites of subjugation* relate to the western direction and embody the functions of the left Gonad centre. The qualifying Jina is Amitābha, and the associated sense-consciousness is that of sight. The concept of subjugation involves the use of *manas* to control the turbulences of the Waters. This differs from the *rites of enrichment,* where the Watery-Earthy Element is exemplified, making control difficult.

Consideration of the Gonad centres will complete our understanding of the functions of the first level minor centres below the diaphragm, except for the pairs of *chakras* at the soles of the feet, knees and hands.[28] These *chakras* form pentads of energy that are absorbed into the Sacral centre when the Stomach and Liver centres are also counted. They are arranged in the usual *iḍā* and *piṇgalā* streams. The *iḍā* line is directed by the left Hand centre, whilst the *piṇgalā* line is directed by means of the right Hand centre. The hands are generally controlled by strong emotions or desire, in which case the *maṇipūra chakra* becomes the directing agent. Later they are directed by the *manasic* input from the eyes. The five fingers to each hand are modes of expression of the five *prāṇas* into the material world.

This group of ten minor *chakras* convey the circulation of Earthy *prāṇas,* whilst the Feet centres are responsible for the most Earthy of these *prāṇas.* The Knee centres convey the Earthy-Airy *prāṇas,* being the substratum for the *prāṇic* circulation of the system. The two Hand centres channel the general Earthy-Fiery *prāṇas*, the Stomach and Liver centres channel the Earthy-Watery *prāṇas,* which are the dominant *prāṇas* of the system. Finally, the Gonad centres are responsive to the Earthy-Aetheric *prāṇas.* They are the most refined of all the *prāṇas* generated at this level of *prāṇic* circulation. The incorporation of the *prāṇic* essence of these pentads into the Gonad centres is necessitated in the function of procreation, where formative forces are directed to produce the appearance of forms. For this reason, and because the *prāṇas* of the other centres are absorbed into their petals, the *Bardo Thödol* focuses upon the Gonad centres.

The Gonad centres form a triad with the Sacral centre. Each centre possesses six major petals, making eighteen in all, twelve for the two Gonad centres (allowing the complete utilisation of the creative potencies associated with the twelve signs of the zodiac), and a synthesising, controlling six for the Sacral centre. The Sacral centre effectively wields the *suṣumṇā* dynamic for the *iḍā* and *piṇgalā* streams of *prāṇas* flowing through the twin groups of five minor *chakras.* This then presents the foundational basis to the yab-yum embrace between a male deity and his Consort found depicted in Tantric art. The energies from the

28 The pairs of *chakras* at the soles of the feet, knees and hands are not incorporated in the *Bardo Thödol*, therefore will not be explained here, except in the way that they fit into the overall scheme.

Gonad centres represent the *śakti/prajñā* to the male deity embodying the Sacral centre. Being the place of integration of all Earthy *prāṇas* it allows the liberation of the *kuṇḍalinī* potency. *Kuṇḍalinī* is literally the Fiery energy that integrates the form into unity.

The Sacral centre needs five petals to process each of the pentads of minor *chakras* integrated with it, plus one extra petal to admix the *prāṇas* and to redirect the *saṃskāras* to their appropriate destinations. It thus becomes the prime centre for the assimilation of the proceeds of external sense contact, primarily of a tactile nature, and consequently of all forms of relationships with objects of the material domain. With respect to the expression of the Earthy Element through the Sacral centre the five sense-consciousness are represented, plus the integrating 'sixth sense' that manifests as the intellect. The Sacral centre therefore represents the *'manasic'* reservoir of the *prāṇas* of these five minor centres.

In contrast, it should be noted that the Solar Plexus is the major synthesising centre for the Watery energy of the entire Inner Round circulation. It directs the expression of these minor *chakras* above and below the diaphragm. It is the place wherein all *saṃskāras* concerning the activities of the personal-I are processed, added to, transformed if necessary, and redirected to the centres where the new volitions can be appropriately utilised. Six of its petals are relegated to processing the *prāṇas* coming from the minor centres. The Liver and Stomach centres become the mediatory source of the in and outgoing Watery *prāṇas*,[29] whilst the Sacral centre plays a similar role with respect to Earthy *prāṇas*. Its six petals are also capable of absorbing the *prāṇas* of any grouping of the Īśvarī. The major function of the Solar Plexus centre concerns the integration of all these *prāṇas* with the Watery *saṃskāras* derived from purely emotional considerations and their *manasic* associations. The term synthesising centre refers to the centre that is the final absorbing repository (the *ālayavijñāna* reservoir) for a specific category of *prāṇas*. Briefly:

- The Sacral-Base of Spine centre unity is the synthesising centre for all Earthy *prāṇas*.

29 As well as processing Earthy *prāṇas* the Stomach and Liver centres are also an integral part of the direct Watery circulation of the *nāḍī* system.

- The Solar Plexus centre is the synthesising centre for all Watery *prāṇas*.
- Splenic centre I is the synthesising centre for the Fiery *prāṇas* developed by the minor centres below the diaphragm. It directs their most refined *prāṇas* to the major centres above the diaphragm, which from this perspective signifies liberated space.
- The Heart centre is the synthesising centre for the Airy *prāṇas* of the body.
- The Throat centre is the synthesising centre for the Fiery *prāṇas* of the body.
- The Ājñā centre coordinates and directs all of these *prāṇas,* integrating them into the Head lotus.
- The Head lotus is the synthesising centre for the *prāṇas* of the entire system, incorporating also the Aetheric *prāṇas.*

The twelve petals of Splenic centre I allow the interrelation between the Airy *prāṇas* derived from the Heart centre and the Fiery *prāṇas* from the Throat centre with the predominantly Earthy *prāṇas* that were derived from the Sacral centre, as well as the Watery from the Solar Plexus centre. The transformative process of the base Earthy *prāṇas* happens in Splenic centre II, and their refinement in Splenic centre I, so that the centres above the diaphragm can assimilate them. All processed *prāṇas* from below the diaphragm are channelled to the centres above it. When integrated into the Heart's circulation the cycle of the generation of *saṃskāras* that are based on a concept of an 'I' are made void.

The synthesising centres are also the domains of expression of the five Jinas, whereby their respective wisdoms can be evoked. We thus have:

1. The Earthy *iḍā* (left Gonad centre) and *piṅgalā prāṇas* (right Gonad centre), integrated with the Sacral and Base of Spine centres, are governed by Amoghasiddhi's All-accomplishing Wisdom.
2. The Solar Plexus centre conveying the Watery *prāṇas* of the minor centres are governed by Ratnasambhava's Equalising Wisdom.
3. Splenic centre I, conveying mainly Fiery *prāṇas* of the minor centres, plus the transformative Fires from above the diaphragm, is governed by Amitābha's Discriminating Inner Wisdom.

4. The Heart centre, conveying liberating and transmutative Airy *prāṇas* expresses the potency of Akṣobhya's Mirror-like Wisdom.
5. The Throat centre governs the overall empirical directives of the sum of the *prāṇic* circulation. The (Fiery-Aetheric) attributes of Vairocana's Dharmadhātu Wisdom is utilised here.
6. These *prāṇas* eventually find their way to either the right (*piṇgalā*) or left (*iḍā*) lobe of the Ājñā centre, which becomes their place of integration. The Ājñā centre is the 'all-seeing Eye' because each lobe of this *chakra* has 48 petals. The number 48 relates to the number of main petals to the major *chakras* below this centre. The influence of the Consort of the Ādi Buddha assists in the integration of the *prāṇas* from the minor centres prior to absorption into the Head lotus.
7. The synthetic reception and absorption of all *prāṇic* streams into the organisational structure of the 1,000 petalled lotus, the *sahasrāra padma*. This centre represents the zone of residence (Shambhala) of the representative Buddhas and Bodhisattvas controlling the development of consciousness for the entire system. It is the final synthesising centre governed by the influence of the Ādi Buddha.

The seven Rays can also be assigned to this list, starting with the organisational rhythm of the seventh Ray of Ceremonial, Cyclic Activity for the Earthy stream. The Watery stream comes under the auspices of the sixth Ray of Devotion. The Fiery stream is organised by the methodology of the fifth Ray of Intelligence, Scientific Reasoning. The Airy stream comes under the auspices of the second Ray of Love-Wisdom. The Aetheric domain is ruled by the third Ray of enlightening, Mathematically Exact Activity. The integrating function of the Ājñā centre is governed by the fourth Ray of Beautifying Harmony overcoming Conflict. Finally, the synthesising, directive *maṇḍala* of the Head lotus comes under the sway of the first Ray of Will or Power.

The Īśvarī, enacting the rites of subjugation, govern the circulation of the six petals of the left Gonad centre. The *Bardo Thödol* states:

> In the minor channels of the western outer courtyard of one's skull,
> [Stand] the six Queens of Yoga who enact the rites of subjugation:
> Vulture-headed Bhakṣasī, greenish red, and holding a club;
> Horse-headed Ratī, red, and holding a human torso;

Garuḍa-headed Rudhiramadī, pale red, and holding a cudgel;
Dog-headed Ekacāriṇī Rākṣasī, red, and holding a vajra;
Hoopoe-headed Manohārikā, red, and firing an arrow from a bow;
And deer-headed Siddhikarī, greenish red, and holding a vase.
O you, the six yoginī from the west, who enact the rites of subjugation,
Perform the rites which assure our independence during the intermediate state![30]

We have a presentation of pairs of deities (three birds and three animals), where the birds are found in the northern hemisphere of the *chakra,* and administer *prāṇas* to and from the higher centres. The animals are found in the southern petals, which administer *prāṇas* to and from the sex centres. This is because they represent the strongest forces generated, as needed for the sexual and generative function. The energies to and from the Stomach and Splenic centres are supportive and hence not so strong. The birds also refer to flights of fancy, to quick impulsive desires. Representing the expression of the elementary evolution of mind they bring the relatively fleeting *manasic* input into the overall gonadic circulation, hence that which assists in the generation of the *iḍā nāḍī* stream.

The rule of mind (*manasic* impressions) is at this stage generally swamped by the overwhelming animal-like desires, especially that of sexual impulses. This centre emanates the form-building *prāṇas* that mould the growing foetus. The higher symbolism that can be attributed refers to the foetus of the mind, as governed by Amitābha's purpose. (Governing the direction west.) The rites of subjugation come about as the mind is developed and it begins to control the forces of strong desire, embodied by the animal-headed deities (manifesting a *piṇgalā* function of desire, sexual allurement and attachment) along the six lines of expression as symbolised by the theriomorphic deities of the petals of this centre.

The problematic, strongly manifesting *prāṇas* from each petal must be subjugated in turn if the procreative forces are not to run rampant in the generation stages of the liberation of *kuṇḍalinī*, especially if the Tantric aspects of sexuality are contemplated. Preceding this stage, however, first comes the generation and later the subjugation of the

30 Gyurme Dorje, 85-86.

various attributes of desire, as a prelude for their transformation into *bodhicitta*. This centre interrelates with the Sacral centre as part of the process responsible for the foundation of the *iḍā nāḍī* that lays the conditions for the manifestation of 'actual *dharmas*'; the *saṃskāras* that support consciousness. (This Gonad centre is therefore linked to the petal of the Sacral centre governed by Varāhī.) Attributes of mind must eventually rule base desire impulses, hence we see the qualities of desire-mind generated in these petals, rather than a relatively pure *iḍā* or *piṅgalā* stream.

With respect to the qualities developed by the deities of both Gonad centres only three Elements are expressed: Earth, Water and Fire. This is because only the most foundational level of *manas* are generated, that are only capable of being garnered from the three worlds of human livingness—the physical, astral, and mental domains. Each of the spokes of the left Gonad centre has an *iḍā* quality (bird) at one end and a *piṅgalā* (animal) quality at the other, indicating the nature of the basic sense-consciousness aspect developed. We thus have:

1. The greenish red vulture-headed Bhakṣasī, who holds a club, occupies the northern petal. A vulture purveys the entire earthy scenario below it for deceased entities; the carrion, and offal, the basest form of food to consume. The club is a primitive weapon used to pound the elementary Earthy *iḍā saṃskāras* into the desired shape.

   These *prāṇas* represent those that have been rejected from Splenic centre II circulation and that must be further processed in the left Gonad centre before they can be returned with view of being incorporated into the circulation of the higher centres. They also represent the most Earthy *prāṇas* from the centres that can be utilised for form building (of a child) or for gonadal secretions. Being rejected by the activity of Splenic centre II they appear death or corpse-like with respect to the higher, more vitalised *prāṇic* flow of the major centres.

   The gonads are the gateway to the next lower level of minor *chakras*, the 49 small centres. The *prāṇas* from these centres can be considered 'carrion, offal' with respect to those from the first level minor centres represented by the Gonad centres. Yogically, everything concerning the form is regarded as death-like and death dealing, appropriately guarded over by vultures and other carrion-eaters.

2. The red horse-headed Ratī, holding a human torso, stands at the southern petal to the northern position of Bhakṣasī. The *prāṇas* from Splenic centre II flow from here to the Sacral and Base of Spine integration with each other and the Gonad centres. The horse is a bearer of human consciousness (the human torso), and here it conveys the most *manasic* attributes of the Earthy *prāṇas* possible to the Sacral centre and generative organs, so that they can be appropriately utilised for procreation. The horse indicates that these desire-mind impulses bear the rudiments of the development of *manas* that are to be cycled through the general gonadic circulation. It can then also bear and help regulate the force of the sacral impulse when it arises.
3. The pale-red Garuḍa-headed Rudhiramadhī, holding a cudgel, occupies the northeast petal of this centre bearing *iḍā* (*manasic*) energies from the Stomach centre. Garuḍa feasts on serpents, the purpose is to eliminate most of the little serpents of desire and lust that are coupled with rudimentary mind so that they no longer affect consciousness in a problematic way. Upon the yogic path, they will be cudgeled into shape and controlled so that sexual images and strong desire that prevent the generation of a serene mind will not permeate the psychic constitution. It should be noted that the desire-mind represents the deadliest combination combating the meditation-stream of all hearkening to be wise. The Garuḍa-headed deity must be most vigilant, because even the smallest serpent can grow into a viper or Hydra of monstrous proportion.
4. The red dog-headed Ekacāriṇī Rākṣasī holds a *vajra* and occupies the southwest petal of this *chakra*. From here emotional *piṅgalā prāṇas* of animal-like desirous propensity evolve after the *manasic* Stomach centre energies from the northeast (polar opposite) energies have been admixed with the general Gonad centre energies. The product is an affectionate, desire based disposition of mind. Of all the animals, the dog is the most devotional and affectionate to humans, but can also be ferocious and aggressive. Therefore, the dog represents the generation of thoughts and ideals of love, strong affection, and companionship with respect to one's sex life, or else the many aggressive attitudes, jealousies, and forms of animosity

that also come from it. It therefore aptly symbolises the relatively strong *iḍā-piṅgalā* interrelation associated with this petal. Watery attributes of Earthy *iḍā prāṇas* are then directed to a small *chakra* associated with the procreative function, to control the entire form-building propensity. These emanations plus those derived from the mineral kingdom build the form of the child of whatever is to be. The functioning and secretions of the actual physical organ are affected. The 'club' pummels the associated physical forces and secretions so that they don't override consciousness with too much desire. The *vajra* indicates that the full force of the five sense-consciousnesses need to be projected to fulfil this function. Later the experiences gained can act as a base to generate basic wisdoms because the principle of devotion, loving disposition, and good will has been established, coupled with the development of elements of mind (as governed by the Stomach centre's activities).

5. The red Hoopoe-headed Manohārikā, firing an arrow from a bow, governs the northwest petal of the left Gonad centre. The hoopoe has a well-defined crest, symbolising many little thoughts coming from the mind. The insects and small invertebrates eaten relate to nagging worries and doubts, irritations and frustrations. Here these are generally of a sexual nature or concerned with human relationships. These energies can consequently be quite strong, even overwhelming, if not properly controlled. This is a Fiery (*iḍā*) petal of Gonadal activity, which directs the desire-mind *prāṇas* generated to the Stomach centre, hence the use of a bow and arrow. (They can then be absorbed and properly processed, as the Stomach centre can handle strong and even violent emotional thoughts.) On the path of liberation, Manohārikā fires the arrows of well-directed thoughts to the higher centres, assisted by the Gonad centre. For proper yogic control and discipline, such arrows will have to be fired continuously and forcefully to the target arenas of the sexual psyche to effectively transform all aspects of the desire principle into their loving correspondences.

6. The greenish-red deer-headed Siddhikarī, holding a vase, governs the southeast petal of the left Gonad centre. Here *manasic* attributes of *piṅgalā prāṇas* generated as a consequence of form building

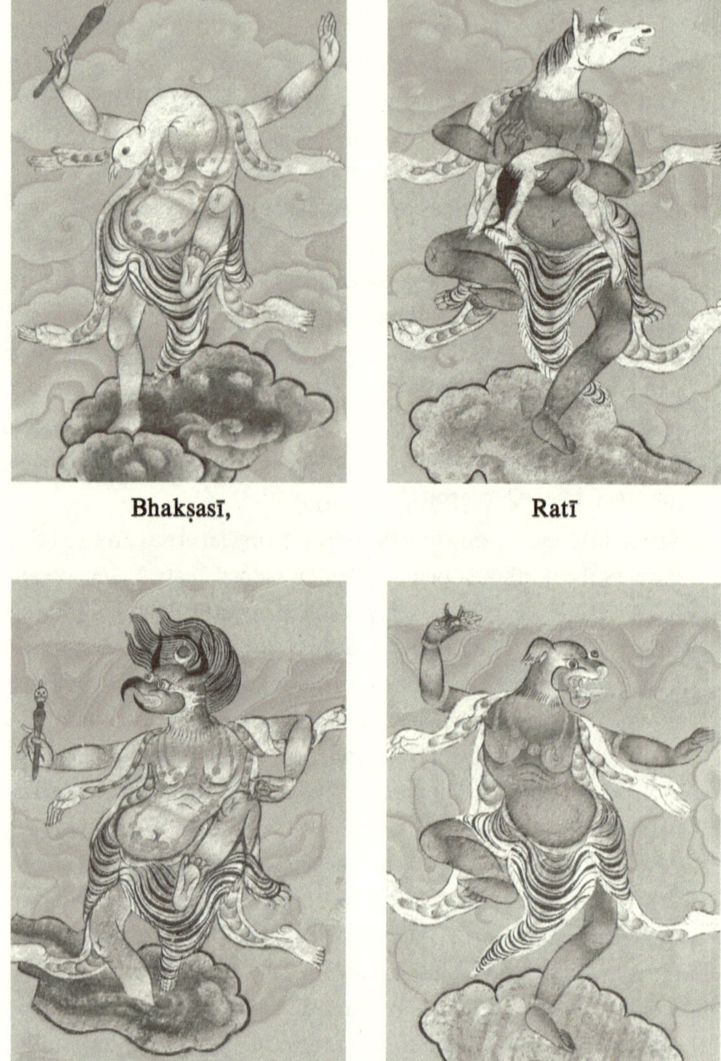

Bhakṣasī, Ratī

Rudhiramadhī Ekacāriṇī Rākṣasī

Plate 24. The Īśvarī of Subjugation; Bhakṣasī, Ratī, Rudhiramadhī and Ekacāriṇī Rākṣasī

Manohārikā **Siddhikarī**

Plate 25. The Īśvarī of Subjugation; Manohārikā and Siddhikarī

come from a small centre concerned with the procreative function. It controls the entire form-building propensity. The deer is considered one of the mildest and gentlest of animals, which indicates the relatively benign nature of the life-supporting energies coming from the bodily form, which Siddhikarī contains in her vase.

The two Gonad centres are directly linked to each other and to the Sacral and the Base of Spine centres. For the most part they function as an integral unity. This interrelation lays the foundation for the way the petals of the Solar Plexus centre are organised, and the mode this lotus awakens.

The six 'Queens of Yoga' projecting the rites of enrichment

These 'Queens of Yoga' manifest the attributes of the southern direction and embody the functions of the right Gonad centre. The corresponding Jina for below the diaphragm is Ratnasambhava, with the associated sense-consciousness being that of touch.

In the minor channels of the southern outer courtyard of one's skull,
[Stand] the six Queens of Yoga who enact the rites of enrichment:
Bat-headed Vajrā, yellow, and holding a razor;
Crocodile-headed Śāntī, reddish yellow, and holding a vase;
Scorpion-headed Amṛtā, reddish yellow, and holding a lotus;
Hawk-headed Saumī, whitish yellow, and holding a vajra;
Fox-headed Daṇḍī, greenish yellow, and holding a cudgel;
And tiger-headed Rākṣasī, blackish yellow, and drinking from a blood-filled skull.
O you, the six yoginī from the south, who enact the rites of enrichment,
Perform the rites which enrich pristine cognition during the intermediate state![31]

Because the Gonad centres are minor *chakras* the potencies of their individual petals are not as strong as those of the major centres. The main importance of the Gonad centres is that they are focal points of application reinforcing the sexual functions and field of desire with respect to Sacral centre activity. This right Gonad centre interrelates with the foundational petal in the Sacral centre for the *piṇgalā nāḍī,* denoted 'a specific moral process'.

With reference to the phrase 'rites of enrichment', one may ask 'what indeed is enriched by these rites?' One intention of Tantric practice is to positively enrich *prāṇas* and thus convert the *saṃskāras* to produce a consequent ennoblement of a person's character. The development of various forms of social mores enriches the principle of desire and all types of human interrelationship refine this principle. Desire is converted into truly loving dispositions when people develop wisdom. Upon the path of yogic control desire is transformed into right aspiration. This occurs when *saṃskāras* of loving dispositions are enriched to produce compassionate undertakings, wherein human relationships and sexuality are equanimously seen as a means of union with the governing forces of Nature. Ratnasambhava's Equalising Wisdom is thereby developed, integrating all disparate forces into unity.

As the Gonad centres deal specifically with the sexual function, incorporating some of the next level of smaller *chakras* of the Inner Round, the complete mode of their activity cannot be fully revealed.

31 Gyurme Dorje, 85.

Daṇḍī Rakṣasī

Saumī Amṛtā

Plate 26. The Īśvarī of Enrichment; Daṇḍī, Rakṣasī, Saumī and Amṛtā

Śāntī Vajrā

Plate 27. The Īśvarī of Enrichment; Śāntī and Vajrā

The subject is also complicated by the differences between the male and female sexual anatomy, for which explanation would have to be provided (as well as that related to the gestation of a child) in any detailed account of this arena of the *nāḍī* system. Such explanation lies outside the scope of this present work.

Regarding the *prāṇic* circulation at the level of expression of the Gonad centres we should note that the normally forceful and generally overriding passions of the emotions, strong desires, and attachments to things material or sensual are dominant. These passions exemplify the potency of the *piṅgalā* line and the *prāṇic* forces to be borne by the petals of the right Gonad centre. They are significant forces that also must be wielded by the Sacral centre. Instead of the flighty birds depicted for the (*iḍā*) left Gonad centre we therefore have much more powerful, dangerous animals manifesting in the right Gonad centre. Even in the case of the hawk we have an efficient predator.

1. The greenish white fox-headed Daṇḍī, holding a cudgel, stands at the northern petal of the right Gonad centre that channels *prāṇas* to and from Splenic centre II. These *prāṇas* are the most refined (Earthy-

Aether) that this *chakra* can express, though they also represent what Splenic centre II rejects along the *piṇgalā* line, needed reprocessing. Consequently, they are forceful potencies of desire-sexuality which the wily fox obtains to gain what is desired or to obtain that which is most pleasurable by stealth and cunning, rather than through brute force. *Saṃskāras* concerning the generation of the object of desire thus come into play. Later the cudgel is utilised to pummel out unwanted, unwholesome desires and wrongly directed deceitful sexual impulses.

2. The blackish tiger-headed Rakṣasī (meaning a 'cannibal demon') drinking from a *kapāla* guards the southern petal. Rakṣasī directs the most refined manasic attributes of this *piṇgalā* line to be integrated with the *prāṇas* of the Base of Spine and Sacral centres. The tiger represents the *saṃskāras* of strong passions that are well hidden in the jungles of desires, and which can spring out at any moment to overwhelm the individual. Such passions are eventually transformed into the ambrosial *bodhicitta* contained in the skull cup, signifying the mastery of all aspects of human relationships and sexual union. The *(kuṇḍalinī)* potency veiled by the Base of Spine centre will then be conveyed into the entire Earthy circulation of the Gonad centres. Until then the cup contains the intoxicating liquor of infatuation with the pleasure of the gratifications of the form and loving relationships, which the tiger stalks at first. Later he yogically seeks out the inner Fire of the psychic heat.
3. The whitish hawk-headed Saumī carries a *vajra* and guards the northeast petal of the right Gonad centre. The hawk spots its prey from a great height, here indicating the conveyance of the Earthy-Airy *prāṇas* projected from the Liver centre into the desire-based energy pool of the right Gonad centre. The emotional potencies from the Solar Plexus centre are also mainly expressed via this route. They generally manifest in the strong Watery desires of the Scorpion-headed Amṝtā (the polar opposite southwest petal). Therefore this centre conveys the potent *saṃskāras* that manifest the general emotional disposition of the person as far as attachment to objects of the form are concerned. These *saṃskāras* manifest via the Gonadic centre's dispensation in the form of loving disposition found in human relationships between

couples and during courting rituals. The 'prey' constitutes images of the members of the opposite sex or any other significant desirous object. Upon the higher way the *vajra* indicates the transformation of this loving disposition into the true selfless service for others that is the hallmark of the Bodhisattva. The 'prey' is then all aspects of the *dharma* that can assist in this task.

4. The reddish-yellow scorpion-headed Amṛtā, occupying the southwest petal, holds a lotus. The scorpion is considered a desert living entity with a very painful sting that can kill, and so is feared by most travellers. The environment it resides in and its death-dealing sting is a symbol for the hardships of *saṃsāra.* Note that *amṛtā* means 'deathless state', immortality. It thus refers to the elixir of immortality, soma, ambrosia, a purified, transmuted mixture of the *saṃskāras* that formerly produced painful ego-clinging. Heightened emotional intensity from the Liver centre, fuelling desire, is conveyed by the scorpion to a small centre governing the function of the pleasure of the sex act.

   At this stage, therefore, the *amṛtā* relates to sexual pleasure. The scorpion then expresses the myriad emotional stings that people suffer through their sexual relationships. The lotus at first indicates that many of the *saṃskāras* that vitalise and are conveyed by the minor centres are generated in relation to consideration of this act. Many flowers bloom as a consequence.

   Upon the upward way the stings and poisons experienced upon the wheel of rebirth in *saṃsāra* are eventually converted into the 'deathless' qualities of the wheel of *dharma.* (Of which each *chakra* manifests it own version.) This is because a function of the sex act is to convert basic desire to loving relationships, the foundation for the eventual generation of the Will-to-Love. This happens directly via the *piṇgalā* line, allowing *bodhicitta* to be expressed by the *yogin* or *yoginī* concerned. We can see here that the fusion of the masculine-feminine attribute of compassion and wisdom inherent in the two parts of this compound word (*bodhi* and *citta*) has its foundation in the sex act, and produces the ultimate goal of the nondual union of a Buddha with his Consort. It is important, however, to realise that it is the internal yogic fusion of male and female *prāṇas* within the psyche that produces this enlightenment, not the physical plane act. The death-dealing proclivity of the scorpion's sting is there to remind all *yogins* of this important fact.

5. The reddish-yellow crocodile-headed (or rather, Makara-headed) Śāntī holding a vase occupies the southeast petal of this *chakra*. The vase contains the expression of the Watery Element at this level of basic desirous-*saṃskāras*. They represent the returning *prāṇas* of having obtained the objective of desire. These *prāṇas* have come from a small *chakra* governing the pleasurable function of the sex act, thus with the gain of physical desire.

   The aggressive, dangerous king of reptiles (the crocodile) symbolises the generation of some of the most base, reptilian-like sexual *saṃskāras* that can manifest in a decidedly unpleasant manner, where sex is sought after only for the temporal pleasures it can bring. It also concerns the type of environment that such people reside in. Therefore, as well as representing the physicality of this act by an animal that lives part on land and in the water, there is also implicated some of the more problematic expressions of people's sexuality.

   Note that *śāntī* means 'tranquillity', referring here to the conversion of impulsive desire-ridden or sexual behaviour into tranquil, peace-abiding attributes. This is the objective of the disciple in dealing with all of these sexual impulses. Upon the higher way the vase is utilised to contain these transformed, controlled *saṃskāras*, preventing them from escaping and causing havoc for the *yogin's* austerities (*tapas*).

6. The yellow bat-headed Vajrā holding a razor occupies the northwest petal of this *chakra*. The bat lives in dark caves, symbolising relatively unimportant, dimly lit *chakras*. Here a *nāḍī* to the Liver centre is implied, and represents the flow of *prāṇas* that are the experiential gain from the field of desire. Generally, this gain is relatively inconsequential as far as the development of wisdom is concerned because the person seeks to satiate the objective of desire over and over again. Pleasure is sought, as well as the consequential myriad *karma*-creating forms of emotional highs and lows. Ignorance is thus perpetuated, hence the bat flies in darkness,

seeking out various nooks and crannies within the caves wherein this animal finds residence. The caves also represent the next level of small *chakras* that the sexual centres are gateways to, which are also the bat's habitat.

The razor Vajrā holds is a very sharp instrument, quickly able to cut through relatively smallish undesirable *saṃskāras,* as is consistent with the second minor level Inner Round circulation of *chakras* that concern us here. The enlightenment-bound one must be able to consistently sever such ties with this razor if the upward way to the higher centres is to be trodden.

In this explanation of the Īśvarīs I have omitted interpretation of their colours because their relationship to the respective Jina families should be clear enough.

The six 'Queens of Yoga' demonstrating the rites of pacification

The *rites of pacification* are associated with the eastern direction and govern the remaining six petals of the Solar Plexus centre. These rites refer to the major function of this *chakra* with respect to the wilful Watery *prāṇas* generated below the diaphragm. They have been cleansed as much as possible from wrongly coloured, dirty, or muddied dross through the processes of wrath, subjugation and enrichment. Now they may be thoroughly controlled (pacified), before being directed to the respective *chakras* that best suit their characteristics.

> In the minor channels of the eastern outer courtyard of one's skull,
> [Stand] the six Queens of Yoga who enact the rites of pacification:
> Yak-headed Manurākṣasī, brownish white, and holding a vajra;
> Snake-headed Brahmāṇī, yellowish white, and holding a lotus;
> Leopard-headed Raudrī, greenish white, and holding a trident;
> Weasel-headed Vaiṣṇāvī, bluish white, and holding a wheel;
> Brown Bear-headed Kaumārī, reddish white, and holding a short pike;
> And black bear-headed Indrāṇī, white, and holding a noose of entrails.
> O you, the six yoginī from the east, who enact the rites of pacification,
> Perform the rites which pacify our fears of the intermediate state![32]

32 Gyurme Dorje, 85.

The functioning of the Solar Plexus centre *(maṇipūra chakra)* is somewhat complex, as was stated in Volume 2, chapter 4 of this treatise, from which Figure 11 was derived. This *chakra* is the place of generation of the emotions and of self will, utilising the principle of desire, around which the entire construct of the personal-I is formed. There are ten petals to this centre, arranged in the form of two groups of five petals. One pentad expresses the more Airy-Fiery attributes of Watery *prāṇas* and the other the more Earthy attributes.

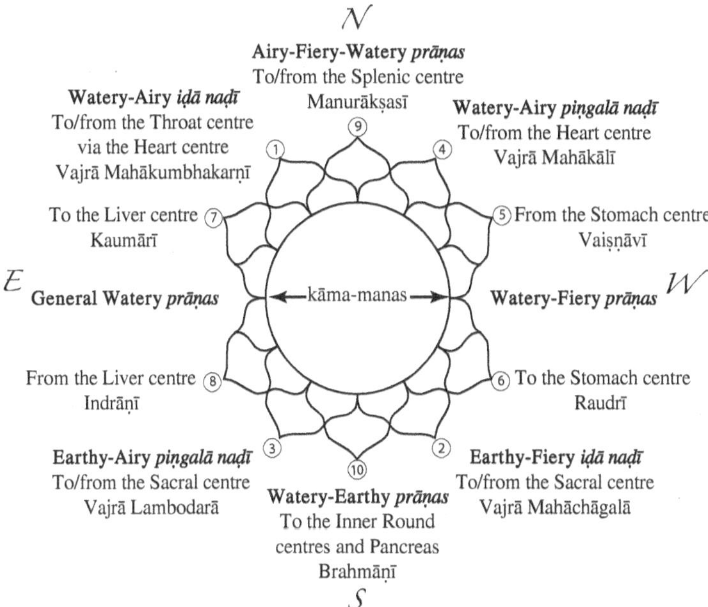

Figure 11. The *maṇipūra chakra* and the Īśvarī of Emanation and Pacification

The pentads have a north-south orientation. There is also an east-west focus towards the Liver and Stomach centres, which deal with the dominant Watery-Fiery aspects of the Solar Plexus centre. The *prāṇas* directed north have a predominant Airy overtone. Those directed south are predominantly Earthy, those directed east (to the Liver centre) are predominantly Watery, whilst those directed west (to the Stomach centre) have a Fiery flavour. The east-west direction demonstrates the potency of the desire or emotional-mind *(kāma-manas)* that is the major attribute generated by this centre and the associated minor ones. This then is the overview of the general *prāṇic* flow, but the major orientation of the *prāṇas* is in terms of two groups (hands) of five petals.

We can analyse the 'two hands' of petals depicted in Figure 11 in terms of *prāṇas* conveyed in the individual petals as fingers of energies. The Airy *piṇgalā* line (3-4) is concerned with the development and expression of the taste sense-consciousness (signifying the ring finger). The Fiery *iḍā* line (2-1) similarly concerns the sight sense-consciousness (the index finger). The petals representing the dexterity of the thumbs (6-7) express the major Watery *saṃskāras* of this centre, and the touch sense-consciousness. The hearing sense-consciousness is conveyed by the central Earthy finger (9-10). The smell sense-consciousness and the embryonic ability to respond to Aetheric impressions is conveyed by the little finger (8-5). Generally only four *prāṇas* are experientially developed, the fifth (Aether) being too subtle and abstract for most to utilise in the form of *saṃskāras*. It represents the most refined *prāṇas* the minor centres are capable of generating.

The main activity is between the Solar Plexus and Sacral centres, as well as the general Inner Round circulation of minor and small *chakras*. The Stomach and Liver centres are then the main onus of expression, whilst the Splenic centres actively play their roles of recycling and converting *prāṇas*. Upon the Bodhisattva path all the pentads of *prāṇas* are expressed and transformed. At first the energies from the Heart centre are drawn to the Solar Plexus centre to effect the necessary transformations. Later the cleansed and transmuted *prāṇas* find abode in the Heart centre.

The Stomach and Liver centres may be viewed as extensions of the Solar Plexus centre, as they are the reservoirs for its *piṇgalā* and *iḍā prāṇas* respectively, though they are not specifically agents for the transformation of *saṃskāras*. Consequently, no further detail of their activity is given in the *Bardo Thödol*.

In analysing the characteristics of the animal-heads of the Īśvarī performing the rites of pacification we see that they manifest as three pairs of entities: two bears, two carnivores, and two other animals.

In the northern direction the brownish white yak-headed

Manurākṣasī

Brahmāṇī

Raudrī

Vaiṣṇāvī

Plate 28. The Īśvarī of Pacification; Manurākṣasī, Brahmāṇī, Raudrī and Vaiṣṇāvī

Kaumārī

Indrāṇī

Plate 29. The Īśvarī of Pacification; Kaumārī and Indrāṇī

Manurākṣasī,[33] who holds a *vajra,* governs the *prāṇas* coming to and from Splenic centre I. Splenic centre I directs its Watery-Fiery reject *prāṇas* needing recycling to the Solar Plexus centre, whilst the Solar Plexus centres sends to it for further refining the most Airy aspect of its general Watery-Earthy *prāṇas.* The yak is a peaceful grazing animal that forages on the greenery it resides in. In a similar fashion this Splenic centre processes the general *saṃskāras* foraged in the symbolic green fields of *saṃsāra* represented by the verdure of the Solar Plexus centre and the entire Inner Round *chakras* it synthesises. The purpose of the power of a *vajra* is to use the most potent forces possible to effect the necessary transformations of *saṃskāras,* which allows the *prāṇas* to be accommodated by Splenic centre I and sent to the centres above the diaphragm. The attributes that vitalise and transform the centres below the diaphragm are thereby developed. The *prāṇas* coming from Splenic centre I are a wash of energies representing muddied accumulations of

33 The term 'Manu' comes from the root 'man', 'to think', thus the name Manurākṣasī refers to a flesh eating demoness, who devours evil spirits (the denizens of the lower strata of the astral and mental realms) with the power of thought.

saṃskāras needing to be refined ('pacified') through being experienced upon a higher cycle of activity.

In the southern direction stands the yellowish-white snake-headed Brahmāṇī who holds a lotus. She embodies the functions of the petal that directs *prāṇas* to the pancreas, whose secretions represent the physical externalisation of the energies of the Solar Plexus centre,[34] as well as to the Inner Round of small *chakras*. Being a physical organ the pancreas therefore is a repository of the most Earthy *prāṇas* from the Watery Solar Plexus centre. The lotus symbolises the attributes of all the small *chakras* that ascribe to the potency of the vitalisation from the Solar Plexus centre, the central processing organ and directing agent for their *prāṇas*.

The greenish-white leopard-headed Raudrī, holding a trident, is one of a pair of carnivores directing Watery-Fiery *prāṇas* to and from the Stomach centre (the western direction) which processes the forceful predatory *saṃskāras* of mental-emotions, aggression, as well as the general *manasic* propensities developed by the emotions through sense contact. The carnivores are represented here because they express the energies of the will, and the stalking tendencies associated with ambitious and aggressive activities. These are *iḍā* in nature because the necessities of the hunt tends to develop the attributes of the mind. Raudrī, who *prāṇically* embodies the ambidexterity of the left thumb, directs the most powerful *kāma-manasic prāṇas* the Solar Plexus centre has developed to the Stomach centre. The powerful leopard consequently is used to symbolise this *prāṇic* flow. It is quite capable of seeking out the desirous propensities of mind within the jungles of *saṃsāra*. The trident allows Raudrī to control the general Watery disposition of the Solar Plexus by means of the attributes of mind.

The second of the carnivores, the bluish-white weasel-headed Vaiṣṇāvī, holding a wheel, directs the *manasic prāṇas* from the Stomach centre. Because *manas* is subservient to the Watery disposition of the Solar Plexus, but in time must come to fully control it, so the comparatively diminutive weasel is implicated. The mental element fused with the emotions and desire produces the cunning, deceit or

---

34 It secretes digestive enzymes, and the hormones insulin and glucagon, needed for carbohydrate (sugar) metabolism into the bloodstream.

craftiness implied by this animal, juxtaposed to the more forcefully aggressive leopard. The weasel represents the relative extent of *manasic* control that most people have over their emotions. The relatively diminutive Aetheric little finger of the top hand is implicated. The wheel held by Vaiṣṇāvī relates to the ability of *manas* to sort out the forms of emotionality and to appropriately direct them.

The pair of bears suggest the most powerful energies developed by people, the total strength of their Watery emotions and desires directed to and from the Liver centre in the eastern direction. As the main *prāṇas* of the Solar Plexus are *piṇgalā* in nature so it is natural that the large and powerful bears symbolise the general intensity of people's emotional proclivities. We thus have the reddish white brown bear Kaumārī holding a short pike regulating the direction of *prāṇas* to the Liver centre and the white coloured black bear-headed Indrāṇī holding a noose of entrails. She channels the *prāṇas* coming from the Liver centre that have been digested, processed, and then stored therein for the sum of the Inner Round circulation.

The pike can produce the penetrating sharpness of many emotions. Yogically, however, it relates to controlling the attributes of nastiness, or forceful, unthinking emotional incentives, and relegating them to their rightful place, preventing their ability to harm. The entrails relate to the general Watery disposition that has been stored in the Liver centre, and which can be projected into the *prāṇic* circulation at need. The fact that the entrails are in the form of a noose means that particular attributes can be lassoed and appropriately controlled by the individual.

The *bījas* and the *maṇipūra chakra*

The ten characteristics of *bījas* presented in the *Treatise on Thirty Verses on Mere-Consciousness* correspond to the ten petals of the *maṇipūra chakra. Bījas* manifest as a consequence of the wilful volition associated with this *chakra* and are actualised via one or other of its petals.

> The 'seeds' are the different potentialities found in the fundamental consciousness *(ālayavijñāna).* They immediately produce their fruits or the actual *dharmas.* The *bījas* in relation to the *mūlavijñāna* and the fruit are neither identical nor different. They are real entities. However their reality is not the same as *tathatā.* They exist as they are produced

> through causes and conditions. The *bījas* depend on the substance *(t'i)* of the eighth consciousness. They are part of *nimittabhāga,* as they are taken as object by *darśanabhāga.* According to Dharmapāla, there are two kinds of *bījas* – (i) natural *bījas* and (ii) *bījas* born of perfuming. The natural *bījas* are the potentialities which have existed innately in the *ālaya* by the natural force of things *(dharmatā).* They produce mental elements, sense-organs and the seeming external objects. The other kind of the *bījas* are those which have come into being as a result of the 'perfuming' of actual *dharmas,* the 'perfuming' being repeated again and again from beginningless time. The seeds stored in the *ālayavijñāna,* being perfumed by seven other consciousnesses, are caused to grow, resulting in the appearance of things.[35]

Only the most pertinent qualities for these petals shall be given, presenting the list according to the numbers depicted in Figure 11 of the *bījas* and the *maṇipūra chakra.* Volume 2, chapter 4 of this *Treatise on Mind* needs to be consulted for added detail concerning the main characteristics of the *bīja* qualities. The first four numbers relate to the four female Gatekeepers of Emanational Rites. They manifest in the form of a *mutable cross* (despite the west-east-south-north orientations assigned to them).

1. At the *western* gate we have the red lion-headed Vajrā Mahākumbhakarṇī.[36] The *bīja* keynote is 'The "seeds" are the different potentialities found in the fundamental consciousness *(ālayavijñāna)'.* These *prāṇas* come from the Throat centre, which directs Fiery energies to seed the *maṇipūra* with *manasic* impressions. We therefore have the main ideas that feed the emotional body with the images of what the 'I' wants. The Solar Plexus centre then draws *bījas* from its collective pool that will instantaneously clothe the images with the weight of the propensities developed from the past. These *saṃskāras* are expressed in new *karma*-formations (volitions). This inwardly demonstrates the way people's desire-minds function to imprint the *maṇipūra* with aspects of *ahamkāra*, the 'I am' consciousness; providing self-identity for

35 Swati Ganguly, *Treatise on Thirty Verses on Mere-Consciousness,* 40.

36 The directions are given according to the corresponding colour of the associated Dhyāni Buddha.

each new incarnation. Via this petal, therefore, the various *bījas* of consciousness-volitions, the *saṃskāras* of identity with things in relation to the 'I', arise. Consciousness then grows in the nine ways associated with the other petals, when these Fiery *bījas* are progressively clothed with the Watery qualities associated with the *maṇipūra chakra* and the outward going *prāṇas.*

2. At the *southern* gate we have the yellow goat-headed Vajrā Mahāchāgalā who directs *iḍā prāṇas* to and from the Sacral centre. There they are grounded into actual concretion as physical action via the field of desire by means of the sense contacts and related perceptions so familiar to us. This relates to the phrase 'They immediately produce their fruits or the actual "*dharmas*"'. This is because the Sacral centre directs the vitality of the entire bodily organism, and is specifically concerned with the process of identification (with that which is material in nature), hence we have concretion. The appearing *saṃskāras* therefore compellingly cause us to identify with the things corresponding to forms of activities formerly undertaken but still perpetuated. Here *dharmas* refer to the attributes of unavoidable bits of *karmic* law with which one must reckon.

3. At the *northern* gate (with respect to the Sacral centre) we have the dark green snake-headed Vajrā Lambodarā, with the key phrase being 'the *bījas* in relation to the *mūlavijñāna* and the fruit are neither identical nor different'. The *mūlavijñāna* is the root form of consciousness *(vijñāna),*[37] therefore with respect to *prāṇic* circulation it is concerned with the nature of the sense-consciousnesses garnered from the field of desire. This involves the returning *prāṇas* from Sacral centre activity along the *piṅgalā* line that develop consciousness. It becomes the basis for the expression of the forms of emotional self-identity associated with the *maṇipūra chakra.* The phrase 'the fruit are neither identical nor different' can

37 *Vijñāna,* consciousness, in all its attributes, from which is appropriated the mind (*manas*), discriminative knowledge. An awareness which is knowing and luminous. *Vijñāna* is composed of the prefix *vi,* meaning 'to divide', and the root, *jñā,* which means 'to perceive', 'to know'. Thus, *vijñāna* is the faculty of distinguishing or discerning or judging.

here refer to the fact that this fruit (referring to *karmic* effects) is of like nature. Having grown from the soil of *saṃsāra,* it is constituted of the originating *bījas* (which therefore are not different) plus that which has been derived from them (thus are not identical).

4. At the *eastern* gate we have the white cuckoo-headed Vajrā Mahākālī, the *bīja* quality given: 'They are real entities. However their reality is not the same as *tathatā'.* Here the *prāṇas* cross over to the Heart centre from the Solar Plexus centre after they are cleansed of their Watery dross. They then become 'real entities' by virtue of being absorbed into the general reservoir of the Heart's potency *(bodhicitta).* The Heart is the source of the entire process of gaining enlightenment, the Real. Addiction to forms of illusion no longer concern the individual, rather, the aspiration is to consciously encapsulate forms of *bījas* stemming from the *dharmakāya.* The types of self-identification associated with the Solar Plexus centre have been swept away by the vitalising *prāṇas* from the Heart centre. Only that which is most refined and akin to the Heart's own substance can now flow up the Airy *piṅgalā* channel. Within the general *prāṇic* pool of the Heart lotus the *prāṇas* are 'not the same as *tathatā*' because they are expressions of the five non-sacred petals of the Heart centre at this stage and need further refinement (rectification) before *tathatā* is the result.

The next six deities together form a fixed cross of resolute purpose orientated in the north-south, east-west direction within the Solar Plexus centre. They are 'fixed' because though individual emotions are volatile, the overall strength of emotionality remains constant, and are mastered with difficulty. The fixed cross integrates all *prāṇas* into the *maṇipūra* circulation, and directs the most appropriate *prāṇas* to either the Heart or Sacral centres, depending upon their resolved qualities.

5. The bluish-white weasel-headed Vaiṣṇāvī processes the *prāṇas* of digestion coming from the Stomach centre. This relates to the dependence of the *bījas* 'on the substance *(t'i)* of the eighth consciousness', the *ālayavijñāna.* The natural state of the Stomach centre is a *manasic* disposition for the Inner Round, garnered from qualities developed in the past, which can be considered the basic

modifying qualities for any future *kāma-manasic* transaction. The *bījas* therefore depend upon the quality of this predisposition for their formation and expression. If for example the Stomach centre is seeded with the disposition for violent mental actions from past lives, then such predisposition can come to the fore in the *bījas* that form in the present. We see, therefore, that the *prāṇas* that pour from this centre to the Solar Plexus centre will tend to intensify the self-will of the personal-I when that 'I' thinks in terms of itself in relation to the world around and the objects of desire that can be manipulated for personal gain.

As the substance of the eighth consciousness is the basis of the entire evolutionary growth of consciousness, (here being the elementary *citta* that is foundational to the activity of the mind), so the wheel held by Vaiṣṇāvī is the wheel of the *dharma* concerning the development of mind for the *chakras* below the diaphragm. These *manasic* impulses are generally quite strong and irrational in the average person because of the uncontrolled nature the desire and emotions impacting upon basic *manas*. The Stomach centre's *manasic* wheel is spun, often very forcefully, as the *saṃskāras* associated with the *ālayavijñāna* are processed by it.

6. The greenish-white leopard-headed Raudrī directs regulating *prāṇas* to the Stomach centre. The *bījas* that 'are produced through causes and conditions' are an outcome of the type of experiences processed by the Stomach centre, after the major part of the *kāma-manasic* experiences have been digested in the Solar Plexus. The *iḍā bījas* below the diaphragm specifically find their onus of expression in the Stomach centre, where aspects of mental-emotions are selectively processed so that the *ālayavijñāna* (as it relates to the personal-I) is created.

The elemental Fiery *prāṇas* generated stimulate the mechanism of self-awareness and self-identity. This causes the ability to modify our perception of things, therefore the *bījas* are altered, or else new *bījas* come into being. This produces the arena of the conditions associated with the mental-emotional world that is the natural quality of this Stomach *chakra*. It draws the predominantly Fiery-Watery *prāṇas* from the Solar Plexus centre to it for processing. Raudrī uses a trident to direct all attributes of these *prāṇas* in terms of the three *guṇas* (here of the Elements Earth, Water and Fire), to be further developed by this minor centre when the person is to express attributes of the Fires of mind.

7. The reddish white brown bear-headed Kaumārī directs *piṅgalā prāṇas* to the Liver centre, consisting of the general Watery environment of the Solar Plexus centre. The Liver centre stores the *saṃskāras* of the loving, affectionate disposition of humanity, their general run-of-the-mill day to day forms of activity, of all activities of mind 'occasioned by good and bad'. The aphorism here being 'They are part of *nimittabhāga* (occasioned by good and bad), as they are taken as object by *darśanabhāga* (the path of seeing)'.

   The *saṃskāras* of the basic lessons of life, that all forms of attachment to transient things ultimately lead to pain and suffering, are stored in the Liver centre. They lay the foundation for the inevitable comprehension of the Buddha's Four Noble Truths. The path of seeing concerns the upward-looking way that is gained once the miasmas and fogs (the swirls of emotionality that most people are immersed in) have been clarified somewhat by consciousness so that individuals can find their way to enlightenment. That which is 'occasioned by good and bad' are the *bījas* of the Watery *saṃskāras* of past actions; the *karmic* heirloom that the person must experience and cleanse. The short pike held by Kaumārī symbolises the activity of the *maṇipūra* to regulate the sharp wilful *iḍā saṃskāras* so that they do not overpower the general loving disposition associated with the Liver centre.

8. The white coloured black bear-headed Indrāṇī that receives the *prāṇas* from the Liver centre. There are two kinds of *bījas* represented here, which according to the *Treatise on Thirty Verses on Mere-Consciousness* are: '(i) natural *bījas* and (ii) *bījas* born of perfuming. The natural *bījas* are the potentialities which have existed innately in the *ālaya* by the natural force of things (*dharmatā*).[38] They produce mental elements, sense-organs and the seeming external objects'.

---

38 *Dharmatā*, actual reality, ultimate truth of phenomenon, *śūnyatā*. Also, the natural force of things. Inherent nature, essence of existence.

The returning *prāṇa* will either enter into the general circulation of the Solar Plexus centre for normal Watery expression, or else they will be cleansed enough to be projected with the Airy quality of Love to be abstracted into the Heart centre. The '*bījas* born of perfuming' in this respect are those *saṃskāras* that have been seeded by the Sambhogakāya Flower, and which have caused the karmically induced experiences and perceptions that have so far been described with respect to the *maṇipūra* circulation. 'The natural *bījas*' represent the development of compassionate aspects of the emotions that are so thoroughly refined that they manifest as *bodhicitta.* They seed the Heart centre with the gain of the evolutionary process of the Watery attributes that have been 'dried' and hence are now Airy. This then evokes 'the natural force of things *(dharmatā)*' from the Heart centre and which engenders the radiance of Mind. This energy also vitalises the entire bodily organism with health. The tendencies to sickness consequently are vanquished, and the yogin naturally becomes a healer. The *bījas* therefore seed the conditions wherein consciousness can arise and find its natural play. When the *prāṇas* from the *maṇipūra* centre have been sufficiently cleansed of their dross they resemble the quality of the natural *bījas* contained in the Heart centre. The sum total of the Heart's circulatory process must occur before *dharmatā* is experienced in consciousness.

The production of 'mental elements, sense organs and the seeming external objects' here refers to the Yogācāra doctrine of all is mind/Mind. What is meant here is that all is an emanation of the emptiness that is a natural endowment of the Heart's Mind when manifesting via the lower centres that are the organs of the generation of phenomena, experienced as conventional truth. From this metric the centres above the diaphragm are concerned with the experience of the 'ultimate truth'.[39] The two truths effortlessly manifest as one once the *prāṇas* of the lower centres have been sufficiently purified to contain the *dharmatā* flowing from the Heart centre. A *siddha* then arises that has mastery over the appearance of phenomena.

---

39 See Volume 1, chapter 2, for an explanation of the two truths.

The noose of entrails that is held by Indrāṇī symbolises all of the attributes of consciousness that are digested by the normal person whose centre of focus is this *chakra* and which must be thus converted. The black-white colouration of this bear implies the contrast between the selfish emotional substance signified by the entrails (the cause of the darkness of ignorance) and the white colouration associated with compassionate activities.

9. The brownish white yak-headed Manurākṣasī, who holds a *vajra,* governs the *prāṇas* coming to and from Splenic centre I. This concerns those *bījas* 'which have come into being as a result of the "perfuming" of actual *dharmas,* the "perfuming" being repeated again and again from beginningless time'. These *prāṇas* (carrying the *bījas*) seed the various factors or aspects of existence that consciousness takes to be real. The originating source of the *bījas* that are expressed are those that have been rejected from the Heart centre's Airy form of activity. They are recycled through the Watery *maṇipūra* system, so that the quality of Love that can be expressed within the Heart centre is generated over time. The 'perfuming' is continuously repeated until the desired outcome of generating *bodhicitta* and the ability to travel the Bodhisattva path is gained.

   The *vajra* held by Manurākṣasī here integrates the rejected *prāṇas* that have been directed from the five non-sacred petals of the Heart centre into the general *maṇipūra* circulation. When registered by consciousness they are mixed with those from the Inner Round, which express the qualities of the 'actual *dharmas*'.

10. The yellowish-white snake-headed Brahmāṇī holding a lotus and directing *prāṇas* to the pancreas assists in fostering the growth of 'the seeds stored in the *ālayavijñāna,* being perfumed by seven other consciousnesses are caused to grow, resulting in the appearance of things'. Our concern here is with the awareness of the dense form and its relationships, as a consequence of 'digestion', the mental comprehension gained through food intake, metaphorically caused by the pancreatic secretions. This intake then assists in the development of the sense-consciousnesses. The intermediate step, however, before the externalisation of the activated *bījas* in the arenas of physical expression, involves the circulation of the *prāṇas*

of the 'seven other consciousnesses' of the Yogācāra philosophy through the Inner Round small *chakras*. In a sense these *chakras* properly digest all *bījas* that affect the physical form, the illusional appearance of things. The activation of this entire level of circulation of *prāṇas* is symbolised by the lotus held by Brahmāṇī. She guards over the qualities of the *saṃskāras* developed at this level of *prāṇic* circulation.

We thus have the means whereby people identify with things via their sense-perceptors. All seven aspects of consciousness come into play with such identification, producing the major glamours that people are besotted by. The seeds that externalise in the bodily form grow through their activities, literally by adding the Watery Element to the Earthy, by which they swell, expand and germinate. The Fiery Element can then play its role.

In viewing the two pentads of petals of the *maṇipūra chakra* in terms of the fingers of two hands, we see that the northern pentad can be considered to bear the mainly Fiery-Airy *piṇgalā prāṇas* of the right hand, and the southern pentad the mainly Earthy-Fiery *iḍā prāṇas* of the left hand. In both cases these *prāṇas* are aspects of the overall Watery dispensation.

The *prāṇas* of the sense of touch (the Watery Element) move via the five fingers into the external universe, producing perception of the things touched. Each finger conveys the *prāṇa* of a particular Element, as shown below:

- The thumb—which is very dextrous and adaptable, is the major exponent of Watery *prāṇas*.
- The forefinger—the Fiery *prāṇas*, pointing the way. (The extension of the mind.)
- The middle finger—the Earthy *prāṇas*, extending to impress the densest (lowest) domain.
- The ring finger—the Airy *prāṇas*, that integrate all of the other potencies (with the principle of Love).
- The little finger—least used and developed, as is the Aetheric Element for most people.

The fingers of the northern, *piṅgalā,* or right hand from this perspective are: Kaumārī, the Watery thumb, Vajrā Mahākumbhakarṇī as the Fiery forefinger, Manurākṣasī as the Earthy middle finger, Vajrā Mahākālī as the Airy ring finger, and Vaiṣṇavī as the Aetheric little finger. The fingers of the southern, *iḍā,* or left hand have Raudarī as the Watery thumb, Vajra Mahāchāgalā as the Fiery forefinger, Brahmāṇī as the Earthy middle finger, Vajrā Lambodarā as the Airy ring finger, and Indrānī as the little Aetheric finger.

We see here that the thumbs convey the major Watery flow, the ring fingers express *piṅgalā* flow. The index fingers convey the *iḍā* flow. The middle fingers unite the highest to the lowest expression of the *maṇḍala* of the Solar Plexus centre along the Earthy line. Though denoted Aetheric, the little fingers simply convey the most refined *prāṇas* from the Liver or Stomach centres to the Solar Plexus centre that each hand is capable of expressing. Though the thumbs and little fingers are polar opposites to each other relatively little energy flows between them for processing.

In the above account, the ten theriomorphic deities are explained with respect to the normal functioning of the *maṇipūra chakra.* These qualities need to be positively developed and refined by those engaged in visualisation techniques in the process of mastering the types of *saṃskāras* evoked on the upward path to the Heart's awakening. For *yogins* and *yoginīs,* however, the development of the *siddhis* via the awakening of *kuṇḍalinī* is a major concern. The awakening of the minor *siddhis* produces changes in the activity of this centre. This subject has been explained somewhat in Volume 2, chapter 4 of this treatise and summarised in Figure 12.

The groups of seven Īśvarī

It should be noted that the *Bardo Thödol* also organises the Īśvarī into four groups of seven:

> And as we roam [alone] in cyclic existence [driven] by deep-seated confused perceptions,
>
> May the seven Īśvarī of the east draw us forward,
>
> Leading us on the path of radiant light,

Which is [a vibrance of] sounds, lights and rays.
May the seven Īśvarī of the south support us from behind,
May the seven Īśvarī of the west support us from the perimeter,
And may the seven Īśvarī of the north destroy [and liberate] our enemies,
And thus [encircled] may we be rescued
From the fearsome passageway of the intermediate state
And be escorted to the level of an utterly perfected buddha.[40]

The entire philosophy of the seven Rays, 'the path of radiant light' that leads us through all the stages of consciousness to liberation, is implicated by the inclusion of the four groups of seven Īśvarī. The four female Gatekeepers enacting the emanational rites that govern the *iḍā* and *piṇgalā nāḍīs* to and from the Solar Plexus centre manifest as the synthesising agents for the four groups of 'six Queens of Yoga'. The *iḍā* and *piṇgalā nāḍīs* convey all of the most refined *prāṇas* derived from below the diaphragm to those above it. Septenaries are needed because the attributes of the seven Rays (that govern the entire life processes) are developed and become refined through the activities of the Īśvarī. Specifically, the centres below the diaphragm express the sub-rays of the four lower Rays of attribute. The three higher Rays of aspect (the first, second and third Rays) are evoked by means of the activity of the Head, Heart and Throat centres. This is important because both the Ājñā and the Head centres are constituted to process these septenaries that signify the development of people's psychology. In summary it can be stated that:

1. The 'seven Īśvarī of the east' that are asked to 'draw us forward' are directed by white cuckoo-headed Vajrā Mahākālī and the *piṇgalā nāḍī* to the Heart centre. The awakening of this centre is a major objective of the activity of the Īśvarī in their entirety. All *prāṇas* are consequently refined so that they can be propelled upwards thereto. The 'Queens of Yoga' that empower the final stages of this process, thereby drawing 'us forward', are those governing the rites of pacification (the remaining six petals of the Solar Plexus centre). By pacifying the turbulent and often volatile emotions, the way to

40 Gyurme Dorje, 87.

the Heart is made clear. The fourth Ray of Beautifying Harmony overcoming Conflict governs this process.

2. The 'seven Īśvarī of the west' are directed by the red lion-headed Vajrā Mahākambhakarṇī, who governs the *iḍā nāḍī* to the Throat centre, thus developing the way of the evolution of Mind. This evolution supports us 'from the perimeter' that represents the extent of the development of consciousness-space. The Īśvarī concerned are those enacting the *rites of subjugation* and that embody the functions of the left Gonad centre. This centre represents the place of generation of the *iḍā prāṇas,* of the *manas* that grows from the minute 'I' of the ego-centred personality to the vastness of abstract space. The mind is that which subjugates all to its will. The fifth Ray of Scientific Reason is here implicated.
3. The 'seven Īśvarī of the north' are directed by the green snake-headed Vajrā Lambodarā governing the *piṅgalā* flow to and from the Sacral centre. These Īśvarī are those that govern the rites of wrath, which must be utilised to 'destroy and liberate our enemies'. The 'enemies' here are not just the forces of darkness, but more specifically the unruly *saṃskāras* and psychological traits that prevent the onset of enlightenment. The wrath therefore starts from the foundational Sacral-Base of Spine centre combination and is directed ever upwards until the entire Head lotus is ablaze with Fiery light. The Ray line is the sixth of Devotion to noble ideals, which drives the entire quest for liberation. All of the serpents of desire symbolised by the snake must eventually be transformed into the elements of wisdom and the awakening of the Fiery *kuṇḍalinī.*
4. The 'seven Īśvarī of the south' that are to 'support us from behind' are directed by the yellow goat-headed Vajrā Mahāchāgālā, governing the *iḍā nāḍī* to and from the Sacral centre. The overcoming of desire through the development of mind that arises from this foundational Sacral centre activity supports the enlightenment that will inevitably come. The Īśvarī concerned are those that govern the rites of enrichment and the Ray line is the seventh of Ceremonial or Ritualistic activity. The sure-footed goat symbolises the ability to climb the mount of Initiation to liberation.

Note that the green colour of the snake and the yellow of the goat implicate an eventual reversal of the attributes people normally develop by those upon the yogic path. (Green is the colour relegated to Amoghasiddhi and his All-accomplishing wisdom, which empowers the seventh Ray, whilst yellow is the colour of Ratnasambhava and his Equalising wisdom, that empowers the sixth Ray.) The reason for this lies in the fact that the Sacral centre governs the entire domain of desire and of sexuality. The complimentary attributes to what normally would be expressed must therefore be developed in these foundational petals (for the *iḍā* and *piṇgalā nāḍīs*), if sex magic is not to be the outcome through a too focussed one-sided development. Hence the *prāṇas* generated must be appropriately integrated with the complementary attributes.[41]

The demonstration of the minor *siddhis*

Only a few comments shall be added here to what was previously presented, leaving the reader to make the necessary correlations for proper comprehension. Here we see that in relation to the mastery of the Liver and Stomach centres the major orientation of the (minor) *siddhis* is east-west. The focus is then clairvoyance and clairaudience, to which the other *siddhis* (apart from *dharmatā)* generate the fundamental support. Later the orientation shifts from below the diaphragm to above, in which case *dharmatā* becomes the base for the awakened Vision and Powers of the combined Head centres.

In this arrangement of petals we have an awakened eight-petalled lotus, to which the orientations of the eight-armed cross of direction in space apply. The east-west petals work to direct the *kuṇḍalinī* flow to all of the minor *chakras*. The energies then vitalise Splenic centre II with *kuṇḍalinī* so that the sum of the Inner Round *chakras* can be awakened with the Fire and the remaining *saṃskāric* obscurations burnt up. *Kuṇḍalinī* moves from an initial south-north line to east-west, manifesting thereby in the form of a fixed cross of steadfast liberating activity. The *iḍā* flow going west and the *piṇgalā* flow to the east. All *chakras* are thus included in one integral fusion of Fiery bliss. *Kuṇḍalinī*

41 *Prāṇically* this is one interpretation of the coital embrace depicted in Buddhist art between a Buddha and his *prajñā*.

is the conclusion of the successful work of one's own mind integrated with the work of all the Peaceful and Wrathful Deities. Tum mo is a name for *kuṇḍalinī* that has awakened to vitalise elements of the form with its Fiery warmth.

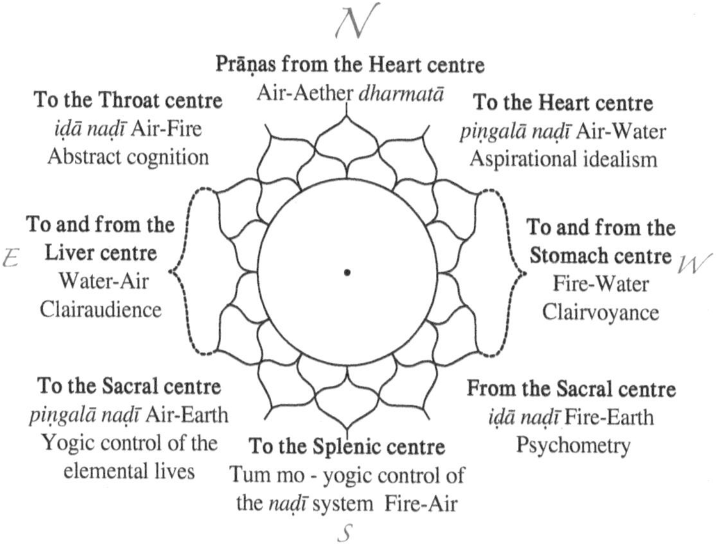

Figure 12. The *maṇipūra chakra* and the *siddhis*

As well as manifesting as an eight-armed cross and thereby aligning with the functions of the diaphragm centre, the east-west direction of *prāṇic* flow literally incorporates the Liver and Stomach centres as major petals of the Solar Plexus centre. These two major petals (energy streams) can be added to the ten to make the twelve that align with the Heart centre. Effectively the Solar Plexus centre then reflects the attributes of the Heart centre. When this occurs the energies of the Heart centre dominate the centres below the diaphragm so that *bodhicitta* can affect every expression of the three-fold personality.

Practitioners should take great care, as the process leading to the development of such *siddhis* necessitate firstly the cultivation of *bodhicitta*. There can be no equivocation concerning this. If the will is evoked without prior rightful cleansing and transformation of the *prāṇas* and *saṃskāras* concerned, as explained above, then the gravest dangers of falling into the dark path will manifest. The Wrathful Deities exist to try to protect practitioners from falling into egoistic and desire-ridden traps (because they still possess unrefined unruly *manas*) when awakening the *siddhis*. These Deities help protect the unwise from the dire consequences of any such premature eventuation. Otherwise the possibility of myriad violent, disease-engendering and pain-causing serpents will course through the *nāḍīs*.

A properly qualified preceptor; a master of yoga of the white *dharma*, must be sought and found that will truly reveal the illumined path that awakens the *siddhis*. Let the seeker also beware, as the charlatans professing to be enlightened gurus are myriad. The true Master of the white *dharma* is rare and consequently most precious. Auspicious *karma* is needed for the most earnest and gifted seekers, such as Milarepa had when he sought and found Marpa. The *karma* must ripen to allow this, and only then the fruit of past life's beneficence may be plucked, not before. The enlightened teacher appears only when the time is right. Such teachers shun the limelight, material wealth, and do not have time for adoring crowds of students. Nor will they kowtow to the demands of the unready, and few indeed there are who can ride the cleansings of their *saṃskāras* through to enlightenment. In the meditation-Mind, however, the Master can always be found.

The mind must be rightly controlled through the development of the Will-to-Love, thence the generation of *bodhicitta* as the emotions come to be mastered. (The generation of *bodhicitta* is incongruous with the expression of the emotions, as they are contradictory qualities.) Let the prospective practitioner be warned. If all warnings are ignored because of abject forceful desire to manifest psychic power at all cost, then the consequences of serious karmic repercussions will be theirs. In stating so the author is absolved from the ensuing *karma* of wilful psychic manipulation by those that read these words and heed not this well intended advice.

6

The Deities of the Bardo Thödol Part Five: Vajrakīla Heruka and the five Jñāna Ḍākinīs

The ninth stage of the evolutionary process and the Herukas

We now come to the next stage of the evolutionary process for humanity.

Stage 9. The psycho-spiritual striving to wisdom by aspirants, world innovators, and helpers of humanity.

This involves the type of activities producing the evolution of Bodhisattvas and the eventuation of the higher *bhūmis*. It is inclusive of the liberating forms of striving as presented in the Sūtrayāna, the Prajñāpāramitā texts (the teachings relating to the nature of the Void) and all classes of Vajrayāna up to the highest *uttaratantra* class of Tantras. We also have the process producing the attainment of the third and higher Initiations by the stalwart victors of the human race.

The third Initiation concerns mastery of the Fiery energy, liberating *kuṇḍalinī,* and awakening the thousand petalled lotus. Thereby the Clear Light that is the natural state of Mind is experienced. The fourth Initiation concerns mastery of the Airy Element and absorption into *śūnyatā.* All the pentads in Nature that produce the attainment of the wisdoms of the five Jinas at the fifth Initiation are then mastered. To attain these Initiations one must effectively conquer the obstacles presented by the five wrathful Buddha Herukas and Consorts. Consequently, one must effectively wield the power of Vajrakīla Heruka and the five Jñāna Ḍākinīs.

Plate 30. Vajrakīla Heruka

The five Buddha Herukas are empowered by Vajrakīla Heruka, who signifies the demonstration of the Will or Power that masters all attributes of the lower centres and their incorporation into the Head lotus. Together the Herukas help to produce the tenth stage of the evolutionary process, the attainment of liberation. With respect to this process the Herukas and Consorts represent the activity of the conversion of the major *saṃskāras* necessary for the development of Wisdom. Vajrakīla and the five Jñāna Ḍākinīs assist in the refinements of consciousness and the liberation of the Fires needed for enlightenment. These sixteen deities are related to the number of petals of the Throat centre, which governs the evolution of the Fires of Mind throughout Nature and within the human persona. Vajrakīla's Consort (the seventeenth deity) represents the *kuṇḍalinī* Fire that dances with its master, the bearer of the *kīla* and the mantric power that directs its course through the *nāḍīs*. The flames surrounding the Herukas are then attributes of this primal Fire. The five Jñāna Ḍākinīs, coupled with Vajrakīla and Consort then embody the attributes of the seven levels or layers of *kuṇḍalinī*.

All of the pentads are an emanation of the *manasic* Fires governing the expression of the diversity of lives found throughout Nature. A major objective of all such activity is to produce the conversion of all attributes of mind into wisdom-principles via the generation of *bodhicitta*. The second Ray of Love-Wisdom in its full glorified splendour is thereby evolved via the activity of mind.

Information concerning the five wrathful Buddha Herukas in relation to their embodiment of the functions of the five Knowledge petals of the Sambhogakāya Flower was presented earlier. In reference to the Wrathful Deities in general we see that their principal function is to assist the process of transforming all attributes of mind into their Void aspects. What remains then are the elements of Mind existing as the nexus between *śūnyatā* and *saṃsāra*. These elements are the foundation for the expression of *dharmakāya*, the Mind of all Buddhas. The earlier depiction of the function of the five wrathful Buddha Herukas (the protectors or guardians of the *dharma*) and their Consorts concerned transformation of the *bījas* of the various classes of knowledge into the wisdoms of the five Jinas. The Herukas thereby help transform gross consciousness-volitions of desire, envy, lust, etc., into their harmless and virtuous qualities before they are acceptable to the Sambhogakāya Flower.

Previously I stated with respect to this Flower that the *Knowledge-Sacrifice petal* is the expression of Amoghasiddhi and his All-Accomplishing Wisdom.[1] This petal governs the sum of the qualities derived from *saṃsāra* and their transmutation into the corresponding wisdoms. His energy is necessary if *saṃsāra* is to be totally and irrevocably mastered. Amitābha's energy is also needed to appropriately transform the awareness and energy from everything gained from incarnation. The qualities of Amitābha and Amoghasiddhi together help to transform the *bīja* seeds in the Knowledge petals. In a similar

1 See Vol. 3, page 444.

manner Akṣobhya and Ratnasambhava are the overseeing Dhyāni Buddhas for the Love-Wisdom petals, and Vairocana is the overriding or synthesising Dhyāni Buddha of the Sacrifice petals. Vairocana is also part of an identifying couplet with the Ādi Buddha.

In attributing the Herukas to the five Knowledge petals we saw that:

- Amitābha's Discriminating Inner Wisdom rules the overall expression of the five Knowledge petals because this wisdom is responsible for the assimilation of the Fires of consciousness into the *dharmakāya*. The fiery flames surrounding each of the Herukas, within which they dance, are constituted of the Element he embodies. All *prāṇas* of the Herukas therefore have a predominant fiery quality to them.
- Buddha Heruka, an emanation of Vairocana, with his Consort Buddhakrodheśvarī, is assigned to the *Sacrifice—Knowledge petal*. The Element is Aether-Fire. The *vayū* developed is *vyāna*.
- The *Love-Wisdom—Knowledge petal* is governed by Vajra Heruka, an emanation of Vajrasattva-Akṣobhya, and his Consort Vajrakrodheśvarī. The Element is Air-Fire. The *vayū* developed is *prāṇa*.
- The *Knowledge—Sacrifice petal* is governed by Padma Heruka, an emanation of Amitābha, and his Consort Padmakrodheśvarī. The Element is Fire-Fire. The *vayū* developed is *udāna*.
- The *Knowledge—Love-Wisdom petal* is governed by Ratna Heruka, an emanation of Ratnasambhava, and his Consort Ratnakrodheśvarī. The Element is Fire-Water. The *vayū* developed is *samāna*.
- The *Knowledge—Knowledge petal* is governed by Karma Heruka, an emanation of Amoghasiddhi, and his Consort Karmakrodheśvarī. The Element is Fire-Earth. The *vayū* developed is *apāna*.
- The *symbol* for this group of petals is the moving *swastika,* which turns the Wheel of Life onwards in time and space.

We saw that each of the Herukas had three faces, six arms and hands holding implements, and four feet. The feet were said to trample upon the *saṃskāras* of the four main Elements. They can also be visualised to dance upon the four petals of the Base of Spine centre, which represents the foundation of all the expressions that emanate from *saṃsāra*. From the pristine cognitions of these petals evolve all of the distorted perceptions and the arousal of the *saṃskāras* that need to be trampled upon by the wrathful emanations of one's own mind.

The four feet can also be viewed to 'trample upon' (meaning here to empower with energies) the activities of all twenty-eight powerful animal-headed goddesses (Īśvarī), consisting of four Gatekeepers and four groups of six theriomorphic deities. The weapons in each of the six hands of the Herukas are capable of transforming any *saṃskāra* from the categories of theriomorphic deities, or with each group as a unit. They can cleanse any line of *prāṇas* stemming from whatever petal of the Base of Spine-Sacral centre is empowered by the Heruka. The combination of six arms and four legs can also be correlated to the emanations from the ten petals of the Solar Plexus centre with respect to their division of six plus four petals, as presented in chapter 4. All *saṃskāras* of the desire-mind and emotions can thereby be converted.

The three faces of deities always indicate the ability of the deity to visualise the three times: past, present, and the future, and to deal appropriately with all associated *saṃskāras*. Yogically we have the emanations of the *iḍā nāḍī* (the past, because expressive of the *manasic* propensities long mastered by the *yogin* or *yoginī*), the *piṇgalā nāḍī* (the present, because expressive of the *bodhicitta* that the *yogin* is demonstrating), and *suṣumṇā* (the future, because its further ramifications will expose the full glory of the *dharmakāya*).

It should be noted that the view presented here is that the *Bardo Thödol* teaching is of the class of the Anuttarayoga (highest yoga) Tantra. The aim, therefore, is to foster the highest stages of the Bodhisattva path by gaining awakened vision, and thereby to become a *siddha*. It is necessary for the *yogin* to serve humanity by utilising the most skilful means possible, having mastered base *saṃskāras* and transformed them into the potencies that the Peaceful Deities veil.

The Tantras

The Nyingma tradition lists three outer Tantras (Kriyāyoga, Caryāyoga, and Yogatantra). These yogas represent the stages where deities are first contacted through appropriate action (Kriyāyoga). Their nature and the qualities within the *maṇḍala* of which they are a part are then thoroughly visualised and comprehended (Caryāyoga). Finally, in

Yogatantra the qualities of the deities come to be embodied in the process of transforming the base *saṃskāras,* so that the enlightened attributes of the Clear Mind can be gained. Next we have the development of the three highest Tantras, Mahāyoga, Anuyoga, and Atiyoga (rDzogs Pa Chen Po). They are called the three inner Tantras. Their purpose at first is to transform base attributes into the divinities of the *maṇḍala* (here of the *Bardo Thödol*), and so ultimately these Tantras embody the qualities of the *dharmakāya.* One must next ride through all of the manifestations of *saṃsāra* that appear as the *karma* unfolds and to transform them into the enlightenment that is the basis of the all. The end attainment can be considered to be the Clear Mind, *dharmatā,* or *dharmakāya,* with their nuanced differences, as defined in my works. The exoteric teaching relating to rDzogs-Chen concerns viewing *saṃsāra* as *nirvāṇa,* and *nirvāṇa* as *saṃsāra,* therefore utilising *saṃsāra* fearlessly with skilful means to gain liberation the quickest possible way. Methods of attainment, generally described as 'esoteric instructions' are provided in the texts and translations, to which the student may refer for elucidation, therefore they need not be repeated here. They should be compared by practitioners to the form of esoteric teachings presented throughout this series of books, which I have termed the Dharmakāya Way, if a complete view is to be established.

The statement found in Tantric texts, that if one follows the yoga practice one can attain liberation in merely one life, is misleading, because it presupposes that the person is at the highest Bodhisattva level, with many previous supporting lives of yogic accomplishment to do so. There is never more than a few such Bodhisattvas incarnate at any time. Therefore most practitioners are simply not qualified, because of lack of karmically ripened (auspicious) background to be able to do this. It is rare for one such as Guru Rinpoche, Milarepa, or a Tsong Ka Pa to appear with such auspicious *karma.* It is best therefore for most practitioners to honestly ascertain where they actually are on the Bodhisattva ladder and work to master its relative level of enlightenment, then yogically strive to conquer the level ahead. Prideful endeavour will hinder their practice if they think they can jump to the level of the highest yogas (Anuyoga and Atiyoga) before having actually mastered the lower levels of Tantric practice.

The manifold forms of pride destroy the path to high spiritual achievement for the great majority of aspirants. Forms of pride are however almost universally found in seekers for high achievement. Therefore let those who are striving for high achievement first deal with this aspect in their psyche. Many are the obstacles and testings presented by enlightened teachers, who work with the law of *karma* to overcome this attribute in their students.

Many lives of attainment have developed the perfection of that yoga, and the *saṃskāric* accomplishments follow naturally into each successive life. Such lives also do not generally follow the way of the Rinpoche tradition of Tibetan Buddhism. *Karma* works in a far wiser, enlightened, and thus mysterious way than that to propel the highest Bodhisattvas into multifarious service work all over the world. They are not then straitjacketed by having to fulfil the roles of ecclesiastical nobility. The pride of 'past life accomplishment' is generally too woven into the consciousness of many Rinpoche's for them to adequately overcome the stranglehold of this hydra.

Vast are the meditations of the Lords of *karma* that mould all interrelations into the intricate web of human life. Indeed, the rDzogs-Chen practice exists to make one a Lord of *karma*. Precious ones (Rinpoches) certainly may exist, but they do not follow a prescribed method of incarnating according to the exoteric concepts of 'lineage'. Rigid formulations and proscriptions of *dharma* (in terms of what is written in the texts) and adherence to exoteric forms of ritual is not the way of the enlightened. Esoteric lineage *(guruparamparā),* however, definitely exists, according to the way of manifestation of the Council of Bodhisattvas, because they are a Hierarchy of enlightened beings. A Master therein knows how to appropriately educate his students, and of the *dharma* and karmic links between them. The entire world is always the field of application of this Hierarchy, not just that viewed in terms of the Tibetan diaspora and their adherents.

When practitioners comprehend the natural sequence of events manifesting from past lives that *karma* directs, it will allow the right teacher to be found. Victory is assured via an enlightened teacher that shows them how to appropriately transform *saṃskāras* according to the way that group *karma* manifests. Understanding group *karma* is necessary, as many such *saṃskāras* were generated as part of a group (e.g., of *yogins),* and require the reappearance of that group for their transformation. The externalising *maṇḍala* is important, based upon the paradigm of a subjective one. The dictates of *karma* assist the inherent recognition by the practitioner of what is right and what must be done to gain the enlightenment ahead. The degree of self will applied to produce the necessary transformations to faithfully follow the instructions of the incarnate Master, and the earnest group of fellow practitioners must be of the highest integrity.

Resilience and persistence must be generated for many years, and often decades, to stay the course. Many practitioners generate initial enthusiasm because of many internal impressions, but disillusionment imperils the practice when seemingly little is happening because of expectancy of results. Manifold are the subjective hurdles to overcome self-centred posturings. Candidates for high attainment are carefully observed by the Master for extraordinary patience and steadfast compassionate endeavour in the path to produce superlative refinements of consciousness. The Wrathful Deities can accordingly assist those that prove steadfast meditative focus upon selflessness and compassion. The objective for the *dhāraṇīs* engendered is therefore not primarily self-enlightenment (though that is a necessary side-effect), but so that others may benefit and the all enriched accordingly. Thus the forces of the Heart centre can be evoked and its *prāṇas* used to cleanse the lower four *(chakras).* Only then can *kuṇḍalinī* be safely released through ritual internal use of the phur ba *(kīla)* and empowerment by the associated deities accomplished. In this way the three jewels of Buddhism, the Buddha (Master), the *dharma* (correct instructions), and *saṇgha* (group) manifesting at the appropriate time produce the unfolding *maṇḍala* of group Initiation. The three are a coherent unity of expression.

Logically, the Mahāyoga level of attainment will produce mastery of the path that allows one to fully demonstrate the accomplishment of the Herukas in transforming maladroit regressive *saṃskāras.* The Anuyoga level of practice successfully attained will bring one to the level of being able to correctly identify one's part within the (extended) *maṇḍala* of the Mahābodhisattvas. The Atiyoga level of practice will produce the attainment of *dharmakāya.* Essentially, Mahāyoga will thus produce the *ālayavijñāna* level of enlightenment, and Anuyoga the *śūnyatā* level of enlightenment. The student must, however, not concretise too much, as much overlapping occurs of attainment in the uneven development of the meditation minds of practitioners and in the redemption and transformation of the *saṃskāras* to be conquered. Effectively these three forms of yoga are practiced simultaneously, and differentiation only emerges at the final stages, when the meditative *saṃskāras* that are the *karma* from past attainment propel the Initiated practitioner into the state of Clear Light, *dharmatā*, or *dharmakāya* that is possible to attain in that life.

All lives proceed as a continuum, everything is integrated, and nothing arises in isolation from anything else. The momentum of enlightenment pushes all forward accordingly. Thus is revealed the secret of the potency of *bodhicitta*. The nature of the generation of *bodhicitta* then becomes the mechanism of determining the level of Tantra that is achievable in one life. There are questions that when answered determine the level of practice possible in any life. 'Is *bodhicitta* something to be worked at, to be generated with some effort, or does it arise spontaneously, effortlessly, and in an all-encompassing manner?' 'Are there limitations to the nature and depths of its expression in the aspirant's life?' Also, 'what is the relative strength or force with which *bodhicitta* flows via the prospective *yogin's* achievements?' *Bodhicitta* simply is, yet also must be generated through overcoming lethargy and the impediments of karmic dross that the weight of *saṃsāric* involvement in former lives has produced. The deeper the mire or weight of *saṃsāra* that one has been addicted to, the harder it is to transform the related *saṃskāras*. It becomes increasingly difficult to unravel the substance that veils the potency of *bodhicitta's* possible flow.

Once the transformations are being accomplished with the aid of theriomorphic deities, Herukas, and Bodhisattvas, then the revealed *bodhicitta* flows with time to produce the accomplishments of the great service of world transformation ahead. To the degree that the dross of *saṃsāra* is cleansed by transforming *saṃskāras* into their enlightenment attributes, so the potency or intensity of that flow increases. The nature of the differing intensities of *bodhicitta* capable of being expressed at any time determines the true Bodhisattva level of the candidate for enlightenment. It is therefore an all-pervasive non-static energy of compassion. This is the basis by which the nature and practice of the three inner Tantras may be understood.

The forty-two Peaceful Deities

The Wrathful Deities so far presented relate to the three times. The past relates to the twenty-eight powerful animal-headed goddesses, and concerns the Solar Plexus and Sacral centre emanations that the sincere practitioner no longer generates. The present relates to the activities of the Mātaraḥ and the Piśācī because their concern is with the process of transforming *saṃskāras* to be fully incorporated into the *chakras* above the Diaphragm centre. The future relates to the activities of the twelve central blood-drinking deities because they are actively engaged in the transmutation of all *prāṇas* so that they can be absorbed by the Heart centre to reveal aspects of the Void. This represents the goal of most practitioners.

Each of the three faces of a Heruka regulate the expression of one or other of the three *guṇas,* and therefore all trinities in manifestation, such as *iḍā, piṅgalā* and *suṣumṇā,* Father, Son and Mother.

In the future an increasing number of individuals will manifest practices that will eventually awaken *kuṇḍalinī.* For this the wrathful emanations of Mind (Wrathful Deities) must be drawn upon to trample and convert the undesirable *saṃskāras* that arise. Each individual must follow the Bodhisattva path for this to be safely accomplished. Historically, it also involved the rise of organised religions, where proper ethics and right moral conduct were established and taught by seers and prophets. The *buddhadharma* represents the epitome of the wisdom-religion for humanity because it exemplifies the teaching of the Bodhisattva path as the way to liberation, as per the generation of both wisdom and compassion. The basis to this is the science of yoga, as exemplified in the Tantras. The wisdom tradition grew as the centuries evolved, rather than degenerating, as in the case of its sister religion, Christianity. The entire progress of travelling the wheel of the *dharma* as a Bodhisattva necessitates the awakening and active functioning of the Heart Centre. The focal point here is the activity of the Mirror-like

Wisdom of Akṣobhya that reflects into manifestation the energies of the forty-two Peaceful Deities associated with the liberating powers of the Heart. These Deities are summarised below, as arranged into five groups.

i. The Āḍi Buddha and Consort.

ii. The five Dhyāni Buddhas and Consorts.

iii. The eight Mahābodhisattvas and Consorts.

iv. The six Buddhas of the Bhavacakra (Sidpa'i Khorlo) who govern the six realms of Buddhism, and are considered emanations of Avalokiteśvara.

v. The four Guardians of the cardinal directions and their Consorts.

The five Dhyāni Buddhas in the manner shown below qualify these five groupings.

i. Vairocana can be considered to be an emanation of the Āḍi Buddha.

ii. The expressions of the Dhyāni Buddhas as a whole are reflected by the Mirror-like Wisdom of Akṣobhya, from which develops the organising patterns of the petals of the Head lotus. The mirror also reflects the qualities of the Dhyāni Buddhas into the planetary Heart centre, wherein resides the Council of Bodhisattvas.

iii. The activities of the eight Mahābodhisattvas and Consorts are directed via the western paradise of Amitābha. These Bodhisattvas are directive agents governing the activity of the kingdom of the Sambhogakāya Flower upon the domains of Mind. The functions of this *tathāgatagarbha* aspect of humanity are organised according to the qualities of the eight directions of the compass. There are sixteen petals assigned to the Throat centre (that rules the activity of mind/Mind) governed by Amitābha. The eight Bodhisattvas and their Consorts embody the functions of these petals in Nature in the way that they regulate the activity of this centre for humanity. The Throat centre conveys mental energies that tend to produce the dissecting, critical, separative, segregating nature of the mind. The ways that these qualities manifest in humanity consequently need careful monitoring by this Council, who tirelessly work to offset these and other negative tendencies developed by humans.

Here lies much of the mystery concerning the 'war' between

the dark and white Brotherhoods, where those of the left hand path find it exceedingly easy to foster such qualities via various forms of scheming to control the human world.[2] Masses of sorcerers and black magicians would evolve out of humanity if it were not for the dynamic work of the Bodhisattvas manifesting their modifying compassionate purpose. They therefore continuously incarnate to offset the malicious scheming of the dark ones. By the state that the world presently is in we see how difficult their task is. Humanity as a whole are still at a stage of generating maligned *saṃskāras* rather than converting them into enlightened tendencies. Consequently, theriomorphic forces act as Lords of *karma* ravaging the human species with the consequences of their desire-mind impulses. The great yogic transformative battles amongst humanity for control over all forces conditioning them still have far to go. Selfishness rather than compassion is still humanity's onus. Bodhisattvas have much work to do to offset this. Only in the far distant future will it be possible for humanity to fully control the manifestations of the Throat, with its ability to command the mantras governing their own psyche and the forces of Nature. All will happen according to the dictates of evolutionary Law in accord with the originating mantric directives from the Ādi Buddha and Consort.

iv. The symbolism of the six Buddhas of the Bhavacakra esoterically relates to the mode of the awakening of the *chakras* governing all of Nature, of the planes, realms and kingdoms. Such activity is an expression of the compassionate force that Avalokiteśvara represents. Ratnasambhava's equalising energies assists in pacifying unruly *saṃskāras,* so that they can be modified by compassionate forces. The liberating force in Nature can then shed light and clarify the blindness of those ensnared by *saṃsāric* allurements. The function of this force is similar to the action of sunlight upon growing plant life. Human units can be considered to be a type of plant, with roots in *saṃsāra,* wherein the personal-I gathers

2 Such ones generally incarnate into situations that allow them to amass much financial, political, military or propagandistic power over the great mass of people of our nations. (The masses are easily manipulated by those who with great cunning scheme to do so.)

nutrients. Its stem is the triune central *nāḍī* system, the foliage being the many tiny *chakras* of the system, and the major liberating force being the Sambhogakāya Flower. Here also the entire Hierarchy of the domain of the Bodhisattvas come into action, being symbolised by Avalokiteśvara's activities, the prototype Bodhisattva. Every level of expression (Bardo) wherein human units are found can then be illuminated.

v. The four Guardians of the cardinal directions and their Consorts are part of the armoury of Amoghasiddhi's All-accomplishing Wisdom. They help to prevent the activities of self-focussed ones who would practice forms of yoga to attain *siddhis* for selfish motives. They help prevent the foolish from amassing the *karma* that would accrue if such powers were utilised prematurely. They guard the liberation of the Fire from the petals of the Base of Spine centre, and allow only the most refined of *prāṇas* to enter the realms of the higher centres upon the Initiation path. All others are to be recycled until converted into the desired Bodhisattvic qualities. The function of the *devas* come to the fore here as the guardians of the *karma* generated by all beings.

The five Jñāna Ḍākinīs and Vajrakīla Heruka

The nature and expression of the emotions and desire in humans must be comprehended, then fully mastered upon the path to enlightenment. Amoghasiddhi governs the process that brings this about at its most fundamental level. His potency rules over the control of this faculty of desire and sexuality with respect to the functioning of the Base of Spine and Sacral centres. The associated esotericism is vast because it concerns all of the procreative forces in Nature, the male-female interrelationships, thus of the balance of forces underlying the entirety of *saṃsāra*. Amoghasiddhi instigates the various types of 'magic' in the form of the *siddhis* evoked, whereas his Consort governs the appearance of things. Here we also have veiled the awesome potency of the *kuṇḍalinī śakti,* hence the activity of these centres must be fiercely protected. The strong forces of these *chakras*, ruling the function of desire (*kāma*), are protected by the emanations of the powerful Vajrakīla

Heruka[3] and his Consort Samayatārā. The process starts with the Base of Spine-Sacral centre interrelation. Our focus is upon the last of the sets of deities that though supplementary, are esoterically an integral part of the *maṇḍala* of deities of the *Bardo Thödol*. They are the five Jñāna Ḍākinīs and Vajrakīla Heruka and his Consort. Lauf states:

> The seven additional deities are situated in the two lowermost cakras, the mūlādhāra-cakra (T. gSang-gnas dkyil-'khor) and the maṇipūra-cakra (T. lTe-ba'i dkyil-'khor). In Chapter II (4E) we were introduced to the lowest cakra in the perineum as the location of the protective deity Vajrakumāra, or Vajrakīla-Heruka. This cakra is also associated with karmic activity (T. Phrin-las) and with Buddha Amoghasiddhi and is usually referred to in the bardo texts as the sukhapāla-cakra (T. bDe-skyong 'khor-lo). Here the powerful protective deity Vajrakīla-Heruka watches over the place of desire (kāma). Between this cakra and the heart-lotus is the maṇipūra-cakra, also called nirmāṇacakra (T. sPrul-pa'i 'khor-lo). Here, in the place of karmic merit (S. guṇa) and of Buddha Ratnasambhava, appear the five "Wisdom-Ḍākinīs" (T. Ye-shes mkha'-'gro lnga).
>
> They form a five-petalled lotus or a hexagram with the five mantric seed-syllables Bam, Ha, Ri, Ni, and Sa. In the centre appears the white Buddha-Ḍākinī, in the east the blue Vajra-Ḍākinī, in the south the yellow Ratna-Ḍākinī, in the west the red Padma-Ḍākinī, and in the north the green Karma-Ḍākinī. They are initiation-goddesses, known in Buddhist symbolism also as emanations of the tantric Ḍākinī, Vajravārāhi (T. rDo-rje phag-mo).[4]

Omitted in the text is the fact that the Base centre is a composite of two *chakras*, the four petalled Base of Spine centre (*mūlādhāra chakra)* and the six petalled Sacral centre (*svādiṣṭhāna chakra)*, of

---

3 Vajrakīla is the alternative name for Vajrakumāra Heruka. The term *kīla* (Tib. Phur ba) a ritual dagger, with a triune blade, symbolising the integration of the three main *nāḍīs*, and the focused projection of their forces. The *kīla* protects the sacred boundaries during a ritual. (Vajrakīla's body is often depicted as integrated with this dagger.) The combined meaning of the names can be interpreted as 'the adamantine *(vajra)* wrathful (Heruka) perpetual youth *(kumāra)* wielder of the power of the *kīla*'. Samayatārā here signifies the sacred pledge *(samaya)* to accomplish the *kila's* purpose through compassionate means *(tārā)*.

4 Lauf, 154-155.

which considerable information has already been presented. The Sacral centre is only hinted at in the phrase 'place of desire'. This centre is specifically responsible for the emanation and eventual control of the principle of desire *(kāma)*. In Tantric texts the Sacral centre is often veiled as being 'the secret centre', or omitted. The reason for this is that its potency and relationships are dangerous for practitioners to visualise without an illumined instructor. One needs to consider that the strength of the factor of desire, if intensified through yogic practices, facilitates the possibility of the generation of sex magic. We then have the problems associated with possible undue sicknesses arising because this centre governs the vitality of the system.

Plate 31. Vajrakīla Heruka and the five Jñāna Ḍākinīs

The qualities of this centre have been unveiled in this Series because the time is right for further exposé of many esoteric doctrines to the world. Increased esoteric revelations with sufficient background presented are in line with the outpouring of information in this technologically advanced era. The explosion of understanding what was formerly hidden is expected to significantly advance the progress to enlightenment for the word's aspirants scattered all over the face of this earth, which is the prayer and hope of the Council of Bodhisattvas.

The Wisdom Ḍākinīs are assigned to both the Solar Plexus and the Sacral centres. This assignment is correct when the five lower petals of the Solar Plexus centre are considered to accommodate the energies from five of the petals of the Sacral centre. Also, as Vajrakīla is the controlling deity for the Base of Spine centre then these Ḍākinīs must assist in the control of the *prāṇas* coursing through the Sacral centre to the Solar Plexus centre.

The *chakras* are not static entities, but are wheels, vortices of energies spinning, revolving at their own rates, depending upon the nature and quantity of the *saṃskāras* to be processed. The energies from one wheel find a reciprocation in another one that spins at a similar rate and direction. The internal motion of *prāṇas* within each petal can also be considered to represent a similar, smaller wheel within a *chakra*. This is the basis for the flow of *prāṇas* moving from one petal to another.

The assignment of deities to specific petals is therefore somewhat generalised, as there are wheels of petals within the main structure that deal with the energies coming to and from them that also come under their jurisdiction. There is also the nature of the turning of a wheel from right to left and left to right and commingling of *prāṇas* from one petal to another to take into account. *Prāṇas* can circulate around or cross over from one petal to another along its spoke. However, the main petals channel the quality of the energies accumulated in the organising arena they govern, to which the attributes of the deity may then be assigned.

The Sacral centre is the place for the generation of the *iḍā and piṅgalā nāḍīs,* however, the associated petals may change places in time because at first the expression of either *prāṇa* is most elementary, weak and muddied for a great deal of the early evolutionary process. The wheels then turn opposite to what is later seen as normal evolutionary flow. It takes considerable evolutionary time to redirect and consolidate this 'left hand' flow to the 'right hand' *prāṇic* direction depicted in the figures in this book. There is another, different cross-over of *prāṇas* at the Diaphragm centre, as already explained, where this centre acts as a type of mirror. This movement is later rectified by a cross-over of *prāṇas* from the Ājñā to Head centres. Similarly, the eye receives impressions from the external environment and sends electrochemical energies in a cross-over manner to the visual cortex in the brain, which interprets and inverts them to present the images we see in our minds.

The Base of Spine/Sacral centre interrelation can be viewed from different perspectives, stemming from the relationship of the petals. There are ten petals in this interrelation, and if we subtract two, as one petal from each *chakra* overlaps the other, then eight petals remain. The petals that overlap are the place of the evocation of *kuṇḍalinī.* Three petals remain for the Base of Spin*e chakra* and five for the Sacral centre. Therefore we have the solution to the mystery of the peculiar wording of Lauf's statement above in relation to the numbers five and six: the Wisdom Ḍākinīs 'form a five-petalled lotus or a hexagram with the five mantric seed-syllables Bam, Ha, Ri, Ni, and Sa'. Here the Sacral centre takes the function of either a five or six petalled lotus. In these numbers lie the basis for the information presented in the extract above concerning the five Jñāna Ḍākinīs and the essentially triune Vajrakīla Heruka and Consort. These eight *prāṇic* pathways, plus the central overlapped duo of petals effectively express the nine-pronged *vajra* that Vajrakīla holds in his first pair of hands.

The logic is that the Solar Plexus flow is altered as described earlier upon the onset of *kuṇḍalinī,* whilst the Sacral centre changes its flow because it is the place of the generation of the Fires. The awakening of *kuṇḍalinī* implies a reversal (turning about) of Sacral centre functioning. The normal expressions of this centre, the factor of desire and of attachment to material things, no longer exist. This centre is then purely a distributor of energies. The evocation of *kuṇḍalinī* means that the *prāṇas* of the five sense-consciousnesses (gained through contact with material objects) are conveyed in terms of the related *siddhis.*

- Smell—Tum mo, the white central Buddha Ḍākinī.
- Taste—aspirational idealism, the blue eastern Vajra Ḍākinī.

- Sight—abstract cognition, the red western Padma Ḍākinī.
- Touch—control of elemental lives, the yellow southern Ratna Ḍākinī.
- Hearing—psychometry, the green northern Karma Ḍākinī.

These five then 'reach out' to the Solar Plexus centre via its lower five 'fingers', to integrate with its energies, thereby turning its energies into a form of Fire-mist that is the basis for the *siddhis*. The Solar Plexus centre adds the transformed factor of the three extra attributes of the eight consciousnesses. The intellect then morphs into clairvoyance; *kliṣṭamanas* converts into clairaudience, and the *ālayavijñāna* is integrated with *dharmatā,* to form the *saṃsāra-śūnyatā* nexus. The top two petals of the Sacral centre (the *iḍā* and *piṅgalā* pair) change positions because there is no internal muddying, desire based resistance in the *chakra* to deflect the *prāṇas* to the sides (as depicted in Figure 10, where two *iḍā nāḍīs* are on the west side and the *piṅgalā nāḍīs* are on the east side). The bottom two petals are where these *nāḍīs* arise, hence the *prāṇas* simply cross and firmly establish the channels with the rising of *kuṇḍalinī.*

The three petals of the Base of Spine centre allocated to Vajrakīla represent the three blades of the dagger *(kīla)* that is the distinctive symbol of this deity, and which shall be explained below.

Vajrakīla and the five Jñāna Ḍākinīs control the overall functions of the deities below the diaphragm when *kuṇḍalinī* is evoked. These Ḍākinīs then direct the activities of the five groups associated with the twenty-eight animal-headed female deities (Īśvarī), whilst Vajrakīla and Consort control the activities of the eight Mātaraḥ and the eight Piśācī. All *prāṇas* are thus rightly directed via the eight spokes of each wheel the Mātaraḥ and Piśācī embody. The 'eight-petalled' Solar Plexus centre[5] then also comes into play. All are integrated with the eight-petalled arrangement of the Sacral-Base of Spine centre. There are thus four eight-petalled lotuses that appear below the diaphragm at the time of the awakening of *kuṇḍalinī,* each manifesting the attributes of the eight armed cross of direction in order to distribute this Fiery energy appropriately throughout the *nāḍīs* of the minor centres. The heart of

---

5 See Figure 12.

this system is the twelve-petalled Splenic centre I, which integrates the *prāṇas* from the Heart centre *(dharmatā)* into the entire field of expression. It allows an unimpeded flow of *kuṇḍalinī* throughout the *nāḍīs*, and the *siddhis* thereby awaken.

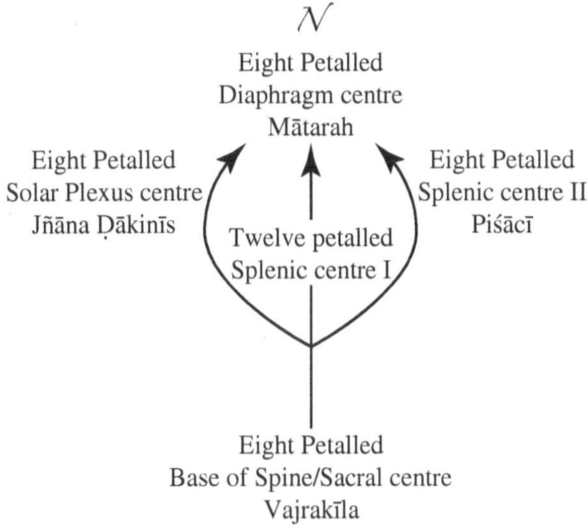

Figure 13. Vajrakīla's three-edged blade pointing upwards

Here lies the esoteric symbolism of the phur ba,[6] of which Vajrakīla is the deity. The normal symbolism relates to the *kīla* pointing downwards to control the potency of the *chakras,* especially of the Watery Element. Here the *kīla* points upwards, but esoterically it can point in any of the eight directions, according to the purpose of the *siddha's* visualisation. The figure depicts the triune blade in the form of a trident used to control the Watery energies of the system by means of the liberating Fires.

At this stage of the liberation of *kuṇḍalinī* the Watery *prāṇas* below the diaphragm have been 'dried up', allowing the *siddhis* to be awakened via the three blades of the *kīla* that are emitted from the mouth of a Makara, the goat-fish. The serpents from Makara's mouth signify that *kuṇḍalinī* is liberated, fusing the three principal *nāḍīs* into one, because energies that awaken the *siddhis* in the three directions of the blade have been mastered.

6 Also spelled: phur pa.

In this presentation of the *kīla* the central blade (Vajrakīla's focus) points to the Diaphragm centre (to empower the Mātaraḥ), and thus inevitably to the centres above the diaphragm. Another blade points in the eastern direction to the Solar Plexus centre (empowering the Wisdom Ḍākinīs) so that the minor centres can be made ablaze. The western blade is directed to Splenic centre II so that the entire *nāḍī* system is made radiant. The Piśācī are empowered here and the *saṃskāras* directly pertaining to enlightenment generated. We thus have the *iḍā* (west) and *piṅgalā* (east) flow of *kuṇḍalinī,* with the *suṣumṇā* flow manifesting in the northern direction.

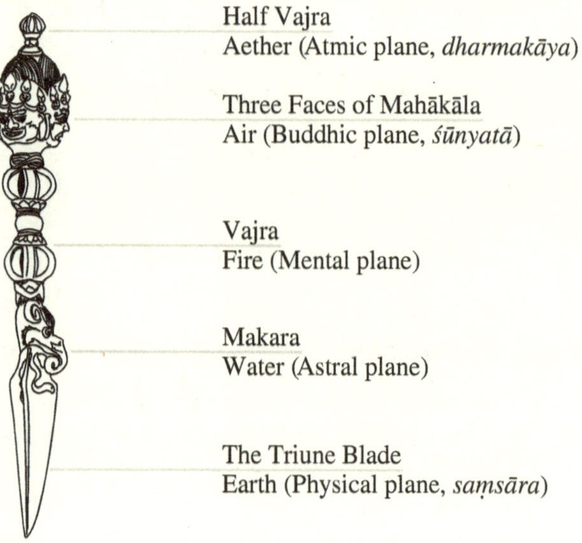

Figure 14. The phur ba

Here the Makara represents the power to control the Watery dispensation of the *chakras* that normally generate them. The *vajra* represents the place of generation of *kuṇḍalinī* that is projected in this three-fold manner. Mahākāla, from which the *vajra* is derived, represents the three remaining petals of the Base of Spine centre. They are associated with the qualities of the three planes of human livingness that are now controlled. The surmounting *uṣṇīṣa,* or else half of a *vajra* upon the head of Mahākāla, represents the yogic process that needs to continue if all of the forces of the three planes (mental, emotional and physical) are to be mastered so that *saṃsāra* becomes the vehicle of *dharmakāya*. To do so the eastern orientation must be the focus, to draw the integrated Heart and Solar Plexus energies up the spinal column via the threefold cord that becomes fused into one integral *mahāmudrā* of expression. This necessitates the conversion of mind into Mind. In so doing, the path of Initiation, the Dharmakāya Way into the Mysteries of being/non-being is traversed.

As a ritual implement the phur ba is quite significant in Tantric practices amongst the Nyingma. Accordingly, it possesses five levels of symbolism in the more exoteric account, which shall be described below.[7]

1. The triune blade, used to cut through the illusions of the three poisons, to master the three planes and Elements of *saṃsāra,* the Earthy physical domain, the Watery emotional (astral) realm, and the Fiery mental plane. Inevitably, yogic prowess in the evocation and control of the three principal *nāḍīs* must be accomplished. All of the above is symbolised by the serpents that normally run through the centre of each blade. The blade is pointed, signifying the focal point of the energy visualised and projected by the *yogin.* The focus is first upon mastery of the allurements of the physical domain. In this respect the phur ba means 'a peg' that is driven into the ground for exorcising the earth.

2. A Makara surmounts the triune blade. From its mouth emanates the blade plus a serpent that runs down the centre of each of the three blades.[8] The Makara is a mythological beast (the vehicle of Varuṇa, the god of the Waters and king of the serpents) that governs the Element Water and thus of all the serpents of desire, myriad maggots of the emotions, and even the full-blown hydra associated with this domain.

3. Above the Makara is a *vajra*, here an emanation of the higher mental plane, signifying that the mind must be completely mastered to conquer the Makara, and also to emanate the powers of the wisdoms

7 The most common attributes will be explained, as there are some variations in the types of phur ba's used.

8 Often a pair of serpents is depicted, symbolizing the *iḍā* and *piṅgalā nāḍīs.*

of the Dhyāni Buddhas. The power of their united wisdom must thereby dominate the sum of *saṃsāra.*

4. The three faces of Mahākāla, the Lord of time, generally surmount the *vajra.*[9] These faces govern the appearance and disappearance of all the triads in Nature, the three *guṇas,* the major *nāḍīs,* the three aspects of time, etc. The Element associated is the Air, signifying the process where all is absorbed into *śūnyatā,* the ultimately real.

5. The heads are surmounted by either an *uṣṇīṣa* (top-knot of hair symbolising the potency of the awakened energies), a half *vajra,* or Hayagrīva, the wrathful manifestation of Avalokiteśvara. The Element is Aether, signifying that the compassionate potency of the *dharmakāya* inevitably governs the *dhāraṇīs* involving the use of the phur ba to control all wayward energies in the *nāḍīs.*

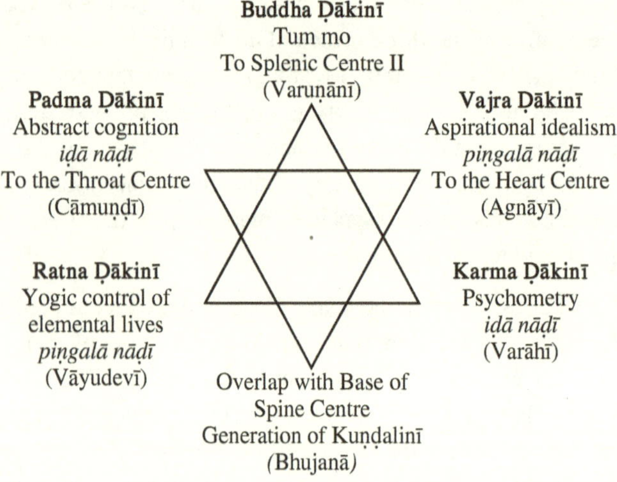

Figure 15. The Wisdom Ḍākinīs

The Wisdom Ḍākinīs help control the *prāṇic* circulation below the diaphragm and that of the entire Inner Round by means of their

9 *Mahākāla,* 'great time' or 'great black one' (of the charnel grounds) is the protector of the three jewels of Buddhism by wrathfully transforming all forms of evil. Consequently he is the principal deity depicted upon the phur ba.

embodiment of the pentads of petals via which the Solar Plexus and Sacral centres manifest. The Solar Plexus centre has two groups of five main petals each, plus two inner tiers of twelve smaller petals governing the overall direction and intermingling of the *prāṇas* for the *chakras* it administers to. As earlier stated, the Solar Plexus centre is the central driving power house for all Watery *prāṇas* in the body. It integrates the principle of desire with all emotions and emotional attachments that a human unit is capable of expressing, thus manifesting the ubiquitous emotional-mind.

As the four female Gatekeepers of pristine cognition embody the petals of the Base of Spine centre they do not technically come under this control, neither do the twelve central blood-drinking Herukas and Consorts. The numbers twelve and four relate to the sixteen petals of the Throat centre that control the flow of Fiery *prāṇas* via these two groupings. Vajrakīla Heruka is the child as well as the father of the developed consciousness-space obtained through cleansing and transforming the *saṃskāras* associated with the theriomorphic deities. The Base of Spine centre grounds the Head centre, whilst the blood-drinking Herukas and Consorts are directed via the Heart centre. This allows direct control of all minor centres below the diaphragm by the accomplished *yogin* through these three major centres when the liberating fires (*kuṇḍalinī*) are being evoked. The Ājñā is the central organ of direction for all these *prāṇas*.

By the colours of the Jñāna Ḍākinīs we see that they convey the feminine (wisdom) aspects of the Dhyāni Buddhas. The central white Buddha Ḍākinī generates the Dharmadhātu quality of the Wisdom of Vairocana. The green Karma Ḍākinī of the northern direction generates the similitude of the All-accomplishing Wisdom of Amoghasiddhi. The red western Padma Ḍākinī generates the Discriminative qualities of the Wisdom of Amitābha. The yellow Ratna Ḍākinī generates the similitude of the Equalising Wisdom of Ratnasambhava, and the eastern blue Vajra Ḍākinī generates the reflective qualities of the Mirror-like Wisdom of Akṣobhya.

The Sacral-Base of Spine centre combination is responsible for the generation of the pool of *saṃskāras* that are conveyed in the form of the *iḍā* and *piṅgalā nāḍīs*. The *iḍā nāḍī* first emanates from the top left hand petal of the Sacral centre and the *piṅgalā nāḍī* from the top right hand petal. (As stated this interrelation later turns around.) The five Wisdom Ḍākinīs are the personifications of the *prāṇas* in these channels. Each *nāḍī* conveys five *prāṇas,* which are expressions of the attributes of the five Elements. The Sacral-Solar Plexus combination generates Earthy-Watery *prāṇas* but must be prepared to channel the Fiery attributes of these Ḍākinīs.

With respect to the Sacral centre we saw previously that the activity of the petals is governed by the Īśvarī of wrath. The difference between these Īśvarī and the Wisdom Ḍākinīs is that the Īśvarī are concerned with the regulation and transformation of *saṃskāras* during the yogic process of attainment, hence the need for wrath. The Wisdom Ḍākinīs deal with the accomplished gain, hence with the proceeds of the awakening *kuṇḍalinī.* The Wisdom Ḍākinīs, Vajrakīla and Consort therefore help regulate the manifestation of the lower *siddhis* of the awakened Solar Plexus centre, except *dharmatā,* which is an emanation of the Heart centre. Clairaudience and clairvoyance (of the east-west direction in Figure 12) manifest via the two main lobes of the Ājñā centre when the Fiery-mist from the Solar Plexus centre activates them. All experiences associated with the *lokas* (dimensions of perception) of the lower centres can then be adequately visualised and comprehended and the inner Voice or Secret Mantra heard. The right lobe of the Ājñā centre (controlling clairvoyance) is governed by Vajrakīla Heruka and the left lobe (controlling clairaudience) by his Consort.

The white Buddha Ḍākinī directs the Tum mo Fire (inner heat) governing the yogic control of the *nāḍīs* as they circulate from the Solar Plexus centre to all of the minor centres, and via Splenic centre II and the Sacral centres to the Inner Round. These Fiery *prāṇas* represent the essence of the *dharma* as they awaken all aspects of the general *prāṇic* circulation below the diaphragm and express the highest *saṃskāric* qualities possible to be conveyed by these centres at any time. The Fiery *prāṇas* will lift the refined, transformed *prāṇas* of the Sacral centre to vitalise every other centre. The entire form can then become one fiery conflagration. Tum mo (elementary *kuṇḍalinī)* moves up the central *suṣumṇā* channel, the centre of each of the major *chakras,* manifesting in the minor *chakras* (the southern direction) via the Solar Plexus centre to the Stomach and Liver centres. The entire process must be rightly controlled by the Mind, and can be quite dangerous if elements of desire-mind intercede in directing the Fires. Varuṇānī governs the qualities of 'the *bīja* is the dharma' to lay the foundation for the liberation of this Fire. The north-south alignment with Bhujanā, who represents the Earthy admixture of all the *prāṇas* coming from the Base of Spine centre, overlaps with the southernmost petal of the Sacral centre. This integration process helps in the liberation of *kuṇḍalinī.*

The other four Wisdom Ḍākinīs signify the generation of the *prāṇas* derived from the four feet of the elephant (Bhujanā) as they integrate with and further develop the attributes derived from the four petals of the Base of Spine centre. (Agnāyī the human-like *prāṇas,* Cāmuṇḍī the animal-like ones, Vāyudevī the plant-like ones and Varāhī the Earthy ones.)

Desire for things pleasurable represents the base from which the *piṇgalā nāḍī* from the top right hand petal flows in the form of 'the homologous and uninterrupted series'[10] governed by Agnāyī (and the sense of taste). As these *prāṇas* flow up the spinal cord, being successively processed by the *chakras* they pass through, so desire is steadily converted into devotion, then aspiration. Eventually we have the evocation of *bodhicitta* when processed by the Heart centre and the reflective nature of Akṣobhya's Mirror-like Wisdom. This allows the liberation of *kuṇḍalinī* and the activity of the blue Vajra Ḍākinī, who projects the Fires through the *piṇgalā nāḍī* in an Airy form. When viewed in terms of the lower *siddhis* it manifests as aspirational idealism. The aspiration here is to penetrate the attributes of the highest planes of perception (awakening the Head lotus), and to bring the resultant revelatory visions into practice. These impressions are the keys of destiny for the entire Bodhisattva path. Prescient vision is awakened, manifesting as compassionate insight into the nature of people's true emotional needs, thoughts and identifications, of the bonds of *karma,* and how to rightly direct these so that enlightenment is the gain. Love and wisdom is generated to appropriately serve upon ever higher domains of realisation. The idealism is at first to make it so, and later with full awakened vision to complete the Bodhisattva steps to Buddhahood.

10 See Figure 10.

Attachment or clinging to that which is desirable is the foundation for 'the production of own fruit' (sight, Cāmuṇḍī). As these *prāṇas* are successively refined by the *chakras* they pass through they produce knowledgeable attributes, and finally much *manasic* capability. The associated *saṃskāras* are later fully processed by the Throat centre (*viśuddha chakra*) and the Discriminating Wisdom of Amitābha. Once the *prāṇas* are sufficiently refined, the red western Padma Ḍākinī can then project *kuṇḍalinī* throughout the *iḍā nāḍī,* lighting up the petals of the minor and major *chakras* with Fiery *prāṇas*, producing a *maṇḍala* of *manasic* light, a living form where every aspect is controlled by the Mind, denoted here as the *siddhi* 'abstract cognition'. The entire Head lotus then becomes illumined, allowing the many subtle discernments of resilient and expanding wisdom to be accomplished. The path of the higher Initiations thereby awakens.

Avaricious pursuit of things desired, selfishness and sensuality, often proceed hand in hand, producing many of the base appetites that the human personality is capable. These *saṃskāras* are denoted as 'the *bījas* belonging to a specific moral process' and are processed by Vāyudevī (the sense of touch). This petal of the Sacral centre represents the place of generation of *piṇgalā* attributes, through integration with the *prāṇas* from the right Gonad centre. The principle of desire and how it affects all aspects of sexuality and concepts of union with the opposite sex (or other) must be understood. The concept of harmony between the sexes through their union and equalisation is eventually transmuted into the equality or unitary nature of all things, as espoused by Ratnasambhava's Equalising Wisdom.

The yellow Ratna Ḍākinī can then help channel *kuṇḍalinī* to her correspondence in the Solar Plexus centre, producing 'yogic control of the elemental lives'. These lives are the theriomorphic forces, the *devas* that are the builders of the form, embodying the sum of its nature. Thus they produce the expression of sicknesses or well being, the entire health aura of the individual. They are the child of revelation for the bodily form and need to be protected through compassionate and wise perception so that perfect health eventuates, and not crippling psychic ills because of deleterious thoughts and energies. Once rightly controlled and imbued with the living Fire, then the true psychic healer appears, able to properly help others with their ailments, by utilising the magnetism of the body and purified *prāṇic* effects. The incongruent bodily ails are therefore expelled or rectified and harmonised into one unitary expression of well-being. The objective is not just for the unit, but also to heal all ailing units and to integrate them into one healthy community emanating good will for each other. This is the basis to the art of true psychic healing.

Pure lust and the desire to satiate the insatiable demonstrates the expression of that *bīja* field known as 'conditions for actual *dharmas'*, and the sense of hearing, governed by Varāhī. The *saṃskāras* generated manifest via the left Gonad centre, which is responsible for the general physical urges, appetites, and attraction amongst the sexes. It concerns the attractiveness that brings them together to manifest forms of sexuality. Through eventual control of the entire sexual function the All-accomplishing Wisdom of Amoghasiddhi is eventually established. All Earthy *prāṇas* may then be mastered in this petal of the Sacral centre that represents the place of generation of *iḍā* attributes. Once mastered, the green Karma Ḍākinī helps to channel *kuṇḍalinī* to awaken the *siddhi* denoted 'psychometry', where facts about the (psychic) history of an object or person can be gleaned by touching it. One must then learn to rise above this foundational realm of experience, to touch the awareness-states of the *chakras* embodying all levels of expression. Compassion, in the form of the abstract cognition of all things, arises and brings the limited state of sentience (associated with the form embodied) to a higher state of awareness.

The Throat centre (governing the output of the mind/Mind) is the higher correspondence of the Sacral centre. The Throat centre acts as a sink for the Sacral centre's energies, and must control sacral output at the time of the rising of *kuṇḍalinī.* The five Jñāna Ḍākinīs therefore can be considered attributes of the Throat centre that finally bring the Sacral centre's forces under control. Weaknesses of the Sacral centre therefore have a reciprocal effect in the Throat centre and vice versa. The power of mantra is also implicated here, but is not a subject of study in this Treatise.

Rulership of the Base of Spine centre

As the forms of activity associated with the Wisdom Ḍākinīs are now established, we can progress to the Base of Spine centre, ruled by Vajrakīla Heruka. Lauf states:

> In the lowermost lotus, the sukhapāla-cakra, the dark-blue Vajrakīla or Vajrakumāra-Heruka appears as a powerful personal protective deity. He has three heads, six arms, and four legs and stands on a lotus with his light-blue female counterpart. Vajrakumāra also has the wings of a garuḍa and wears the tantric death's-head buddha-crown. In his first pair of hands he holds a ninefold vajra (T. rDo-rje rtse-dgu) and a burning flame; in the second pair he caries a vajra and a long trident; in the third pair he holds a magic dagger and at the same time embraces his Prajñā. The magic dagger, also called a vajra dagger (S. vajrakīla; T. rDo-rje phur-pa), is an important ritual tool in the tantric rites of Tibet. Its handle is a vajra and it has a three-edged blade. The deity is himself named after this attribute. The dagger is used in Tibet for ritual exorcism and annihilation of harmful and demonic beings, and especially of serpent-spirits. According to the Tibetan Book of the Dead the magic dagger is associated with the sukhapāla-cakra in that it is the three-edged tool for annihilating the "three basic evils" or "three poisons" of all human activity, which continually lead to karma and attachment. The "three poisons" (T. Dug-gsum) are ignorance, hatred, and the passions.[11]

The Base of Spine centre has four petals, each of which ascribes to one or other of the four kingdoms of Nature. The petal that is overlapped with a petal from the Sacral centre is devoted to the generation of plant-like *prāṇas*. The characteristics of this overlapped petal manifests as the foundational basis for all else that manifests in the *nāḍīs*.[12] The *maṇḍala* of the *nāḍī* system is therefore generated here, allowing the conveyance of all *prāṇas*. The polar opposite of this petal governs the expression of the Earthy Element, the mineral kingdom *prāṇas*. When the internal fires of this kingdom are yogically directed then we have

11 Lauf, 155.

12 The *nāḍī* system and the *chakras* (flowers) represent the plant kingdom in the body. The 'plant' comes out of the 'soil' of the Earthy Element at the point of overlay of these two petals.

the generation of psychic heat. The triune Vajrakīla Heruka directs the *prāṇas* that pour through the remainder of the petals of this *chakra*. They control the vitality of all the organs of the dense form. These organs have a propensity to sicknesses, disease, or health, viewed both from a psychic as well as a mundane perspective. The *kīla* (phur ba) is a ritual implement assisting in focussing healing *prāṇas* and to ward off evil potencies or entities, therefore it is specially venerated and utilised for this purpose in Nyingma Tantric practices. The three blades of the phur ba represent mastery of the qualities or *saṃskāras* of the three planes of human livingness (*saṃsāra*), the mental, emotional (astral), and dense physical. These planes are symbolised by the qualities of 'the three poisons': ignorance (dense physical involvement), the passions (of the Watery universe), and hatred (with its *manasic* input). Under the guise of the cock, serpent, and pig they are depicted as the central hub of the great Wheel of the Six Realms of death and rebirth, and the entire saga of Dependent Origination (*pratītyasamutpāda*).

Each pair of hands holding implements of the six arms of Vajrakīla Heruka symbolise the qualities of the *iḍā* and *piṇgalā nāḍīs*. The nine pronged *vajra* and a burning flame that he holds in his first pair of hands refers to the qualities of the mental plane. This *vajra* is the power behind the evocation of the *prāṇas* of the eight petals of the overlapped Base of Spine-Sacral centres, plus the central integrated pair. It generates the masculine *piṇgalā* attribute of *manasic* Fires which feed all aspects of consciousness. This *vajra* symbolises the attributes of the combined adamantine wisdoms of the Dhyāni Buddhas (the cardinal directions of the prongs), and their Consorts (the intermediate directions), as well as the functions of the eight directions of space. The *burning flame* refers to the generation of the *cittavṛtti,* the general substance of the mind. Here the feminine *iḍā* aspect is evoked, as sustained by the activity of the Wisdom Ḍākinīs, symbolising the generation of the five sense-consciousnesses and the intellect.

In the second pair of hands he carries a *vajra* and a trident. (A simplified version of the *khaṭvāṅga.)* With them all of the vicissitudes of the Watery astral plane can be mastered. This relates to the majority of the defilements generated by an individual, which are collectivised by the term *kliṣṭamanas.* The *vajra* and the trident are two of the most powerful weapons possessed by a *yogin* and are needed to control these unruly *saṃskāras*. Such weapons are also specifically needed because Watery *prāṇas* are the basis of the common *siddhis* first developed by *yogins*.

The *vajra* refers to the inception of *prāṇas* that will eventually develop into the ten higher supramundane *siddhis* (the Buddha-attributes) as expressed by the five Jinas and their Consorts. They result from the foundation of the converted Watery into Airy *prāṇas* in the *piṅgalā nāḍī* stream which produces the mundane *siddhis*. The *siddhis* are transformed into their supramundane version when the related *iḍā* qualities are similarly mastered and all *prāṇas* are appropriately accommodated in the Head lotus. (Without the *piṅgalā* attributes being properly developed first the *iḍā* qualities produce *siddhis* associated with the dark brotherhood.)

The trident of this base centre, possessing three prongs, represents the qualities of the three Elements; Earth, Water and Fire that embody the attributes of *saṃsāra*. It eventually grows into a *khaṭvāṅga,* held in the hand of a Tantric master, such as Guru Rinpoche once all of the Elements of the entire multidimensional world have been mastered. We saw that this Tantric ritual staff represents the opposite sex of the one who holds it,[13] thereby symbolising non-dual union of great bliss and emptiness. The male version is sealed with a *viśvavajra* at the base and tipped with a *vajra*, symbolising compassion or skilful means. The female version is tipped with a trident, symbolising the wisdom aspect (non-duality). However, more accurately, the three prongs of the trident actually symbolises the triune *nāḍī* system and in fact all triads in nature. The non-dual attribute can be interpreted here to mean that the *iḍā* and *piṅgalā* function become fused in the central prong, representing the *suśumṇa nāḍī.*

In the third pair of hands Vajrakīla Heruka holds a 'magic dagger' (phur ba) and 'at the same time embraces his Prajñā'. The downward-pointing dagger signifies that all attributes of the physical plane must be mastered, including all aspects of the sexual function (when integrated with the *iḍā* and *piṅgalā* fusion of wisdom and compassion symbolised

13 Esoterically this signifies the crossing over of the energies from below the diaphragm to above it at the Diaphragm centre, as well as within *chakras*. That which stands above the diaphragm represents the masculine forces and that below the feminine forces.

by this embrace), which therefore includes the principle of rebirth. First the phur ba is used to fully control the generation of the feminine *kuṇḍalinī*, and the associated psychic practices (which need not concern us here) known as the yoga of the psychic heat, Tum mo. Implied is the control of all sexual forces, to manifest non-dual liberating bliss. Such bliss is the result of the union of masculine and feminine in the form of the *suṣumṇā* energy that flows up the central spinal column. This happens in meditation after the masculine *piṅgalā* and the feminine *iḍā* energies have been integrated in the Base *chakra,* and the dynamic father energy from the Sambhogakāya Flower has descended down the spinal column to fuse with the feminine *kuṇḍalinī.*

Without the input of this vertical (masculine) descent (and its associated mantric potency) the feminine energy would not be enticed to travel up the column of ascent prepared through yogic activities. Rather, its tendency would be to burn pathways to the lower centres, producing many psychic and physiological maladies. Here lies the extreme danger of premature focus upon this centre and its energies. The yogic path generates the *bodhicitta* that lines the *nāḍīs* with the protective blue (of Akṣobhya) that will safely convey the Fires.

One important attribute of the symbolism associated with Vajrakīla (that he has four legs) is omitted from the account above:

> As the personification of the ritual dagger (*kila*), Vajrakumara is here depicted as a three-faced and six-armed figure. With his four legs, he dynamically stands in the *pratyalida* posture, as he tramples triumphantly on the symbols of delusion and ego. The male Rudra lies face down under Vajrakila's right leg, while Rudra's female consort lies on her back. Iconographically, the lower part of Vajrakumara's body is sometimes portrayed in the form of a triple-edged *kila*, literally symbolizing the pinning down of the demon of ego.[14]

The four legs symbolise the 'four corners' of the material domain, the four cardinal points of the compass. This indicates the levels wherein all karmic volitions are enacted and cleansed: the dense physical, the etheric substratum, the Watery astral realm, and the Fiery mental realm.

---

14 Huntington, John C., and Dina Bangdel, *The Circle of Bliss: Buddhist Meditational Art.* (Serinda Publications, Chicago, 2004), 503.

The male Rudra represents all of the defilements associated with the *piṇgalā* circulation, whilst the female Rudra is concerned with the corresponding *iḍā nāḍī* defilements. They have to be trampled by means of the activity of the wielder of the *kīla*. This is done through the ritualistic obeisance to the Tantric vows that will enable one to pass Initiation testings.

The form of Vajrakīla portrayed with his lower torso as a ritual dagger is the most important aspect of his symbolism. The *kīla* which he embodies in totality, not only concerns the mechanism of mastering the three poisons of ignorance-delusion, desire-attachment, and enmity-hatred, but also everything concerning the evocation of the *iḍā, piṇgalā* and *suṣumṇā nāḍīs,* of body, speech, and mind. (The three worlds of *saṃsāra.)* This mechanism assists to focus the energies of mind (by utilising *dhāraṅīs*) upon whatever task the practitioner wishes to achieve. Many rituals developed by shamans, Nyingma, and Bön pa priests utilise the *kīla* for the subjugation of evil spirits, for healing purposes, for the evocation and focusing of energies for a specific task, and for working with *chakras* in a knowledgeable way.

The *kīla* pierces a prostrate human figure, signifying the means of penetrating the mysteries of the sum of the human form and its experiences in the various Bardos, over which the Heruka manifests the full glory of mastery. He wears a flayed human skin, signifying that he is a 'cemetery dweller', a *yogin* who has outgrown mere considerations of the human form, the trappings of which he wears disdainfully as a cloak that veils his full regal splendour. He is crowned with the death heads of the perfected endeavour of many lives of achievement. He also wears the wings of a Garuḍa, which has a similar meaning as attributed to his brother Herukas.

Perhaps one of the traditions concerning the origins of Vajrakīla given in *The Circle of Bliss* would be a fitting conclusion to assist in the comprehension of the nature of this most powerful protective Deity.

> Another narrative records that Vajrakila was emanated as the son of all Buddhas from the heart of Vajrasattva in his form of Varja Heruka. In this context, Vajrakila was born as the wisdom manifestation of all Buddhas. He thus embodies the enlightened activities of Buddhas and has potential power in the struggle against evil. On the other hand,

> he also originates from Rudra and his retinues, who are symbolic of all negative forces that would cause obstacles to the teachings and practicing of the esoteric path. In this sense, the Vajrakila incorporates the characteristics of both Buddhas and demons, manifesting in the most terrifying form yet profoundly compassionate nature in order to subjugate the delusions and negativity along the path to enlightenment. A practitioner may, therefore, realize the absolute truth of every human condition, from the best to the worst, by meditating upon the single image of Vajrakila. Through recognizing and defeating one's own Rudra (demon), one may attain liberation from samsara.[15]

Because the highest realm (*dharmakāya*) finds its grossest reflection in the totality of *saṃsāra,* so this lowest plane of perception holds the keys to the highest. If one can therefore transform and pacify the Herukas into their peaceful correspondences, then the *dharmakāya* comes within one's ken at the *śūnyatā-saṃsāra* nexus. The process of pacification concerns mastery of the *saṃskāras* collected and conveyed by the petals of the *chakras,* over which the various Wrathful Deities preside.

15 Ibid.

7

The Deities of the Bardo Thödol
Part Six:
The Wrathful Deities above the Diaphragm

The tenth stage of the evolutionary process

The process associated with the conversion of *saṃskāras* so that the *chakras* are sufficiently cleansed in order to awaken the normal *siddhis* has been analysed, along with some of the symbolism associated with the liberation of *kuṇḍalinī* and all of the salient features concerning the circulation below the diaphragm. This allows analysis of the *tenth stage* of the evolutionary process whereby the supramundane *siddhis* are awakened. Our vision is thereby directed to the major centres above the diaphragm and finally to the Head lotus. Because the attributes of the Throat and Heart centres have been dealt with generally throughout this Treatise they need not be considered here in any detail.

Stage 10. Evolutionary perfection, the appearance of liberated beings.

During this stage all pentads associated with the human psyche and within Nature are conquered, thereby generating the attributes of a Jina. A glorious, victorious one thereby roars out the song of liberation. This process produces the attainment of the sixth to the tenth Bodhisattva *bhūmis,* signifying the undertaking of the third, fourth and fifth Initiations. The third Initiation is the *ālayavijñāna* enlightenment, the fourth Initiation is the attainment of *śūnyatā* and the fifth Initiation concerns the mastery of all correspondences of the five sense-consciousnesses seeded aeons ago by the Ādi Buddha.

The entire process of converting the subtlest of *saṃskāras* to produce enlightenment is presided over by Mahottara Heruka and Krodeśvarī (the wrathful form of the Ādi Buddha and his Consort). The Head Lotus (*sahasrāra padma*) and the Ājñā centre can thus become totally awakened. There are five tiers of petals to the Head Lotus, three being major, containing the *bījas* for the activity of the consciousness-stream for the various periods and cycles of Life. The two innermost tiers only fully flower at the highest stages of the Bodhisattva path. These five tiers (levels) of *saṃsāric* expression are governed by the functions of the five Dhyāni Buddhas, with Amoghasiddhi governing the activity of the outermost tier, wherein all types of knowledgeable attributes are extracted from *saṃsāra*.

Great beauty and wisdom is seen underlying the overall schema of the human constitution and its evolution; from the interplay and awakening of the Inner Round, then the Base of Spine/Sacral, Solar Plexus, Splenic, Heart and Throat centres, through to the fifth level of the combined Head lotus. All is but one grand interlocking and enmeshing of wheels (vortices) of energies of different colours and the lines of interrelation (*nāḍīs*) linking one centre to the other.

The main function of the Head lotus is to incorporate and process Fiery *prāṇas*. These *prāṇas* are also later integrated with the energies from the Heart centre. This activity manifests in the three outermost petals. They process the five Elements in terms of their Fiery subdivisions. The eventual product is the *ālayavijñāna* enlightenment. The two innermost petals process Airy and Aetheric *prāṇas,* the gain being the *śūnyatā* and *dharmakāya* enlightenments. The three outermost tiers, the arena of Fiery activity of this regal flower crowning a person, constitute the major part of evolutionary time to awaken. They are consequently the main subject of this chapter, coupled with the organisation of the integrated Ājñā centre. The functions of the three outermost tiers of petals can be outlined as below:

a. The outermost and largest tier of petals incorporate the Fiery *prāṇas* governing the normal unfoldment of *manas* within the human consciousness as one undergoes the trials and tribulation of the activities of the entire life process. Watery and Earthy *prāṇas* are also processed here, thus this tier represents the Solar Plexus in the head (the Solar Plexus tier). These petals are by far the most numerous and complex in the Head centre. Here the final processing of mental-emotional *saṃskāras* occur.

b. The next inner tier of petals of the Head lotus, here termed the Heart in the head (the Heart Tier), process the Fiery-Airy *prāṇas*. This tier is concerned with the types of activity that generate *bodhicitta,* hence the attainment of the second Initiation (mastery of the Watery Element, and the expression of the minor *siddhis).* It then helps generate the experience of *śūnyatā,* associated with the attainment of the fourth Initiation, after the second innermost tier of petals (of the pentad of tiers) has been properly awakened.

c. The Fiery-Aetheric *prāṇas* are processed in the third innermost central tier, here called the Throat in the head. It awakens the full potential of the Head Lotus, enlightening one by respect of being able to express the attributes of the lowest level of expression of *dharmakāya* at the third Initiation. There is a natural progression of refinement of *prāṇas* from the first Initiation (of mastery of attitudes to physical plane livingness) of the outermost tier of this centre to the third Initiation. When the *kuṇḍalinī śakti* is evoked and fully expressed an *arhat*[1] appears with this Initiation that produces mastery of the *saṃskāras* of mind. The fifth Initiation is attained when all five tiers of the Head lotus are aligned and conveying energies to maximum capacity. The two innermost tiers of the Head lotus are then fully vivified, and all of the twelve major petals are fully vibrant.

The coursing of the Fiery *prāṇas* awakens the three outermost tiers of petals of the Head Lotus. The Airy *prāṇas* produce the vivification of the second and fourth innermost tier of petals, whilst Aetheric *prāṇas*

---

1 *Arhat* (Tib. dgra bcom pa): From the root *arh,* meaning 'worthy or deserving'. Thus a worthy one, foe destroyer, also, *'arhan'.* One who has attained freedom from the cycles of existence, associated with the Theravādin (*śravakayāna*) tradition. A solitary meditator. A title given to those that have journeyed to the 'other shore' of *saṃsāra* by this tradition, thus a 'non-returner'. Esoterically, Initiates of the third degree that have mastered the Fiery attributes of Mind, of conscious integration with the Sambhogakāya Flower, producing the 'self'-absorbed contemplativeness described in the texts. They however do 'return' as later a new personal-I is rayed into cyclic existence that manifests as a Bodhisattva.

awaken all tiers of petals and the rapid spinning of the twelve major petals of this crown of crowns. This produces the *uṣṇīṣa* (top-knot of energies, signifying omniscience), depicted as a bundle of hair in representations of Buddhas and highest level Bodhisattvas.

- Mastery of the Inner Round *prāṇas* below the diaphragm associated with Sacral centre activity produces the first Initiation.
- Mastery of the Solar Plexus forms of activity produces the second Initiation, awakening the ordinary *siddhis*.
- At the third Initiation there is mastery of the full integration of the Throat and Heart centre energies into the Head centre.
- At the fourth Initiation the *śūnyatā* experience allows complete awakening of the All-seeing Eye.
- The fifth Initiation necessitates the vibrant awakening of all petals of the Head lotus. The entire *maṇḍala* of accomplishment is now revealed, with wheels spinning within wheels, according to a primal paradigm established as the basis for the appearance of Shambhala.

Mahottara Heruka and his Consort Krodeśvarī control the activity related to the transmutation of the *prāṇas* of the Head lotus. Vajrakīla Heruka and Consort (Samayatārā) govern the activity of the Ājñā centre, allowing the regulation, control, and direction of all of the ordinary *siddhis*, where the focus is upon the *prāṇas* generated below the diaphragm. The awakening and development of the supramundane *siddhis* is deferred to the Head lotus proper. From these two centres therefore the activity of all Wrathful Deities and their Consorts are regulated. There is an obvious correlation between Mahottara Heruka and Krodeśvarī to Vajrakīla Heruka and Consort (Samayatārā), as the Base of Spine/Sacral centre represents the foundation for that which later appears fully manifest in the Head lotus. In fact the entire *maṇḍala* of Peaceful and Wrathful Deities that can be found contained in the lower centres is established in the Head lotus, as the Mind is the real and all phenomena is born in it and is carried by it. Verily, all is Mind. All attributes of *dharmakāya* are expressions of the primordial Mind of the Ādi Buddha.

There are higher levels of attainment relating to the sixth and higher Initiations. The *eleventh stage* of the evolutionary process produces the appearance of Buddhas within the earth sphere, with Shambhala being their place of residence, preparatory to their abstracting journey into the vast space of cosmos. The *twelfth stage* of the evolutionary process involves the return of cosmically trained Buddhas to establish world spheres as Ādi Buddhas. In this schema of twelve we inevitably have the completion of the turning of the petals of the Heart centre of a grand Logoic entity that lies far beyond the ken of all but the highest Bodhisattvas upon the earth.

The goalpost for what constitutes a liberated being has changed throughout the millennia, a fact needing to be comprehended by religious historians. Higher spiritual teachings than were ever broadcast before are periodically released by the Lords of Wisdom and Active Compassion. With the information herein given concerning the functioning of the Head lotus, this will later be presented concerning the constitution of Shambhala, from where the peaceful and wrathful forces emanate to transform aberrant *saṃskāras* on a planetary scale. The process of enlightenment for the entire human race is similar to that of the liberation of an individual and is the object of meditation for the Council of Bodhisattvas. How to transmute massed human *saṃskāras,* the processes and entities involved, plus the stage of evolution of the various categories of humanity and arenas of activity is a subject of their meditation. Accordingly, Bodhisattvas incarnate at the level where the next major stage of overcoming theriomorphic forces is possible for the massed areas of human activity, or for targeted groupings. Vast is the needed vision over the aeons of human evolution to see the process through to conclusion, considering the multitudinous diversity of the human family and their differing needs. Here we see the vaster application of the teachings of the *Bardo Thödol.*

The overall more esoteric number for the Wrathful Deities is 60 (5 x 12), rather than the 58 normally ascribed to them. One must also add to the 58 the wrathful emanation of the Ādi Buddha (Samantabhadra), the fearsome red-brown Mahāśrī-Heruka (Che-mchog Heruka) in union with his Consort. They are all protectors of the *dharma*, guarding all of the pathways to the 1,000 petalled lotus. This number is symbolic, a convenient shorthand notation, signifying the way of manifestation of the Great Perfection. The number twelve governs the organisation of the petals of this *chakra,* as it essentially extends the functioning of a Heart *chakra* into the domain of Mind. It must do so because Love is what governs all that is, otherwise *bodhicitta* and the Bodhisattva path could not evolve Buddhas. The process of manifesting *bodhicitta* awakens the twelve main petals of the Heart in the Head centre.

The number 60 = 5 x 12, assigned to all the Wrathful Deities, informs us that there are five major pathways (of the sense-consciousnesses) for the *saṃskāras* of mind entering this Head lotus. They relate to the five Elements multiplied by the twelve qualities of the petals of the Heart centre. Sixty Protectors are needed to ensure that all negative *prāṇas* of mind are diverted from the sacred spaces of Mind, and are recycled until they can be properly transmuted into their higher octave, allowing them to play an enlightening role. What stands true for a human Head centre also manifests on a far vaster scale for Nature. Of these sixty, the twelve major Protectors of the *dharma* focus upon safeguarding the twelve main petals of the Head Lotus, and forty-eight guard either lobe of the Ājñā centre, depending upon the nature of the flow of *prāṇas.* (If our view is just upon the physical characteristics of the petals. We will later see that the arrangement is far more complex.) In the Ājñā centre most of the work related to organizing the *prāṇas* to be absorbed into the Head centre is carried out, hence the necessity of the forty-eight female protectors in the Ājñā centre.

Quoting 'the Tibetan treasure-discoverer Padma gling-pa before his students in the Kun-bzang-gling monastery in eastern Bhutan' Lauf states:

> He emphasizes the psychological significance of the deities: "One's own body is the home of the peaceful and wrathful deities." Then from out of the powerful Mahāśrī-Heruka (T. Che-mchog Heruka), the wrathful manifestation of Ādibuddha Samantabhadra, there unfolds the group of five blood-drinking deities in order to annihilate the five principal failings of human behavior (T. Khrag-'thung rigs-lnga). With them appear the five Heruka-Ḍākinīs to enlighten the five elemental realms (T. Khams-lnga kro-ti-shva-ri-ma). They are followed by the eight wrathful Keurima and the eight animal-headed Phra-men-ma for the enlightenment of the eight kinds of awareness and their realms of operation (T. gNas-brgyad yul-brgyad ke'u-ri bcu drug).

> These are the wrathful counterparts of the eight Bodhisattvas and the Ḍākinīs from the maṇḍala of the peaceful deities. Then from the four cosmic directions of the visionary space follow the four theriomorphic female Guardians, whose purpose is to indicate to awareness its "four boundaries" (T. rTag-chad mu-bzhi sgo-ma bzhi). At the end there is a wild round-dance of animal-headed Furies who appear in groups of seven wrathful Ḍākinīs from each of the inner regions of the head, from its eastern, southern, western, and northern parts. They conquer all karmic hindrances in order to liberate the world of awareness from all passions and attachments. For only on the image-less level can the realm of transcendence be attained.[2]

This final section on the Wrathful Deities integrates the symbolism of the combined Head centres (the Ājñā centre and the Head Lotus) that form a functioning unity. The Head lotus takes the role of the masculine Deity, where the Ājñā centre becomes the place of the union (or Son) with the Consort, the feminine mechanism of interrelationships that represent the five major *chakras* existing below the head. In these five lower centres the attributes of the five sense-consciousnesses are evolved and mastered. The Head lotus absorbs, integrates and perfects their qualities, whilst the Ājñā centre is the agent that acts as a mechanism of interrelationship. It directs and coordinates the *prāṇas* evolving as the child (the consciousness principle) in the Womb of the great Mother (Krodheśvarī), the entire phenomenal appearance of things. The Ājñā centre also integrates the incoming *saṃskāric* incentives (forces) from the body into the Head lotus. In integrating both spheres of activity it becomes the 'all-seeing Eye'. When awakened and gazing upwards it visualises via the twelve main petals of the Head lotus and manifests as the Eye of Reality. It can view the liberated Lives constituting the expanse of *dharmakāya,* thus conquering space and time. Once all past life events (the '777 incarnations' embodied by the petals of the Head lotus) can be known, then the sum of the corruptible nature of phenomena will have been controlled and conquered, allowing the preservation of an incarnation body for the duration desired.

When viewing outwards, the Ājñā manifests in terms of the pristine cognitions to view the multidimensionality of all forms via any of the

---

2 Lauf, 143.

five main *chakras*. The phenomena of the sum of the appearance of things then becomes known and the major *siddhis* are generated that control all such appearances.

When viewing downwards the Solar Plexus centre becomes the Ājñā's natural organ of expression, with its clairvoyance and telepathy. Hence it discriminately views the subjective events and processes conditioning *saṃsāra* via all of the centres of the Inner Round.

The petals of the Ājñā centre

There are 96 petals to the Ājñā centre, arranged into two lobes or wings of 48 (2 x 24) petals each. The significance of the number 24 was explained earlier in chapter three. The number 4 x 24 = 96 produces a receptivity to the four petals of the Base of Spine centre. The four petals of this centre effectively stand as the basis of the expression of *saṃsāra,* and when we multiply its qualities with the twelve petals of the Heart *chakra* (which project the qualities of *bodhicitta*), then we get the number of petals of one lobe of the Ājñā centre. Of the two lobes (2 x 48 petals), one lobe directs the *piṅgalā nāḍī* energies, and the other directs the *iḍā nāḍī* energy. The *piṅgalā nāḍī* is said to be anchored in the Heart centre and the *iḍā nāḍī* in the Solar Plexus centre (for normal human *kāma-manasic* thought processes).

At the inner base of the *maṇḍala* of this centre are twelve petals, from which both lobes of petals emanate. These petals integrate the *prāṇas* of the twelve major petals of the Head lotus with the general qualities of the Heart centre, as well as all bodily *prāṇic* circulations via all groupings of twelve petals found therein. All petals convey the energies of the Heart of Life, from where the energy of *bodhicitta* emanates. Two times 48 plus twelve makes the sacred number 108, necessary to account for all *prāṇas* associated with the circulation of the principle of Life (*jīva*) from the Heart centre. If a group of 48 *prāṇas* of either lobe is integrated with the central twelve representing the jewel of this lotus, then we get the number 60, the significance of which was explained above.

In relation to the mathematics of the petals, the number 96 (8 x 12) should be emphasised as this is the main number from which all further calculations are derived. The number 8 x 12 immediately coordinates the energies and qualities of the eight Mahābodhisattvas into our thinking, via the basic number twelve associated with the Heart of all Life.

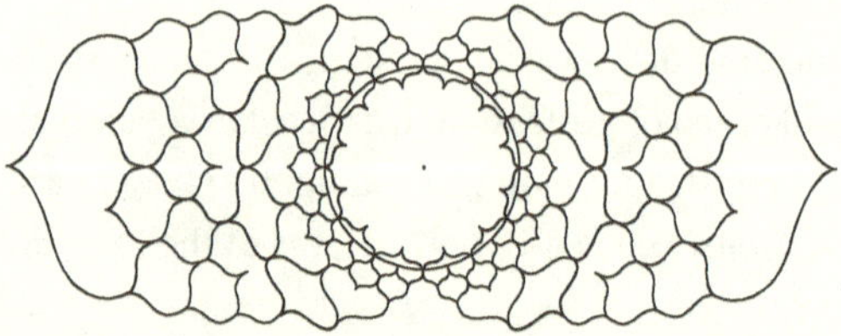

Figure 16. The *Ājñā* centre

We can integrate the deities presented in the previous quote in terms of seven Ray statements. These seven Ray potencies are the underlying force organising the 'groups of seven wrathful Ḍākinīs from each of the inner regions of the head'. The central sphere incorporates a group of twelve (petals) that project the major *prāṇas* to the Head lotus, and therefore help govern the overall movement of *prāṇas* via the twelve major petals of that lotus. The incoming *prāṇas* to the Ājñā centre are the Buddha Herukas and their consorts. The Herukas guard the five major *prāṇas* entering the right lobe of the Ājñā (the five outermost petals), which control the movement of the *prāṇas* of the *piṇgalā nāḍī.* Their consorts similarly guard five *prāṇas* and *saṃskāras* entering the left lobe of the Ājñā and thus the movement of the *prāṇas* of the *iḍā nāḍī.* The Rays can now be assigned to the seven groups of Wrathful Deities.

1. Mahāśrī (Mahottara) Heruka (Tib. Che-mchog Heruka), the wrathful manifestation of Ādi Buddha Samantabhadra, with his consort, the Ḍākinī Krodheśvarī. Theirs is the potency of the first Ray of Will or Power which they utilise to destroy the five poisons of ignorance, hatred, passion, pride, and envy. They do this via coordinating the activities of all the subordinate deities associated with the rest of the *maṇḍala.*[3] Mahottara presides over the general protection of the Head lotus, whilst his consort coordinates the work concerning the

3 Though Mahottara Heruka and Consort are depicted here in terms of a human Head centre, this depiction also represents a minute reflection of what transpires in the planetary Head centre, Shambhala.

prāṇas entering the Ājñā centre. Mahottara's presence is found in the central eye (jewel) of this centre. The masculine deity is oriented towards the right hand lobe and his consort to the left hand lobe. Their work is assisted by the general influence of the five Dhyāni Bodhisattvas and their Consorts. Their purpose is not so much to guard from harmful influences (as that has been accomplished by the Buddha-Herukas), but rather to rightly place all *saṃskāras* within the constitution of the Head lotus, and vice versa with respect to the emanations from this lotus to the major *chakras*. All *saṃskāras* are consolidated in the Head lotus according to compassionate considerations. Wisdom must be expressed to ascertain where the *saṃskāras* are to be assigned and the resultant outcome.

2. The five wrathful blood-drinking Herukas and their Consorts are said to annihilate the five principal failings of human behaviour. This is done via the ability of their guardianship of the innermost (Aetheric) petals of this third Eye, that allows them to direct all *prāṇas* coursing through the two main *nāḍīs*. The corrected *prāṇas* can then be directed to the necessary petals of the Head centre, according to the pattern of the pentads of *prāṇas* explained in Volume 4 of this treatise. They work closely with the Dhyāni Bodhisattvas, and are thus their protective extension, guarding the purity of expression and manifestation of the second Ray of Love-Wisdom. The development of this quality is the purpose of incarnation in *saṃsāra,* and its evocation constitutes the way of walking the path of Initiation, over which these Herukas guard.
3. The eight wrathful Mātaraḥ (Keurima) are the terrifying aspects of the eight peaceful Bodhisattvas. All have human heads and are the Wisdom Ḍākinīs of the eight kinds of awareness. They therefore assist in the development of the pure expression of the third Ray of Mathematically Exact Activity, which is the way the expression of the potential of the Mind manifests.
4. From the four cosmic directions of the visionary space follow the four animal-headed female Gatekeepers of pristine cognition,[4] whose

4 Lauf uses the term Guardians here, but as stated in an earlier chapter I shall use the term Gatekeeper for the wrathful female deities.

purpose is to reveal its 'four boundaries' to consciousness. This work comes under the auspices of the fourth Ray of Beautifying Harmony overcoming Strife. This Ray at the centre of things facilitates access to all directions in space.

5. The eight animal-headed Piśācī (Phra-men-ma) stand for the enlightenment of the eight kinds of awareness and their realms of operation. They are the wrathful counterparts of the Consorts of the Bodhisattvas. Four have bird heads, and four have animal ones. We therefore have the beneficent auspices of the fifth Ray of Intelligence, Scientific Reasoning, governing the activities of the many types of awareness to be processed.
6. Twenty-eight animal-headed female deities[5] (Īśvarī) who appear mainly in groups of six Ḍākinīs that deal wrathfully with the emotio-mental *saṃskāras* generated by the personal-I. They transform the *saṃskāras* into beneficent attributes for the long-term goal of enlightenment. Working to liberate the world of awareness from all passions and attachments requires them to draw upon the potency of the sixth Ray of Devotion, which therefore colours all their activities.
7. Vajrakīla Heruka and Consort govern the overall movement of the *prāṇas* in the Ājñā centre and their relation to the Head lotus in accordance with the consequences from the primary energies derived from the four petals of the Base of Spine centre. They thereby link the highest to the lowest in one grand interlocking scheme, utilising the organising Power of the seventh Ray of Ceremonial Cyclic Activity to do so.

Points three to six of this list are concerned with the 48 female theriomorphic deities who were explained previously with respect to the centres below the diaphragm. These *ḍākinīs* also have their higher directive correspondences in the Head lotus.[6] It should be noted that all

5 Lauf utilises the term Furies here, which refers to mythological entities that execute the effects of curses pronounced upon criminals, with the agony of their conscience, and pestilence. Generally the term can be considered to represent angry or violent forces.

6 Esoterically, the feminine *deva* kingdom exists as a basic duality, similar to the distinction between the abstract and concrete minds. The masculine human kingdom on the other hand, exists as a basic trinity, which is symbolised by the three bodies of a Buddha, *nirmaṇakāya, sambhogakāya,* and *dharmakāya.*

deities have their primary activity with respect to the organisation of the Head lotus. In this analysis of the Ājñā centre we will see that the basic structure of some groups of deities is based upon the number four (modelled upon the petals of the Base of Spine centre). Each such quartet can be considered guardians of the gates of the subdivisions of the Head lotus, possessing twelve major petals subdivided into groups of four. Alternatively there is the number six associated with the Sacral centre.

The number 48 is divided into two groups. The first group consists of twenty entities (2 x 4, 2 x 4, and 4), making five groups of four. They are the representatives of the eight Mātaraḥ (with their two sub-groups embodying the fixed and mutable crosses). Similarly, the eight Piśācī possess two subgroups to which we add the four female Gatekeepers of pristine cognition. These five groups correspond to the expression of the five non-sacred petals of the Heart centre, whose primary purpose is to channel the *prāṇas* of the five sense-consciousnesses in accordance with the four major Elements of which these *saṃskāras* are composed.

Next we have the *prāṇas* of the twenty-eight animal-headed female goddesses (Īśvarī). We saw in the previous chapter that they were organised in groups of 4 + 6 + 6 + 6 + 6, which deal with the *saṃskāras* associated with the Solar Plexus, Sacral and the two Gonad centres. These five groups are concerned with processing the categories of *saṃskāras* of the five sense-consciousnesses. With respect to the internal arrangement of absorption of these *saṃskāras* into the Ājñā centre we see that they are also integrated as groups of 7 x 4 *saṃskāras*. Here any of the groups of six are directed by a respective female Gatekeeper (thus conditioned by one or other of the four Elements). They are organised by means of the primary *maṇḍala* of the four petals of the Base of Spine centre, according to the primacy of the *prāṇas* of Earth, Water, Fire and Air. They also incorporate the attributes of the seven Ray qualities, as associated with the seven sacred petals of the Heart centre. Each of the Gatekeepers enacting rites manifests the functions of the first Ray of Power to appropriately direct or work to transform the *saṃskāras* flowing through them for the group of six Īśvarī under their jurisdiction.

In addition, we also need to observe the actual layout of the petals of the Ājñā centre. We see that for each lobe there is an innermost tier of seven petals, followed by twelve petals, then tiers of eleven, five, four, three times two, five, four, and one. (Incorporating therefore nine strata of petals.[7]) This arrangement allows for all main *prāṇic* combinations associated with the eight consciousnesses to be directed to the Ājñā centre.

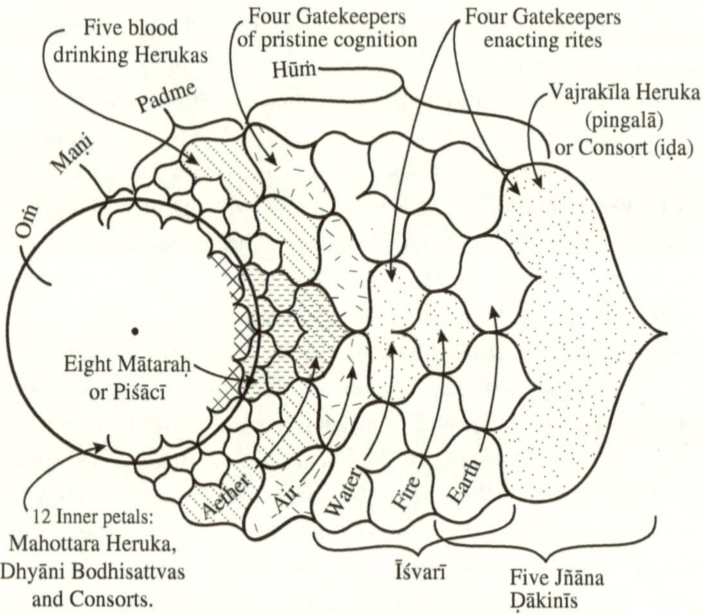

Figure 17. Detail of the Ājñā centre

The nine tiers of petals can be arranged into three groups. First we have an innermost tier of twelve petals. They direct organised *prāṇas* to and from the twelve major petals of the Head lotus. Seven of these innermost petals are utilised by each lobe of the Ājñā centre, where they share two of the petals of this circle of twelve. For each lobe the seven innermost petals can channel the seven Ray potencies, plus the *prāṇas* originating from the seven sacred petals of the Heart centre. The remaining five petals relate to the non-sacred petals. They are expressed in the opposite lobe of whatever lobe one is focused upon at any time, for either the *iḍā* or *piṇgalā* circulation. This represents

7 There is a correlation between these 9 + 1 levels of the Ājñā centre (counting also the central sphere) to the ten stages of evolution, starting from the outermost petal to the inner sphere.

the Will tier that can project the most refined *prāṇas* from each lobe to the Head centre.

As these twelve petals integrate both lobes of the Ājñā centre they can be viewed as one wheel turning. Interlocking with this wheel is another that consists of 12 + 11 + 5 + 4 petals, making 32 altogether. This number represents twice the number of petals to the Throat centre, allowing the conveyance of its *iḍā* or *piṇgalā prāṇas.*

Of these 32 petals the inner twelve can be viewed as integrating the *prāṇas* from the lobe concerned to the innermost twelve petals, plus conveying the potencies from the Head lotus. This then leaves the 11 + 5 + 4 arrangement, making twenty altogether, whose main purpose is to transmit the Airy *prāṇas* of the system. These *prāṇas* represent the general mix of the most refined attributes to be channelled to the Head lotus. The number twenty can be thought of as expressing the energies of the five sense-consciousnesses in terms of the four Elements. When integrated with the major petal from whence either *iḍā* or *piṇgalā prāṇas* flow then we have 21 = 7 x 3 petals implicated. (This allows the conveyance of the energies of the seven Rays in terms of the three *guṇas.)* They represent the general energies evoked by the centres above the diaphragm.[8]

The 20 petals are also able to convey the *prāṇas* that originated from the ten petalled Solar Plexus centre, plus the ten petals of the combined Sacral-Base of Spine centres.[9] This allows incorporating the processed Watery *prāṇas* of the system (desire-mind and the emotions). The number 10 + 10 also allows the expression of the *iḍā* or *piṇgalā prāṇas* from any of these *chakras.* All of the Watery and Earthy attributes of the *saṃskāras* of the four Elements in their most refined attributes can thereby be accommodated.

The 32 petals represent the Love-Wisdom tier, that is also constituted to accommodate the energy of *bodhicitta* when generated by the individual. For most individuals, however, we have the processing of the most refined aspects of emotional-mind attributes developed. The *piṇgalā prāṇas* of the Heart centre are, however, the onus of attention.

---

8 Eleven plus one petals for the Heart centre, and the number 5 + 4 implicates the organisation of the Throat centre. See Figure 1, in Volume 5 part B.

9 It also correlates to the group of twenty Wrathful Deities earlier mentioned.

Finally the outer, Activity (Īśvarī) tier is concerned mainly with the processing of *prāṇas* associated with the development of desire-mind in the objective world of the senses. There are fifteen (6 + 5 + 4) petals involved altogether, reflecting the extraction of the *saṃskāras* of the five sense-consciousnesses associated with the three Elements: Earth (the number 4), Water (the number 6) and Fire (the number 5). They therefore reflect the development of the qualities of the three main *chakras* below the diaphragm, under the auspices of the generation of Throat centre *(iḍā) prāṇas*. The *manasic* qualities processed are the main input from the experiences of the five sense-consciousnesses. These Fires of the mind are needed for all of life's activities.

The interrelations of all the above are further qualified by the fact that each lobe of the Ājñā centre receives either the *iḍā* or *piṇgalā nāḍī* flow. Each of these *nāḍīs* is also inherently dual, and contain the refined *saṃskāras* of all the petals of the various *chakras* that have contributed to the *prāṇic* flow.

The eight tiers of petals

The twelve innermost petals exist purely for interrelationship with the Head lotus, for the *prāṇas* from the remainder of the Ājñā centre. They channel *prāṇas* to and from the Head centre via batches of twelve, seven, five, four, three or individual petals. There are four groups of three *prāṇas* (or three groups of four) possible, related to the qualities of the four cardinal directions, or to the way these four Elements are expressed. The direction of these triads of petals come under the jurisdiction of the eight Mātaraḥ or Piśācī, as will later be explained.

This leaves eight tiers of petals to each lobe of the Ājñā centre which in general command the expression of the eight types of consciousness, depending upon the focus of the expression of any of these eight consciousnesses at any time. All of the deities embodying the functions of the petals assist in the projection of the associated *saṃskāras,* according to the role that a particular deity plays. The remaining tiers of petals are arranged as below:

1. An inner group of 12 petals, which are capable of bearing the potency of any arrangement of *prāṇas* from the innermost twelve petals in a two way flow.

2. The next layer of eleven petals, which integrate all *prāṇas* with the major petal, thus making twelve petals in all, similarly allowing a conveyance of any combination of the *prāṇas* mentioned above.
3. A group of five petals, able to convey the five types of *prāṇas* expressed by any *nāḍī*.
4. A group of four petals that specialise in the qualities of the four main Elements by which the *prāṇas* are categorised.

This completes the inner circle of petals of the Ājñā centre. Their focus is the *prāṇas* from above the diaphragm. Next we have the 3 + 1 tiers of outermost petals, whose focus is the *prāṇas* that originate below the diaphragm. Thus we have:

5. A group of six (3 x 2) petals, which have a direct correlation to the desire, sensual, and sometimes violent and aggressive *saṃskāras* that have their origination in the major petals of the Sacral centre and its affiliates within the Inner Round *chakras*.
6. A group of five petals, which convey the mental-emotional, generally Watery *saṃskāras* derived from either of the pentads associated with the Solar Plexus centre.
7. A group of four petals that channel the Earthy *prāṇas* associated with attachment to the form. They therefore have an affiliation to the qualities engendered by the four petals of the Base of Spine centre.
8. The overall petal that integrates all *prāṇas* into one unified stream, allowing the third Eye to focus that stream towards any direction or target area in the entire *nāḍī* system, or upwards towards the Head centre.

In terms of the eight consciousnesses, the first tier consisting of twelve petals can be considered to process the *kliṣṭamanas* (defiled-mind) level of expression, in groups of 2 x 6, thus allowing the six *vijñānas* to be expressed via their *iḍā* and *piṇgalā* interrelations. The significance of the number six hints at the six petals of the Sacral centre, and hence the desire principle that defiles the pure principle of mind. These twelve petals effectively process the Watery-Airy *saṃskāras* that need further refining before they can be accommodated by the Heart centre.

The next tier is constituted of eleven inner petals. They project the *prāṇas* which may be flowing via any Aetheric petal (possessing 4+3+1 petals). These Aetheric petals sum up the *manasic* propensities of an entire lobe of the Ājñā centre and distribute them to this second tier so that they can be incorporated into the appropriate petal of the twelve major petals of the Head lotus.[10] The 3+4 subpetals of the Aetheric petal process the *manasic prāṇas* constituting the sum of the five sense-consciousnesses and the abstract Mind. They also categorise these consciousnesses into the seven Ray attributes. Here three of these petals pass their *prāṇas* into two pairs of petals (of the twelve inner petals) within an Aetheric petal. These four inner petals (which consequently categorise the *prāṇas* in the form of septenaries) then reflect these energies into an innermost triad of petals.

There is thus a mirroring effect of three passing into four and the four projecting energies into three, from the macrocosm (here the Head lotus) to the microcosm (the subsidiary *chakras).* The three, four, three interrelation symbolises the nature of the appearance of phenomena from subjective space. The higher three represents the spiritual triad: *ātma, buddhi, higher manas,* the 'real' or liberated space, the domains of enlightened being. 'The four' represents the appearance of the form, of the three planes of human livingness: the physical, astral and mental domains (body, speech and mind), interrelated by a fourth embodying a mirroring principle. As the energies from the 'real' impact upon the unreal, the phenomenal form, so it produces constant change and periodical mutations. Such transience would be meaningless unless there is a containment of the gain of the transformations whereby the movement from the real to the unreal, and vice versa, can be experienced. This necessitates the appearance of a mechanism of exchange, a container of consciousness or sentience, a mind, and the mechanism of its preservation, the Soul-form (Sambhogakāya Flower). This movement is termed 'the fall of the three into the four' and is symbolised by the interlaced triangle. Much more could be added here, but would diverge us from the main theme. The ten stages of the evolutionary process is also veiled by the 3-4-3 interrelation.

10 It should be noted that the level of attainment of the individual denotes the type of *prāṇas* expressed through any grouping of petals. This account is in reference to aspirants working to gain enlightenment.

The eleven petals constituting the totality of an Aetheric petal is divided in terms of the three abstracted inner petals (projecting *prāṇas* from the 'three planes' or the abstract Mind to the Head lotus) plus the remaining eight, which also process the *prāṇas* of the eight sense-consciousnesses.

The five tiers of petals categorised in terms of the five Elements are organised to integrate the *prāṇas* of the five sense-consciousnesses. They are incorporated in terms of *kāma-manasic saṃskāras* of all these forms of sensory input in the two tiers of five petals in Figure 17. There are also two tiers of four petals that convey the *iḍā-piṇgalā* attributes of the four main Elements. These eight petals also allow the integration of the *prāṇas* coming from any of the eight-petalled lotuses of the Inner Round in terms of their mutable or fixed cross aspects. There is also one tier of six petals that predominantly deals with Watery *prāṇas*.

The third of the eight tiers of petals of this consideration consists of five petals that specialise in the assimilation of Aetheric *prāṇas* associated with the smell sense-consciousness. They synthesise the most refined attributes of the five sense-consciousnesses.

The four petals of the next (fourth) tier specialises in assimilating Airy *prāṇas* associated with the taste sense-consciousness. Only four petals are required because this perception integrates the Airy Element with the qualities obtained through interacting with the material domain of body (Earth), speech (Water) and mind (Fire). The Aetheric expression is too refined for these general base physical plane *saṃskāras*.

This completes the consideration of the middle circle of petals, whereby abstraction of *saṃskāras* into their most refined attributes is possible. The remaining three tiers of the outermost circle concern the direction of the *prāṇas* developed through experience in the three worlds of human livingness—the mental, emotional and physical domains.

The fifth of the tiers in this consideration concerns the touch sense-consciousness. It consists of six petals arranged in pairs, thus we have 3 x 2 petals. This allows the assimilation of all the Watery qualities of desire and the emotions in terms of the three *guṇas* as the desire-emotional principle wedded to mind. This tier incorporates the Elements associated with the mental, emotional and physical domains via the way of expression of the energy directives of the six petals from any of the six-petalled lotuses below the diaphragm, such as the Sacral centre. Here the *kāma-manasic iḍā-piṅgalā* attributes are processed in a way that can be accepted in the innermost tier of twelve petals. As the desire and emotional attributes dominate the normal person, this tier acts as a final processing agent before the *prāṇas* are incorporated in the Head lotus, whose twelve major petals can adequately absorb all of the potencies from the Sacral and associated centres.

The sixth of these eight tiers concerns the sight sense-consciousness governing the direction of the Fiery *manasic* propensity of the individual. All *saṃskāras* developed by the mind require five petals to be processed.

The seventh tier of this consideration concerns the hearing sense-consciousness, thus of the direction of the Earthy *prāṇas,* necessitating four petals. They allow the incorporation of all *prāṇas* originally stemming from any of the four petals of the Base of Spine centre.

The final petal is the major synthesising petal dealing with the sum of *manasic* propensities, as governed by the *ālayavijñāna.* This petal governs the major direction of any individual or group of *prāṇas* of the Ājñā centre to and from it and the rest of the *nāḍī* system.

The Ājñā centre and Initiation

The above account concerns the generalised movements of *prāṇas* in the average person. When upon the path of Initiation, where the *yogin* is consciously working with the transformation and transmutation of *saṃskāras,* then entire groups of petals of the Ājñā centre are utilised. Many are the unwanted *saṃskāras* that need to be consciously transformed with the assistance of the Wrathful Deities.

The seven petals of the innermost tier of a lobe of the Ājñā centre channels the (seven Ray) potencies from the sacred petals of the Heart centre or those from the Head centre. Next are the twelve petals that help process the energies coming from the Heart centre, or to project potencies from the Head centre thereto. The expression of the energy of *bodhicitta* is implicated here. The next tier of eleven inner petals, plus any of the five Aetheric petals,[11] process the energies of the Throat centre, where the Aetheric petal integrates the *prāṇas* of a major petal

11 Each of these five Aetheric petals can be considered to specialise in conveying the most refined *prāṇas* of one or other of the five sense-consciousnesses. The appropriate petal then processes the dominant *saṃskāra* flowing at any time.

of the centre. The eleven petals coupled with either the outermost major petal or the inner sphere project *manasic* attributes to, or receive them from, the twelve inner petals of the Throat centre. Thus the energies of mind/Mind (as conveyed by the eight petals of an Aetheric grouping) can be assimilated into, or directed by, the Head lotus. The arrangement of 4 + 3 + 1 petals of an Aetheric petal also incorporates the ability of these petals to accommodate the incoming energies of one or all of the four major petals of the Throat centre, plus of the three inner petals that support it.[12] Also, the Head lotus can manifest empirical directives to the Throat centre via this arrangement. The five Aetheric petals allow the proceeds of all five sense-consciousnesses or attributes of the Jina Wisdoms to be conveyed in this way.

When the *prāṇas* from a tier of four petals (of the next Airy level) are incorporated with this group then the energies of the Throat centre can be utilised to direct the four main Elements, plus the *prāṇas* that stem from the Base of Spine centre onwards. When utilising the outer (Fiery) group of five petals then the *prāṇas* of any of the pentads associated with the Solar Plexus can be directed by the Head and Throat centres. Similarly with the major *prāṇic* flows in the *nāḍīs*. When focused via the tier of six petals then the Sacral centre can be controlled and its potencies utilised for yogic purposes. The triads of energies therein (that are directed downwards or upwards) can be specifically utilised. At a later stage this allows the direction of *kuṇḍalinī* in the way desired. When one or all of the five Aetheric Petals are focussed via the four Airy petals then the Heart centre can be influenced via its five non-sacred petals. When the focus of the Aetheric and Airy petals is via the three petals that consist of two Watery and one Fiery petal, it allows the control of the sum of the Inner Round *prāṇas* via the transformative potency of the twelve-petalled Splenic centre. This combination implicates the potency of the force empowering the four Gatekeepers enacting rites, projected via a major *iḍā* or *piṇgalā* petal of the Ājñā centre. (In each case the Solar Plexus centre is the organ of distribution of the energies below the diaphragm.)

When the Ājñā centre is focused upon the Head centre then the group of six petals can be utilised to direct *prāṇas* to any of the associated six

12 The organisation of these petals are explained in Part B, Figure 1.

layers of minor petals within any major petal of the Head centre. (This happens during the normal *kāma-manasic* activity of an individual.) When a group of four Airy petals are utilised then purifying *prāṇas* can be directed to control the sum of the petals associated with the incorporating (Watery) level of petals of the Head centre. The path of aspiration and probation to Initiation has then begun. (The reference here being to Figure 23 titled 'The Next Seventy Incarnations' found in Volume 4, chapter 7 of this treatise.) Each Watery petal in the Head centre is constituted of ten minor petals (4 + 3 + 2 + 1) that are also capable of absorbing any group of five *prāṇas* at this level. (This allows the complete development of the five sense-consciousnesses.) There are two times three petals making two smaller (bud) petals for the larger Watery petals. They absorb the *prāṇas* associated thereto from any of the triads of the Sacral centre. When this tier of petals is consciously vitalised with purified *prāṇas* by a *yogin* it allows complete *prāṇic* control of the *nāḍīs* at the level denoted as Tum mo in the texts. (Meaning that the first stage of the awakening of *kuṇḍalinī* has manifested the generation of inner heat that signifies bodily control.)

At the next higher Initiation level (the second) all five of these Watery petals of the Head lotus can be vitalised at once with transformed *prāṇas*, allowing expression of the minor *siddhis*. The process is accomplished via the Aetheric group of five petals of the Ājñā centre. Consequently, the mind must then control all Watery dispositions and the Mind be in the process of being developed. The *prāṇas* of these petals can then be directed to any of the four Fiery petals of the Head lotus. (The next level up petals, each incorporating 100 petals.) When the purified, transformed *prāṇas* from the middle five tiers of petals of the Ājñā centre (of 5 + 4 + 6 + 5 + 4 petals) can be directed to vitalise these four Fiery petals then the third Initiation is possible. When the innermost twelve petals of the Ājñā centre, drawing *prāṇas* from the awakened Heart centre, can be utilised to direct *prāṇas* to the two Airy petals then the fourth Initiation (the *śūnyatā* experience) is possible. When the sum of the petals of any lobe of the Ājñā centre utilises the *prāṇas* of both the awakened Throat and Heart centres then the fifth Initiation is possible, and the *dharmakāya* becomes the ken of the Initiate.

The Ājñā centre is also an expression of the simple *vajra*, and is organised accordingly.[13] Thus with respect to the mantra Oṁ Maṇi Padme Hūṁ, the Oṁ can be considered to integrate the organisation of the consciousness-space of the central sphere (iris) of this Third Eye. The term Maṇi then refers to the direction of the integrated energies from the innermost twelve petals of this lotus, which then represents the central jewel or matrix of energies, from which the power governing the entire structure is derived. This lays the foundation for integrating this *chakra* with the general *prāṇas* of the Head lotus. The term Padme concerns the actualisation of the *prāṇas* to the next major tier of petals (signified by the five Aetheric petals of each lobe) and their interrelation with the entire construct. It therefore coordinates the movement of the *prāṇas* of an entire lobe of this *chakra* (or else integrates incoming *prāṇas* towards the Head centre). The evocation of the Hūṁ then incorporates the *prāṇas* of all the remaining petals and projects them onwards towards the fulfilment of their purpose. Clearly that purpose must be predetermined as part of the meditative *dhāraṇī* of the *yogin* or *yoginī*.

We saw that the 11 + 5 + 4 inner petals process *prāṇas* to and from the centres above the diaphragm. The normal *manasic* propensity of the Throat centre is accommodated by the eleven inner plus five Aetheric petals, where the gain of the sense-consciousness is processed. These petals also process the proceeds from the five non-sacred petals of the Heart centre. The number 11 + 5 produces the necessary sixteen types of *prāṇas* needed to energise the sixteen main petals of the Throat centre. This generates the wisdom attributes of the Throat centre. In projecting *prāṇas* through the next tier of four Airy petals to govern the unfoldment of the four petals of the Base of Spine centre, Fiery *prāṇas* can proceed through all *chakras* on the way to the Base of Spine centre. The foundation for the entire creative expression of evolutionary being thereby comes under the control of *manas*.[14] This interrelation then

13 The figures of the *chakras* presented are two dimensional representations and should be visualised three dimensionally. The *vajra* may then appear in consciousness once the appropriate energies are flowing that link up the petals concerned.

14 Note that the two way flow of *prāṇas* between centres should always be understood to be implicated, where one way concerns the generation of the required attributes, and the other way represents the process of their mastery.

becomes the mechanism of empowerment of the Head lotus with Fiery *prāṇas.* Upon the path of enlightenment the focus of the activity of the Ājñā centre moves to the twelve inner petals and the evocation of the Heart centre's disposition. The engendering of the Airy Element is then the onus of consciousness. The outer four petals of the Throat centre and the four petals of the Airy fourth tier of petals of the Ājñā centre then become subordinate to the Heart centre's emanations. The focus is consequently upon one or other of its four main gates for the expression of the Throat centre's creative Fires. The compassionate attributes of *manasic* activity are thereby expressed. The inner twelve petals for receptivity of the Heart centre's energies convey these compassionate attributes, whilst the 11 + 1 petals express the wisdom attributes. Overall, the Heart centre's expression is the compassionate attribute *(bodhi)* of *bodhicitta,* whereas the Throat centre's contribution is the *manasic* or wisdom attribute of *bodhicitta* (*citta).* If the combination concerns the inner group of twelve petals then one can project energies to the Heart centre and focus upon any particular major petal. The *bodhicitta* associated with its related attribute is then directed to the arena of need.

When the focus is via the outer triad of 6 + 5 + 4 major petals plus the major integrating petal (making the number 15 + 1) then the Ājñā centre can project *prāṇas* to control the centres below the diaphragm. (In this case the energies are projected via the four petals of the outermost tier.) Various permutations of these numbers allow control of any of the ten petals of the Solar Plexus centre, the six petals of the Sacral centre, the Gonad centres and the Splenic centres, via groups of six or four petals. The number 15 + 1 = 16 also indicates that the mode of focussing the *prāṇas* of either lobe of the Ājñā centre is by means of the mind/Mind, as controlled by the Throat centre. This is needed because the sense-consciousnesses are developed by the centres below the diaphragm, the *prāṇas* of which are controlled by Throat centre activity.

Fifteen major petals are utilised for the circulation below the diaphragm because here effectively we have the number 3 x 5 needed to convey the three *guṇas* of the *nāḍīs* to the system, with respect to the five sense-consciousnesses, of which all these *prāṇas* are really aspects.

One could also incorporate the mantra Oṁ Āḥ Hūṁ in this discussion. As Govinda states, these three seed syllables correspond to the three principles of body, speech and mind, and after the meditator has integrated all forces and psychic perceptions in his Mind, they are consequently transformed by means of the mantrạ into:

1. The principle of the all-embracing universal body ('OṀ'), realized in the Crown Centre;
2. The principle of all-embracing, i.e., mantric speech (Tib. gzuṅs) or creative sound ('ĀḤ'), realized in the Throat Centre;
3. The principle of the all-embracing Love of the Enlightened Mind (*bodhi-citta;* Tib. byaṅ-chub-sems) of all Buddhas ('HŪṀ'), realized in the Heart Centre.[15]

Here the Oṁ integrates the *prāṇas* of the two inner tiers of petals, and the Āḥ the *prāṇas* of the next five layers of petals. Finally the Hūṁ expresses the *prāṇas* of the sum of the Ājñā centre, focused upon the one integrating petal. It directs the sum towards any specific petal of the Heart centre so that it becomes the key expression controlling the life purpose in the centres below the diaphragm.

The role played by the deities

Having explained the generalised, overall *prāṇic* flow of the Ājñā centre, the role played by the deities can now be discussed. They symbolise or effectively embody the controlling factors directing the flow of the various groups of *prāṇas,* according to the inherent qualities of the associated *saṃskāras.*

The five tiers of larger petals conveying the Elements have a certain organisation that expresses the main patterns of energies associated with the Īśvarī, Mātaraḥ, Piśācī, blood-drinking Herukas and Gatekeepers of pristine cognition. The *prāṇas* of the five innermost tiers are focused via the four petals of the Airy tier. They are the foundation for the pure elementary *prāṇas* of the entire *nāḍī* system, hence we have the qualifying phrase 'pristine cognition' for their Gatekeepers. Similarly, the Watery, Fiery and Earthy *saṃskāras* of the three outer tiers must pass through the Airy tier in order to be incorporated in the remainder

15 Lama Anagarika Govinda, *Foundations of Tibetan Mysticism,* (Samuel Weiser, Maine, 1982), 185.

of the *chakra*. We see, therefore, that this Airy tier is the effective door between the inner domain and thus the centres above the diaphragm, and the outer world of the sense-consciousnesses. The Airy Element expresses the quality of the Heart centre and the domain represented by *śūnyatā,* and the Gatekeepers 'guard' these foundational *prāṇas* and stages of development upon the path of Initiation. They represent the 'doors' for the expression of each of the four ethers, the substance of etheric space that can convey the properties of the *nāḍīs*. These ethers form a septenary with the three Elements constituting the dense physical plane (Earth, Water and Fire). The ethers represent substance of increasing subtlety that must be attained through the living process if the potencies of the associated *chakras* are to be awakened. The centres below the diaphragm are to be found in the fourth ether. The Throat centre is found in the third ether, the Heart centre in the second ether, and the combined Head centres in the first ether. The ethers are void of cognitive perceptions, hence pristine, as they serve to convey the *saṃskāras* of human consciousness in an unadulterated fashion. These four Gatekeepers therefore guard the pathways to the above mentioned centres, so that only the appropriate grade of *prāṇa* can be channelled to them.

We can think of the pristine cognitions as those that originated in their pure elementary form via the four petals of the Base of Spine centre (including also the central point of this centre). These cognitions over the course of the evolutionary process developed into the five classes of *saṃskāras*. Once refined and cleansed they become the foundation of the wisdoms of the five Jinas, whose cognition is thereby pristine. Of these the *dharmadhātu* (expanse of reality) wisdom of Vairocana manifests as the centre of the *maṇḍala* of the Jinas. The rest of the *maṇḍala* encompasses the four directions of space. The four Gatekeepers of pristine cognition therefore guard the transformations of the *prāṇas* that originated in the four petals of the Base of Spine centre into the wisdoms of the Jinas embodying the four directions. These wisdoms are mirror-like for Akṣobhya, the ability of humanity to reflect cosmos into *saṃsāra* (east). We also have the discernment of inner reality governed by Amitābha, for the mind/Mind that originally developed in the animal kingdom (west). Next, the wisdom of equality, or sameness of Ratnasambhava for the quality developed from the plant kingdom (the *chakras),* that equanimously convey all types of *prāṇas.* The complete mastery of the *nāḍī* system is here implicated. From the perspective of the Base of Spine centre the direction is north, from that of the Head lotus, south. Finally we have the accomplishment associated with Amoghasiddhi's wisdom of mastering the entire material domain. (The north or south direction.)

We have seen that the 48 petals of each lobe of the Ājñā centre manifest a basic duality associated with the distinction between what is above and below the diaphragm; with three outer tiers of petals representing the *chakras* below the diaphragm and the inner tiers representing those above the diaphragm. The outer tiers of petals are relegated to integrating the *prāṇas* from the twenty-eight Īśvarī. They are derived from a special arrangement of the six-petalled tier, the five-petalled tier and the four-petalled tier. (These tiers then specialise in conveying the Watery, Fiery, and Earthy *prāṇas* of normal human interrelationships.) They stand upon the group of four Airy petals of the four Gatekeepers of pristine cognition, which are doorways for integrating the mundane *prāṇas* into the general circulation of the Head lotus.

There are four groups of six Īśvarī represented by pyramids of six petals each, for which the four Airy petals of the four Gatekeepers represent a seat of power. Each of the bases of the pyramids are constituted of three of the Watery petals, their apex being one or other of the four Earthy petals. Thus when the four Earthy petals are multiplied by six, then we get the four groups of six theriomorphic entities constituting the Īśvarī, not counting the Gatekeepers enacting rites. The group of Watery petals are counted as either six single petals, or as three groups of two. When counted singly they manifest as above, however, when as three groups and integrated with the Fiery petal then they also take the role of the four Gatekeepers enacting rites. Here there is also an integration with the major petal, which takes the role of the fourth Gatekeeper at the level of channelling mundane *saṃskāras* of the individual. It directs the function of the major *saṃskāra* to be conveyed at any time via either the *iḍā* or *piṇgalā* flow, as controlled by the associated four petals of the Solar Plexus centre.

The tiers representing the Wrathful Deities

When analysing the petals that principally deal with the circulation above the diaphragm, we should note that there are five Aetheric petals that are expressions of the Consorts of the five blood-drinking Herukas for the *iḍā nāḍī* lobe of the Ājñā centre, and the Herukas themselves for the *piṅgalā* lobe. (Only one lobe shall be taken into account below, though all processes are mirrored for the other one.) If we omit the innermost tier of twelve petals that are relegated to the activity of Mahottara, the Dhyāni Bodhisattvas and Consorts, then we see that each of these five Aetheric petals are really the apex of pyramids consisting of eight petals each. They are capable of conveying the *prāṇas* of all eight consciousnesses. Here, in a compact formula of petals, the relation between the five blood-drinking Herukas and the eight Mātaraḥ and Piśācī manifest. We see that the blood-drinking Herukas regulate the abstracted qualities of the sense-consciousnesses, allowing the attributes of *kliṣṭamanas* and the *ālayavijñāna* (of the two innermost tiers of petals) to be directed to and from the Head lotus. The Mātaraḥ and Piśācī bring to them the converted *prāṇas* from the corporeal body. They can then be utilised or rejected by the blood-drinking Herukas. These Herukas, therefore, will wrathfully reject all *prāṇas* deemed unsuitable for Head centre circulation. (In practice the true effect of this is seen in consciousness only in the latter stages of development, upon the path producing the third Initiation.)

The Herukas also generally govern the overall activity of the five main tiers of petals of the Ājñā centre wherein the five Elements are processed. Buddha Heruka and Consort oversee the processing of the Aetheric petals, Vajra Heruka and Consort the Airy petals, Padma Heruka and Consort the Fiery petals, Ratna Heruka and Consort the Watery petals and Karma Heruka and Consort the Earthy petals.

The Ājñā centre is not static, the central twelve petals revolve, allowing any combination of *prāṇas* coming from any group of petals to be absorbed by a central grouping of three, four or seven of these petals. Each petal can also be viewed in terms of wheels of energies spinning, with a point of exit and entry of *prāṇas*.[16] They then direct

16 Such a point of exit and entry of *prāṇas* is a *nāḍī*, also called a 'gate', hence

the associated *prāṇas* to the corresponding major petals of the Head lotus. The group of three petals integrate the *prāṇas* from either the Mātaraḥ or Piśācī. The group of four petals manifest similarly with respect to the Gatekeepers. Finally the group of seven petals integrate the *prāṇas* of an entire lobe, according to the seven Ray potencies.

The various deities also act automatically, independent upon the conscious input of the thinker. Only at the latter stages of the path, that of active transformation of *saṃskāras,* does the *yogin* come into contact with them, and may have to placate their wrathful emanations.

The outer groups of petals associated with the Īśvarī direct their *prāṇas* via the Gatekeepers of pristine cognition[17] to the pyramids of eight petals governed by the Herukas. (Also, the five Herukas process the five sense-consciousnesses.) All aspects of the eight consciousnesses garnered through empirical experience can then be directed into the Head centre. The tiers of petals governed by the Īśvarī process mainly the *iḍā prāṇas* of the system. The petals associated with the middle tier process mainly the *piṇgalā prāṇas.* The innermost Maṇi petals convey all of these energies, and when evoked the *suṣumṇā prāṇas* are conveyed within the central sphere.

By including three of the innermost Maṇi petals, then each of the five Aetheric (Padme) petals of the Herukas will possess ten petals, plus one integrating petal, making eleven altogether. Each completes the number twelve when their *prāṇas* are projected via the major petal at the apex of each lobe. The rotation of the innermost tier of twelve petals in the Heart conveys the directives from the Head lotus and defines the qualities expressed by these Wrathful Deities. (There can of course be a two-way direction of *prāṇas.*) When the influences associated with the Dhyāni Bodhisattvas, or Mahottara Heruka and their Consorts is incorporated into a lobe of the Ājñā, it ensures a compassionate grounding for all energies directed to and from the Head centre. Mahottara and the Dhyāni Bodhisattvas then govern the *piṇgalā* lobe, whilst their Consorts govern the *iḍā* lobe.

---

the concept of 'Gatekeepers'. They consequently control the flow of what inevitably moves in and out of each wheel.

17 As above mentioned, the function of the Gatekeepers is to embody the expression of the *nāḍī* system as a whole.

When both lobes of the Ājñā are taken into account the two groups of five Aetheric petals make ten petals in all. They are linked to the ten petals of the Solar Plexus centre via its associated pentads of petals. The Solar Plexus centre literally becomes the focal point of the all-seeing Eye when its focus is upon *saṃsāra* at the stage of development where the Herukas are evoked. The integration between the Ājñā and Solar Plexus centres thereby allows the expression of such *siddhis* as clairvoyance and clairaudience. When the Ājñā centre is similarly focused upon, then petals in the Head lotus, or the entire centre, and the higher spiritual perceptions concerning the domains of Mind awaken the higher *siddhis.* With respect to the Solar Plexus centre, the blood-drinking Herukas work via the upward focused pentagram and their Consorts with the inverted pentagram.

The *maṇḍala* of twelve petals, (completed when the eleven petals of any of the Wrathful Deities or Consorts manifests outwardly via the major petal of the particular lobe they are in), is important. It allows the inception of energies from the twelve major petals of the Head centre, and inevitably of *bodhicitta.* When this energy guides the projected *prāṇas* then the target *chakra* or petal becomes rightly stimulated. Alternatively it allows the Ājñā centre to see through the Heart and to work directly with any of its potencies.

If the innermost Maṇi tier of petals is omitted in our consideration then we have groups of eight petals to consider at the Aetheric level. Here then manifest the domains of influence of the eight Mātaraḥ and Piśācī. (The tiers relegated to the Herukas therefore double up for the Mātaraḥ and Piśācī, depending upon the nature of the *prāṇas* conveyed and the purpose of the directive Eye.) Of these there are 5 x 8 = 40 petals for each lobe of the Ājñā centre (making 80 petals all told), if all combinations of the sense-consciousnesses are to be taken into account. We would also have the ability to project the *prāṇas* of the eight types of consciousness via the eight directions in space to any or all of the ten petals of the Solar Plexus centre. However, in practice all of these *prāṇas* are not evoked simultaneously. Rather the focus is upon one or other of the groups of eight petals, which becomes the centremost group whenever the Maṇi wheel turns, so that the sense-consciousness embodied by a particular group becomes the desired focus of attention, the focal point of the Eye. (Such a group is shaded in Figure 18.)

The eight-fold energisation is then projected to influence the target *chakras* possessing eight petals, such as the Diaphragm centre or Splenic centre II, to produce the desired effects in the *nāḍī* system. When the right lobe of petals of the Ājñā centre is the focus then the Mātaraḥ manifest their forms of duty. When the left lobe is the focus then it is the turn of the Piśācī.

It should be noted, however, that all eight petals would normally only be affected when a *yogin* works directly with wilful intent to focus upon the activity of an entire *chakra*. Normally we see that the energisation happens via a group of four petals (of Mātaraḥ or Piśācī), or else of single petals. This would be the case for the normal non-aware consciousness of the average person. The *saṃskāras* generated are of a relatively high order, being concerned with the evocation of wisdom and of compassionate activities. Accounting for the nature of the flow of *prāṇas* and of their quality thus depends upon the stage of development of the individual concerned. The clear demarcation between the inner and the outer tiers of petals of each lobe of this *chakra* can also refer to the processing of Solar Plexus, Sacral and Base of Spine energies in the outer circle, and that of the Splenic and Throat centres in the inner circle, prior to the awakening of the Heart centre proper. It is important to note that this account is intended for those upon the path of discipleship and of Initiation, where one would expect the readers of this text to be.

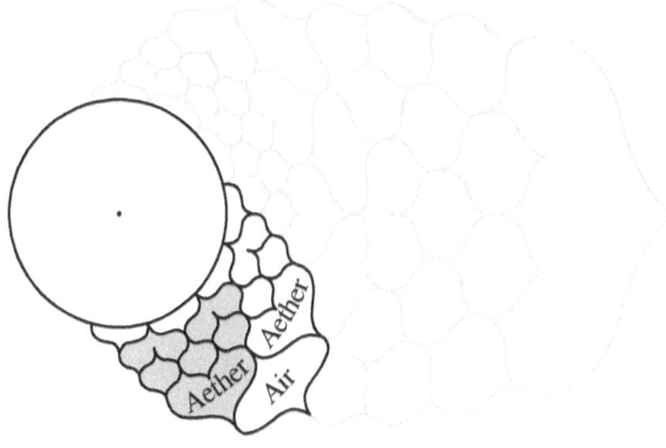

Figure 18. An Airy petal of the Ājñā centre

The tiers of petals controlled by the qualities of the four Gatekeepers of pristine cognition can now be considered. They are the Airy petals supporting the activities of the Īśvarī. As the refinement of perception (inner vision) transpires, untoward *prāṇas* must be warded off as much as possible before they enter the inner tiers of petals of the third Eye. This middle tier of petals are of significant importance in the overall *maṇḍala* of the Ājñā centre. They occupy the juncture between the inner and outer tiers of the Ājñā centre because they process the consequences of the *prāṇas* from the foundational Base of Spine centre. (The pristine basis for what later emerges as the *iḍā* and *piṅgalā nāḍīs*.) Their focus can therefore be an integral part of the circulation of *prāṇas* from below the diaphragm that stem from this base centre (directed towards the petals relegated to the Īśvarī). They can also direct the *siddhis* developed as a consequence of awakening *kuṇḍalinī* and which the all-seeing Eye regulates. Here the two lobes of this centre must be taken into account, where the left lobe directs the mutable cross aspect of the *siddhis*: abstract cognition (northeast), psychometry (southeast), clairaudience (southwest) and clairvoyance (northwest). The right lobe directs the expression of the fixed cross aspect: *dharmatā* (north), aspirational idealism (east), yogic control of the elemental lives (south), and Tum mo (west). The *siddhis* of the mutable cross represent control by means of the developed Mind. The fixed cross positions necessitate the compassion aspect to be exemplified.

From this perspective each Airy petal (incorporating two Aetheric petals) is a large synthesising petal constituting five rows of petals if the innermost Maṇi circle of petals is counted, four if omitted. Of these four tiers the most refined Watery *prāṇas* are processed by the innermost tier of six petals. The most refined Fiery *prāṇas* are processed by the next tier of five petals. The most refined Earthy *prāṇas* by the two Aetheric petals, and the Airy petal. They become the place for the integration of all inner *prāṇas* with those from the three outer tiers, designated Water, Fire and Earth. The three inner tiers incorporated by an Airy petal are fundamentally Fiery in nature, whilst the three outer tiers of the Ājñā centre that first process the incoming *prāṇas* of the *iḍā* or *piṅgalā* are Watery. The integration of the two helps the

Ājñā centre to process and control the attributes of the emotional-mind, or *kāma-manas,* which is the major mode of thinking of most people. Again we have a symbolic 3-4-3 arrangement; of the three inner tiers of an Airy petal and the three outer tiers, that are mirrored into each other by a fourth principle, here the four petals of the Airy tier. (The three outer tiers being able to project *prāṇas* into any of the Airy petals.) From another perspective they can control the petals of the two 'hands' of the Solar Plexus centre.

The Airy petals are also the fifth tier travelling from the outermost petal going inwards. From the point of view of the Airy petals representing the place of generation of the *iḍā* and *piṅgalā nāḍīs* (the effect of the Base of Spine-Sacral centre overlap) this concerns the way of assimilating the *prāṇas* from below the diaphragm into the higher centres. The Airy designation of these petals relates to the generation of these *nāḍīs,* albeit at this stage at an Earthy level.

The tiers of petals labelled Earth, Fire, Water, Air and Aether represent the five stages of the evolutionary flow of *prāṇas* (the five *vayūs*) whereby the wisdoms of the Jinas are eventually evoked, via the mastery of the Solar Plexus centre forces. When the *prāṇas* of the five Elements are dominated by either the Throat or Heart centres, after being integrated into the Ājñā centre from the *chakras* below the diaphragm, and answering the directives from the Head lotus, then we have the possibility of generating *siddhis.* The all-seeing Eye can then rightly direct their expression according to the governance of wisdom. We also have the projection of energies from the Base of Spine centre to the Head lotus implicated. These five tiers of petals also integrate the attributes of the five Elements with the activities of the five Jñāna Ḍākinīs, where the Aetheric tier is energised by the activities of Buddha Ḍākinī, the Airy tier is vitalised by Vajra Ḍākinī, and so forth.

The four Airy petals represent the place of overlap of the Base of Spine and Sacral centres (whose *prāṇas* are processed in the six petals of the next, Watery tier). The five Aetheric petals supporting the Airy petals can then project the potency from the Head centre to awaken *kuṇḍalinī* at the appropriate time, as well as to receive the liberated Fires.

The two Aetheric petals within an Airy petal are governed by two of the five blood-drinking Herukas or Consorts.[18] The energies supporting their activity are thereby derived from the Gatekeeper of pristine cognition that governs the Airy petal they are part of. From this perspective one of the Herukas (or Consort) will process the *prāṇas* of the *iḍā* (will, mind) *nāḍī*, and the other the *piṇgalā* (love, devotion, emotion) *nāḍī*. Each of the Airy petals can then transform one of five groups of *saṃskāras* from below the diaphragm. The *saṃskāras* need to be capable of being expressed in the form that can be channelled to either the Heart or Throat centres. The Herukas work in pairs here to discern whether the *prāṇas* are to be directed to either of these two centres, because of their fundamental *iḍā* or *piṇgalā* dispensation.

Within an Airy petal there are four petals of the innermost Maṇi tier that convey the generalised Airy *prāṇas* to the Head lotus. (This Element being the conveyor of all the *prāṇas* of a *nāḍī*.) The next tier of six petals convey the most refined Watery *prāṇas* that have come from the Solar Plexus centre via the Heart centre. The tier of five petals convey the most refined Fiery *prāṇas* from the Throat centre. The two Aetheric petals, plus the Airy one convey the most abstracted Fiery, Watery or Earthy *prāṇas* from the petals of the outer portion of the Ājñā centre, hence from the centres below the diaphragm. The overall characteristic in these inner tiers is Fiery, with an Earth-Air hue for the left lobe, and Water-Air for the right lobe. Upon the path of enlightenment the Watery aspect dries up completely and consequently one lobe of the Ājñā centre becomes predominantly Fiery and the other Airy.

The difference in the account between the four tiers of the Airy petal earlier described and this description of the five tiers is that the earlier account relates to the normal function of the Ājñā centre, whilst the latter account concerns the yogic path of conscious transformation of *saṃskāras*.

For each major Airy petal (a Gatekeeper of pristine cognition) there are 4 + 6 + 5 + 2 + 1 = 18 petals. The petals are arranged according to a innermost grouping of four from the Maṇi tier, which help process the

18 Remembering here that in the right lobe of the Ājñā centre we find the activity of a Heruka, or else that of a Mātaraḥ. In the left lobe we have the activity of the Heruka's Consort, or else of a Piśācī.

four *prāṇas* emanating from the Base of Spine centre (physical plane activity), or being directed thereto to produce controlling effects upon the entire corporeal form. The refined attributes of the sum of *saṃsāra,* of the four kingdoms of Nature, and the quaternary of the personal-I, can then be directed to the Head lotus (and vice versa). Next there is a tier of six petals that help to process and control the *prāṇas* that have emanated from the Sacral centre (or affect it). The tier of five petals have a similar function with respect to one or other of the pentads of petals of the Solar Plexus centre. A pair of petals then function to control the *iḍā* or *piṅgalā prāṇas* directed via either the Throat or Heart centres. From them the centres below the diaphragm can be directed to transform *saṃskāras.* The focus is then upon the petals relegated to the blood-drinking Herukas. The main function of the Gatekeepers of pristine cognition therefore concerns the meditative or yogic control of the forces of the three above-mentioned *chakras.* The final integrating petal of each Gatekeeper (labelled Air) represents the place of admixing all of the *prāṇas* of this directive flow.

The number 18 also signifies the number of *lokas,* here the sub-planes of perception, associated with human livingness in *saṃsāra* wherein *saṃskāras* are generated and must be transformed. They are the seven physical sub-planes (four etheric and three concrete), the seven astral sub-planes, plus four for the empirical (concrete) mind. These tiers of petals therefore project the directives to effect the necessary transformations in all these levels of perception.

If we omit the four innermost (Maṇi) petals in this consideration then there are fourteen petals in all, 6 + 5 + 2 + 1. They effectively deal with the seven Ray potencies from the sacred petals of the Heart centre (6 + 1 petals) or from their correspondence in the Throat centre (5 + 2 petals). The 6 + 1 arrangement concerns the expression of *bodhicitta,* where it evolves from the transmuted aspect of the principle of desire (the number six) into Love by means of the right application of the will (the number one). The 5 + 2 combination relates to the evocation of Love-Wisdom (the number two) via the perfection of the expression of the five sense-consciousnesses in such a way that Mind takes the place of mind.

Finally, when we project outwards from the central group of eight petals associated with the Mātaraḥ or Piśācī, then at the apex of the group we find a little acorn of three petals, plus at their tip is the major synthesising petals governed by either Vajrakīla Heruka or his Consort. As stated, these three petals plus the major one embody the functions of the *four Gatekeepers enacting rites*. They protect and properly regulate the *prāṇic* streams flowing to and from the *piṇgalā nāḍī* via Vajrakīla Heruka's petal, as well as the *iḍā nāḍī* side of the Ājñā centre via the petal governed by his Consort. They guard the major *kāma-manasic prāṇic* flows of the *nāḍī* system from any untoward *prāṇas*, so that only the appropriate *saṃskāras* can be integrated into the Ājñā centre. This allows the major function of the third Eye to manifest without impediments. The major lobes are thus needed to receive the associated *prāṇas*, or their projection from the Head centre. The attributes of the major lobes of the Ājñā centre are therefore necessarily governed by the most powerful of the deities, wielding the full potency of the phur ba (*kīla*) to do so.

A triad of petals of these Gatekeepers enacting rites sits upon a pair of Airy petals (of the Gatekeepers of pristine cognition), making a group of five petals. They allow the processing of a complete *nāḍī* of five *prāṇas* (conveying the five sense-consciousnesses), to cause the flow of the *iḍā* and *piṇgalā nāḍīs* from their inception onwards. This integration also depicts the relation between the two types of Gatekeepers. The main expression over which the Gatekeepers enacting rites guard is *kāma-manas,* desire or emotional-mind, as the Watery emotions produce major obstacles to developing wisdom. The pair of Airy petals also sit upon a triad of Aetheric petals, involving therefore the potencies of the associated Herukas in the conveyance of the forces of *iḍā* and *piṇgalā nāḍīs* to control *saṃskāras*. These eight petals can then process the eight consciousnesses, plus the groups of eight petalled centres below the diaphragm needed for the evocation of *siddhis*.

The outermost (Earthy) petals of the Īśvarī can also be viewed as 'gatekeepers' of sorts, delineating the limitations of the types of materialistic and form-obsessed addictions (desires) that obscure the development of consciousness. The four outermost (Earthy) petals, plus the major integrating petal, can double up as the petals utilised by the five Jñāna Ḍākinīs to control the sum of the Earthy *prāṇas* that are directed by the Ājñā centre, or integrated into the Head lotus. This control is necessary for *kuṇḍalinī* to be liberated. These *prāṇas* are those associated with experiences derived from normal waking consciousness, where most that are incarnate are focussed.

The Wrathful Deities and the Head centre

The Head centre's circulation is much more complicated than that of the Ājñā centre. There are five major tiers of petals to the Head centre, which have a direct association with the emanations of the five Jina wisdoms and the integration of the *saṃskāras* of the five Elements into this centre. The information presented in Volume 4, chapter 7 (see Figure 23) of this *Treatise on Mind* refers to the outermost tier of this *chakra*, denoted as the Solar Plexus in the Head. By this is meant that it is principally concerned with the expression and integration of the sum of *manasic* propensity of the *prāṇas* below the diaphragm into the Head centre. This outermost tier's purpose is to generate the empirical mind and its eventual transformation. The Wrathful Deities help to assimilate and process *manasic saṃskāras* in this tier of the *maṇḍala* of the Head lotus to produce revelatory thoughts.

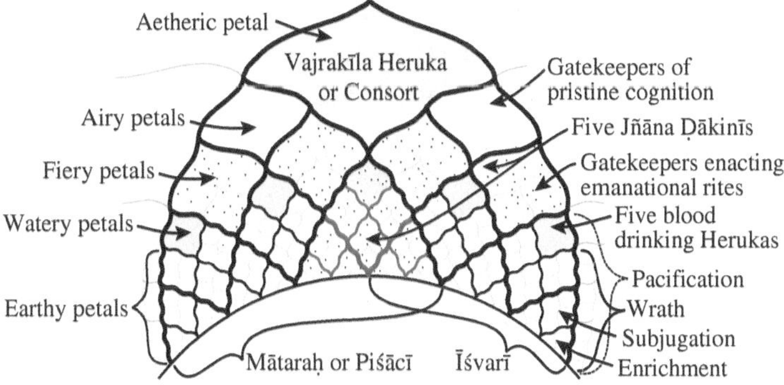

Figure 19. The Head centre and the Wrathful Deities

This analysis will be concerned purely with the level of the 'seventy incarnations' of the outer tier of petals of the Head lotus. It deals with the *saṃskāras* generated at the latter stages of the evolutionary process when the emotions begin to be comprehended and mastered by the mind. We thus have the process of converting Solar Plexus energies into qualities that can be accommodated above the diaphragm in either the Throat or Heart centres. The main source of energisation for the outer tier of the Head lotus are the refined Fiery energies directed by the four Gatekeepers enacting emanational rites to all of the petals that derive energies from them. Their work is integrated with that of the blood-drinking Herukas. Next are the tiers of petals manifesting the activities of the Īśvarī. In their simplest arrangement the four groups of six Īśvarī can be viewed in terms of the four acorns of six petals each for each Fiery petal.

Each Fiery petal is embodied by one of the Gatekeepers enacting emanational rites, as indicated in Figure 19. They are divided into an *iḍā* and *piṇgalā* grouping by the two integrating Watery petals governed by the blood-drinking Herukas. There are five of these Heruka petals for a major petal of the Head lotus. They are arranged in such a way that one Fiery petal synthesises the *prāṇas* from two such petals. (Each Fiery petal thereby shares two Watery petals.) This is necessary to accommodate the *iḍā* and *piṇgalā* flow of the *prāṇas* of each petal. There is therefore a de facto 2 x 4 = 8 petals utilised by the four Fiery petals, signifying the way of categorising consciousness in terms of the five sense-consciousnesses and the eight consciousnesses.

Note that the Head centre's main function is to convey *manas* (Fiery attributes of mind). All *prāṇas* absorbed into its sphere of influence are *manasic* in nature. Consequently the four petals of the Head lotus, designated 'Fiery petals', manifest the attributes of the abstract (higher) Mind, which is the gain of the pacification of all the aspects of mind. (The view here is at an advanced stage of development of an individual.)

The Watery and Earthy petals of the Head lotus therefore represent the attributes of the four sub-planes of the concrete (empirical) mind. Three of these sub-planes are labelled 'Earthy', and the synthesising one is labelled 'Watery'. By this is meant that these Earthy petals represent aspects of the empirical mind that is focussed upon normal day to day activities and observations in the material world. They produce *manasic saṃskāras* that have their foundation in desire, which causes attachment to the objects of the senses. (Processed by the bottom six petals of a Fiery petal.) We then have the development of the five sense-consciousnesses, processed by the next five petals. Together they develop desire-mind and the mental emotions *(kāma-manas),* which is the major quality developed by most people. All of these propensities are aspects of the four main Elements, and through the mechanism of wrath, subjugation and enrichment they become more refined and Airy. These *prāṇas,* in their dual capacity of being either *iḍā* or *piṇgalā,* are then expressed in the four Earthy petals (each consisting of six subsidiary petals) to every Fiery petal. (There are ten of these Earthy petals to every major petal of the Head lotus.)

The petals designated 'Watery' represent the more fluid, vibrant attributes of *manas,* when the emotions and desire principle have been, or are, in the process of pacification so they can be converted to the attributes of the Clear Light of Mind. The five Watery petals therefore represent the most refined *prāṇas* of the five sense-consciousnesses in the process of becoming enlightened perceptions. The Waters must be evaporated if one is to become enlightened. This represents the purpose of the activity of the five blood-drinking Herukas relegated to these petals. The Watery petals are therefore named as such because under their auspices Watery *prāṇas* are processed, pacified, and their *saṃskāras* transformed by way of mind into Fiery attributes. This tier (which incorporates and synthesises the Earthy petals) stands at the junction between the four concrete sub-planes of mind (representing the highest of these) and the three abstract sub-planes of Mind, to which the refined attributes of the five sense-consciousnesses can be directed.

When viewed in terms of the sub-planes of the mental plane, the seven tiers of petals of a major petal of the Head lotus are arranged so that all aspects of mind can be mastered. The *ālayavijñāna* enlightenment (the third Initiation) can then be gained. This level of attainment is the focus of the teachings here because most that are vying for enlightenment are at the stage where this Initiation is possible. Only a fraction of the many who thus strive will however achieve this attainment in that life. Of them only a small number will advance to take the fourth, Śūnyatā Initiation. Of them only a few at most have the capacity to take the fifth, Dharmakāya Initiation. Nevertheless, as the centuries pass an ever-increasing number of people will be vying for the higher Initiations, consequently information such as is here presented must be available to them.

The two petals denoted Airy petals can therefore be interpreted in terms of the second sub-plane of the mental, or in terms of the development of the *prāṇas* that relate to *śūnyatā,* depending upon whether the third or fourth Initiations are possible in that life. Similarly the Aetheric petal can be interpreted as either relating to the development of the qualities of the highest mental sub-plane (the Clear Light), or else conveying *prāṇas* that awaken *dharmakāya* (if the fifth Initiation is possible in that life). For the great mass of people, therefore, the higher three tiers of petals are mostly dormant.

The following elaborates the activity and unfolding of the tiers and groups of petals constituting a Fiery petal (relegated to the Īśvarī) in the Head centre:

1. In the six small petals at the base of the Fiery petal we have the work of the Īśvarī ('queens of yoga') concerned with *the rites of enrichment.* Here the types of *prāṇas* originally emanating from the right Gonad centre are appropriately processed. They pass the purified (mainly Watery) *prāṇas* from the rest of the petal governed by a Gatekeeper to the next inner sphere of petals of the Head centre, the Heart in the Head (the Heart tier) for assimilation. The enriching process of these six petals helps to produce the foundation for the generation of loving attributes. The relation between the Solar Plexus and Heart centres is here viewed in terms of an esoteric interpretation of the sexual function. There is a magnetic attraction between the Watery emotional *prāṇas* processed in the Solar Plexus in the Head and the attributes of Love processed in the Heart in the Head.
2. Sitting atop of the six petals is a tier of five petals that are also incorporated in these activities. Each of the five petals consists of a triad of small petals that assimilate the types of foundational *manasic prāṇas* generated by the left Gonad centre. The Īśvarī manifesting the *rites of subjugation* work to regulate these basic desire-mind attributes and to develop them in terms of more refined aspects of the five sense-consciousnesses.

Subjugation and enrichment work as a functional unity because first the unruly *saṃskāras* must be subjugated to eliminate undesirable attributes, then the extract can be enriched, so that which is most desirable manifests with increasing power and clarity. The five petals associated with this act of subjugation (of Earthy *saṃskāras)* are concerned with the development of *manas* via the five sense-consciousnesses. The mental qualities developed then act to suppress what is not wanted. The triads of petals (of which there are eleven for a major lobe of the Head lotus) are the main petals where the assimilation and processing of *kāma-manas* occurs. Each of these petals are accompanied by two of those concerned with the rites of enrichment, making 33 petals altogether for a major lobe of the Head lotus. The number 33 is accounted for by the energies from the twelve petals of the right and left Gonad centre petals, the six Sacral centre petals, the *saṃskāras* derived from the two hands of the Solar Plexus centre, plus the originating *prāṇas* of the five sense-consciousnesses derived from the Sacral-Base of Spine centre overlap.

Both of these triads manifest in the form of the three *guṇas,* where with the petals arranged in sixes, we have the Sacral centre manifesting as the will aspect *(sattva),* the right Gonad centre as the love aspect *(rajas),* and the left Gonad centre as the activity aspect *(tamas).* Similarly with the triad of pentads, with the one pointing north representing the *sattvic* aspect, that pointing south the *rajaistic* aspect, and the Sacral-Base of Spine centre interrelation the *tamasic* aspect. (*Tamasic* because more Earthy.)

3. The four acorns of six petals (within the constituency of a Fiery petal) governing the general consideration of the Īśvarī also represent the function of the *rites of wrath* for the Earthy *prāṇas* coursing through these petals. They are needed to convey and further develop the *prāṇas* of the four main Elements and qualities derived from the petals of the Base of Spine centre. The entire Sacral centre activity is now involved with respect to the generation of the flow of the *iḍā* and *piṇgalā nāḍīs.* The major *saṃskāras* of desire and attachment are processed. Significant wrath must be utilised at the appropriate time to convert strong desire elements into attributes of

desirelessness. The assimilation and conversion of the sum of Earthy *prāṇas* developed in terms of the three *guṇas* of body, speech and mind for this Element are here the concern. All three attributes of the threefold personality are dealt with via physical plane activity. The energy of wrath represents the intensified effects of speech (emotions), subjugation necessitates development of the mind, and the entire bodily process engendering *prāṇas* producing health and vitality is enriched. The Sacral centre *prāṇas* conveying all desire based activities must be dealt with, requiring wrath to overcome because of their potency. The Īśvarī are evoked to assist in the process. The war-like intensity of Fiery-Water is often demonstrated. Either aggressive or vibrant thoughts are generated in the desire to carry through the idea conceived.

The three tiers of petals governed by the process of wrath correspond to the three outer tiers of petals of the Ājñā centre. There are also six, five and four petals involved. The Ājñā centre *prāṇas* are directed to this Earthy triad within the Head lotus, where they are stored and utilised, swaying actions, or later converted, requiring the demonstration of forms of wrath. The Head lotus is consequently the generator of thoughts, based upon the accumulation of stored *saṃskāras,* and manifests the directive impulses influenced from various sources: from above or below the diaphragm, from past lives, from the mental-emotional environment one is in, and from the inner realms via the domain of the Sambhogakāya Flower.

The twelve innermost petals from a lobe of the Ājñā centre direct their *prāṇas* to the Aetheric petals, of which there are twelve to the Head lotus. (All *prāṇas* to be processed in the Head lotus must pass through these petals, however the innermost petals only process the most refined Aetheric *prāṇas* that are too subtle for the other petals to appropriately accommodate.) The next tier of eleven petals (plus the major petal) direct their *prāṇas* to the Airy petals of the Head lotus. The five Aetheric petals of the Ājñā centre direct *prāṇas* to the Fiery petals of the Head lotus, and the four Airy petals of the Ājñā centre to the Watery petals of the Head lotus. The Head lotus thus integrates all of the incoming *prāṇas* and stores them. The conscious will then makes its decisions, and the *prāṇas* are automatically utilised as per the effect of the above mentioned influences.

4. Having dealt with processing the Earthy *prāṇas* in the Head centre we can now analyse the Īśvarī enacting *rites of pacification.* This concerns control of the Watery Element, consisting of one's mental-emotions. They can be quite volatile and the process of pacification involves more than just suppression. The Fires of the mind must be developed to convert them into clear, logical thought-streams. All forces of the Solar Plexus centre must be controlled by the mind, if emotional thoughts are to be tamed so that they become submissive to creative impulse and do not run amok with strong desire. The sum of the activity of the Īśvarī manifest, as all of their factors are integrated into the functioning of the Īśvarī enacting *rites of pacification.* Because the *saṃskāras* generated mainly from the east-west orientation of the Solar Plexus centre towards the Liver and Stomach centres are here processed with view of control, so the entire Inner Round must become dominated by the Fires of mind. Once purified, controlled and enriched, the resultant Fiery Waters can pass through the six petals designated 'enrichment' to the Heart tier of the Head lotus. This enrichment of the expression of the five sense-consciousnesses also implicates the conveyance of *iḍā* and *piṅgalā prāṇas* to produce an overall Fiery disposition. The entire Fiery petal of *prāṇas* embodied by a Gatekeeper enacting emanational rites is also utilised in this pacification process, which is necessary to produce enlightened thinking. These *prāṇas* are those controlled by the Throat centre, when inevitably influenced by the emanations of the Heart centre. The term 'inevitably' is utilised because it implies a process of conversion of the empirical mind into the attributes of the Heart's Mind.

The work of converting the attributes of the empirical mind is carried out in the four tiers of petals (6 + 5 + 4 + 2 petals) within the Fiery petals. The process of moving from enrichment, subjugation, wrath and pacification first involves the purification of the general Watery *prāṇas* of the five sense-consciousnesses, so that a higher enriched quality of the emotions is the gain. Next there is the subjugation of these qualities so that they are completely dominated by the mind. This process awakens the perception of the illusory nature of *saṃsāra* and of how attached one is to various objects of the material form. To conquer materialism necessitates the use of significant force, hence the concept of wrath. This entire yogic process comes under the auspices of the developing, increasingly refined mind, which then works at the pacification of the mental constitution via the techniques of *śamatha* (calm abiding). This process is governed by the activities of the Herukas, who only let pass into the enlightened domains the most abstracted of the *manasic prāṇas.* These *prāṇas* flow according to an *iḍā or piṅgalā* disposition, which are directed by the Gatekeepers enacting emanative rites. The work thus concerns the ability to project *antaḥkaraṇas* (consciousness-links) from the concreted to the abstracted levels of mind/Mind. This is consistent with the general flow of the *nāḍīs* below the diaphragm (whose *prāṇas* this set of petals incorporates) to above the diaphragm.

When viewing the overall number of petals concerned, of all the subpetals constituting the four Fiery petals, then we need to multiply the 1 + 2 + 4 + 5 + 6 petals by four, making 72 petals altogether. This number implicates the process that converts the sum of the field of desire (6) into the way of the Heart centre (12). This necessitates mastery of the entire material domain and the four Elements constituting it.

The pacification of the *kāma-manasic prāṇas* incorporated into the Head centre therefore constitutes all five levels of petals governed by a Gatekeeper enacting emanational rites. The Gatekeepers absorb the refined Fiery essences of this activity of pacification and directs them to where they must go. The most logical and refined thoughts can thereby be produced, which become the main fare of all intellectually and meditatively creative pursuits of the individual. Because much effort is needed to control emotional *saṃskāras,* these rites of pacification incorporate the combined activities of wrath, subjugation, enrichment, and the protective ferocity of the Herukas. Inevitably, proper ritualistic yogic austerities are generated to emanate meditative awareness and sound thoughts.

The Sacral centre is the distributive organ of *prāṇas* throughout the system, where five petals are needed for the five sense-consciousnesses, plus one for their admixture (which becomes the basis for the expression of the 'sixth sense', the intellect). The six petals associated with the rites of enrichment reflect this function in the Head centre. They therefore act as conveyors of *prāṇas* to and from the Heart tier. There are twelve of these petals to one major tier of petals of the Head lotus, signifying their ability to convey *prāṇas* to all twelve petals of the Heart centre. (Here represented by the twelve major petals of the Head lotus, the major subdivision of this centre.)

The next group (rites of subjugation) consists of 5 x 3 petals that convey *prāṇas* originating from three pentads of petals, two from the Solar Plexus centre and one from the Sacral centre. Here the attributes of the five sense-consciousnesses are thoroughly processed (hence the need for their subjugation and control). There are eleven of these triads in a major tier of the Head lotus, the significance of which has already been explained.

The four groups of six petals embodied by the rites of wrath process the complete field of desire and attachment to phenomena via the *prāṇas* originating from the six petals of the Solar Plexus centre (omitting the four concerned with the *iḍā* and *piṇgalā nāḍīs),* those of the Sacral centre, and the six petals of each of the two Gonad centres. This 'wrath' therefore concerns the effect of the complete activity of all the Īśvarī (except the Gatekeepers) to control the formidable desires of a person. Overall there are ten such petals in a major tier of the Head lotus. They are thereby able to store and process all of the *saṃskāras* of the accompanying emotional-mind generated via the ten petals of the Solar Plexus centre.

A single group of ten petals governed by the rites of pacification deals with the *saṃskāras* generated after the wrath has proceeded and the energies of the Solar Plexus centre and the Inner Round are controlled. There are five of these petals to a major tier of the head lotus, allowing all five sense-consciousnesses to be completely mastered.

The Gatekeepers enacting emanational rites each govern a pair of these decades of petals, allowing the processing of the *iḍā* and *piṇgalā nāḍī* flow that has been incorporated in the Head lotus. They contain the sum of the *prāṇas* derived from the entire evolution of the *nāḍī* system. There are four of these Fiery petals, governing therefore the *nāḍīs* associated with the four main Elements, each categorised in terms of their *iḍā* and *piṇgalā* aspects. The *prāṇas* must also be integrated with the qualities stemming from the four petals of the Base of Spine centre, allowing control of the entire corporeal world. The pacification of the emotional *saṃskāras* associated with consciousness is a major function of the Īśvarī because *manas* must rightly rule the mind and not the erratic egoistic desire and emotional based hubris associated with the lower *chakras*.

The higher synthesising petals

Though the Herukas are ascribed to the five decades of Watery petals controlling the activities of the Īśvārī, their influence in fact pervades the five groups of petals governed by the Elements. (Our focus being the attainment of the *ālayavijñāna* enlightenment.) Buddha Heruka guards the incoming *prāṇas* of the Aetheric tier, Vajra Heruka the Airy petals, Padma Heruka the Fiery petals, Ratna Heruka the Watery petals, and Karma Heruka the Earthy petals. The main onus of their activity, however, lies in the conversion of Watery *saṃskāras* into Fiery attributes, as here the great transmutative battles are fought. The work of the Herukas involves increasingly refining the proceeds as the *prāṇas* move up the column of petals.

The Aetheric petal synthesises the *prāṇas* of the two Airy petals and with them the qualities of all the other petals. The Aetheric petal manifests as the fifth synthesising level for the Fiery Element that governs the purpose of the entire construct of the Head lotus. Its activity is controlled by the attributes of either Vajrakīla Heruka or his Consort, depending upon whether the major *prāṇa* channelled is *iḍā* or *piṇgalā*. As with the Ājñā centre these petals should be analysed as a pair to properly assess their function. Vajrakīla's Consort governs a major petal that is the polar opposite to that of Vajrakīla. A large version of the Ājñā centre (viewed also as a *vajra)* is thereby established capable of directing the activities of the supramundane *siddhis* once *kuṇḍalinī* has ignited the petals with dynamic Fire.

From this perspective the two Airy petals governed by the functions of the Gatekeepers of pristine cognition embody the refined *saṃskāras* derived from the four petals of the Base of Spine centre. This centre is in a north-south (the plant and mineral kingdom petals) and east-west (the human and animal kingdoms petals) orientation. This is reflected in the Head lotus in that two Airy petals of a major petal governed by Vajrakīla process the *prāṇas* derived from the east-west orientation of the Base of Spine centre, whilst the polar opposite petal, governed by his Consort, processes the *prāṇas* from the north-south orientation of that centre. The Aetheric petal therefore represents the place of overlap between the Sacral and Base of Spine centres, wherein *kuṇḍalinī* is evoked. At the appropriate time, once the necessary subjugation, enrichment and pacification of *prāṇas* have been accomplished, pristine Fiery energy can awaken all of the petals of the Head lotus via this (and its brethren Aetheric) petal. There are six such pairs in the Head lotus, and when combined with the integrating central point, makes a sevenfold energisation.

The Airy petals processing the *prāṇas* originating from the east-west petals of the Base of Spine centre embody an Airy-Fiery potency. The petals processing the *prāṇas* originating from the north-south petals of the Base of Spine centre embody the Airy-Earthy potency. The smaller petals each Airy petal embodies are concerned with the transformation of Water into Air by means of Fire. The two pairs of petals therefore embody a masculine-feminine polarity viewed in terms of energy interrelationships.

When interpreting the two Airy petals and the Aetheric petal of one of the twelve major petals of the Head lotus, our view is of them being the repositories for the *iḍā, piṅgalā* and *suṣumṇā nāḍīs* that have risen from one major *chakra* to another up the spinal column. *Kuṇḍalinī* can arise when the Head centre has been prepared and the webs of etheric substance in the spinal column that act to prevent premature arising of the Fires have also been distilled away. Consequently, all four Gatekeeper petals are needed to hold the Fires in the Head lotus. These four contain the thoroughly en-Flamed distillates from the quaternary of the concrete mind. All reifying attributes have been eliminated, and the quaternary is subservient to the triad of abstract Mind. At this stage the triune Fires of each male and female polarity are also integrated by the Fire rising through the centre of the Head lotus. *Kuṇḍalinī* is seven layered and its serpent has seven heads.

One Aetheric petal, two for the Gatekeepers of pristine cognition and four for the Gatekeepers enacting emanative rites manifest the 3 + 4 arrangement that allows the inception of all seven Ray potencies into a major petal of the Head lotus.[19] The Rays then flow through to the Īśvarī via a pentad of ten (4 + 3 + 2 + 1) petals embodied by a blood-drinking Heruka. Also, the major petals embodied by Vajrakīla Heruka or his Consort can channel the *suṣumṇā* when awakened. With respect to Vajrakīla, the five Jñāna Ḍākinīs embody the attributes of Mind that control the activity of the five Elements with view of their refinement. The petals associated with this activity are the four Fiery petals, plus any Watery petal, seen as an extension of the central decades of petals from the Throat and Heart tiers (see Figure 21). Their work facilitates the awakening of *kuṇḍalinī,* and empowers the transformative activity of the five sense-consciousnesses by the five blood-drinking Herukas, and of the Gatekeepers enacting emanative rites. These fourteen entities (fifteen including Vajrakīla Heruka or his Consort) are therefore responsible for the final stages of the process of converting mind into Mind so that *kuṇḍalinī* can en-Flame all petals of the Head lotus with vibrant Fire. The third Initiation is the result of this process.

When viewing one of the Airy petals governed by a Gatekeeper of pristine cognition we see that there are eight base petals, allowing all *prāṇas* to manifest in terms of the eight directions in space and the eight consciousnesses. This subject will be detailed when dealing with the Mātaraḥ and Pīśācī.

Two of the Fiery petals assigned to the five Jñāna Ḍākinīs support one of the Gatekeepers of pristine cognition petals during the *kuṇḍalinī* flow. This incorporates three of the petals governed by the five Herukas. The *saṃskāras* of the five sense-consciousnesses are processed by the

---

19 These Rays have been explained throughout this Treatise. One should note that each of the Ray lines have seven sub-rays, making 49 Ray potencies all told. They are normally denoted by the formula 1/2, 1/3 etc., where the first number represents the Ray and the second the sub-ray.

intellect, during the normal course of human livingness. The Jñāna Ḍākinīs help convert the contents of the intellect into wisdom attributes. However, the main consideration of the Jñāna Ḍākinīs (which work as a septenary with Vajrakīla Heruka and his Consort) relates to the processes associated with the generation of the common *siddhis,* as previously explained. The activities of pacification, etc., must by then have been satisfactorily accomplished. The Jñāna Ḍākinīs handle the five attributes of mind/Mind supporting the awakening *kuṇḍalinī,* whereas Vajrakīla Heruka and Consort are concerned with its two highest Ray attributes.

For each major petal of the Head centre the two Gatekeepers of pristine cognition manifest as part of a triad with the Aetheric petal, which conveys the energies from the three-fold cord in the spinal column via their Airy directives. This represents the normal *prāṇic* flow to the innermost tiers of petals (the Heart and Throat in the head) of the Head lotus. (Or outwards to the *nāḍī* system.) The sevenfold directive mentioned above is mainly expressed upon the path of Initiation. During the life of the normal person, the main *prāṇic* flow is via the *iḍā* and *piṇgalā* pairs of the four petals governed by the Gatekeepers enacting rites. If Aetheric qualities are generated for any Element then it is conveyed via a major petal.

The *vajra* that manifests from a pair of major petals situated opposite to each other is *prāṇically* aligned to the one constituting the Ājñā centre. If we take a similar pair of major petals at right angles to this then we get the *viśvavajra* in the process of developing the full expression of its powers. The *viśvavajra,* with its prongs oriented in the four cardinal directions, determines the movement of the *prāṇas* of the Head lotus. When its activity is consciously controlled then we have the activity of an enlightened being in any of the stages of demonstrating the wisdoms of the Jinas. If oriented in the intermediate directions then the qualities of their Consorts is expressed.

One must visualise the *chakras* in a state of constant activity, of moving wheels within wheels of *prāṇas.* The outer tier of the Head centre turns around the inner Heart tier like clockwork motion one petal at a time, and later in groups of three or six, then ten as the larger circles of petals are vivified. All are in motion, thereby *prāṇas* (consciousness-streams) flow from one arena of the *chakra* to the next. There is a weeding out of the gross types of *prāṇas* unsuited for storage in the petals of the tier concerned, *prāṇas* then pass from this tier to other tiers where they can be assimilated and further refined. These *prāṇas* also have their own inherent colourations and intrinsic sound. The effect of continuous refinement is the beauteous display of a radiant aura around an awakened one.

With respect to the numbers of petals we can summarise that the number five relates to the assimilation and direction of the five sense-consciousnesses. When doubled to make the number ten, then the *iḍā* and *piṇgalā* form of these consciousnesses are represented. This number also allows complete integration with the *prāṇas* from each or all of the ten petals of the Solar Plexus centre. The number three allows the natural division of the reaped *prāṇas* in terms of the three *guṇas*. (Expressed as three types of Fires.) Numbers such as six, eight, twelve, and sixteen interrelate *chakras* through numerical affinity. Male-female deities also show that a dual activity manifests. The feminine deity directs the activity of the *prāṇas* reaping the consequences of past action, or of the *iḍā* stream. The male produces new thought directives, moving the entire activity in new directions. The *piṇgalā* stream is considered masculine.

The four petals governed by the Gatekeepers enacting emanational rites focus the main Fiery impetus of the Head lotus as far as *manas* is concerned via the four Elements, to manifest via the fixed or mutable positions of the eight directions in space. Depending upon the level of evolution, these Gatekeepers control the final transformation of the Watery Element (the mental-emotions) into *manas* (the natural development as a consequence of the rising of the *iḍā* and *piṇgalā nāḍīs*). We then see the development of the attributes of the abstract Mind. They do the foundational work so that the Jñāna Ḍākinīs can prepare the petals for the outpouring of *kuṇḍalinī.*

Fiery *prāṇas* manifest through various triads, hexads, quadruples, and pentads of smaller petals because the *manasic* input is via the sense-perceptors, spurred by desire, and experienced via the three worlds of human livingness, as conditioned by the four Elements. The Herukas appropriately refine these *manasic prāṇas* by distilling them from the general Watery mix of the Head lotus, so that the emotions may be controlled. They therefore need a full decade of petals, allowing control of the qualities of the ten major petals of the Solar Plexus. This conditions the desire-mind *prāṇic* tone for the remainder of the minor *chakras*. By the time the *prāṇas* reticulate through the higher centres the predominant *iḍā* or *piṅgalā* flavour becomes ever more refined with the complementary characteristics.

We can also see that any of the groups of six 'queens of yoga' can integrate with any one of the Gatekeepers enacting emanative rites when their attributes are required by the indwelling thinker, allowing the qualities associated with the seven Ray potencies to be expressed.[20] The Ray attributes governing all human activity can thus be properly processed and refined. They are incorporated into human livingness in terms of the four qualities or Elements that humanity develop during normal *saṃsāric* activity. We saw that these qualities are represented as sensual and tactile (the Earthy), emotional (Watery), intellectual (Fiery), and loving (Airy). They are arranged in a *maṇḍala* of the four directions, and have their foundational instigation in the four petals of the Base of Spine centre. Also, when the four Gatekeepers of pristine cognition can be vivified with Airy energies via the transforming activities of the Īśvarī, then the Solar Plexus centre can convey *siddhis*.

For the most part the activity of the Gatekeepers enacting emanational rites and the Īśvārī dominate the Head centre. Once the *prāṇas* have been sufficiently enriched then the energy of the major Airy petal ruled by the Gatekeepers of pristine cognition can properly manifest. Eventually the entire lotus comes under the impetus of the pure Fires of Mind, with the total *ālayavijñāna* environment coming into ken. The Aetheric petal can be awakened, and from it the dynamic Fiery Will (and mantric sound) can descend to the Base of Spine *chakra* to awaken *kuṇḍalinī*. Such activity is controlled by the wrathful Vajrakīla Heruka responding to this directive sound from the (masculine[21]) Sambhogakāya Flower that governs the Aetheric petal. This illustrates the esoteric function of the phur ba *(kīla)* that he wields. The energy descends, producing a reciprocal ascent of (feminine) Fire, awakening the *chakras* as *kuṇḍalinī* rises up the spine and en-Flames the Head lotus with brilliant incandescence.

---

20 The seven dancing Īśvarī of the four cardinal directions of space earlier explained.

21 Seen in terms of energy expression. The originating impetus is Monadic.

The petals of the Head and Ājñā centres influence each other via numerical affinity, and through the deities governing the interrelated petals. The group of petals controlled by the Mātaraḥ, for instance, are able to direct *prāṇas* to their correspondences in the Ājñā centre, then to their subordinates governing the petals of the *chakras* above the diaphragm, and finally those below it. Overall, therefore, this implies five levels of Wrathful Deities: that relate to the controlling potencies from the Sambhogakāya Flower, the Head lotus, the Ājñā centre, the *chakras* above the diaphragm, and those below it. The usual correspondences with respect to the five Elements, etc., can then be assigned to them.

All mental-emotional attributes developed in the lower centres can be stored in the Head lotus, however, base human emotions and psychicism have no true place in this lotus. As all emotional inputs are effectively viewed as feminine attributes, so the deities guarding against and converting them are also feminine.[22] They represent the most troubling aspects of the defiled *saṃskāras* and need to be converted into attributes that will inevitably awaken *bodhicitta*. The entire *chakra* system exists to bring this conversion about. Also, we have seen that all *ḍākinīs* are really agents of *karma* that work to propel appropriate *karma* for the education of a person at the right time. The gross *saṃskāras* also represent types of *karma* to be rejected (or cleansed) by these deities, leaving only the enlightenment-attributes to pass their scrutiny. Inevitably, intelligence must be converted into the higher abstract reasoning pertaining to wisdom, and consequent enlightenment.

The feminine reference to the emotions is correct, though problematic, as they are the basis to developing compassion, which the Buddhist *dharma* considers masculine. The *manasic* content of the *saṃskāras* on the other hand are needed to generate wisdom, which is viewed as feminine. The esoteric rationale is that the feminine attribute is really *manasic*, because Nature is feminine and all of its aspects are governed by the vicissitudes of mind, via the feminine agencies that control it, the *devas* and *ḍākinīs*. When viewing the human kingdom as Sambhogakāya flowers, on the other hand, it is masculine, because

---

22 The male Wrathful Deities therefore guard against the more concreted and forceful attributes of *manas* from defiling the mind.

it is innately an expression of the Will-of-Love. (Humans therefore are fundamentally embodiments of this energy, despite all of the outer seeming of the selfish and aggressive qualities of those in our societies.) The rationale is that the principle of Love is integral to the constitution of the Sambhogakāya Flower, thus is the guiding power of the *tathāgatagarbha,* the Buddha-embryo of each human. The *vajra* of the Head lotus exists to integrate the masculine and feminine polarities into a unity, a non-duality. We see, therefore, that the entire constitution of *saṃsāra* is feminine because it is ever-changing, transient activity that evokes the qualities of mind. Wisdom is developed when the mind is impregnated with Love. Wisdom and compassion are therefore aspects of each other, but *manas* is a necessary ingredient of wisdom, whereas compassion utilises wisdom, integrating it with direct non-conceptual insight. The enlightened Mind, the wisdom of compassionate insight, is consequentially non-dual. *Manas,* wisdom, and insight are integrated in one vast expanse of lucid awareness. *Saṃsāra* and *nirvāṇa* manifest in terms of one reality. These attributes are incorporated in the term *bodhicitta (citta* is mind, *bodhi* is compassion).

The petals governed by the Mātaraḥ and Pīśācī

When analysing the petals attributed to the eight Mātaraḥ (representing the functions of the Diaphragm centre) or Pīśācī (manifesting the attributes of Splenic centre II) we see that the associated petals sit upon a base of eight smaller petals. The eight petals allow the complete processing of *saṃskāras* of the eight consciousnesses via the orientation of the eight armed cross of direction in space. With respect to the Pīśācī in the Head lotus we have the process of transformation of thought-substance that is mostly Watery in nature with view of the generation of more refined *piṇgalā* attributes. The focus, therefore, is the transformation of *kliṣṭamanas* into *bodhicitta.* From this perspective the Īśvārī mainly deal with the reception of the *prāṇas* of the *iḍā nāḍī,*[23] thus with *manasic* content. The generation of attributes of the *ālayavijñāna* is their goal. The Pīśācī integrate all of the *prāṇas* from

23 When speaking of the *iḍā* and *piṇgalā nāḍīs* one must remember that each of them is dual, with the *iḍā* having a *piṇgalā* component and the *piṇgalā* an *iḍā* one.

the activity of the Īśvārī, refining all categories of substance into more clearly defined *iḍā, piṅgalā* and *suṣumṇā* attributes. Airy qualities, rather than the Fiery aspects of the sense-consciousness per se, become the major gain. They work with refining all attributes of consciousness, viewed in terms of the three *guṇas* of Īśvārī, so that the *prāṇas* can be directed to the inner Heart and Throat tiers of the Head centre. We see here that most of the work of the transformation of consciousness is accomplished by the Īśvārī, whilst the Pīśācī focus upon refining Watery-Earthy substance within the context of the activity of the Īśvārī.

The Mātaraḥ incorporate the most refined qualities developed by the Pīśācī with the *prāṇas* sent to them from the inner Heart and Throat tiers of petals. These *prāṇas* concern the upward arc of thinking relegated to contemplative and meditative thoughts. The gross attributes of the groups of petals of the Solar Plexus tier must be refined in order to accommodate without adulteration the refined *prāṇas* of expressed love and wisdom. Nevertheless, in the earlier stages of the path of discipleship the possible clarity is distorted via loving-minded and well-meaning, but often opinionated idealism. What then arises is sectarianism, emotional puritanism, fanatical religious beliefs and their counterparts in the scientific, socio-economic or philosophic communities.

Within the embrace of one Airy petal there are five tiers of petals to consider. They process the attributes of the five sense-consciousnesses in terms of:

Petal groupings	**Total petals**
1. Eight base petals of enrichment	8
2. Seven triads of subjugation	21
3. Six hexads of wrath	36
4. Two times twenty petals	40
5. Three decades of Herukas	30

Briefly, the first three of this list process Earthy *prāṇas* in terms of the attributes of the three worlds of human interrelationships. The fourth point distils Watery *prāṇas* from the *kāma-manasic* attributes embodying the thoughts developed by most people, so that only pure *manas* remains. The fifth point deals exclusively with Fiery energies.

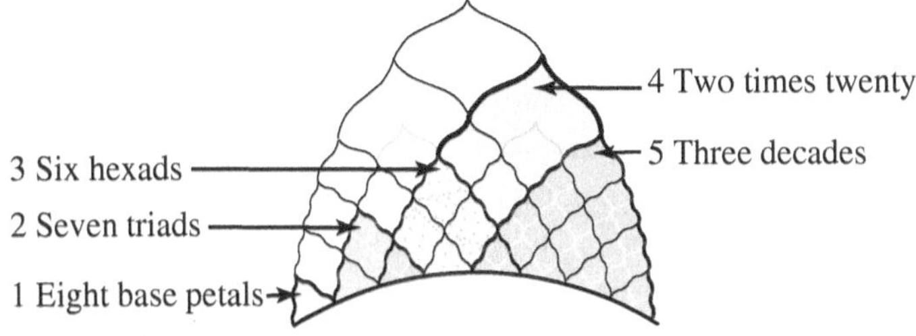

Figure 20. An Airy petal detailed

- The significance of the number eight has been earlier explained. Here we can also think in terms of the eight gates of direction and reception of *prāṇas* to and from the inner Heart tier of petals. The Watery nature of such energies esoterically implicates the sense of touch. The Heart tier is 'touched' by means of these base petals, and thereby attributes are transferred from one tier to the next.

- The number 7 x 3 relates to the subjugation and enrichment of the images formed by means of the colourations of all seven Ray lines. The sense of sight is consequently the main sense developed. The Rays manifest via the dense, astral and mental planes to produce desirable outcomes.

- The number 6 x 6 refers to the entire *maṇḍala* of the form that must be mastered by means of the agency of the mind. The subjugation of the *prāṇas* is assisted by (mantric) sound, thus the sense of hearing. Thoughts are spoken in the mind to assist in the comprehension of the images. They are then subjugated in terms of desired concepts and integrated into the knowledge banks of the mind. This Earthy *maṇḍala* is constituted of interrelated hexads[24] all fed by a central reservoir of energy via their central points. The primary hexad in the body is the Sacral centre, from which stems the energy that empowers the sum total of desire and the organisation of petals of the *chakras* and the energies directed to them. All factors of desire and attachment to phenomenal things can be converted by controlling these hexads of petals. The force of the energy utilised manifests as 'wrath' because the emotional energy impelling desire

24 Each hexad being in the form of interlaced triangles.

is integrated with the mind to produce a forceful determination to sever ties to attachments that produce suffering. Mental images are first moulded in terms of the desire or will of the thinker, later developing into compassionate considerations that demand *manasic* control. All knowledgeable pursuits can then be pursued allowing material phenomena to be conquered. Consequently, wisdom is developed through comprehension of the fundamental illusionality of phenomena in terms of the means to alleviate suffering.

- The numbers 8 + 21 + 36 produce 65 petals all told, which *maṇḍalically* implicates a central foundational grouping of five (sense-consciousness) surrounded by twelve such groups. This implies energising all twelve petals of the Head centre with the attributes of the five sense-consciousnesses derived from interrelating with material things.

- The 2 x 20 Fiery petals govern the transformation process of the four sub-planes of the empirical mind in terms of their *iḍā* and *piṇgalā* constituency. The three decades of Herukas for one Airy petal embody the attributes of the three sub-planes of the Mind, and the process of the conversion of the substance of the *saṃskāras* into their Void Elements. The gain is the experience of *śūnyatā.*

- The 30 and 40 petals of the list relate to the process of gaining mental mastery of all factors pertaining to the seven Ray attributes (30 + 40 = 70). Subtle discernments of thought (the sense of taste) are conceived or perceived from higher (enlightened) sources and developed to suit the mental narrative. A complete mental appreciation of everything that *saṃsāra* can teach for the symbolic 'seventy incarnations' of this level of expression of the Head lotus can therefore manifest.

Together there are 135 = 15 x 9 petals. This number relates to the inception into the nine whorls of petals of the Sambhogakāya Flower the gains of *saṃsāric* experience in terms of the three *guṇas* of the five sense-consciousnesses. The Knowledge petals of this Flower are thereby specifically awakened. The Airy petals of the Head centre serve to convey these *prāṇas* to the Sambhogakāya Flower. They effectively represent the continuance of the *iḍā* and *piṇgalā nāḍīs* thereto. There is consequently a two-way flow of attributes between the two centres. There are two Airy petals per major petal of the Head lotus, allowing the conveyance of twenty-four such streams of *prāṇas.*[25] This number allows the *iḍā* or *piṅgalā* aspect of the Heart centre to influence evolutionary space. We see, therefore, that consciousness is organised to awaken the way of the Heart centre. Even the Sambhogakāya Flower has twelve petals when the inner three bud petals are counted.

Observing the number of petals to *one entire major petal* at the level of the 'seventy incarnations', and as far as the complete demonstration of the Fires of mind are concerned, we see that there are:

	Petal groupings	Total petals
1.	12 base petals of enrichment	12
2.	11 triads of subjugation	33
3.	10 hexads of wrath	60
4.	5 decades of the Herukas	50
5.	8 decades governed by the Gatekeepers enacting rites	80

All five are integrated within the context of two Airy petals governed by the Gatekeepers of pristine cognition. From these numbers much can be deduced according to the nature of how the attributes of mind/ Mind are developed, and the overall sweep of governing forces at play in the organisation of mental factors at the level of the generation of wisdom attributes.

- The number 12 here indicates the integration of the energies of the Heart centre into the entire organism of the Head centre via their incorporation into the inner Heart tier of petals. All thoughts have been seeded with the wisdom of the Heart. Eventually the attributes of the Clear Light of the Mind are produced.
- The number 33 relates to the symbolic 33 *crore* (33,000,000,000) deities in Hinduism. They are the attributes of mind that have gained evolutionary perfection (3 x 10) and then adeptship (3 x 11) of all the forces and processes involved. Mastery of all forms of mental activity has been accomplished. The inner hearing of a Jina has

25 They are extensions of the innermost tier of the Ājñā centre, plus the twelve inner petals of either lobe.

been awakened and the nature of all deities (the images forming in the mind) comprehended. A Master of Wisdom has thereby evolved, who has subjugated all base desires and glamour forming thoughts and illusions. The Sacral centre then acts as a mechanism for the regulated projection of all energies within the *nāḍīs*. The blocks (squares) in consciousness have consequently been overcome, allowing the triangulation of all aspects of consciousness (*iḍā, piṅgalā* and *suṣumṇā*) whereby *kuṇḍalinī* can rise. The rising Fires have awakened the potencies of the *chakras* which are consciously utilised at will.

- The number 60 implies mastery of all attributes of desire and emotions.
- The number 50 refers to the perfect control of the images and resultant mental processes of all attributes of the sense-consciousnesses. The nature of every sensory input has been mastered and integrated into the thought structure so that all factors of *manasic* activity produce enlightened considerations. Emotional or desire based motivations are no longer involved.
- The number 80 signifies the perfection of the eight directions of space for all thought processes. The Fiery Element then has complete unimpeded access to every aspect of mind/Mind. There are no blocks or hindrances to the expression of enlightened Thought, as the *chakras* and wheels in the entire body based upon the number eight are fully awakened, including those producing the lower *siddhis*. The greater wheels of the Head centre are consequently awakened, with an unimpeded energy flow, allowing the supermundane *siddhis* to be demonstrated.

If we add 2 x 135 = 270 petals for the two Airy petals to the 235 petals explained above, then we have 505 all told, where the five hundred here is seeded with an initial five sense-consciousnesses. If these five are subtracted from the number 505 we have the number 500 of absolute perfection of the aspects of mind/Mind.[26] When the polar opposite petal is included in our analysis then we have the number 1,000 (plus 10),

---

26 The symbolism of the numerology is important here rather than the exact accounting of the *prāṇas* from the petals. The 'initial five sense-consciousnesses' can be thought of in terms of the petals effectively occupied by the five Jñāna Ḍākinīs channelling pristine energies from the Base of Spine centre admixed with the form sustaining *kuṇḍalinī*.

which is one reason why Alaya Avalokiteśvara, the downward looking Lord, is depicted with 1,000 arms. The Head lotus looks downwards upon all the other *chakras*.

Another way of viewing the numbers pertaining to the Earthy tiers is that there are 105 (12 + 33 + 60) petals that correspond to the 'Lords of Flame'.[27] They are a major part of the constituency of Shambhala, and govern the factors of the evolution of mind/Mind within the sum of *saṃsāra*.[28] This incorporates the three levels of experience of human livingness, denoted above in terms of the three Earthy petals. This leaves twelve major petals governing the activity of the rest (five Watery, four Fiery, two Airy and one Aetheric petal). They can be considered as a unit because their direct concern is with the subjective (peaceful) energies above the diaphragm. The activity associated with the 105 petals involves the development of consciousness within corporeality, hence the (forceful) forces evolved below the diaphragm, plus the transitional processes and factors producing their conversion. The number 105 can also be arranged in terms of 12 + 33 = 45 (3 x 15) and 60 (4 x 15), or 7 x 15 conditioning energies, allowing the seven Ray potencies to govern the manifestation of all the *guṇas* of the five sense-consciousnesses (3 x 5), and of the quaternary of the form (4 x 5). Verily all is hid in the symbolism of numbers.

Of the twelve petals embodying factors or attributes of the Heart centre, five petals can be ascribed to the Herukas. These five relate to the non-sacred petals, dealing with the attributes of the five sense-consciousnesses and the processing of their *saṃskāras*. The remaining seven are sacred petals, hence channel the seven Ray potencies. Together they synthesise all *manasic* factors into the Heart of Life (the entire twelve petals of the Sambhogakāya Flower, or eventually into the Monadic Eye).

The number 105 + 12 = 117 is the number pertaining to the sum of the Peaceful and Wrathful deities of the *Bardo Thödol*, inclusive of

---

27 See H.P. Blavatsky, *The Secret Doctrine*, (Theosophical Publishing House Madras, 1962, six volume edition), iii, 31, 85-7. Also A.A. Bailey, *A Treatise on Cosmic Fire* where they are also called Kumaras (mind-born sons of Brahmā), specifically 387-8.

28 Bodhisattvas of high degree have presently taken their place within Shambhala, freeing them to do other service in cosmos.

the supplementary deities. The twelve synthesising petals of the Head lotus, each incorporating twelve integrating petals, process the *prāṇas* from the foundational petals governing the processes of enrichment, subjugation, wrath and pacification. The result is the pristine cognition that evolves from *manasic* activity. Thus the major sweeps of energy manifest through yogic control, meditation involving the calm abiding *(śamatha)* of the main petals, and the insightful penetration *(vipassana)* needed to accommodate the rest. They represent the *piṇgalā* and *iḍā* of the methodology of the inherent dualities of the petals, to achieve wisdom and compassion and the awakening of the all-seeing Eye of revelation.

Though other aspects of numerological considerations could be considered, the above suffices for this analysis.

In conclusion, we need to observe another arrangement that these protectors of the *dharma* can generally manifest. This concerns the *prāṇas* coming from the major *chakras*:

- The twenty-eight animal-headed Īśvarī process, help protect and transform the general mix of Earthy *prāṇas* coming from below the diaphragm centre. Twelve come from the Splenic centre, ten via the Solar Plexus centre and six via the Sacral centre.
- The wrathful, central blood-drinking Herukas protect the Head lotus from any aberrant Watery *prāṇas* that may come via the Heart centre. As stated, seven petals of the Heart centre are sacred as their (Airy) *prāṇas* are clean, the remaining five need to be converted into pure carriers of undefiled *prāṇas*. The pristine attributes of Mind and the Void Elements pertaining to *śūnyatā* must thereby be wrought.
- The eight Mātaraḥ and the eight Piśācī protect the Head Lotus from the Watery attributes of the Fiery *prāṇas* coming via the sixteen petals of the Throat Centre.
- The four animal-headed female Gatekeepers of pristine cognition protect the Head Lotus from defilements within the general Airy *prāṇas* (*iḍā* and *piṇgalā nāḍīs*) originating from the Base of Spine *chakra* onwards.
- Vajrakīla Heruka, his Consort and the Jñāna Ḍākinīs help protect the Head lotus from all of the above *saṃskāras*.

The Wrathful Deities do not just protect the Head Lotus from the forceful demands of a wilful *yogin* prematurely desirous of obtaining *siddhis*. They also function in the normal course of awakening the personal-I to higher states of awareness. They are an integral part of the equipment of the Sambhogakāya Flower, allowing it to control the nature of the *saṃskāras* that it absorbs into its petals, and also to project into the personality what it deems necessary for the mind to learn from. As Lauf states:

> All these deities should be recognized as manifestations of one's own mind. The 42 peaceful deities come from the radiance of the dharmakāya, and the 58 wrathful deities come from the radiance of the sambhogakāya.
>
> The Tibetan Book of the Dead mentions another consequence of the transformations of the visionary deities in case one flees from these images out of fear. Then all the peaceful deities become forms of the protective deity Mahākāla, and all the wrathful deities change into the most extremely negative and threatening aspect of the god of death, Dharmarāja (T. Chos-kyi rgyal-po). The peaceful deities assume the aspect of power which represents protection through wisdom and knowledge. Mahākāla, the great and powerful protective deity, is indeed a wrathful figure, but in the positive sense. Therefore he is also called Ye-shes mgon-po, the "protector of knowledge and wisdom." If, even under this positive aspect of warding off ignorance, the person does not become aware that all manifestations of the deities in the bardo are not external to his own mind, but rather are inherent in it, then the wrathful deities will suddenly all appear in the form of Yama or Dharmarāja, the god of death. For all manifestations of one's own thought, in the form of "images" of psychic projection, but not recognized as such or else they could be withdrawn, are now annihilated.[29]

We can say that some Wrathful Deities stand at the bridge between the *saṃskāras* of the empirical mind and those of the abstract Mind (which necessitates evoking the unifying quality of the Will-to-Love that generates *bodhicitta*). We then have the appearance of the Peaceful Deities in the *yogin's* mind. The point of transition from the aspects

29 Lauf, 152-153.

of mind into those of Mind is governed by the fearsome attributes of Mahākāla so that the enlightened attributes of Mind are not made aberrant by untoward *saṃskāras*. *Saṃskāras* are seen in terms of the sum of the expression of the three times. Other Wrathful Deities work to convert emotions into pure aspects of mind so that the higher conversions can be accomplished.

Not only must the past and present effects of unruly *saṃskāras* be warded against, but also any that might arise in the future. This is another significant aspect of the phur ba *(kīla)* in the symbolism of its ritual use, to one-pointedly help to cleanse all defilements of mind through yogic practices so that the gain can be projected upwards via the *antaḥkaraṇa* (consciousness link) to the Sambhogakāya Flower.

Because *bodhicitta* is generated in the Heart centre, so the way to experience the Peaceful Deities is in the Heart, through engendering the qualities of the seven Rays associated with the positive aspects of the sacred petals. These seven Ray qualities allow one to approach Bodhisattvaship via seven different pathways, not just that of religion or devotion. This is important to realise, as religionists often demonstrate an aura of pride, thinking that theirs is the only way to salvation or to liberation. Their way may indeed facilitate the process, but may also be harmful if the devotee focuses upon the wrong concepts, images of gods, or to processes based upon glamour or dogma, rather than truth.

To become fully enlightened one must develop expertise via these Ray lines and so master all forms of ignorance and fear. For each individual, however, a specific Ray line or pathway of the Heart will be their forte, the road to the highest truths. Such truths inevitably incorporate comprehending the functioning of the 1,000 petalled Lotus. All we see around us can be viewed as being aspects of *chakras* unfolding within a grand liberated Being, a Logos. The attributes of life are *prāṇic* lives expressed within that Being's *nāḍī* system. Such concepts lead to higher considerations as to what constitutes the *dharmakāya* that lie outside the scope of this present book. The Peaceful and Wrathful Deities then stand at all transcended levels of consideration. Logoi also have versions of such Entities to consider. The meanings of the statement 'verily all is Mind' is then expanded to vast proportions.

The inner Throat and Heart tiers of the Head centre

The next major tier of petals (the fourth of the five, counting from the centre) was denoted as the Heart in the Head (the Heart tier) because it is principally concerned with integrating the Watery-Airy *saṃskāras* from the general circulation in such a way that the Will-to-Love and the Will-of-Love are generated. The attributes of the Heart's Mind *(bodhicitta)* are thereby awakened and inevitably *śūnyatā* can be experienced. The third, central tier of petals, represents the Throat in the Head (the Throat tier) as it coordinates the mastery of the *saṃskāras* of mind in such a way that selfish will is overcome by the generation of knowledgeable pursuits and the wisdom attributes of Mind. Eventually the third Initiation is attained. The purpose of this tier therefore is to generate and anchor the expression of the abstract Mind, allowing the complete potency of the Mind to be experienced.

The detail provided concerning the nature of the activity of these two inner tiers of petals will indicate the complexity of the activity of these petals. However, a full explanation would need to systematically include the various stages of evolution from an average individual to a fully enlightened being. Interpretation of the effects of the deities occupying the petals would then change to accommodate the complete evolutionary process. Consequently, my focus shall be upon the path of those seeking enlightenment. The two tiers of petals work together to integrate the way that the Heart and Throat centres interrelate, which includes their interrelation with the circulation below the diaphragm. As the wheels spin there is a conveyance of energies to and from any one petal in the outer tier of petals (the Solar Plexus in the head) or any combination of groups of petals. Groups of *prāṇas* from the inner tiers of petals to the outer one can then flow, depending upon the focus of consciousness at any time.

The twelve major petals of the Throat in the Head centre are arranged in groups of four petals that project *prāṇas* into one major petal of the Heart tier. These four in turn incorporate the *prāṇas* of five decades of petals that come under the general auspices of the five Vidyādharas. They help in the complete processing of the qualities of the five sense-consciousnesses into wisdom principles. Broadly speaking, the four main petals represent the domain of the four Guardians. They guard consciousnesses from any nefarious influences that may manifest in the *prāṇas,* facilitating the Initiation process. (Their Consorts embody the polar opposite petals.) They therefore reject the qualities that are harmful for the attainment of enlightenment, and prepare the petals for the inception of the *prāṇas* travelling up the *suṣumṇā nāḍī.* All expressions of the Fires of Mind that the evocation of *kuṇḍalinī* will bring (via any combination of ten petals associated with the Solar Plexus centre or of the combined Sacral/Base of Spine centres) can then be awakened.

When *kuṇḍalinī* is awakened, then any improper direction of this Fiery energy is guarded against by the function of Vajrakīla Heruka and Consort, who at this stage will appropriate control of the central pair of petals of the four main ones in question.

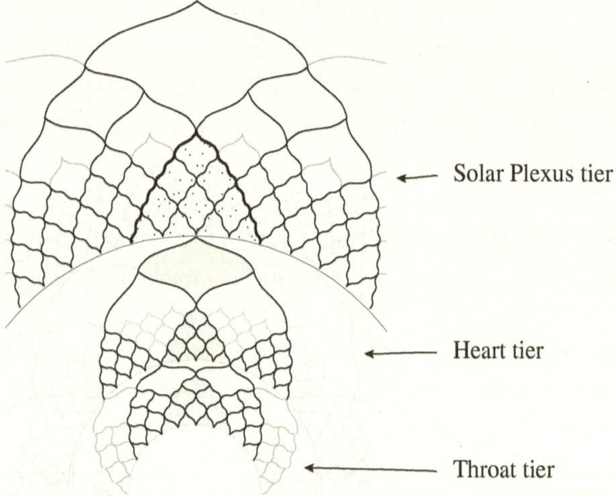

Figure 21. Part of the Heart and Throat tiers in the Head centre

Together the above mentioned four plus five decades of petals make nine major petals to consider for this Throat tier in the Head. Also, from one perspective we can count 18 = 2 x 9 petals for any of the four major petals embodied by a Guardian[30]. (The petal also consists

30 The Guardians are Trailokavijaya, Yamāntaka, Hayagrīva, and Amṛtakuṇḍalin and their Consorts. As per usual, when analysing the petals of any lotus the Consorts govern the polar opposite petals to those being considered.

of two Vidyādhara decades of petals, making twenty-one from another perspective.) The organisation of the *prāṇas* into groups of nine is significant because they can then be directed to the nine major whorls of petals of the Sambhogakāya Flower. The *prāṇas* find themselves in one or other of these petals according to the quality conveyed. The nature of the incoming *prāṇa* depends upon the focal point of the direction of the Mind. The number eighteen also has significance with respect to the three worlds of human livingness whereby experiences are gathered. There are seven dense sub-planes to consider (three concrete and four etheric), seven astral sub-planes of subjective experiences garnered via the emotional body, and four levels of the empirical mind, making eighteen in all.

There are three levels of *prāṇic* flow indicated by Figure 21. The *first* (Will) level integrates both tiers of petals. This happens via a central acorn of ten petals in the Throat tier[31] for each wheel passing *prāṇas* to the major petal of the Heart tier via a decade of petals in that tier. These twenty petals express the will to control the circulation of the major *prāṇas below* the diaphragm. The central decade of the Throat tier is concerned with the Sacral-Base of Spine centre combination, and the decade of the Heart tier projects *prāṇas* to the Solar Plexus centre. Each decade can be considered to represent the forces of the Vidyādharas and Consorts and of the way that the energies of the Dhyāni Buddhas and Consorts influence them. (Thereby necessitating twenty petals to accommodate the combination of energies.) The forces of desire and the emotions must be thoroughly commanded by the stern regime of the will disciplining the mind. Once desire and emotions no longer function as conditioning factors, then the attributes of the Will focussed via these petals can direct the expressions of the *siddhis* as they develop.

The *prāṇas* are channelled through one major petal of the Heart tier, making 21 petals from this perspective, allowing the conveyance of the energies of the seven Rays in terms of the three *guṇas*.[32]

The *next* major (Love-Wisdom) grouping consists of three groups *(guṇas)* of ten *prāṇas* embodied by two major petals of the Throat

31 The Will petals are coloured grey in the figure.

32 This number also relates to the seven sub-planes of the three worlds of human livingness (mental, astral and physical) that must be mastered.

tier focused upon one acorn of ten petals of the Heart tier, making 42 petals altogether (when counted in terms of decades of petals, plus the integrating two of the Throat tier). The *prāṇas* are then directed to one major petal to the Solar Plexus tier of the Head lotus. We saw earlier that this pentad is governed by one of the Jñāna Ḍākinīs at the time of the arousal of *kuṇḍalinī,* the stage of *manasic* development indicated here. Prior to this the *prāṇas* also assist in the transformative activity of *kāma-manas* by the Herukas. The combined *prāṇas* convey the general potencies of the 42 Peaceful Deities, which are implied by the term Love-Wisdom *(bodhicitta).* A major petal of the Heart centre can then be vitalised with the attributes of Love-Wisdom via a group of ten such petals via one major petal of the Heart tier and the refined *prāṇas* of one Watery petal of the Solar Plexus tier. Any group of ten petals can convey the combined energies of the Dhyāni Buddhas and Consorts, their Bodhisattvas and Consorts, the Vidyādharas and Consorts or Herukas and Consorts, depending upon the quality of energy needed at any time.

The *third* Activity level consists of five groups of ten petals in the Throat tier shown in Figure 21, with their *prāṇas* gathered by four larger petals. They pass *prāṇas* to three acorns of ten petals in the Heart tier. Together, therefore, there are eight groups of ten petals that embody the regulatory potency of the eight Mātaraḥ, thereby empowering the attributes of the eight consciousnesses, the eight directions in space, or the eight petalled lotuses in the body. The activities of the eight Mahābodhisattvas are also *prāṇically* incorporated in these petals in terms of their compassion and wisdom. By the time an individual functions via these petals the developed Bodhisattvic virtues are a fait accompli. The sum of the energies of the four pairs of Deities mentioned in the Love-Wisdom level can also be accommodated in this grouping of petals. All of these *prāṇas* are gathered by the four large Throat tier petals and two major Heart tier petals, and then directed by its major petal to the outer Solar Plexus tier of the Head lotus. (The four plus three produces seven organising and integrating petals in terms of the seven Ray qualities for all of the *prāṇas*.)

These energies are generated by the activity of the Throat centre at the various stages of its development, hence we have the complete evolution of *manas*. The emphasis is upon the five groups of ten petals of the Throat tier that process the enlightened consequences of the attributes of the five sense-consciousnesses. At first the energies of the Piśācī are activated to accomplish the major transmutative battles upon the path of yogic austerities. The energies of the Mātaraḥ can then refine the subtle discernments of mind to express wisdom.

Depending upon the level of development of consciousness the *prāṇas* of the four larger petals are regulated by the Guardians, their Consorts, or the Gatekeepers of pristine cognition. They are arrayed to absorb the *manasic* attributes of the four Elements and levels of the empirical mind and are aligned to the four major outer petals of the Throat centre.

As well as the seven Ray attributes organising the flow of all these energies in the major petals of the Throat and Heart tiers, there are nine decades of petals altogether in the Heart tier and five in the Throat tier. They signify the ability to project the perfected expression of the five sense-consciousnesses to the nine whorls of petals of the Sambhogakāya Flower. There are also 14 x 10 (7 x 20) *prāṇic* streams viewed in terms of the seven Ray attributes. The focus being mastery of the *saṃskāras* from the twenty petals of the Base of Spine, Sacral and Solar Plexus centres by organising them in terms of their Ray combinations, so that they can be expressed by the seven sacred petals of the Heart centre. We therefore have the perfection of the energies of Love-Wisdom.[33] Here each decade represents the attributes of the Dhyāni Buddhas and Consorts, which are conditioned by one or other of the Rays that qualify their expressions in the fields of activity.

Also shown is that when the five *manasic* pentads of the Throat tier project their *prāṇas* into three decades of the Heart tier all attributes of consciousness can be utilised and governed by Love-Wisdom *(bodhicitta)*. The 5 + 3 combination implies the way of mastery of the sum of the aspects of the eight consciousnesses so that the wisdom principle can utilise any of these aspects at need. This triad also represents the *guṇas* of expression of these wisdom characteristics.

---

33 Numerologically symbolised by the number 2. The number 20 refers to the second Ray multiplied by the number 10 of evolutionary perfection. The seven Rays are esoterically considered as sub-rays of the second Ray.

When considering only two major petals of the Throat tier[34] we see that there are 24 + 2 petals in all, with eight petals at the base. These eight petals help convey the most refined attributes of the eight consciousnesses to the innermost tiers of the Head centre. They thereby become the evolved foundation for the manifestation of *dharmakāya*. They represent the essence of the transformations and transmutations of *saṃskāras* accomplished by the meditative process.

The number 24 (12 x 2) allows the complete energisation of the petals of the Heart centre, and directs the *piṅgalā* flow for the *nāḍī* system. Also, the Heart tier receives the consequence of the Heart centre's *prāṇic* flow for the normal activity of human consciousness. The two major petals represent the regulating power of Vajrakīla Heruka and Consort to ensure that this *piṅgalā* flow is freed from defilements, whether in their *iḍā* (the Consort's focus) or *piṅgalā* attribute. Such directives are part of a *yogin's* meditative purpose at an advanced stage of development. The Fire of *kuṇḍalinī,* once awakened, is anchored in this Throat centre tier, thus Vajrakīla's regulatory energies are needed to handle the potency. The five decades of petals of this Throat tier then represent the supporting activity of the Jñāna Ḍākinīs.

The two central major petals are focussed upon an acorn of ten petals within the Heart tier, which with the 26 petals of the Throat tier makes 36 (3 x 12) *prāṇic* potencies. These potencies incorporate the *iḍā, piṅgalā* and *suṣumṇā* flow empowering the *bodhicitta* of the Heart centre. The major petal of the Heart tier that focuses these potencies is embodied by the characteristics of one or other of the Dhyāni Buddhas, Mahottara Heruka, or of their Consorts. Thus it conveys the particular attribute of Love-Wisdom *(bodhicitta)* expressed by an enlightened one at any time. These attributes are also qualified by the twelve signs of the zodiac, esoterically interpreted. The twelve signs therefore represent modes of delineation of an enlightened Mind.

From another perspective there is a triad of ten petals, each integrated by the two major petals, making 32 petals altogether, twice the number of major petals to the Throat centre. This number was explained above with respect to the Love-Wisdom grouping of petals, and also when a similar number of petals appeared in the Ājñā centre.

34 Marked with bolder lines in Figure 21.

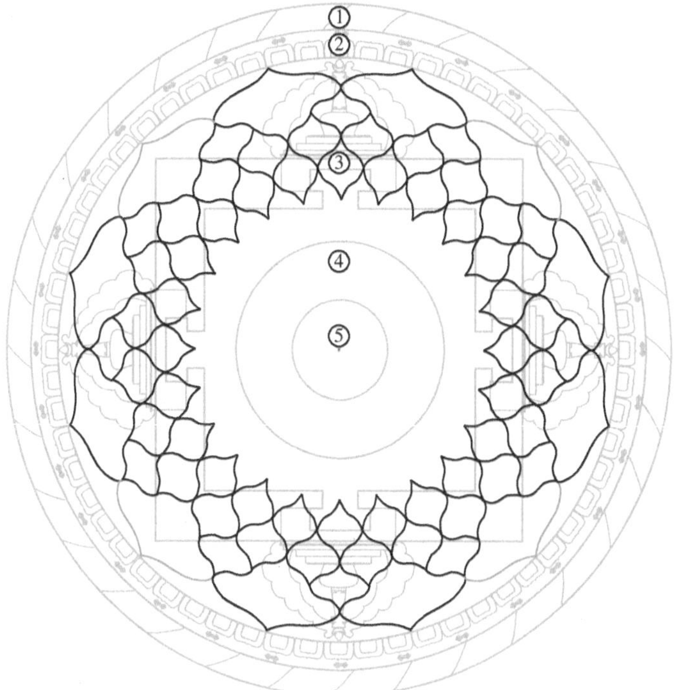

Figure 22. The Throat tier in the Head centre as a *maṇḍala*

Taking the Throat tier as a unit we see that there are twelve orientations of such couplets possible, but the major expression is of four such groupings manifesting the fixed cross orientation, leaving four major petals (each consisting of two decades of petals) oriented in the intermediate mutable cross positions. (The fixed and mutable cross directions of these petals empower the orientations of the two types of *viśvavajra*.) There are therefore 32 petals orientated north-east-south-west and 21 petals orientated in the intermediate positions. Here we have the significance presented in many Tibetan *maṇḍalas*, of a central square containing the four gates of the celestial mansion of protective deities, surrounded by two concentric circles, the outer one signifying the burning ground and the inner one symbolising the potencies of the Heart centre. Most *maṇḍalas* are based upon the Head lotus, but some, for instance, are centred upon the *chakras* below the diaphragm. Different Tantras not only have different central deities, but the artists depicting them may choose the basic symbolism in individualistic ways. Therefore there can be variations shown in Thankas depicting the same *maṇḍala*.

Figure 22 depicts the petals of the Throat tier superimposed upon the inner part of a typical *maṇḍala* for a Head lotus. The information here can be correlated with Volume 4, chapter 5 of this *Treatise on Mind* where the basic elements of a *maṇḍala* were explained in terms of the Initiation process. The numbers refer to:

1. The outer perimeter of Fire.
2. The charnel grounds.
3. The gates to the celestial mansion.
4. The abode of the Deities.
5. The point of abstraction (from which all comes and returns), becoming the central deity and consort.

Dudjom Rinpoche states that there are two traditions of meditation, one emphasising the Tantras (Mahāyoga, consisting of Father, Mother, and non-dual Tantras), and the second that emphasises 'the class of means for attainment'. There are:

> Five classes of means for attainment of the deities of pristine cognition, namely, the Means for Attaining the Body of the Sugatas by Relying on the Four Centres of Mañjuśrī the Body[35]...the Means for Attaining the Lotus Speech by Relying on the Three Neighs of Hayagrīva...the Means for Attaining the Indestructible Reality of Mind by Relying on the Genuine and Unique Accomplishment, the Awareness and Naturally Present Pristine Cognition which is Yangdak the Mind[36]... the Means for Attaining Nectar Attributes which Perfectly Reveal All Things of Saṃsāra and Nirvāṇa as the Enlightened Attributes of Mahottara...and the Means for Attaining the Enlightened Activity of Vajrakīla which Emphatically Teaches the Skilful Means for Training Malicious Beings by the Rites of Sorcery of Vajrakīla.[37]

---

35 The deity referred to here is Yamāntaka, the wrathful form of Mañjuśrī, the Bodhisattva embodying wisdom. See Dudjom Rinpoche, *The Nyingma School of Tibetan Buddhism,* (Wisdom Publications, Boston, 1991), part two, 141.

36 The deity referred to is Śrīheruka, Ibid., part two, 141.

37 Ibid., part one, 361-2.

From this quote we see that the information presented in this chapter relates to the second of the traditions of meditation.

First we have Yamāntaka, the wrathful, bull-headed form of Mañjuśrī (the embodiment of wisdom), governing the ending of the cycles of death and dying, as ruled by desire and attachment to phenomena. He embodies the general form of the *maṇḍala* of the Head lotus, and the transformation of *saṃskāras* by means of trampling upon them via Fiery Wrath. This activity is exoterically depicted in the *maṇḍala* by the outer perimiter of Fire of the five concentric circles, explained in my book on *maṇḍalas*[38]. Taking Yamāntaka as the integrating deity for all incoming *saṃskāras* implies that the purpose of the *maṇḍala* is the generation of wisdom from the sense-perceptions, which is the major purpose of the outer tier of the Head lotus. We can think of this *maṇḍala* in terms of a five dimensional representation (relating also to the qualities of the five Jinas) in this form of meditation.

In this Fiery outer perimeter (signifying the Solar Plexus tier of the Head lotus) most *saṃskāras* are processed. This tier (1) is generally depicted in terms of three, four or five bands of coloured flames. The Fiery impetus is carried right through to the central Throat tier. As well as relating to the development of the attributes of the Dhyāni Buddhas (according to the colours presented), these numbers also represent the petals of wrath, subjugation and enrichment within the Solar Plexus tier, where most of the transformations of *saṃskāras* pertaining to the Head lotus occur.

The 'four centres of Mañjuśrī' refer to the four main *chakras* below the Head/Ājñā centre combination (Throat, Heart, Solar Plexus and Sacral-Base of Spine centres) that govern the activities of the form and the evolution of the four main Elements. With them the attributes of wisdom are generated, as per the symbolism of Mañjuśrī. Also the quaternary of the personality structure can here be implicated, as well as the four concreted levels of mind. A Sugata is a Buddha, and the means to develop the three bodies of a Buddha *(dharmakāya, nirmāṇakāya* and *sambhogakāya)* are here implicated in the terms 'Body, Speech and Mind'.

---

38 See Volume 4, 160-167.

The 'Body' normally incorporates the five *skandhas* in accordance with the qualities of the five Elements. 'Speech' yogically incorporates the sum of the psychic constitution, of the *nāḍīs* conveying the *saṃskāras* developed from interrelating with consciousness, which is normally Watery in nature. Where *kāma-manas* was earlier generated, we now have *bodhicitta*. The *kāma-manas* was controlled by mantra, *smṛti* (mindfulness) and *dhāraṇīs* (the means for fixing the mind upon ideas, concepts in meditation). 'Mind' refers to the Fiery impetus of consciousness, where logical *manasic* characteristics overcame emotional and desire based incentives, producing enlightenment.[39]

The next deity mentioned is the wrathful aspect of Avalokiteśvara, Hayāgriva, (of which there are said to be 108 forms), who represents the generation of the compassionate qualities of the Heart tier (2) in the Head lotus. This tier constitutes the charnel grounds, signifying the Heart tier wherein the refined Watery *prāṇas* are accommodated. Here the charnel grounds refer to the process producing the death of all unwanted *saṃskāras* so that the *prāṇas* entering this Heart tier are thoroughly transformed. Though there are various depictions of this tier in the Thangkas, a common theme is that of a circle of lotus petals (signifying that a *chakra* is depicted), which are often surrounded by a ring of *vajras*. They signify the potency needed to be wielded at the charnel ground before the enlightened attributes of the inner tiers of the *maṇḍala* can be obtained. The 'three neighs of Hayāgriva' refer to the mantras needed to produce the enlightened attributes of 'Body, Speech and Mind'. The Watery *saṃskāras* conveyed by the triune central *nāḍīs* can then be accommodated in terms of the compassionate attributes associated with the petals of the Heart tier.

The third, Throat tier (3), is that of the celestial mansion, which contains a square with four gates of the *dharma* in the fixed cross position containing the four Guardians. The complete attributes concerning the development of Mind, the 'Naturally Present Pristine Cognition', is symbolised by this tier, thus there is significant detail portrayed in the *maṇḍalas*. The *manasic* attributes of this tier is produced by the activities of Śrīheruka (Buddha Heruka) and the

39 *Maṇḍalas* are normally interpreted in accord with the triune classification of 'Body, Speech and Mind' in different ways. In the Kālachakra they are presented in terms of aspects of the celestial mansion.

maṇḍala around him. This tier represents the central processes of the *maṇḍala* of the Head centre, thus embodies the Fiery gain developed by the three main petals of the Head lotus. This work is accomplished in the outermost Solar Plexus tier, with the refined *prāṇas* finding their way through the gates represented by the Guardians.

Most descriptions of *maṇḍalas* focus upon the attributes of this portion, generally analysing the terms 'Body, Speech and Mind' in relation to it. All major tiers of the Head lotus come to fruition therein, and are consequently integrated as a unit. From this perspective, this tier sums up the significance of the *maṇḍala* of the Head lotus. The two outer tiers signify the process of incorporation of *prāṇas* from below the diaphragm plus the chest cavity into the Head lotus, whereas this central tier empowers the Fiery attributes of the Mind. It signifies the true gain of all interrelated activity.

Next, (4) is the abode of the Deities wherein eight deities and consorts that are expressions of the central deity are normally depicted. There are normally two spheres of deities to complete the *maṇḍala,* the circle of the eight, plus the central sphere of the presiding deity. Mahottara embodies the qualities of this dual tier in terms of the generation of four Void Elements (pristine consciousnesses) via the eight directions of space. These consciousnesses are depicted as 'Nectar Attributes' in the quote. The manifesting central deity (conditioning the purpose of the *maṇḍala)* embodies the fifth Element and the Dharmadhātu wisdom of Vairocana (the *dharmakāya)* according to the attributes of that wisdom the particular deity exemplifies. (Exemplified in terms of 'great bliss', *mahāsukha.)* The central governing deity (5) expresses the point of abstraction *(bīja)* from which all comes and goes. This deity represents the major qualification of the *maṇḍala,* the objective of the entire meditation to produce. In the case of Mahottara it concerns the generation of the fierce qualities needed to liberate consciousness from all limitations via the work of the sum of the Wrathful Deities.

In the meditation technique, Vajrakīla Heruka manifests as the central point of power, because via him comes the generation of *kuṇḍalinī,* hence the Fiery impetus that awakens all of the powers and transformative processes of this centre associated with an enlightened one. This Fire must be generated if the qualities of the central deity of the *maṇḍala* in question is to be enthroned. *Kuṇḍalinī* is the potency that awakens all of the attributes of the *maṇḍala* through the central deity. Here then is the rationale to the information presented in this volume. The mechanism of the awakening of *kuṇḍalinī* lies at the heart of the liberation process and gaining enlightenment. The 'Skilful means for Training Malicious Beings' refers to the transformation of all negative forces from the Base of Spine centre to the Head lotus, including that of external demonic or malicious psychic entities that try to prevent the engendering of enlightenment. *Siddhis* are therefore utilised to ward off and to convert all such extraneous forces.

The four integrating petals of the inner Throat tier represent the doors of approach to the four Guardians that block the way to undertaking Initiation until the *saṃskāras* projected are of the necessary grade. The complete development of the compassionate factors that lay the foundation to attain Initiation happens at the Heart tier of petals. They represent an exalted level of evolutionary perfection where Bodhisattva attributes are refined and further generated so that the higher *bhūmis* can be attained. The necessary wisdom to know how to rightly give and the prescient vision of the consequence of all such actions is generated at the Throat tier level. Each of these Guardian petals convey the *prāṇas* of two acorns of ten petals (which therefore represent the *iḍā* and *piṇgalā* attributes of the necessary *saṃskāras).* These twenty petals also help control the *siddhis* developed via the twenty petals of the major *chakras* below the diaphragm.

Concerning the Guardians it is said that Yamāntaka overcomes all nihilistic views via the rites of enrichment.[40] He dances upon the corpses of the subtlest aspects of desire and emotional thoughts. Hayāgriva utilises the rites of subjugation, thereby developing the subtle discernments of Mind to overcome all traces of egotism. Amṛtakuṇḍalin utilises the rites of wrath to eliminate the last vestiges of conceptualising the substantial reality of material phenomena. Trailokyavija utilises the rites of pacification to eliminate all desire-mind concepts of a perpetual heaven as a justification for right action. Here we see the nature of the interrelation between the decades of petals synthesised by the Guardians and those embodied by the Gatekeepers enacting emanative rites of the Solar Plexus tier.

40 See Gyurme, 393.

Each major Throat tier petal ruled by one or other of the four Guardians has six minor petals at the base, followed by 5, 4, 2 and 1 petals, making 18 (2 x 9) altogether.[41] The six base petals indicate that the output from the Sacral centre is completely controlled so that its energies awaken *siddhis* that substitute for the sense-consciousnesses and intellect. The 'rites of wrath' have consequently accomplished their purpose. The entire philosophy associated with the conversion process by the six Buddhas within the Six Realms of the wheel of birth and death *(bhavacakra)* can be applied here, when viewed in terms of the attributes of Avalokiteśvara's compassionate action. The number five in this case represents the processes of the Jñāna Ḍākinīs that produce the awakening of *siddhis*. At first ordinary *siddhis* are expressed and later the supramundane ones take their place as the higher Initiations are undertaken. The four petals accommodate the *prāṇas* from the Base of Spine centre. The remaining three petals convey the attributes of the *iḍā, piṇgalā* and *suṣumṇā nāḍīs*. The eighteen petals allow inception of these eighteen Fires into the Will-Sacrifice petals of the Sambhogakāya Flower. It signifies also the will and sacrificial attributes that must be evoked if Initiation is to occur. This produces great spiritual power upon the three worlds of human livingness via the awakened Head lotus. There are also four major petals to five smaller ones in the Throat tier, that similarly project a complete array of these Fiery *prāṇas* to the Will-Sacrifice petals of the Sambhogakāya Flower.

The activity of the Throat tier generates the attributes of the abstract Mind via the five groups of ten petals that incorporate the most refined *prāṇas* of the five sense-consciousnesses. It thus anchors the complete expression of the *iḍā nāḍī* stream. When a group of five decades (50 petals) are viewed in terms of the eight directions of the wheel of direction in space, as consistent with the symbolism of the geometry of the celestial mansion of the *maṇḍala* outlined above, then we have 50 x 8 = 400 different potencies. They can then empower the Fiery activity of the 400 petals of a major Solar Plexus tier petal[42] to produce the activity of an enlightened Mind. The *prāṇas* from the Throat tier pass through the nine

41 The 18 petals allow processing the sum of the attributes derived from the 2 x 7 sub-planes of the physical and astral domains, as well as the four concreted levels of mind.

42 See Volume 4 for explanation of the arrangement of these 400 petals.

decades of petals of a major petal of the Heart tier. Consequently, 490 (7 x 70) *prāṇic* factors can flow to the Solar Plexus tier, manifesting their potency through one decade of petals of the Solar Plexus tier (dotted in Figure 21) that conveys any ideation from the inner tiers to express an enlightened thought. The centres below the diaphragm can then be empowered with the effect of the expression of Mind. When this grouping of ten petals governed by the Herukas is added to the 490 *prāṇic* factors, then we have 500 different combinations of the *manasic prāṇas*. The interrelation with the decades of the Heart tier represents the integration of the *piṇgalā prāṇas,* and the incorporation of the outer ten petals signifies the awakening of *suṣumṇā.* The derivation of the number 500 by such computation may appear arbitrary, but one must understand that here we are concerned with the perfection of mind so that Mind is the outcome. We therefore have the gain of the *ālayavijñāna* Initiation and the evocation of *bodhicitta* implicated. The mode that *bodhicitta* manifests depends upon the turning of the petals of the Heart tier, whilst the projection of this energy via any decade of the Solar Plexus tier determines the minutiae of the way *bodhicitta* is expressed in *saṃsāra.*

A simpler way of stating the above is that when the number 50 is multiplied ten times to produce evolutionary perfection (ten levels of refinement) of the associated *saṃskāras,* then we have the number 500 so often found in the texts, such as the 500 *arhats* that convened the first Buddhist Council after the *parinirvāṇa* of Gautama. *Prāṇically* all forces pertaining to the *ālayavijñāna* environment are accounted for in this arrangement. The Vidyādharas and Consorts actively come to the fore to assist in the assimilation of the attributes of mind and their conversion to Mind. Also, the number 490 = 7 x 70 is important, as it implicates the perfected expression of the 49 Ray and sub-ray potencies via such an enlightened Mind.

If the two Airy petals of the Solar Plexus tier are included, allowing further refinement of the Fiery attributes with those of the Airy (drawing upon the properties of the inner tier of petals of the Head lotus governed by Mahottara), then attainment of the *śūnyatā* enlightenment is possible. Each Airy petal posses 2 x 20 petals = 80 petals for the two Airy petals at the level of the 70 incarnations, and 2 x 30 petals = 120 petals for the two Airy petals at the level of the 777 incarnations. These numbers

(80, 120) allow the complete *prāṇic* expression of the twelve petals of the Heart centre conveyed via the eight directions in space, to be contained in the Head lotus so that the attributes of the Heart centre can thoroughly transmute any base *saṃskāras* in the tiers of the Head centre. These Airy petals are *piṅgalā* in constitution.

We can see from the above that the numerical analysis for the organisation of the petals of the Head lotus admits many different possibilities according to the way the petals are arranged and the proper flow of energies, as conditioned by the deities concerned. There are minor interrelations of energies and major sweeps of *prāṇic* movement to account for.

A similar important interrelation for the Heart tier as shown for the Throat tier can also be analysed. In this case the major conditioning number is twelve (signifying the attributes of a Heart centre). Therefore if we multiply the triad (delineated by the five main petals of the Throat tier) consisting of 3 x 10 petals of a Heart tier by the movement of the directions of the twelve synthesising petals, then we have 12 x 30 = 360. These Heart tier energies are then directed to the Solar Plexus tier where the main focus are the 135 petals of an Airy petal described above. (The Airy energies are the medium of expression of the energies from the Heart centre.) Adding 360 to 135, we get the number 495, and when the energies of Mind from the five major Throat centre petals are added, the number 500 is produced.

Also, when the number 495 is added to the 505 earlier described then the number 1,000 is obtained, the significance of which has already been commented upon. This number integrates the Heart and Throat tiers into one sphere of perfected activity of compassionate Ideation via the Airy petals and the dynamic activity of the Jñāna Ḍākinīs. The number 1,000 also represents the attainment of the Great Perfection that is the *śūnyatā* experience. To achieve this one must also draw energies from the second innermost tier of the Head lotus governed by the energies of Akṣobhya (via a group of five main petals of the Throat tier).[43] The way of developing the Great Perfection refers to each *saṃskāra* undergoing its version of the ten stages of evolution explained

43 The activity of the Throat tier therefore is governed by the energies of Amitābha, the Heart tier by the energies of Ratnasambhava, and the Solar Plexus tier by Amoghasiddhi.

earlier. They are cycled and recycled through ever higher and subtler levels of expression as the dross is cleansed, until eventually only the Void Elements remain.

In such a case all the Wrathful Deities associated with the Airy tier have accomplished their tasks, the Gatekeepers and then the Guardians have not blocked the refined *prāṇas*, as they have been stripped of all defiling characteristics, by undergoing ten levels of alchemical purification. This direct line of energisation represents the mechanism of the *vajrayāna*. When the potencies of the male-female deities are integrated in one field of embrace, as in the case of the number 505, where the opposite petal is sought to produce the significance of the number 1,000, *prāṇically* speaking,[44] then we have the *mahāmudrā*. From this perspective the inner Throat tier can be considered masculine, the outer Solar Plexus tier feminine, and the middle Heart tier the place of consummation of the integrated *prāṇas*. *Bodhicitta* is the outcome.

One can also multiply the nine decades of petals to each major petal of the Heart tier by twelve to produce the number 1080, a version of the sacred number 108.

The Heart in the Head tier

The generation within humanity of the qualities embodied by the Heart tier in the Head Lotus is presently the focal point for the activities of the eight Mahābodhisattvas and their Consorts. These energies are guarded by the fierceness of the eight wrathful Mātaraḥ (Keurima), or at a lower level of expression the eight animal-headed Piśācī. We saw earlier the significance of the eight decades of petals where three decades of this tier are integrated with five decades of petals from the Throat tier. The significance of the number eight also comes to the fore in this tier, as a pair of major petals have eight smaller petals as their base. Next is seen seven triads of petals that integrate the incoming energies in terms of the seven Ray potencies. They process the Airy *prāṇas* of this major petal. The third tier consists of six hexads of petals. They process the Waṭery *prāṇas* incorporated into the Heart tier from the external

44 We therefore have an esoteric reason why the Head centre is called the 1,000 petalled lotus, even though this is not the exact number of petals it contains.

Solar Plexus tier, further refining and perfecting their attributes. The five decades of petals from either of the sub-major petals of a major petal process the Fiery *(manasic)* attributes from the Solar Plexus tier.

We therefore have 8 + 21 + 36 + 50 = 115 (23 x 5) petals altogether. There are also 26 + 1 (3 x 9) petals when the petals are counted individually. The number 3 x 9 relates to directing refined *saṃskāras* to the nine whorls of petals of the Sambhogakāya Flower. When the two major petals within the major Heart tier petal are considered then we have 2 x (8, 21, 36, and 50) petals altogether, making 16, 42, 72 and 100 petals. The significance of these numbers need not be explained here, as they have been explained elsewhere.

All of these potencies are integrated by the major petal and its two subsidiary petals. There being four tiers of smaller petals, making 42 petals (9 + 10 + 11 + 12 petals) signifying the energies of the 42 Peaceful Deities. The twelve small base petals incorporate all aspects of this Heart tier with the energies from the Heart centre and the twelve main petals of the Head centre. (We also saw earlier that this Love-Wisdom tier also garners 42 *prāṇas* when a decade of its petals are integrated with the 32 petals of a major segment of the Throat tier.) Consequently, the sum of the energies of these Peaceful Deities is the basis of the potency directed to the Heart centre.) The major petal and its two subsidiary petals incorporate the sum of their *prāṇas* in terms of the three principal *nāḍīs*.

The eleven triads of minor petals integrate and further process the refined *prāṇas* from the eleven triads concerned with the 'rites of wrath' of the outer Solar Plexus tier. The *saṃskāras* of physical plane activity thereby become thoroughly refined and impregnated with compassionate thought. When projected to any of the triads of the Solar Plexus tier in order to assist the conversion process, then effectively twelve such triads are formed, allowing the complete expression of the energies of the Heart tier to manifest according to the symbolism of the number twelve. These triads integrate the associated *prāṇas* into the Throat tier. The Earthy *prāṇas* from the Solar Plexus tier can then be thoroughly transformed so that the attributes of Mind can be engendered. As well as generating the basis of wise decisions in all thought-form construction, this is necessary if *kuṇḍalinī* is to be safely liberated.

A function of the nine groups of ten petals (as well as directing *prāṇas* to the Sambhogakāya Flower) is to integrate with one Watery petal of the outermost Solar Plexus tier in the head, which consists of ten smaller petals. The Watery Element is the focus of this Heart tier because it is the conduit for the energy of Love. We then have 10 x 10 petals altogether that are responsible for the evolutionary perfection of this Element. Because processing the *saṃskāras* of the emotions and desire are the focus here, one can deduce the importance of this activity with respect to the Solar Plexus tier of petals. It produces the inevitable control of Solar Plexus activity and of the entire Inner Round *prāṇas*.

Each major petal of the Heart tier contains two secondary level petals incorporating five 'acorns' comprised of ten smaller petals each. The significance of groups of ten petals was explained in the accounting of a tier concerned with the 'rites of pacification' in the Solar Plexus in the Head tier. These two groups of five decades of petals utilise Love-Wisdom to further refine the *kāma-manasic prāṇas* directed by the Herukas from the Solar Plexus tier. The objective being to develop good will and the Will-to-Love from the mental-emotional aspects of the sense-consciousnesses. These loving attributes are specifically targeted in terms of their *iḍā* and *piṇgalā* constituents by the two groupings of petals. The total pacification of all emotional *saṃskāras* thereby becomes a major objective of the Heart tier (with the major petal also conveying *suṣumṇā* energies). The meditation practice of *śamatha* (calm abiding) is primarily concerned with consciously manifesting the function of this grouping of petals, so that the potency of the Heart awakens. Consequently, all unruly unregenerated *saṃskāras* are destined to become increasingly refined, transformed, transmuted, and liberated.

This Heart tier anchors the energies from the Heart centre, which is designed to integrate all loving energies into the *nāḍīs,* and also to anchor the Life stream *(sūtrātmā)* from the Monad, the true Buddha within. This energy of Life is thoroughly integrated with those of the Peaceful Deities, becoming the basis for the evolutionary path of all attributes of consciousness. It conveys the seven Ray potencies, which are incorporated into the seven sacred petals.[45] For this reason the Heart centre is the source of compassion and the fount of *bodhicitta.*

45 They are the basis for the demonstration of the energy of *bodhicitta.*

The energies of the Peaceful Deities are also channelled via the inner tier of twelve petals of the Ājñā centre. The focus is then upon any group of eight petals governed by a major Aetheric petal (for the activity of the Mahābodhisattvas), or 11 + 1 petals when three innermost Maṇi petals are included and incorporated with the energy projection of an entire lobe of petals. These three groups of twelve petals are then aligned with the 36 (3 x 12) *prāṇic* potencies earlier mentioned.

When more *manasic* attributes of consciousness of a refined nature are to be directed to the Sambhogakāya Flower then the *prāṇas* of any of the decades of petals in the Heart tier can link to one of the 5 + 4 = 9 petals of the Throat tier. Their main import is the development of Will-Sacrifice, the spiritual power allowing the overcoming of all personality hindrances. This is perceived as sacrifice in the world of human affairs. All of the attributes of the five sense-consciousnesses are thereby incorporated into the Sambhogakāya Flower. The influence from this Flower manifests according to the attributes of the fixed or mutable cross via the modifying influence of any Guardian, Vidyādhara, Mātaraḥ or Piśācī that is the focus of consciousnesses at any time.

Because the Sambhogakāya Flower is the source of the energy of Love-Wisdom to the personal-I, its relation to the Heart tier is dominant. It assists the personality to generate goodwill and the Will-to-Love. The nine acorns of ten petals to a major Heart tier petal facilitates this process. The two smaller main petals wield five acorns of ten each to assist in the integration of the sense-consciousnesses.

If the Solar Plexus, Heart and Throat tiers of the Head centre are viewed in terms of one integral movement of energies, then the *prāṇas* from the 5 + 3 decades of petals of the Heart and Throat tiers (bearing the attributes of the eight-consciousnesses) will be seen to channel transforming *prāṇas* to one decade in the outer Solar Plexus tier. The transformation of Watery *saṃskāras* into the refined impressions that have their originating source in the Sambhogakāya Flower can then be facilitated. This source is viewed in terms of either coming from one petal, a triad of its petals, or from a complete pentad of characteristics. The latter happens from the time of the third Initiation onwards.

With respect to the Mātaraḥ and Piśācī within the Solar Plexus tier that directly interrelate with the Heart tier petals, much depends upon whether the *prāṇas* are predominantly *piṅgalā* in nature (Mātaraḥ) or manifest an *iḍā* quality (Piśācī). Either group align with the members of the four female Gatekeepers of pristine cognition that guard the nature of the flow of *prāṇas* to and from the Head lotus. Rejected or directed *prāṇas* provide the *prāṇic* instruction to the centres below the diaphragm—via the Diaphragm centre and Splenic centre I (Mātaraḥ), or Splenic centre II (Piśācī), where the *prāṇas* are reprocessed. The purpose of all such circulation lays the foundation to eventually attain the second Initiation, which incorporates the activity of the *prāṇas* circulating in the Heart in the head tier.

The eight Mātaraḥ, the terrifying aspects of the eight Mahābodhisattvas, sort the various *saṃskāras* of the consciousness-attributes and direct them to the Head lotus. (The Piśācī are the wrathful emanations of the Consorts of the Mahābodhisattvas.) They work as a type of filtering system via the process of pacification, wrath, subjugation and enrichment that is the role of the Īśvarī. At the level of enrichment the *prāṇas* are of sufficient quality to be absorbed into the next major sphere of activity of the Head centre (the Heart tier). The concourse of *prāṇas* from this inner sphere in the head then issues the directive flow upwards through the major petals of the outermost circle of the Head lotus, the Fiery, Airy, and Aetheric petals of the Solar Plexus (Activity) tier.

In the petals associated with the Mātaraḥ of the Solar Plexus tier the Watery and Fiery qualities are integrated and manifest in the form of *kliṣṭamanas*. Only when the Airy (Love) principle dominates can these *prāṇas* be appropriately controlled and the defiled aspect cleansed to reveal the pure unadulterated *ālayavijñāna* that is Mind. The nature of the unadulterated *ālayavijñāna* environment is experienced in the inner Throat tier of the Head lotus, after the *saṃskāras* of consciousness have been integrated with those of the Sambhogakāya Flower. All *manasic saṃskāras* that have passed through the appropriate stages of purification, rites of wrath, etc., in the Solar Plexus tier of the Head lotus, eventually pass through to the four Gatekeepers of pristine cognition of the Throat tier. The final refinements of thoughts that are then produced are associated with the emanations attributed to these Gatekeepers. They are 'boundless compassion' in the east, 'kindness' in the south, 'sympathetic joy' in the west, and a state of 'infinite equanimity' in the northern direction of the Head lotus. These attributes are also an effect of seeding *bījas* in the Head lotus at the appropriate time by the Sambhogakāya Flower.

In the Solar Plexus tier the Piśācī (who work to transform the eight types of consciousness) are represented by the eight innermost petals of the large acorn of petals embodied by a Gatekeeper of pristine cognition. As noted, these eight gates come to be embodied by the Mātaraḥ when the flow of consciousness from the innermost circles of the Head lotus are to be projected outwards to direct the fields of expression of the target *chakra(s)* in the body. Once enlightenment has ensued then the Mātaraḥ are no longer needed, and the attributes of the Mahābodhisattvas are projected instead. Until then we can see that the work of the Piśācī and Mātaraḥ lay the foundation of awakening the attributes of Mind. The energies they represent are an essential part of the process of converting *kliṣṭamanas* into *bodhicitta.*

The innermost two tiers of the five tiers of the Head lotus are concerned with the attainment of the higher Initiations that produce the *dharmakāya* revelations and liberation from *saṃsāra*. The innermost tier can be considered the place of residence of the energies of Samantabhadra and Consort and the Dhyāni Buddhas and Consorts. It is the *bīja* from which all else proceeds. The next tier embodies the energies of the five Dhyāni Bodhisattvas and Consorts, and are guarded over by the fierceness of Mahottara Heruka and Consort.

The twelve main petals of each major tier of the Head lotus should also be analysed as a unit. They indicate that the expression of all the above processes necessitate repeating the cleansing processes of *prāṇas* in cycles of twelve. The major conditioning energies to each of these petals are those of the twelve signs of the zodiac, which govern all of the factors developed by consciousness on its evolutionary journey. The *prāṇas* qualifying each sign must therefore be developed and mastered for the three main tiers of the Head lotus before Initiation is possible at the level the personality is at. Each incarnation helps to develop the qualities of one or other of the signs of the zodiac. Therefore, as the higher Initiations are developed, knowledge of esoteric astrology is important, and is a major reason why the subject has been emphasised in this Treatise.

In conclusion, the sum of the major petals of the outer Solar Plexus tier of the Head lotus (at the level of 'the seventy incarnations') should be briefly analysed. There are 12 main Aetheric petals, 24 Airy ones, 48 Fiery ones, and 60 governed by the Herukas. This makes 144 = 12 x 12 in all, signifying the cycles of unfoldment of the attributes of the twelve signs of the zodiac, which energise the Head lotus. This allows the complete energisation of the twelve petals of the Heart lotus, and the sum of the circulation of all the *chakras* that become vitalised by it. The general *piṇgalā nāḍī* circulation is thus directed wherein the compassion attributes of consciousness are awakened.

At the level of the five Herukas of the Solar Plexus tier there are an additional four petals that were not included in this discussion. The reason is that as the wheel of the major Solar Plexus tier turns, so they 'click' into position as the next set of Herukas, allowing the *prāṇas* they embrace to be expressed. Their qualities therefore manifest as the background influence to that of a Heruka. (The four become a fifth as the wheel turns.) These nine petals then receive energies from various nine groups of petals of the two inner Heart and Throat tiers, and help convey the *prāṇas* of the Solar Plexus in the head to be channelled to the Sambhogakāya Flower. When we view the major petals from this perspective then there are 9 + 4 + 2 + 1 = 16 x 12 petals to consider. They are orientated to energise the sixteen major petals of the Throat centre (the *iḍā nāḍī* circulation), and to generate wisdom attributes within the mind.

The way of viewing the Head lotus in terms of incorporating the energies from below the diaphragm into the Heart and Throat tiers presents an esoteric view of the nature of the integration of wisdom and compassion. Here we see the nature of the *mahāmudrā* that is the union of a Buddha and his Consort, of the way that one becomes an enlightened being.

The Head lotus and the Initiation process

The complete picture of the Initiation process as far as the Head centre is concerned requires a consideration of the movement of *prāṇas* from the eight decades of petals from the Heart and Throat tiers to the petals of the Solar Plexus in the Head tier. This necessitates the vitalisation of an Airy petal via the gates occupied by the eight Mātaraḥ. The events producing Initiation are then possible. The Initiation concerned depends upon the level of the tiers of petals that have been appropriately cleansed by the action of the Wrathful Deities. The petals are thereby prepared for the oncoming *prāṇas* from the inner tiers.

When the petals previously cleansed by the activity of the Īśvārī of wrath are vitalised through annulling the attachments of Earthy *saṃskāras* then the first Initiation is possible. The effects of Amoghasiddhi's All-accomplishing Wisdom have consequently been evidenced. When the activity of all the Īśvārī have processed the Watery *saṃskāras* and the consciousness-attributes have passed the Doors guarded by the Herukas, then the second Initiation is possible. *Bodhicitta* will also have been generated through activating the three inner Heart acorns of petals, bringing Ratnasambhava's Equalising Wisdom into play. Similarly, when the Fiery *prāṇas* generated via the five petals of ten *prāṇas* of the inner Throat tier have thoroughly dried out the Watery ones, then the third Initiation is possible. (In doing so they pass through and transform the attributes of the three Watery decades of petals within an Airy petal in the Solar Plexus tier.) The Gatekeepers enacting rites have by then accomplished their ritual (cyclic) duties in conjunction with successful meditative disciplines (rites) by the Initiate. Fiery manasic *prāṇas* can then spontaneously circulate unimpededly throughout the Head lotus. These rites consequently awaken *kuṇḍalinī*, assisting its flow to the Ājñā and Head centres, laying the basis for developing the higher *siddhis*. The five Jñāna Ḍākinīs then fully manifest their powers and Amitābha's Discriminating Wisdom can play its role.

The fourth Initiation is possible when the Airy Element is engendered by the liberating Fire, and the inner Heart tier is ablaze. *Saṃsāra* then comes under complete control of the *yogin*. The Gatekeepers of pristine cognition thereby dance upon the attributes of all the qualities of the four kingdoms in Nature veiled by the four petals of the Base of Spine centre. Etheric space (both in its lower Earthy and higher cosmic connotations) is then consciously the true outer form of the Initiate, and the *śūnyatā-saṃsāra* nexus has become the place of residence for consciousness. Akṣobhya's Mirror-like Wisdom now rules.

The fifth Initiation necessitates the entire Head centre to be made ablaze as a consequence of the rising of *kuṇḍalinī* without hindrance up all the prepared channels and centres. It connotes the demonstration of the Vajrayāna because with the empowerment of the Aetheric Element *(ātma)* the total power of the *vajra* manifests. The innermost tier or jewel at the centre of the Head lotus, relegated to the attributes of Vairocana and his Dharmadhātu Wisdom, has been consciously awakened and its energies integrated with the major outermost petal, thus producing the diamond-Mind *(cintāmaṅī).* The *dharmakāya* becomes the modus operandi in the Initiate's consciousness. Such a one is then a resident of Shambhala. The Dharmakāya Way (the Initiation path) has played its role and the Initiate has gained the fruits of its activity.

Further numerological considerations

The overall view of the number of petals that accommodate the processing of the *prāṇas* within the five tiers of petals of the Head lotus can now be enumerated. In this account the complete Head lotus shall be considered. In this broader analysis the sum total of human activity and the associated *saṃskāras* are the concern, rather than being focussed upon discipleship. We therefore have:

a. The innermost tier of twelve petals that are effectively spokes of energy. It directs the synthesised, refined *prāṇas* associated with the complete *maṇḍala* of the Head lotus to the integrating Sambhogakāya Flower. It also allows the governing potencies of the Flower to set the overall pattern of activity for the twelve major groups of petals of the Head lotus via the twelve major petals of the Throat tier. This interrelation also provides a general sphere of receptivity for the twelve energies from the Heart centre. The innermost tier transmits Aetheric-Fiery *prāṇas* and is receptive to the overall influences of the Dhyāni Buddha Vairocana.

b. The second innermost tier consists of twenty-four petals. Twelve petals are the main conduits for anchoring into the person's consciousness the impulses from the Sambhogakāya Flower. The other twelve petals mainly project the *prāṇas* to and from the twelve major petals of the tiers of petals in the Head Lotus that have been sufficiently processed and are able to be absorbed by the Sambhogakāya Flower. The 24 petals of this tier plus the twelve petals of the innermost tier when integrated are specifically affiliated with the 36 main petals of the

Heart tier, and by extension the Heart centre, to which energies are mirrored from the Sambhogakāya Flower. The number 36 represents the number of the Peaceful Deities minus the six Buddhas of the Six Realms (which are but emanations of Avalokiteśvara).

The permutations of the number twelve, and by extension the number 24 that allow the projection of *prāṇas* to and from the Sambhogakāya Flower, have already been discussed. The 2 x 12 petals of the second inner tier can also be considered in terms of either an *iḍā* or *piṇgalā* flow from the twelve petals of any major tier in the Head lotus. They can also manifest in terms of the seven sacred and five non-sacred petals, the eight consciousnesses, the attributes of the four main Elements, or in the field of desire *(kāma-manas)* associated with the six consciousnesses, where the intellect *(manas)* dominates. This level corresponds to the Airy-Fiery Element. The main energising source being derived from the Dhyāni Buddha Akṣobhya.

These two levels can be viewed as a practical unity, corresponding to the Śūnyāta Eye and the three bud-like petals of the Sambhogakāya Flower. The next three levels of the Head lotus have a direct relation to the three major tiers of petals of the Sambhogakāya Flower. They are:

c. The central Throat tier of 96 petals that governs the expression of Fiery-Fiery *prāṇas*. The type of *saṃskāras* that manifest here are normally absorbed by the Sacrifice petals of the Sambhogakāya Flower, which produce the tests of the Initiation process. It mainly integrates the *prāṇas* of the eight types of consciousness (96 = 8 x 12) via the qualities associated with the twelve petals of the Heart centre. The objective being the development of the attributes of abstract Mind. The stimulating effects of the work of the eight Mahābodhisattvas and Consorts directly influence the groups of eight petals when the individual is consciously walking the path to enlightenment. This tier is conditioned by the energy of the Dhyāni Buddha Amitābha.

d. The fourth level of 192 (16 x 12) petals of the Heart tier governs the expression of Fiery-Watery *prāṇas*. We saw how these petals form a functioning unity with the Throat tier and integrates *prāṇas* from the Solar Plexus tier so that the energies of the eight consciousnesses (in their *iḍā* and *piṇgalā* attributes) can be directed to the Sambhogakāya Flower. For the major evolutionary period the emotional aspects are processed in a way that produces kind, considerate and loving qualities. The overall objective of this tier is to generate the attributes of compassion, which is facilitated by the activities of either the eight Mātaraḥ or eight Pīsācī and then the Mahābodhisattvas and Consorts. All help to ensure that the needed quality of *prāṇas* can be directed to and from the overall Love-Wisdom petals of the Sambhogakāya Flower. The Heart tier conveys the general energy of the Dhyāni Buddha Ratnasambhava. *Bodhicitta* is generated via the combined activity of the Throat and Heart tiers and directed by this Heart tier to the rest of the body of manifestation.

e. The fifth level is the Solar Plexus tier, consisting of 8 x 96 = 768 petals, and governs the expression of Fiery-Earthy *prāṇas*. The major consciousness-aspects associated with material plane living are processed here. These *saṃskāras* flow to and from the Knowledge petals of the Sambhogakāya Flower. This fifth level conveys the energy of the Dhyāni Buddha Amoghasiddhi.

If we were to focus just upon the three outer tiers, wherein all of the activity of processing and transforming general *saṃskāras* occurs, then we have 1056 (11 x 96, 22 x 48) petals all told. This number represents the total number for the Head lotus, as the two innermost tiers of petals are principally energy conduits between the Sambhogakāya Flower and the Head lotus. They drive the quest for enlightenment in the individual. The number 1056 can also be considered the true number of hands of Avalokiteśvara, as each of these petals represents a major factor, 'a helping hand', needed to drive forward the compassionate aspects of consciousness to include all that is.

We saw that the innermost spheres of this centre do not awaken into full activity until the process of Initiation has been instigated. When the twenty-four petals of the second tier are added to the 1056, then we get the number 1080, a version of the sacred number 108. When twelve spokes of energy of the innermost tier of petals are added, plus the twelve innermost and the outer 96 petals of the Ājñā centre, then we have the number 1,200 (12 x 100, 25 x 48), signifying the complete (or great) perfection of the sum of the qualities associated with the twelve petals of the Heart centre. It concerns the purpose accomplished by the twelve signs of the zodiac as they cycle through the aeons. Everything concerning the demonstration of the Wisdoms of the Jinas and the expression of *bodhicitta* to convert all aspects of *saṃsāra* into Love-Wisdom comes into play.

There are twelve petals to the Heart centre and ten to the Solar Plexus centre. When these two numbers are multiplied together making 120, it signifies the ability of the Heart centre to perfectly control all of the qualities of the Solar Plexus centre. Because the Solar Plexus centre is the driving agent for all the *saṃskāras* engendered below the diaphragm, and the sum of what constitutes the 'self' concept, so this control signifies the perfection of the individual and the awakening of the *siddhis*. When the number 120 is multiplied by the number 10, the number of perfection (of the ten stages of the evolutionary process), then the number 1,200 is obtained, signifying the Great Perfection, allowing the supramundane *siddhis* to be expressed.

Alternatively, the number 10 can signify the potency of the combined petals of the Base of Spine and Sacral centres, which thus also come under the control of the Heart centre. As in all things esoteric, we see that the ancient adage 'as above, so below' holds true, thus the significance of the number 1,200 of the Head lotus is reflected into the perfection of the centres below it. This allows the appearance of a Mahāsiddha.

The number 25 x 48 is also significant. Here is seen the concept of all permutations of the five sense-consciousnesses (5 x 5) manifesting as the *prāṇic* Fires that vivify the sum of a main wheel of petals, as conveyed by one or other of the lobes of the Ājñā centre. We saw that each lobe is capable of conveying to and from the Head lotus the sum of the *manasic* attributes in either their *iḍā or piṅgalā* flavourings from the entire *nāḍī* system. The number 25 x 48 therefore implicates that not one vestige of the *prāṇas* generated by human consciousness can be outside of the activities of this all-seeing Eye. It directs all, and consequently sees and knows All.

The Throat centre is the other main *chakra* to consider. It consists of 16 (12 + 4, or 2 x 8) major petals. Its purpose is to direct the Fires of mind/Mind to control the nature of the flow of the *prāṇas* in the body. It thus generates the creative Sound (Āḥ) that organises and directs the *prāṇas* to their target *maṇḍala*. The Oṁ concerns the ability to hold the creative Fire *in situ* in the domain of the Mind (the Head centre). It integrates the full *maṇḍala* of expression. The Hūṁ pervades the sound of consciousness to all that is, thus it is the sound of the Heart. It demonstrates the purpose of the *maṇḍala* to all similar forms of expression. This is *nāda,* the silent Voice of the Heart speaking, demonstrating the perfection of being/non-being.

Both the numbers 1056 and 1200 are divided by 16, to produce the numbers 66 x 16 and 75 x 16 respectively. Consequently, the number 66 (33 x 2) relates to the ability of the Throat centre to control all aspects of the manifestation of consciousness, signifying what facilitates the march of the symbolic 33 *crores* of creative intelligences to embody the sum of the awakening mind/Mind of an incarnate personality. It makes incarnation possible. It is interesting to note that the Bible informs us that understanding the extended version of this number (666) is the source of wisdom:

> Here is wisdom. Let him that hath understanding count the number of the beast: for it *is* the number of a man; and his number is Six hundred threescore *and* six.[46]

There are a number of interpretations of the meaning of the term 'beast', one of which is that it embodies the entire field of desire, and which is the cause for the incarnation process. Why the number 666 (literally 600 + 60 + 6) is the 'number of a man' (the thinker) is provided in the arrangement of the petals of the Head lotus. The interpretation here is in terms of the factor of desire, or of the five sense-consciousnesses plus the intellect, thus of the organisation of petals in the three main tiers to accommodate their expression. There is a diminishing number of petals needed to process this factor as we travel from the outer tiers of the Head lotus to the inner ones. Symbolically 600 petals for the Solar Plexus tier, 60 for the Heart tier and 6 for the Throat tier. Effectively, however, groups of 6 x 6 petals in each tier deal with processing the 'six consciousnesses'.

Esoterically it refers to the incarnation process, integrating the qualities associated with the six petals of the Sacral centre with those of the left and right Gonad centres. Whoever undergoes incarnation,

---

46 *Rev. 13:18.* (King James version.)

from a Logos to a human unit, therefore, manifests via this number. Literally, the Sacral and Head centres become integrated by the means of the number six and its powers.

The number 75 = 25 x 3, refers to the significance of the number 25 extended in terms of the three *guṇas* of its expression.

The tabulation below summarises the main structure of the Head lotus.

Jina	Level	Petals	Prāṇa	Sambhogakāya Flower Tier
Vairocana	1st	12	Aetheric-Fiery	The Iris
Akṣobhya	2nd	24	Airy-Fiery	Three bud petals
Amitābha	3rd	96	Fiery-Fiery	Sacrifice petals
Ratnasambhava	4th	192 (2 x 96)	Fiery-Watery	Love-Wisdom petals
Amoghasiddhi	5th	768 (8 x 96)	Fiery-Earthy	Knowledge petals

Table 4. The petals of the Head lotus

The 117 Peaceful and Wrathful Deities have now been analysed. We have seen that they integrate the energies of the various *chakras* in the body with the Head lotus and the Ājñā centre, allowing the *prāṇas* to flow to the Sambhogakāya Flower. To these regulating factors (Deities) the three synthetic, integrating, primordial Ray emanations that condition all manifestation can be added.[47] Or else we can think in terms of the integrating *iḍā, piṅgalā* and *suṣumṇā* aspects to produce the number 120. When multiplied by the number 100, signifying the Great Perfection, the number 1,200 is produced, the number governing the major petals of the combined Head centres. The above mentioned triad of Rays can be thought of in terms of the Will or Monadic aspect (the *dharmakāya),* Love-Wisdom or the Sambhogakāya Flower (the *sambhogakāya),* and the Activity (the *nirmaṇakāya)* aspect that is the Head lotus of a personality. Here we have the mystery of the triune human unit implicated.

47 Viewed in terms of the Father, Son and Mother attributes of deity.

One should not therefore think that only Buddhas possess three bodies of expression (a *dharmakāya, sambhogakāya,* and *nirmaṇakāya* form). Indeed, all humans do, where the *dharmakāyic* aspect is the Monadic Eye, the *sambhogakāya* aspect is the Sambhogakāya Flower, and the appearance of the *chakras* is a *nirmaṇakāya*. The *nāḍī* system is the true human form, as the corporeal body is the great illusion, an automaton. The only difference is that in ordinary humans the lower two bodies are defiled with occluding *saṃskāras*[48] blocking out the guiding influence of the Monad. In Buddhas, all stand expressed in one grand awakened harmony of beauteous, magnificent design.

The *dharmakāyic* aspect (the Monad) can be conceived of in the form of an Eye (effectively manifesting a pupil, the iris, and the spherical main body of dynamic energy), that is focussed upon wherever travel in cosmos is envisaged. The triune *dharmakāyic* Form is only revealed as one masters the testings to the higher Initiations, and thus has cleansed the defilements of mind to the extent that allows the full blaze of that Eye to control the Mind via its Aetheric *(dharmakāyic)* petals. This happens at the fifth Initiation. The sixth Initiation relates to the Initiate being able to fully reside in the Monadic form, then a Buddha appears who can travel in this 'body of *dharma*' to the far reaches of cosmos; wherever there is need, according to the perceptions envisioned by this cosmic Eye. From Eye to Eye is the measurement of cosmic perspective seen.

Oṁ Tat Sāt!

Oṁ Svāhā!

Oṁ!

48 Thus for the Sambhogakāya Flower we have the *nirmalā* and *samalā tathatā,* Suchness (the condition of the *tathāgatagarbha*) apart from *saṃsāric* defilements, and with defilements.

Appendix 1

Website links and resources

Our website has documents that you can download for access to colour versions of some of the imagery included in this book. The images listed below are included in one PDF document. This document includes colour versions of:

Plate 1. Vairocana and Consort Ākāśadhātviśvarī

Plate 2. Akṣobhya with Consort Locanā and surrounding Bodhisattvas

Plate 3. Amitābha with Consort Pāṇḍaravāsinī and surrounding Bodhisattvas

Plate 4. Ratnasambhava with Consort Māmaki and surrounding Bodhisattvas

Plate 5. Amoghasiddhi with Consort Tārā and surrounding Bodhisattvas

Plate 7. The five Vidyādharas and Consorts

Plate 8. Mahottara Heruka and Consort

Plate 9. Buddha Heruka and Consort

Plate 10. Vajra Heruka and Consort

Plate 11. Padma Heruka and Consort

Plate 12. Ratna Heruka and Consort

Plate 13. Karma Heruka and Consort

Plate 30. Vajrakīla Heruka

Plate 31. Vajrakīla Heruka and the five Jñāna Ḍākinīs

Go to the following link on our website to download these as a PDF:
www.universaldharma.com/ud_downloads/resources/appendix_1.pdf

Appendix 2

Deities of the Bardo Thödol

The following pages are guides to identifying the Deities of the *Bardo Thödol*. They include a Layout guide with outlines, and on the opposite page the original graphic. Due to the limitations of printing a book this size, the images are quite small. We have included these images in a PDF download from our website that are at a much larger scale so you can print it out on an A4 page.

Listing 1 is of the Peaceful Deities as painted in the Lachen Gompa murals.*
Listing 2 is of the Wrathful Deities as painted in the Lachen Gompa murals.
Listing 3 is of the Wrathful Deities as painted in a Thangka. There are a few minor differences here between this and the Gompa images.

*Special thanks for the assistance of the Lachen Gompa Rinpoche.

Go to the following link on our website to download these as a PDF:
www.universaldharma.com/ud_downloads/resources/appendix_2.pdf

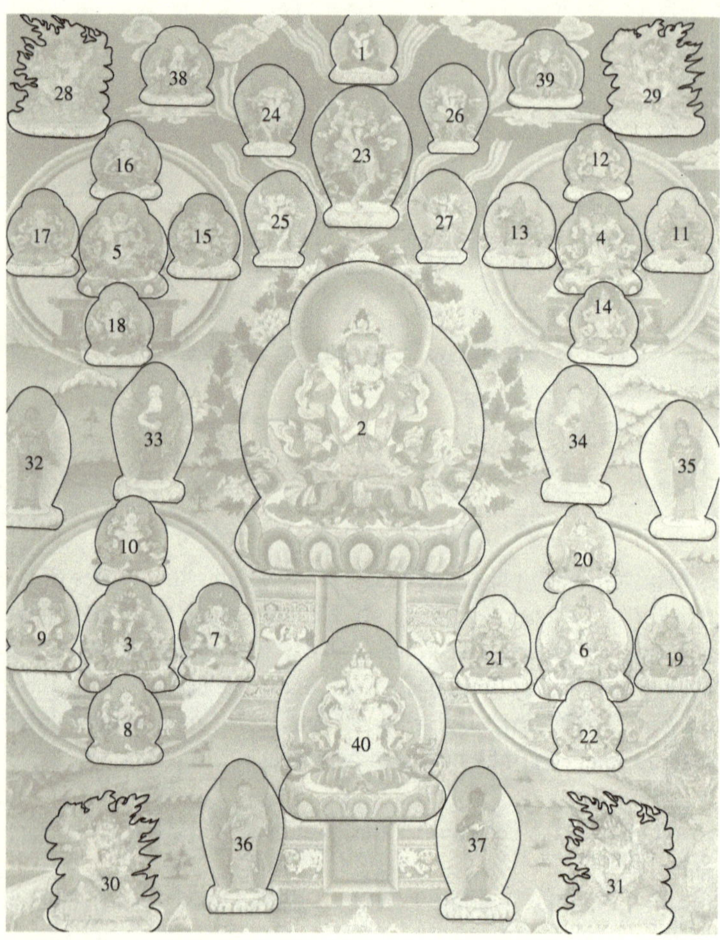

Transcendant Buddhas

1 Samantabhadra as Ādi Buddha and Samantabhadrī
2 Samantabhadra
3 Akṣobhya and Locanā
4 Amitābha and Pāṇḍara
5 Ratnasambhava and Māmakī
6 Amoghasiddhi and Samayatārā

Eight Mahābodhisattvas and consorts

7 Kṣitigarba
8 Lāsyā
9 Maitreya
10 Puṣpā
11 Mañjuśrī
12 Ālokā
13 Avalokiteśvara
14 Gītā
15 Ākāśagarbha
16 Dhūpā
17 Samantabhadra
18 Mālā
19 Vajrapāṇi
20 Nrtyā
21 Viśkambhin
22 Gandhā

The Five Vidyādharas
23 Kāya-Vidyādhara
24 Guṇa-Vidyādhara
25 Citta-Vidyādhara
26 Vāc-Vidyādhara
27 Karma- Vidyādhara

Four Gaurdians
28 Yamāntaka and Vajrapāśī
29 Hayagrīva and Vajraśṛṅkhalā
30 Vijaya and Vajrāṅkuśī
31 Amṛtakuṇḍalin and Vajraghaṇṭā

Six Buddhas
32 Thag-bzang-ris
33 brGya-byin
34 Śākyamuni
35 Seng-ge-rab-brtan
36 Kha-'bar-ma
37 Chos-kyi-rgyal-po

38 Chenrezigs
39 Padmasambhava
40 Vairocana and Ākāśadhātviśvarī

The Herukas and Consorts
1 Mahottara Heruka and Krodheśvarī
2 Vairocana Buddha Heruka and Buddha Krodeśvarī
3 Ratna Heruka and Ratna-Krodheśvarī
4 Padma Heruka and Padma-Krodheśvarī
5 Vajra Heruka and Vajra-Krodheśvarī
6 Karma Heruka and Karma-Krodheśvarī

The Eight Piśācī
7 Lion-headed Siṃhamukhī
8 Tiger-headed Vyāghrīmukhī
9 Fox-headed Śṛgālamukhī
10 Wolf-headed Śvānamukhī
11 Kite-headed Kaṅkamukhī
12 Vulture-headed Gṛdhramukhī
13 Crow-headed Kākamukhī
14 Owl-headed Ulūkamukhī

The Eight Mātaraḥ
15 Gāurī
16 Caurī
17 Pramohā
18 Vetālī
19 Pukkasī
20 Ghasmarī
21 Caṇḍālī
22 Śmaśānī

Four Female Gate-keepers
23 Sow-headed Pāśā
24 Lion-headed Sphoṭā
25 Tiger-headed Aṅkuśa
26 Snake-headed Ghaṇṭā

Four Female Gate-keepers of Emanational Rites
27 Goat-headed Vajrā Mahāchāgalā
28 Cuckoo-headed Vajrā Mahākālī
29 Lion-headed Vajrā Mahākumbhakarṇī

30 Snake-headed Vajrā Lambodarā

Six Queens of Yoga - Enrichment

31 Fox-headed Daṇḍī

32 Tiger-headed Rākṣasī

33 Crocodile-headed Śānti

34 Scorpion-headed Amṛtā

35 Bat-headed Vajrā

36 Hawk-headed Saumī

Six Queens of Yoga - Subjugation

37 Vulture-headed Bhakṣasī

38 Horse-headed Ratī

39 Garuḍa-headed Rudhiramadī

40 Dog-headed Ekacāriṇī

41 Hoopoe-headed Manohārikā

42 Deer-headed Siddhikarī

Six Queens of Yoga - Pacification

43 Weasel-headed Vaiṣṇāvī

44 Brown bear-headed Kaumārī

45 Black bear-headed Indrāṇī

46 Yak-headed Manurākṣasī

47 Snake-headed Brahmāṇī

48 Leopard-headed Raudrī

Six Queens of Yoga - Wrath

49 Ibex-headed Agnāyī

50 Wolf-headed Vāyudevī

51 Sow-headed Varāhī

52 Crow-headed Cāmuṇḍī

53 Elephant-headed Bhujanā

54 Snake-headed Varuṇānī

55 Vajrakila-Heruka and Samayatārā

The Five Ḍākinīs

56 Buddha ḍākinī

57 Vajra ḍākinī

58 Ratna ḍākinī

59 Padma ḍākinī

60 Karma ḍākinī

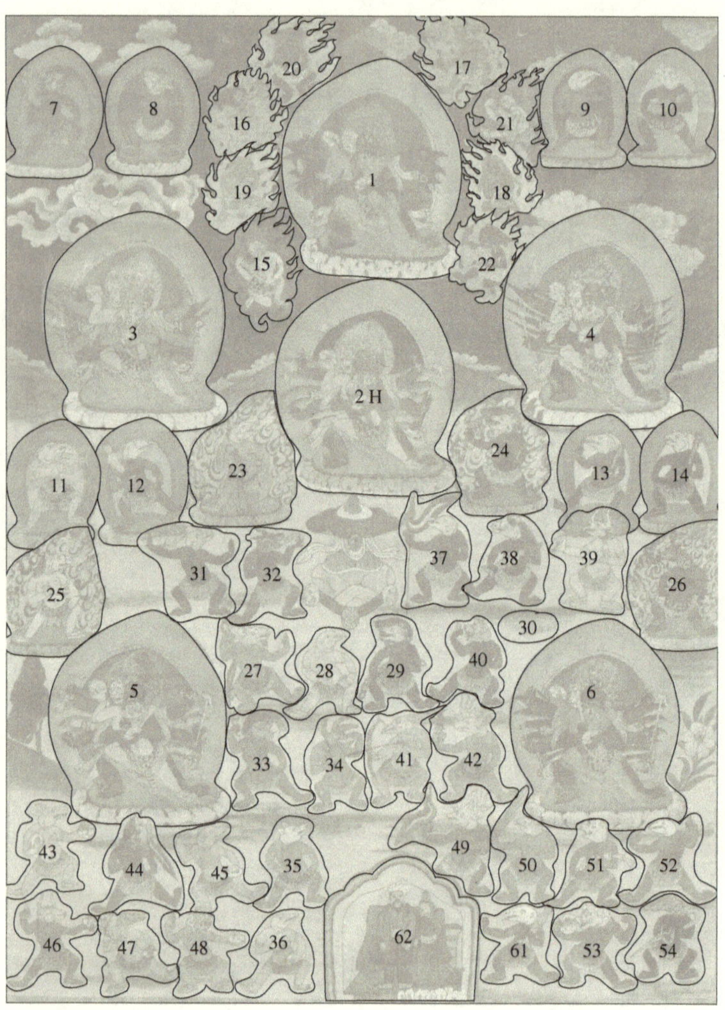

The listings for these Deities are the same as the previous 2 pages except for the following:

Four Female Gate-keepers
25 Horse-headed Aṅkuśa

Four Female Gate-keepers of Emanational Rites
30 Vajrā Lambodarā - is missing

Six Queens of Yoga - Enrichment
31 Bird-headed Daṇḍī

61 unknown
62 Patrons of the Thangkha in Newari appearance

Bibliography

Bailey, Alice A. *A Treatise on Cosmic Fire.* New York: Lucis Publishing Company, 1982.

——. *Esoteric Astrology.* New York: Lucis Publishing Company, 1968.

Balsys, Bodo. *A Treatise on Mind, Volume 4* Sydney: Universal Dharma Publishing, 2014.

——. *A Treatise on Mind, Volume 6* Sydney: Universal Dharma Publishing, 2014.

——. *Karma and the Rebirth of Consciousness.* Delhi: Munshiram Manoharlal, 2006.

Beer, Robert. *The Encyclopedia of Tibetan Symbols and Motifs.* Boston: Shambhala, 1999.

Blavatsky, H.P. *The Secret Doctrine. Vol. 1.* Adyar: Theosophical Publishing House, 1962.

Dorje, Gyurme. Trans., *The Tibetan Book of the Dead: The Great Liberation by Hearing in the Intermediate States.* London: Penguin Books, 2005.

Dudjom Rinpoche, and Jikdrel Yeshe Dorje, *The Nyingma School of Tibetan Buddhism.* Translated by Gyurme Dorje and Matthew Kapstein. Boston: Wisdom, 1991.

Evans-Wentz, W.Y. *The Tibetan Book of the Dead.* London: Oxford University Press, 1960.

Ganguli, Swati. Trans., *Treatise on Thirty verses on Mere-Consciousness. A critical English translation of Hsüan-Tsang's*

Chinese version of the Vijñaptimātratāriṃśikā with notes from Dharmapāla's commentary in Chinese. Delhi: Motilal Barnasidass, 1992.

Govinda, Lama Anagarika. *Buddhist Reflections*. Delhi: Motilal Banarsidass, 2007.

——. *Foundations of Tibetan Mysticism*. London: Century Paperbacks, 1987.

——. *Insights of a Himalayan Pilgrim*. California: Dharma Publishing, 1991.

Gyatso, Geshe Kelsang. *Clear Light of Bliss, A Commentary to the Practice of Mahāmūdra in Vajrayana Buddhism*. Boston: Wisdom Publications, 1982.

Huntington, John C., and Dina Bangdel, *The Circle of Bliss: Buddhist Meditational Art*. Chicago: Serinda Publications, 2004.

Lauf, Detlef Ingo. *Secret Doctrines of the Tibetan Books of the Dead*. Boston: Shambhala, 1989.

Leadbeater, C.W. *Man, Visible and Invisible*. Adyar: Theosophical Publishing House, 2004.

Stcherbatsky, Theodore. *The Central Conception of Buddhism*, Delhi: Motilal Baranasidass, 1994.

The King James Version Bible. London: Oxford University Press, 1922.

Thurman, Robert. *The Tibetan Book of the Dead*. New York: Bantam Books, 1994.

Index

E

F

G

N

P

R

S

About the Author

BODO BALSYS is the founder of The School of Esoteric Sciences. He is an author of many books on subjects centred on Buddhism and the Esoteric Sciences, a meditation teacher, poet, artist, spiritual scientist and healer. He has studied extensively across multiple traditions including Esoteric Science, Buddhism, Christianity, Esoteric Healing, Western Science, Art, Politics and History. His advanced esoteric insights, gained through decades of meditative contemplation, enable him to provide a rich understanding of the spiritual pathway toward enlightenment, healing and service.

Bodo's teachings can be accessed via the School of Esoteric Science's website:
http://universaldharma.com

For any other enquiries, please email
sangha@universaldharma.com

About Universal Dharma Publishing

Universal Dharma Publishing is a not for profit publisher. Our aim is make innovative, original and esoteric spiritual teachings accessible to all who genuinely aspire to awaken and serve humanity. The books published aim in part to provide an esoteric interpretation of the meaning of Buddhist *dharma* with view of reformation of the way people perceive the meaning of the related teachings. Hopefully then Buddhism can more effectively serve its principal function as a vehicle for enlightenment, and further prosper into the future. A further aim is to provide the next level of exposition of the esoteric doctrines to be revealed to humanity following on the wisdom tradition pioneered by H.P. Blavatsky and A.A. Bailey.

Cover Design by
Angie O'Sullivan & Kylie Smith

www.ingramcontent.com/pod-product-compliance
Lightning Source LLC
LaVergne TN
LVHW050912080826
845145LV00001B/63

* 9 7 8 0 9 9 2 3 5 6 8 4 2 *